The Books of Enoch: The Angels, The Watchers and The Nephilim (with Extensive Commentary on the Three Books of Enoch, the Fallen Angels, the Calendar of Enoch, and Daniel's Prophecy)

2nd EDITION

A Volume Containing
The First Book of Enoch (The Ethiopic Book of Enoch)
The Second Book of Enoch (The Slavonic Secrets of Enoch)
The Third Book of Enoch (The Hebrew Book of Enoch)
Fallen Angels, The Watchers, and the Origins of Evil:
With Expanded Commentary on Angels and Prophecies in the Sacred Texts

First time or interested authors, contact Fifth Estate Publishers, Blountsville, AL 35031.

Editng of 2nd Edition by Carol Plum-Ucci

Cover Design by An Quigley

Printed on acid-free paper

Library of Congress Control No: 2011922711

ISBN: 9781936533077

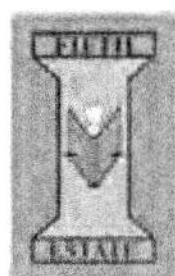

Fifth Estate, 2011

The Books of Enoch: The Angels, The Watchers and The Nephilim (with Extensive Commentary on the Three Books of Enoch, the Fallen Angels, the Calendar of Enoch, and Daniel's Prophecy)

2ND EDITION

A Volume Containing
The First Book of Enoch (The Ethiopic Book of Enoch)
The Second Book of Enoch (The Slavonic Secrets of Enoch)
The Third Book of Enoch (The Hebrew Book of Enoch)
The Book of Fallen Angels, The Watchers, and the Origins of Evil: With Expanded Commentary on Enoch, Angels, Prophecies and Calendars in the Sacred Texts

by Dr. Joseph B. Lumpkin

Table of Contents

Introduction

Our search for deeper understanding often leads beyond the Bible itself. Even in our attempt to fully understand the Bible we must go beyond the book. As we encounter references to social conditions, cultural practices, and even other writings mentioned within the scriptures we are called to investigate and expand our knowledge in order to fully appreciate the context, knowledge base, and cultural significance of what is being taught.

Thus, to fully understand the Bible, we are necessarily drawn to sources outside the Bible. These sources add to the historical, social, or theological understanding of Biblical times. As our view becomes more macrocosmic, we see the panoramic setting and further understand the full truth within the scriptures. Yet, in the case of Enoch, we are not going beyond THE Bible. We are simply going beyond OUR bible. The Book of Enoch is contained in the Bible of the Ethiopic Christian Church.

Popular texts among early Christians

To lead us to sources of information outside of our Protestant and Catholic Bibles we must know which books were popular and important at the time the Bible was being written. There are several books mentioned in the Bible which are not included in our Bible. They are not spiritual canon, either because they were not available at the time the canon was originally adopted, or at the time they were not considered "inspired." In cases when inspiration was questioned, one could argue that any book quoted or mentioned by a prophet or an apostle should be considered as spiritual canon; unfortunately this position would prove too simplistic.

Books and writings can fall under various categories such as civil records and laws, historical documents, or spiritual writings. A city or state census is not inspired, but it could add insight into certain areas of life. Spiritual writings which are directly quoted in the Bible serve as insights into the beliefs of the writer or what was considered acceptable by society at the time. As with any new discovery, invention, or belief, the new is interpreted based upon the structure of what came before. This was the way in the first century Christian church, as beliefs were based upon the old Jewish understanding. However, one should realize pagan beliefs were also added to the church as non-Jewish populations were converted, bringing with them the foundations of their beliefs on which they interpreted Christianity.

In the case of Jude, James, Paul, and others, the Jewish past was giving way to the Christian present, but their understanding and doctrine were still being influenced by what they had learned and experienced previously. It becomes obvious that to understand the Bible one should endeavor to investigate the books and doctrines that most influenced the writers of the Bible.

The Dead Sea Scrolls, found in the caves of Qumran, are of great interest in the venture of clarifying the history and doctrine in existence between biblical times and the fixing of canon. The scrolls were penned in the second century B.C. and were in use at least until the destruction of the second temple in 70 A.D. Similar scrolls to those found in Cave 4 within the 11 caves of Qumran were also found at the Masada stronghold which fell in 73 A.D. Fragments of every book of the Old Testament except Esther were found in the caves of Qumran, but so were many other books. Some of these books are considered to have been of equal importance and influence to the people of Qumran and to the writers and scholars of the time. Some of those studying the scrolls found in Qumran were the writers of the New Testament.

Knowing this, one might ask which of the dozens of non-canonical books most influenced the writers of the New Testament. It is possible to ascertain the existence of certain influences within the Bible context by using the Bible itself. The Bible can direct us to other works in three ways. The work can be mentioned by name, as is the Book of Jasher. The work can be quoted within the Bible text, as is the case with the Book of Enoch. The existence of the work can be alluded to, as is the case of the missing letter from the apostle Paul to the Corinthians.

Books mentioned in the Holy Bible

In the case of those books named in the Bible, one can set a list as the titles are named. The list is lengthier than one might at first suspect. Most of these works have not been found. Some have been unearthed but their authenticity is questioned. Others have been found and the link between scripture and scroll is generally accepted. Following is a list of books mentioned in the Holy Bible:

1. **The Book of Jasher:** "Also he bade them teach the children of Judah the use of the bow: behold, it is written in the Book of Jasher." *(2 Samuel 1:18)* "Is it not written in the Book of Jasher? And the sun stopped in the middle of the sky and did not hasten to go down for about a whole day." *(Joshua 10:13)*
2. **The Book of Wars of the Lord:** "Therefore it is said in the Book of the Wars of the Lord." *(Num. 21:14)*
3. **The Annals of Jehu:** "Now the rest of the acts of Jehoshaphat, first to last, behold, they are written in the annals of Jehu the son of Hanani, which is recorded in the Book of the Kings of Israel." *(2 Chronicles 20:34)*
4. **The Book of the Kings:** "As to his sons and the many oracles against him and the rebuilding of the house of God, behold, they

are written in the treatise of the Book of the Kings. Then Amaziah his son became king in his place." *(2 Chronicles 24:27)*

5. **The Book of Records, Book of the Chronicles of Ahasuerus:** "Now when the plot was investigated and found to be so, they were both hanged on a gallows; and it was written in the Book of the Chronicles in the king's presence." ... "During that night the king could not sleep so he gave an order to bring the book of records, the chronicles, and they were read before the king." *(Esther 2:23, 6:1)*
6. **The Acts of Solomon:** "Now the rest of the acts of Solomon and whatever he did, and his wisdom, are they not written in the book of the Acts of Solomon?" *(1 Kings 11:41)*
7. **The Sayings of Hozai:** "His prayer also and how God was entreated by him, and all his sin, his unfaithfulness, and the sites on which he built high places and erected the Asherim and the carved images, before he humbled himself, behold, they are written in the records of the Hozai." *(2 Chronicles 33:19)*
8. **The Chronicles of King David:** "Joab the son of Zeruiah had begun to count them, but did not finish; and because of this, wrath came upon Israel, and the number was not included in the account of the Chronicles of King David." *(1 Chronicles 27:24)*
9. **The Chronicles of Samuel, Nathan, Gad**: "Now the acts of King David, from first to last, are written in the Chronicles of Samuel the seer, in the Chronicles of Nathan the prophet and in the Chronicles of Gad the seer." *(1 Chronicles 29:29)*
10. **Samuel's book:** "Then Samuel told the people the ordinances of the kingdom, and wrote them in the book and placed it before the Lord." *(1 Samuel 10:25)*
11. **The Records of Nathan the Prophet:** "Now the rest of the Acts of Solomon, from first to last, are they not written in the Records of Nathan the Prophet, and in the Prophecy of Ahijah the Shilonite, and in the Visions of Iddo the Seer concerning Jeroboam the son of Nebat?" *(2 Chronicles 9:29)*
12. **The Prophecy of Ahijah the Shilonite:** "Now the rest of the acts of Solomon, from first to last, are they not written in the Records of Nathan the Prophet, and in the Prophecy of Ahijah the Shilonite, and in the Visions of Iddo the Seer concerning Jeroboam the son of Nebat?" *(2 Chronicles 9:29)*
13. **The Treatise of the Prophet Iddo:** "Now the rest of the acts of Abijah, and his ways and his words are written in the treatise of the prophet Iddo." *(2 Chronicles 13:22)*

There are several books which have come to us entitled, "Book of Jasher." One is an ethical treatise from the Middle Ages. It begins with a section on the Mystery of the Creation of the World: It is clearly unrelated to the Biblical Book of Jasher.

Another was published in 1829, supposedly translated by Flaccus Albinus Alcuinus. It opens with the chapter 1, verse 1 reading, "While it was the beginning, darkness overspread the face of nature." It is now considered a fake.

The third and most important is by Midrash, first translated into English in 1840. It opens with chapter 1, verse 1 reading, "And God said, Let us make man in our image, after our likeness, and God created man in his own image." A comparison of Joshua 10:13 with Jasher 88:63-64 and 2 Samuel 1:18 with Jasher 56:9 makes it clear that this Book of Jasher at least follows close enough with the Bible to be the Book of Jasher mentioned in the Bible.

Missing Epistles

The existence of a lost book can be inferred even if no text is available. This is clearly seen with several missing epistles.

Paul's letter to the Church at Laodicea appears to be missing, according to some scholars. Colossians 4:16 states, "When this letter is read among you, have it also read in the church of the Laodiceans; and you, for your part, read my letter that is coming from Laodicea." Since three earlier manuscripts do not contain the words "at Ephesus" in Ephesians 1:1, some have speculated that the letter coming from Laodicea was in fact the letter of Ephesians. Apostolic fathers also debated this possibility.

In Paul's first letter to Corinth, he predated that letter by saying: "I wrote you in my letter not to associate with immoral people" *(1 Corinthians 5:9)* This could merely be a reference to the present letter of 1 Corinthians.

Book of Enoch may be most influencial

Of all the books quoted, paraphrased, or referred to in the Bible, the Book of Enoch has influenced the writers of the Bible as few others have. Even more extensively than in the Old Testament, the writers of the New Testament were frequently influenced by other writings, including the Book of Enoch.

It is not the purpose of this work to make judgments as to the validity or worth of the Book of Enoch, but rather to simply put forth a meaningful question: *Is not the non-canonical book that most influenced the thought and theology of the writers of the New Testament worth further research and contemplation?*

Before we continue in our study of the Book of Enoch there are several questions we must keep in mind. If a book is mentioned or quoted in the Bible, is it not worthy of further study? If it is worth investigating, is this the book of which the Bible speaks? What knowledge or insight does it add to our understanding of the Bible or the men who wrote it?

The Book of Enoch was once cherished by Jews and Christians alike. It is read in certain Coptic Christian Churches in Ethiopia. Three versions of the Book of Enoch exist today.

Book of Enoch: Discovering it; dating it

Most scholars date the Book of Enoch to sometime during the second century B.C. We do not know what earlier oral tradition, if any, the book contains. Enoch was considered inspired and authentic by certain Jewish sects of the first century B.C. and remained popular for at least 500 years. The earliest Ethiopian text was apparently derived from a Greek manuscript of the Book of Enoch, which itself was a copy of an earlier text. The original was apparently written in the Semitic language, now thought to be Aramaic.

The Book of Enoch was discovered in the 18th century. It was assumed to have been penned after the beginning of the Christian era. This theory was based on the fact that it had quotes and paraphrases as well as concepts found in the New Testament. Thus, it was assumed that it was heavily influenced by writers such as Jude and Peter.

However, recent discoveries of copies of the book among the Dead Sea Scrolls found at Qumran prove the book was in existence before the time of Jesus Christ. These scrolls forced a closer look and reconsideration. *It became obvious that the New Testament did not influence the Book of Enoch; on the contrary, the Book of Enoch influenced the New Testament.* The date of the original writing upon which the second century B.C. Qumran copies were based is shrouded in obscurity. Likewise lost are the sources of the oral traditions that came to be the Book of Enoch. Slowly, over the past 60 years, we have unraveled some of the mystery.

Inspired, authentic or fake?

It has been largely the opinion of historians that the book does not really contain the authentic words of the ancient Enoch, since he would have lived several thousand years earlier than the first known appearance of the book attributed to him. However, the first century Christians accepted the Book of Enoch as inspired, if not authentic. They relied on it to understand the origin and purpose of many things, from angels to wind, sun, and stars. In fact, many of the key concepts used by Jesus Christ himself seem directly connected to terms and ideas in the Book of Enoch.

The theories regarding the authenticity of Enoch vary widely. Some believe Enoch is Midrash; that is an elaboration on a biblical story. In this case it is suggested that Enoch expands Genesis chapter 6.

Parallels between Enoch and the Holy Scriptures

Another more controversial theory has Enoch predating the Genesis story. Like the Book of Enoch, Genesis seems to have several authors with stories intertwined. One of these authors is known simply as "P," owing to the fact he was thought to be a priest. If we compare the "P" contribution of Genesis to the Book of Enoch, parallels leap out.

Enoch	P
Corrupt earth	Human way corrupt on the earth (Gen 6)
eating animals	eating animals (Gen 9)
bloodshed	bloodshed (Gen 9)
364-day year	30-day months (Gen 7)
(12 months x 30 + 4)	365-day year (Gen 5)
Enoch goes to heaven	Enoch goes to heaven (Gen 5)

There are other connections. The name "Azazel" appears in Leviticus. The scapegoat is sent into the wilderness "to Azazel," and through the ceremony of laying on of hands by the priest and people, the goat is sent away, bearing the sins of the people. This reference only makes sense if the writer believed that Azazel was responsible for all human sins and would bear the punishment for it, as the Book of Enoch declares.

In Genesis, it is Cain who bears sins into the wilderness. However, we will see that there are connections between the fallen angels and the descendants of Cain.

The problem with such a connection between Enoch and Genesis is that it does not point to the direction of the transmission. We now can be reasonably sure that Enoch and Genesis are connected, but we cannot be certain which was recorded first. The best evidence we have for the undisputed authenticity of Enoch is not the connection to Genesis, but the faith Jesus and the Apostles had in the Book of Enoch, demonstrated by various references and quotes.

How Jesus and his followers used Enoch

It is hard to avoid the evidence that Jesus not only studied the book, but also respected it highly enough to allude to its doctrine and content. Enoch is replete with mentions of the coming kingdom and other holy themes. It was not only Jesus who used phrases or ideas from Enoch, there are over 100 comments in the New Testament which find precedence in the Book of Enoch.

As we begin looking for connections between the words of or about Jesus and those of Enoch, we cannot look for exact matches. It is possible that what was originally spoken by these men was very close in wording or exact meaning, but after divergent paths of transmission and translations through various languages and cultures they arrive here in the 21st century with many alterations. Like the child's game of "telephone," exact wording has been somewhat altered. Let us look at general ideas within passages.

Jesus	Enoch
Blessed are the meek, for they shall inherit the earth. (Mat 5:5)	And all the elect shall rejoice, and there shall be forgiveness of sins, and mercy and peace and forbearance and joy. There shall be salvation for them, (like/and) a good light. (Enoch 5:7)
the Father judgeth no man, but hath committed all judgment unto the son (John 5:22).	And he sat on the throne of his glory, and the sum of judgment was given to the Son of Man. (Enoch 69:27)
Matt. 19:16 Now a man came up to Jesus and asked, "Teacher, what good thing must I do to get eternal life?" (Jesus said) And everyone who has left houses or brothers or sisters or father or mother or children or fields for my sake will receive a hundred times as much and will inherit eternal life.	...who is set over the repentance and those who hope to inherit eternal life.. (Enoch 40:9)
"Woe unto you that are rich! for ye have received your consolation. (Luke 6:24)	Woe to you, you rich, for you have trusted in your riches, and from your riches shall you depart, because you have not remembered the Most High in the days of your riches. (Enoch 94:8)
Ye also shall sit upon twelve thrones, judging the twelve tribes of Israel. (Mat. 19:28)	And I will bring out in shining light those who have loved My holy name, and I will seat each on the throne of his honor (glory). (Enoch 108:12)
Woe unto that man through whom the Son of man is betrayed! It had	Where will there be the dwelling for sinners, and where the will

been good for that man if he had not been born. (Mat. 26:24)

there be a resting-place for those who have denied the Lord of spirits? It had been good for them if they had not been born. (Enoch 38:2)

between us and you there is a great gulf fixed. (Luke 16:26)

Then I asked, regarding all the hollow places (chasm): 'Why is one separated from the other?'
9 And he answered me and said to me: 'These three have been made that the spirits of the dead might be separated. (Enoch 22: 9)

Luke 1:32 He will be great and will be called the Son of the Most High. The Lord God will give him the throne of his father David, 33and he will reign over the house of Jacob forever; his kingdom will never end."

John 14:2 In my Father's house are many mansions

On that day My Elect One shall sit on the throne of glory and shall try the works of the righteous, and their places of rest shall be. (Enoch 45:3)

that ye may be called the children of light (John 12:36)

And now I will summon the spirits of the good who belong to the generation of light,... (Enoch 108:11)

the water that I shall give him shall be in him a well of water springing up into everlasting life. (John 4:14)

And in that place I saw the spring of righteousness which was inexhaustible. And around it were many springs of wisdom. And all the thirsty drank of them, and were filled with wisdom, and their dwellings were with the righteous and holy and elect. (Enoch 48:1)

Further evidence of Enoch's popularity

Other evidence of the early Christians' acceptance of the Book of Enoch was for many years buried under the King James Bible's mistranslation of Luke 9:35, describing the transfiguration of Christ: "And there came a voice out of the cloud, saying, 'This is my beloved Son. Hear him.'" Apparently the translator here wished to make this verse agree with a similar verse in Matthew and Mark. But Luke's verse in the original Greek reads, "This is my Son, the Elect One (from the Greek *ho eklelegmenos*, literally, "the elect one"). Hear him."

The "Elect One" is a most significant term (found 14 times) in the Book of Enoch. If the book was indeed known to the Apostles of Christ, with its abundant descriptions of the Elect One who should "sit upon the throne of glory" and the Elect One who should "dwell in the midst of them," then the great scriptural authenticity is justly accorded to the Book of Enoch. Then the "voice out of the cloud" tells the Apostles, "This is my Son, the Elect One,"... the one promised in the Book of Enoch.

The Book of Jude tells us in verse 14 that "Enoch, the seventh from Adam, prophesied." Jude also, in verse 15, makes a direct reference to the Book of Enoch (2:1), where he writes, "to execute judgment on all, to convict all who are ungodly." As a matter of fact, it is a direct, word-for-word quote. Therefore, Jude's reference to the Enochian prophesies strongly leans toward the conclusion that these written prophesies were available to him at that time.

Fragments of ten Enoch manuscripts were found among the Dead Sea Scrolls. The number of scrolls indicate the Essenes (a Jewish commune or sect at the time of Christ) could well have used the Enochian writings as a community prayer book or teacher's manual and study text.

Many of the early church fathers also supported the Enochian writings. Justin Martyr ascribed all evil to demons whom he alleged to be the offspring of the angels who fell through lust for women; directly referencing the Enochian writings.

Athenagoras (170 A.D.) regarded Enoch as a true prophet. He describes the angels who "violated both their own nature and their office." In his writings, he goes into detail about the nature of fallen angels and the cause of their fall, which comes directly from the Enochian writings.

Irenaeus (A.D. 180), in his work "Against Heresies," spoke of Enoch, whose translation was a prophetic view of our future rapture: "For Enoch, when he pleased God, was translated in the same body in which he did please Him, thus pointing out by anticipation the translation of the just" (Against Heresies, bk. 5).

How Enoch disappeared

Since any book stands to be interpreted in many ways, Enoch posed problems for some theologians. Instead of reexamining their own theology, they sought to dispose of that which went counter to their beliefs. Some of the visions in Enoch are believed to point to the consummation of the age in conjunction with Christ's second coming, which some believe took place in A.D. 70 (in the destruction of Jerusalem).

This being the case, it should not surprise us that Enoch was declared a fake and was rejected by Hilary, Jerome, and Augustine. Enoch was subsequently lost to Western Christendom for over 1,000 years.

However, some view the Book of Enoch as prophetic, not only as a timeline, but being a picture into what is coming to all those who believe and are obedient to God.

"By faith Enoch was translated that he should not see death; and was not found, because God had translated him: for before his translation he had this testimony, that he pleased God" *(Hebrews 11:5).* Enoch experienced "rapture" in his time before the judgment of the Flood. What Enoch experienced is what some modern Christians believe is waiting for the church. 1 Thessalonians 4:15-17 promises that Jesus will descend from heaven with a shout, with the voice of the archangel and the trumpet of God, and the church will be taken up, or "raptured,"," to meet Him in the air.

Enoch supports Biblical endtime prophecy

The Book of Enoch may inform and prepare us for coming events. Some believe there are prophecies contained in the Book of Enoch that are as applicable as those written in the books of Daniel and Revelation.

The prophecies within Enoch are presented in several ways. There is a list of weeks, much like those of Daniel. There are a list of animals and their actions toward each other. There is a list of generations defining a timeline.

Enoch's "70 generations" was also a great problem. Many scholars thought it could not be made to stretch beyond the first century. Copies of Enoch soon disappeared. Indeed, for almost 2,000 years we knew only the references made to it in the Bible. Without having the book itself, we could not have known it was being quoted in the Bible, sometimes word for word, by Peter and Jude.

"...the Lord, having saved a people out of the land of Egypt, afterward destroyed them that believed not. And angels that kept not their own principality, but left their proper habitation, he hath kept in everlasting bonds under darkness unto the judgment of the great day. Even as Sodom and Gomorrah, and the cities about them...in like manner...are set out as examples...." *(Jude 5-7)*

"For if God spared not the angels when they sinned, but cast them down into hell, and committed them to pits of darkness, to be reserved unto judgment." *(2 Peter 2.4)*

To what extent other New Testament writers regarded Enoch as scriptural canon may be determined by comparing their writings with those found in Enoch. A strong possibility of influence upon their thought and choice of wording is evidenced by a great many references found in Enoch which remind one of passages found in the New Testament.

Famous Christians who accepted Enoch

Enoch was also referenced in other writings, such as the Book of Jubilees, which is canon in the Ethiopic Christian Church, and the Book of Giants, in which one of the fallen angels is called by the name of Gilgamesh.

The Book of Enoch seems to be a missing link between Jewish and Christian theology and is considered by many to be more Christian in its theology than Jewish. It was considered scripture by many early Christians. The literature of the church fathers is filled with references to this book. The early second century apocryphal book of the Epistle of Barnabus makes many references and quotes from the Book of Enoch. Second and third century church fathers like Justin Martyr, Irenaeus, Origen and Clement of Alexandria all seemed to have accepted Enoch as authentic. Tertullian (160-230 A.D.) even called the Book of Enoch "Holy Scripture." The Ethiopian Coptic Church holds the Book of Enoch as part of its official spiritual canon. It was widely known and read the first three centuries after Christ. This and many other books became discredited after the Council of Laodicea. And being under ban of the authorities, it gradually disappeared from circulation.

How Enoch was rediscovered

In 1773, rumors of a surviving copy of the book drew Scottish explorer James Bruce to distant Ethiopia. He found the Book of Enoch had been preserved by the Ethiopian church, which put it right alongside the other books of the Bible.

Bruce secured not one, but three Ethiopian copies of the book and brought them back to Europe and Britain. In 1773 Bruce returned from six years in Abyssinia. In 1821 Richard Laurence published the first English translation. The famous R.H. Charles edition was published in 1912.

In the following years several portions of the Greek text surfaced. Then with the discovery of Cave 4 at Qumran, seven fragmentary copies of the Aramaic text were discovered. This means the text passed from its Aramaic form into Greek, and finally into Geez, an Ethiopian tongue.

Before the discovery of the Aramaic form was uncovered, it was thought that Enoch was written after Jude and borrowed heavily from it. However, after the discovery of Enoch among the texts in Qumran, scholars had to re-examine the evidence. Enoch not only existed long before the biblical book of Jude, it is now obvious that both Jude and Peter read, believed and borrowed heavily from Enoch. This makes the Book of Enoch (1 Enoch) one of the earliest apocalyptic books.

Most apocalyptic literature was written after the destruction of the Jewish temple in Jerusalem in 70 A.D. under the feet of a Roman siege. Rome was considered by the Jews to be an ungodly nation as well as the oppressors and enemy of the Jews. The Jews considered themselves to be the chosen people of God. When the temple of God was destroyed it caused great turmoil throughout Judaism. Why would God let this happen to His chosen people and moreover, to His own house? The answer must be that the Jewish people had sinned and wandered away from the will of God. If this were true then when the Jewish nation repented and came back to God, He would avenge them by allowing the Jews to conquer and crush their enemies. The Jews would once again appear to be the victorious and chosen people they were meant to be. The return of the Jewish nation to the strict will and law of God and the battle and victory through God's help is the basis of most apocalyptic literature.

This is not the case in the first and oldest section of the Book of Enoch, written as early as the 3rd century B.C. The apocalyptic theme in the section we are calling "The Book of the Watchers" is a simple one of blessing the righteous and destroying the unrighteous beings, both human and angelic. More traditional or common apocalyptic themes can be seen in sections of Enoch written around 100 A.D.

How The First Book of Enoch is divided

The First Book of Enoch is not one manuscript. It is a composite of several manuscripts written by several authors over a period of 300 to 400 years.

The Book of Enoch is composed of six main parts. These sections can be subdivided further. It could be argued that, like the writers of the Bible itself, the various authors of Enoch did not foresee their contributions being concatenated into a single volume.

The six basic sections are as follows:

The Book of Watchers **(Chapters 1-36)**
Probably written: Late 3rd century or early 2nd century B.C.
Overall theme: Last judgment
This section is considered to be the most authentic and important part of the Book of Enoch.
Contents:

- Introduction (Chapters 1-5): Last judgment
- The Fall (Chapters 6-36): Fall of the angels by having sex with the women of earth; the evil of the children and the corruption of mankind

The Book of Parables **(Chapters 37-71)**
Probably written: 1st century A.D.
Overall theme: The Messiah and His judgment
Contents:

- 1st parable: Enoch's vision of heaven containing the righteous people, the angels and the Messiah (Chapters 38-44)
- 2nd parable: The messianic judgment (Chapters 45-57)
- 3rd parable: The Son of Man (Chapters 58-71)

The Book of Astronomy and Calendar **(Chapters 72-82)**
Probably written: Late 3rd or early 2nd century B.C.
Overall theme & contents: Elements of weather, movement of stars, planets, sun and moon, and the calendar

The Book of Visions **(Chapters 83-90)**
Probably written: 165-160 B.C. (thought to be written around the time of the revolt led by the Maccabees)
Overall theme: Judgment and history
Contents:

- 1st vision: The deluge as the first judgment (Chapters 83-84)
- 2nd vision: A history of Israel until the revolt (Chapters 85-90)

The Book of Warnings and Blessings of Enoch **(Chapters 91-104)**
Probably written: Early 2nd century B.C.
Overall theme: Warnings, blessings and an apocalypse
Contents:

- The prophecy of the Apocalypse of Weeks (Chapters 91 and 93)
- What will befall sinners and the righteous (Chapters 94-104)

Later Additions to the Text, Book of Noah **(Chapters 105-108)**
Probably written: 2nd century B.C.
Overall theme: Noah and Methuselah
Contents: This section of the book seems to be added as an afterthought. It consists of fragments from other books, such as the Book of Noah.

When the Book of Enoch was found along with other scrolls around the Dead Sea, the Book of Parables was not included. This was because that section was added later. In addition, the Book of Watchers and the Book of Visions were already joined and intact.

Trustworthiness of the Enochian Calendar

During the time period Enoch was written, the Jewish community was torn regarding which type of calendar to use. Enoch seems to taut a solar-based calendar that is 364 days long with a week added as needed to make up for the missing a day and a quarter (1.25). Compare 365.25 days to 364 days. The Enochian calendar began each year on a Sunday. The starting point for the calendar was the spring equinox, which occurs around March 21st or 22nd. Since the year always begins on the same day of the week, and only a full week is added when needed, the calendar is considered to be a calendar of weeks. To put this in perspective, simply assume that instead of adding a day every four years as we do, a week would be added every few years as needed to align the beginning of the years as close to the first Sunday after the equinox. Now assume New Years comes, not on January 1st, but on March 21st. Although this is a bit of an over simplification, it is basically the way the Enochian calendar functioned.

The Book of Enoch tells of the sun traversing the heavens through a number of gates. The passage through the various gates represented segments of a day. The Enochian day is not divided into 24 hours but into 18 segments of one and one-third hours each. Thus, each segment lasted 80 minutes. More detailed information on the calendar will be presented at the end of this book, when we discuss its application to the Prophecy of Daniel.

The Book of Jubilees, which was written in the same timeframe, demands and defends the use of the ancient lunar calendar. Writers of Jubilees reasoned that if one were to worship in strict compliance to the customs presented by the Torah, one had to use the same lunar calendar so one would worship at the proper times and days. The Book of Enoch does not defend the choice of a solar calendar; it simply lays out the math and astronomical movements.

The Hebrew calendar is a lunar-based system. In this system Passover occurs after sundown on the 15th day of the month Nisan. Passover is celebrated for seven days. The first Passover was in the springtime and many thought it should be keep in that period of the year. Since the calendar is based in lunar movements the Hebrew calendar is offset to the solar calendar by about 11 days a year. This meant that Passover would drift from spring, to winter, to autumn, and back again. The drift had become so annoying that in the year 359 A.D. a rabbi named Hillel II began the process of aligning the lunar calendar to the solar calendar by standardizing the lunar months to 29 or 30 days and adding a day to the month of Adar when needed to keep synchronized, just as we would add a day to our leap year.

All of this information will become important as we begin discussing prophecy. So, let's nail down what the Bible says about the first Passover and the date:

Exodus 12
1 *And the LORD spake unto Moses and Aaron in the land of Egypt saying,*
2 *This month shall be unto you the beginning of months: it shall be the first month*
of the year to you.
3 *Speak ye unto all the congregation of Israel, saying, In the tenth day of this month*
they shall take to them every man a lamb, according to the house of their fathers, a
lamb for an house:
4 *And if the household be too little for the lamb, let him and his neighbour next unto*
his house take it according to the number of the souls; every man according to his
eating shall make your count for the lamb.
5 *Your lamb shall be without blemish, a male of the first year: ye shall take it out*
from the sheep, or from the goats:
6 *And ye shall keep it up until the fourteenth day of the same month: and the whole*
assembly of the congregation of Israel shall kill it in the evening.
7 *And they shall take of the blood, and strike it on the two side posts and on the*
upper door post of the houses, wherein they shall eat it.
8 *And they shall eat the flesh in that night, roast with fire, and unleavened bread;*
and with bitter herbs they shall eat it.
9 *Eat not of it raw, nor sodden at all with water, but roast with fire; his head with*
his legs, and with the purtenance thereof.
10 *And ye shall let nothing of it remain until the morning; and that which remaineth*
of it until the morning ye shall burn with fire.
11 *And thus shall ye eat it; with your loins girded, your shoes on your feet, and your*
staff in your hand; and ye shall eat it in haste: it is the LORD's passover.
12 *For I will pass through the land of Egypt this night, and will smite all the*
firstborn in the land of Egypt, both man and beast; and against all the gods of Egypt
I will execute judgment: I am the LORD.
13 *And the blood shall be to you for a token upon the houses where ye are: and when*
I see the blood, I will pass over you, and the plague shall not be upon you to destroy
you, when I smite the land of Egypt.
14 *And this day shall be unto you for a memorial; and ye shall keep it a feast to the*
LORD throughout your generations; ye shall keep it a feast by an ordinance forever.
15 *Seven days shall ye eat unleavened bread; even the first day ye shall put away*
leaven out of your houses: for whosoever eateth leavened bread from the first day
until the seventh day, that soul shall be cut off from Israel.
16 *And in the first day there shall be an holy convocation, and in the seventh day*
there shall be an holy convocation to you; no manner of work shall be done in them,
save that which every man must eat, that only may be done of you.
17 *And ye shall observe the feast of unleavened bread; for in this selfsame day have I*
brought your armies out of the land of Egypt: therefore shall ye observe this day in

your generations by an ordinance forever.
18 In the first month, on the fourteenth day of the month at even, ye shall eat
unleavened bread, until the one and twentieth day of the month at even.
19 Seven days shall there be no leaven found in your houses: for whosoever eateth
that which is leavened, even that soul shall be cut off from the congregation of Israel,
whether he be a stranger, or born in the land.
20 Ye shall eat nothing leavened; in all your habitations shall ye eat unleavened
bread.
21 Then Moses called for all the elders of Israel, and said unto them, Draw out and
take you a lamb according to your families, and kill the passover.
22 And ye shall take a bunch of hyssop, and dip it in the blood that is in the bason,
and strike the lintel and the two side posts with the blood that is in the bason; and
none of you shall go out at the door of his house until the morning.
23 For the LORD will pass through to smite the Egyptians; and when he seeth the
blood upon the lintel, and on the two side posts, the LORD will pass over the door,
and will not suffer the destroyer to come in unto your houses to smite you.
24 And ye shall observe this thing for an ordinance to thee and to thy sons forever.
25 And it shall come to pass, when ye be come to the land which the LORD will give
you, according as he hath promised, that ye shall keep this service.
26 And it shall come to pass, when your children shall say unto you, What mean ye
by this service?
27 That ye shall say, It is the sacrifice of the LORD's passover, who passed over the
houses of the children of Israel in Egypt, when he smote the Egyptians, and
delivered our houses. And the people bowed the head and worshipped.
28 And the children of Israel went away, and did as the LORD had commanded
Moses and Aaron, so did they.

It should be noted that when the Gregorian or Enochian calendars are applied, Passover will last for eight days since the Hebrew day starts at sundown and both the Enochian and Gregorian days start at midnight.

Now, we understand that the Hebrew lunar calendar, the Enochian calendar, and the Gregorian calendar are all slightly different. When we turn our attention to the prophecy in the Book of Daniel, called "Daniel's Weeks of Years," we can now ask the first intelligent question: "What kind of year was the prophecy based upon? You will find an in-depth explanation of the application of the Enochian calendar to prophecy in the section titled "The Calendar for Enoch's and Daniel's Prophecies," starting on page 158. For now, let us turn our attention back to the Book of Enoch.

1 Enoch, 2 Enoch and 3 Enoch: Three different texts

The Book of Enoch will referred to henceforth in this text as 1 Enoch. That is because there exist two other Books of Enoch we will discuss.

Another "Book of Enoch" surfaced, commonly called the Slavonic Enoch or 2 Enoch, as it will be referred to herein. It was discovered in 1886 by Professor Sokolov in the archives of the Belgrade Public Library. It appears that just as 1 Enoch escaped the sixth-century Church suppression in the Mediterranean area, so 2 Enoch survived far away, long after the originals from which it was copied were destroyed or hidden.

Specialists in the Enochian texts believe that the missing original of 2 Enoch, from which the Slavonic was copied, was probably a Greek manuscript, which itself may have been based on a Hebrew or Aramaic manuscript.

2 Enoch has evidence of many later additions to the original manuscript. Unfortunately, later additions and the deletion of teachings considered "erroneous," rendered the text unreliable.

Because of certain references to dates and data regarding certain calendar systems in 2 Enoch, some claim the text cannot be earlier than the seventh century A.D. Some see these passages not as evidence of Christian authorship, but as later Christian interpolations into an earlier manuscript. Enochian specialist R.H. Charles, for instance, states that even the better of the two Slavonic manuscripts of 2 Enoch contains interpolations and is, in textual terms, "corrupt."

The last great book of the Enochian tradition is the Third Book of Enoch, also known as the Hebrew Book of Enoch, or as referred to herein, 3 Enoch. 3 Enoch is a wealth of mystical knowledge. The book claims to be authored by Rabbi Ishmael, a highly respected and brilliant priest living between 90 and 130 A.D.; however, no fragments have been found dating earlier than around 400 A.D. The book was written in Hebrew but has a few Latin and Greek words and cognates. 3 Enoch has its roots in the Metatron tradition, which has Enoch ascending to heaven and being translated into the angel Metatron. He is then given authority over the angels and the earthly nations, much to the protests of the angelic host. The amount of mystical information, along with the angelology contained in the book, is unrivaled. 3 Enoch is obviously a continuation and expansion of the Enochian traditions of 1 and 2 Enoch, which are drawn on for the story's foundation.

1 Enoch is most accepted

We shall examine the three books of Enoch separately in this book with the understanding that it is only 1 Enoch that is considered inspired by some and canon by the Ethiopic Christian Church.

The books of 2 Enoch and 3 Enoch have been of little influence within mainline Christianity. However, 1 Enoch addressed in this work is of major and amazing influence within the modern Christian world, informing our beliefs and concepts of angels, demons, and the world to come.

The translations used for this work are taken from both the Richard Laurence and R.H. Charles manuscripts in addition to numerous sources and commentaries. The texts were compared and rendered for easier reading by the modern "American" English reader as some phrasing from the 18th and 19th centuries may seem somewhat clumsy to our 21st century eyes. When there are clear differences in various texts, a word is added in parentheses to show both paths of translations.

In addition to the translation notes there are Biblical references showing how the Book of Enoch contains various Old Testament sources, or how the 1 Enoch was quoted, referenced, or was possibly used as a source document for New Testament writers. These Biblical references, as well as quotes from other ancient sources, are italicized and the chapters and verses noted. Notes and commentaries from the author are kept in plain text, leaving the bold text to be the Book of Enoch.

Let us now proceed to 1 Enoch.

The First Book of Enoch

1 Enoch

The First Book of Enoch

The *Book of Watchers* (Chapters 1-36):
[Chapter 1]

1 The words of the blessing of Enoch, with which he blessed the elect and righteous, who will be living in the day of tribulation, when all the wicked and godless people are to be removed (from the earth).

2 And he began his story saying: (I am) Enoch, a righteous man, whose eyes were opened by God, and who saw the vision of the Holy One in heaven, which the angels showed me. And I heard everything from them, and I saw and understood, but it was not for this generation (to know), but for a remote one which is to come.

3 As I began my story concerning the elect I said, The Holy Great One will come out from His dwelling,

4 And the eternal God will tread on the earth, (even) on Mount Sinai, and appear in the strength of His might from heaven.

5 And all shall be very afraid. The Watchers shall shake, and great fear and trembling shall seize them all the way to the ends of the earth.

6 And the high mountains shall be shaken, and the high hills shall be laid low, and shall melt like wax in the flame.

7 And the earth shall be completely torn apart, and all that is on the earth shall be destroyed, And there shall be a judgment on all.

Revelation 21: 7-8 He who overcomes will inherit all this, and I will be his God and he will be my son. 8 But the cowardly, the unbelieving, the vile, the murderers, the sexually immoral, those who practice magic arts, the idolaters and all liars – their place will be in the fiery lake of burning sulfur. This is the second death."

8 But with the righteous He will make peace; and will protect the elect and mercy shall be on them. And they shall all belong to God, and they shall prosper, and they shall be blessed. And the light of God shall shine on them.

Revelation 21:23-25 The city does not need the sun or the moon to shine on it, for the glory of God gives it light, and the Lamb is its lamp. [24] The nations will walk by its light, and the kings of the earth will bring their splendor into it. [25] On no day will its gates ever be shut, for there will be no night there.

9 And behold! He comes with ten thousand of His holy ones (saints) to execute judgment on all, and to destroy all the ungodly (wicked); and to convict all flesh of all the works of their ungodliness which they have ungodly committed, and of all the hard things which ungodly sinners have spoken against Him.

Jude 1:14-15 And Enoch also, the seventh from Adam, prophesied of these, saying, Behold, the Lord cometh with ten thousands of his saints, [15]To execute judgment upon all, and to convince all that are ungodly among them of all their ungodly deeds which they have ungodly committed, and of all their hard speeches which ungodly sinners have spoken against him.

[Chapter 2]

1 Observe everything that takes place in the sky, how the lights do not change their orbits, and the luminaries which are in heaven, how they all rise and set in order each in its season (proper time), and do not transgress (defy) their appointed order.

2 Consider the earth, and understand the things which take place on it from start to finish, how steadfast they are, how none of the things on the earth change, but all the works of God appear to you.

3 Behold the summer and the winter, how the whole earth is filled with water, and clouds and dew and rain lie on it.

[Chapter 3]

1 Observe and see how (in the winter) all the trees seem as though they had withered and shed all their leaves, except fourteen trees, which do not lose their foliage but retain the old foliage from two to three years until the new comes.

[Chapter 4]

1 And again, observe the days of summer how the sun is above the earth. And you seek shade and shelter because of the heat of the sun, and the earth also burns with growing heat, and so you cannot walk on the earth, or on a rock because of its heat.

[Chapter 5]

1 Observe how the trees are covered with green leaves and how they bear fruit. Understand, know, and recognize that He that lives forever made them this way for you.

2 And all His works go on before Him from year to year forever, and all the work and the tasks which they accomplish for Him do not change, and so is it done.

3 Consider how the sea and the rivers in like manner accomplish their course but do not change because of His commandments.

4 But you, you have neither held to nor have you done the commandments of the Lord, but you have turned away and spoken proud and hard words with your unclean mouths against His greatness. Oh, you hard-hearted, you shall find no peace.

5 Therefore shall you curse your days, and the years of your life shall perish, and the years of your destruction shall be multiplied and in an eternal curse you shall find no mercy.

Deuteronomy 11: 26-28 See, I am setting before you today a blessing and a curse-- [27]the blessing if you obey the commands of the LORD your God that I am giving you today; [28]the curse if you disobey the commands of the LORD your God and turn from the way that I command you today by following other gods, which you have not known.

6 In those days you shall make your names an eternal curse to all the righteous, and by you shall all who curse, curse, and all the sinners and godless shall curse you forever. And for you the godless there shall be a curse.

7 And all the elect shall rejoice, and there shall be forgiveness of sins, and mercy and peace and forbearance and joy. There shall be salvation for them, (like/and) a good light. And for all of you sinners there shall be no salvation, but on you all shall abide a curse.

8 But for the elect there shall be light and joy and peace, and they shall inherit the earth.

9 And then wisdom shall be given to the elect, and they shall all live and never again sin, either through forgetfulness or through pride: But those who are given wisdom shall be humble.

10 And they shall not again transgress, Nor shall they sin all the days of their life, Nor shall they die of the anger or wrath of God, But they shall complete the number of the days of their lives. And their lives shall be

increased in peace, and their years will grow in joy and eternal gladness and peace, all the days of their lives.

Isaiah 65
1 I am sought of them that asked not for me; I am found of them that sought me not: I said, Behold me, behold me, unto a nation that was not called by my name.
2 I have spread out my hands all the day unto a rebellious people, which walketh in a way that was not good, after their own thoughts;
3 A people that provoketh me to anger continually to my face; that sacrificeth in gardens, and burneth incense upon altars of brick;
4 Which remain among the graves, and lodge in the monuments, which eat swine's flesh, and broth of abominable things is in their vessels;
5 Which say, Stand by thyself, come not near to me; for I am holier than thou. These are a smoke in my nose, a fire that burneth all the day.
6 Behold, it is written before me: I will not keep silence, but will recompense, even recompense into their bosom,
7 Your iniquities, and the iniquities of your fathers together, saith the LORD, which have burned incense upon the mountains, and blasphemed me upon the hills: therefore will I measure their former work into their bosom.
8 Thus saith the LORD, As the new wine is found in the cluster, and one saith, Destroy it not; for a blessing is in it: so will I do for my servants' sakes, that I may not destroy them all.
9 And I will bring forth a seed out of Jacob, and out of Judah an inheritor of my mountains: and mine elect shall inherit it, and my servants shall dwell there.

[Chapter 6]

1And it came to pass when the children of men had multiplied that in those days were born to them beautiful and fair daughters.

Genesis 6:1-3 And it came to pass, when men began to multiply on the face of the earth, and daughters were born unto them, 2That the sons of God saw the daughters of men that they were fair; and they took them wives of all which they chose. 3And the LORD said, My spirit shall not always strive with man, for that he also is flesh: yet his days shall be an hundred and twenty years.

2 And the angels, the sons of heaven, saw and lusted after them, and said to one another: 'Come, let us choose us wives from among the children of men

3 And have children with them.' And Semjaza, who was their leader, said to them: 'I fear you will not agree to do this deed,

4 And I alone shall have to pay the penalty of this great sin.'

5 And they all answered him and said: 'Let us all swear an oath, and all bind ourselves by mutual curses so we will not abandon this plan but to do this thing.' Then they all swore together and bound themselves by mutual curses.

6 And they were in all two hundred who descended in the days of Jared in the summit of Mount Hermon, and they called it Mount Hermon, because they had sworn and bound themselves by mutual curses on the act.

(Author's note: Jared is the Father of Enoch. Mount Hermon is located in the highest point in Israel. It covers an area of about 5,000 acres and is 2814 meters above sea level.)

Jude 1:5-6 I will therefore put you in remembrance, though ye once knew this, how that the Lord, having saved the people out of the land of Egypt, afterward destroyed them that believed not. [6]And the angels who kept not their first estate, but left their own habitation, he hath reserved in everlasting chains under darkness unto the judgment of the great day.

7 And these are the names of their leaders: Samlazaz, their leader, Araklba, Rameel, Kokablel, Tamlel, Ramlel, Danel, Ezeqeel, Baraqijal,

(Author's note: Samlazaz could be another spelling of Semjaza, and possibly be the same entity.)

8 Asael, Armaros, Batarel, Ananel, Zaqiel, Samsapeel, Satarel, Turel, Jomjael, Sariel. These are their chiefs of tens.

[Chapter 7]

And all of them together went and took wives for themselves, each choosing one for himself, and they began to go in to them and to defile themselves with sex with them,

Genesis 5:32-6:6 And Noah was five hundred years old: and Noah begat Shem, Ham, and Japheth. [1] And it came to pass, when men began to multiply on the face of the earth, and daughters were born unto them, [2] That the sons of God saw the daughters of men that they were fair; and they took them wives of all which they chose. [3] And the LORD said, My spirit shall not always strive with man, for that he also is flesh: yet his days shall be an hundred and twenty years. [4] There were giants in the earth in those days; and also after that, when the sons of God came in unto the daughters of men, and they bare children to them, the same became mighty men which were of old, men of renown. [5] And GOD saw that the wickedness of man was great in the earth, and that every imagination of the thoughts of his heart was only evil continually. [6] And it repented the LORD that he had made man on the earth, and it grieved him at his heart.

2 And the angels taught them charms and spells, and the cutting of roots, and made them acquainted with plants.

3 And the women became pregnant, and they bare large giants, whose height was three thousand cubits (ells).

Jubilees 7:21-25
[21] Because of these three things came the flood on the earth, namely, the fornication that the Watchers committed against the law of their ordinances when they went whoring after the daughters of men, and took themselves wives of all they chose, and they made the beginning of uncleanness.
[22] And they begat sons, the Naphilim (Naphidim), and they were all dissimilar, and they devoured one another, and the Giants killed the Naphil, and the Naphil killed the Eljo, and the Eljo killed mankind, and one man killed another.
[23] Every one committed himself to crime and injustice and to shed much blood, and the earth was filled with sin.
[24] After this they sinned against the beasts and birds, and all that moved and walked on the earth, and much blood was shed on the earth, and men continually desired only what was useless and evil.
[25] And the Lord destroyed everything from the face of the earth. Because of the wickedness of their deeds, and because of the blood they had shed over all the earth, He destroyed everything."

4 The giants consumed all the work and toil of men. And when men could no longer sustain them, the giants turned against them and devoured mankind.

5 And they began to sin against birds, and beasts, and reptiles, and fish, and to devour one another's flesh, and drank the blood.

6 Then the earth laid accusation against the lawless ones.

Jasher 2:19-22
[19] For in those days the sons of men began to trespass against God, and to go contrary to the commandments which he had given Adam, to be prolific and reproduce in the earth.

[20] And some of the sons of men caused their wives to drink a mixture that would render them unable to conceive, in order that they might retain their figures and their beautiful appearance might not fade.
[21] And when the sons of men caused some of their wives to drink, Zillah drank with

them.
[22] And the child-bearing women appeared abominable in the sight of their husbands and they treated them as widows, while their husbands lived with those unable to conceive and to those women they were attached.

Genesis 4:8-12
And Cain talked with Abel his brother: and it came to pass, when they were in the
field, that Cain rose up against Abel his brother, and slew him. [9] And the LORD
said unto Cain, Where is Abel thy brother? And he said, I know not: Am I my
brother's keeper? [10] And he said, What hast thou done? the voice of thy brother's
blood crieth unto me from the ground. [11] And now art thou cursed from the earth,
which hath opened her mouth to receive thy brother's blood from thy hand; [12] When
thou tillest the ground, it shall not henceforth yield unto thee her strength; a
fugitive and a vagabond shalt thou be in the earth.

[Chapter 8]

1 And Azazel taught men to make swords, and knives, and shields, and breastplates, and taught them about metals of the earth and the art of working them, and bracelets, and ornaments, and the use of antimony, and the beautifying of the eyelids, and all kinds of precious stones, and all coloring and dyes.

2 And there was great impiety; they turned away from God, and committed fornication, and they were led astray, and became corrupt in all their ways.

Matthew 5:19 (New International Version)
[19]Anyone who breaks one of the least of these commandments and teaches others to do the same will be called least in the kingdom of heaven, but whoever practices and teaches these commands will be called great in the kingdom of heaven.

3 Semjaza taught the casting of spells, and root-cuttings, Armaros taught counter-spells (release from spells), Baraqijal taught astrology, Kokabel taught the constellations (portents), Ezeqeel the knowledge of the clouds, Araqiel the signs of the earth, Shamsiel the signs of the sun, and Sariel the course of the moon. And as men perished, they cried, and their cry went up to heaven.

Jasher 4:18-20
[18]And their judges and rulers went to the daughters of men and took their wives by force from their husbands according to their choice, and the sons of men in those days took from the cattle of the earth, the beasts of the field and the fowls of the air, and taught the mixture of animals of one species with the other, in order therewith to provoke the Lord; and God saw the whole earth and it was corrupt, for all flesh

had corrupted its ways on earth, all men and all animals.
[19]And the Lord said, I will blot out man that I created from the face of the earth, yea from man to the birds of the air together with cattle and beasts that are in the field for I repent that I made them.
[20]And all men who walked in the ways of the Lord died in those days, before the Lord brought the evil on man which he had declared, for this was from the Lord that they should not see the evil which the Lord spoke of concerning the sons of men.

[Chapter 9]

1 And then Michael, Uriel, Raphael, and Gabriel looked down from heaven and saw much blood being shed on the earth, and all lawlessness being done on the earth.

2 And they said to each other: 'Let the cries from the destruction of earth ascend up to the gates of heaven.

3 And now to you, the holy ones of heaven, the souls of men make their petition, saying, "Bring our cause before the Most High."'

4 And they said to the Lord of the ages: 'Lord of lords, God of gods, King of kings, and God of the ages, the throne of your glory endures through all the generations of the ages, and your name holy and glorious and blessed to all the ages!

1Timothy 6:15-16 Which in his times he shall shew, who is the blessed and only Potentate, the King of kings, and Lord of lords; [16] Who only hath immortality, dwelling in the light which no man can approach unto; whom no man hath seen, nor can see: to whom be honour and power everlasting. Amen.

5 You have made all things, and you have power over all things: and all things are revealed and open in your sight, and you see all things, and nothing can hide itself from you.

6 Look at what Azazel has done, who hath taught all unrighteousness on earth and revealed the eternal secrets which were made and kept in heaven, which men were striving to learn:

7 And Semjaza, who taught spells, to whom you gave authority to rule over his associates.

8 And they have gone to the daughters of men on the earth, and have had sex with the women, and have defiled themselves, and revealed to them all kinds of sins.

Genesis 6:4 There were giants in the earth in those days; and also after that, when the sons of God came in unto the daughters of men, and they bare children to them, the same became mighty men which were of old, men of renown.

9 And the women have borne giants, and the whole earth has thereby been filled with blood and unrighteousness.

Genesis 6:5-6 And GOD saw that the wickedness of man was great in the earth, and that every imagination of the thoughts of his heart was only evil continually. [6]And it repented the LORD that he had made man on the earth, and it grieved him at his heart.

10 And now, behold, the souls of those who have died are crying out and making their petition to the gates of heaven, and their lament has ascended and cannot cease because of the lawless deeds which are done on the earth.

11 And you know all things before they come to pass, and you see these things and you have permitted them, and say nothing to us about these things. What are we to do with them about these things?'

Revelation 6:10 (New International Version) They called out in a loud voice, "How long, Sovereign Lord, holy and true, until you judge the inhabitants of the earth and avenge our blood?"

[Chapter 10]

1 Then said the Most High, the Great and Holy One, "Uriel, go to the son of Lamech.

2 Say to him: 'Go to Noah and tell him in my name "Hide yourself!" and reveal to him the end that is approaching: that the whole earth will be destroyed, and a flood is about to come on the whole earth, and will destroy everything on it.'

Genesis 7:4 For yet seven days, and I will cause it to rain upon the earth forty days and forty nights; and every living substance that I have made will I destroy from off the face of the earth.

3 'And now instruct him as to what he must do to escape that his offspring may be preserved for all the generations of the world.'

Genesis 6:13-14 And God said unto Noah, The end of all flesh is come before me; for the earth is filled with violence through them; and, behold, I will destroy them with the earth. [14] Make thee an ark of gopher wood; rooms shalt thou make in the ark, and shalt pitch it within and without with pitch.

4 And again the Lord said to Raphael: 'Bind Azazel hand and foot, and cast him into the darkness and split open the desert, which is in Dudael, and cast him in.

5 And fill the hole by covering him with rough and jagged rocks, and cover him with darkness, and let him live there forever, and cover his face that he may not see the light.

Revelation 20: 1-3 And I saw an angel come down from heaven, having the key of the bottomless pit and a great chain in his hand. [2] And he laid hold of the dragon, that old serpent, which is the Devil, and Satan, and bound him a thousand years, [3] And cast him into the bottomless pit, and shut him up, and set a seal upon him, that he should deceive the nations no more, till the thousand years should be fulfilled: and after that he must be loosed for a little season.

6 And on the day of the great judgment he shall be hurled into the fire.

Revelation 19:20 (King James Version) [20] And the beast was taken, and with him the false prophet that wrought miracles before him, with which he deceived them that had received the mark of the beast, and them that worshipped his image. These both were cast alive into a lake of fire burning with brimstone.

7 And heal the earth which the angels have ruined, and proclaim the healing of the earth, for I will restore the earth and heal the plague, that not all of the children of men may perish through all the secret things that the Watchers have disclosed and have taught their sons.

Romans 8:18-21 For I reckon that the sufferings of this present time are not worthy to be compared with the glory which shall be revealed in us. [19] For the earnest expectation of the creature waiteth for the manifestation of the sons of God. [20] For the creature was made subject to vanity, not willingly, but by reason of him who hath subjected the same in hope, [21] Because the creature itself also shall be delivered from the bondage of corruption into the glorious liberty of the children of God.

8 The whole earth has been corrupted through the works that were taught by Azazel: to him ascribe ALL SIN.'

9 To Gabriel said the Lord: 'Proceed against the bastards and the reprobates, and against the children of fornication and destroy the children of fornication and the children of the Watchers. Cause them to go

against one another that they may destroy each other in battle: Shorten their days.

Genesis 6:7-8 And the LORD said, I will destroy man whom I have created from the face of the earth; both man, and beast, and the creeping thing, and the fowls of the air; for it repenteth me that I have made them. [8] But Noah found grace in the eyes of the LORD.

10 No request that (the Watchers) their fathers make of you shall be granted them on their behalf; for they hope to live an eternal life, and that each one of them will live five hundred years.'

11 And the Lord said to Michael: 'Go, bind Semjaza and his team who have associated with women and have defiled themselves in all their uncleanness.

12 When their sons have slain one another, and they have seen the destruction of their beloved ones, bind them fast for seventy generations under the hills of the earth, until the day of the consummation of their judgment and until the eternal judgment is accomplished.

(Author's note: 70 generations of 500 years = 3500 years)

13 In those days they shall be led off to the abyss of fire and to the torment and the prison in which they shall be confined forever.'

14 Then Semjaza shall be burnt up with the condemned and they will be destroyed, having been bound together with them to the end of all generations.

Fragment from the Book of Giants:
And he answered, I am a giant, and by the mighty strength of my arm and my own great strength [I can defeat] anyone mortal, and I have made war against them; but I am not [strong enough for our heavenly opponent or to be] able to stand against them, for my opponents . . . reside in Heaven, and they dwell in the holy places. And not [on the earth and they] are stronger than I. . . . The time of the wild beast has come, and the wild man calls me. Then Ohya said to him, I have been forced to have a dream and the sleep of my eyes vanished in order to let me see a vision. Now I know that on Gilgamesh [our futures rest].

15 Destroy all the spirits of lust and the children of the Watchers, because they have wronged mankind.

16 Destroy all wrong from the face of the earth and let every evil work come to an end and let (the earth be planted with righteousness) the plant of righteousness and truth appear; and it shall prove a blessing, the works of righteousness and truth shall be planted in truth and joy forevermore.

Genesis 6:7 And the LORD said, I will destroy man whom I have created from the face of the earth; both man, and beast, and the creeping thing, and the fowls of the air; for it repenteth me that I have made them.

17 And then shall all the righteous survive, and shall live until they beget thousands of children, and all the days of their youth and their old age shall they complete in peace.

Genesis 8:22 While the earth remaineth, seedtime and harvest, and cold and heat, and summer and winter, and day and night shall not cease.

Genesis 9:1 And God blessed Noah and his sons, and said unto them, Be fruitful, and multiply, and replenish the earth.

18 And then shall the whole earth be untilled in righteousness and shall be planted with trees and be full of blessing. And all desirable trees shall be planted on it, and they shall plant vines on it.

19 And the vine which they plant shall yield fruit in abundance, and as for all the seed which is sown, each measurement (of it) shall bear a thousand, and each measurement of olives shall yield ten presses of oil.

20 You shall cleanse the earth from all oppression, and from all unrighteousness, and from all sin, and from all godlessness, and all the uncleanness that is brought on the earth you shall destroy from off the earth.

21 All the children of men shall become righteous, and all nations shall offer adoration and shall praise Me,

22 And all shall worship Me. And the earth shall be cleansed from all defilement, and from all sin, and from all punishment, and from all torment, and I will never again send another flood from this generation to all generations and forever.

[Chapter 11]

1 And in those days I will open the storehouse of blessings in heaven, and rain down blessings on the earth and over the work and labor of the children of men.

Malachi 3:10 (King James Version) Bring ye all the tithes into the storehouse, that there may be meat in mine house, and prove me now herewith, saith the LORD of hosts, if I will not open you the windows of heaven, and pour you out a blessing, that there shall not be room enough to receive it.

2 Truth and peace shall be united throughout all the days of the world and throughout all the generations of men.'

[Chapter 12]

1 Then Enoch disappeared and no one of the children of men knew where he was hidden, and where he abode;

Genesis 5:21-24 And Enoch lived sixty and five years, and begat Methuselah: [22] And Enoch walked with God after he begat Methuselah three hundred years, and begat sons and daughters: [23] And all the days of Enoch were three hundred sixty and five years: [24] And Enoch walked with God: and he was not; for God took him.

2 And what had become of him. And his activities were with the Holy Ones and the Watchers.

3 And I, Enoch, was blessing the Lord of majesty and the King of the ages, and lo! the Watchers called me, Enoch the scribe, and said to me:

4 'Enoch, you scribe of righteousness, go, tell the Watchers of heaven who have left the high heaven, the holy eternal place, and have defiled themselves with women, and have done as the children of earth do, and have taken to themselves wives:

5 "You have done great destruction on the earth: And you shall have no peace nor forgiveness of sin:

6 Since they delight themselves in their children, They shall see the murder of their beloved ones, and the destruction of their children, and they shall lament, and shall make supplication forever, you will receive neither mercy or peace."

(Author's note: Although we are led to believe the fallen angels are loathsome and evil, they loved and adored their children according to the above. Further, it was not the angels that became the demons. It was their children, whose spirits were evil and could not be killed.)

[Chapter 13]

1 And Enoch went and said: 'Azazel, you shall have no peace: a severe sentence has been passed against you that you should be bound:

2 And you shall not have rest or mercy (toleration nor request granted), because of the unrighteousness which you have taught, and because of all the works of godlessness,

3 And unrighteousness and sin which you have shown to men.

4 Then I went and spoke to them all together, and they were all afraid, and fear and trembling seized them.

5 And they asked me to write a petition for them that they might find forgiveness, and to read their petition in the presence of the Lord of heaven. They had been forbidden to speak (with Him) nor were they to lift up their eyes to heaven for shame of their sins because they had been condemned.

6 Then I wrote out their petition, and the prayer in regard to their spirits and their deeds individually and in regard to their requests that they should obtain forgiveness and forbearance.

7 And I went off and sat down at the waters of Dan, in the land of Dan, to the southwest of Hermon: I read their petition until I fell asleep.

8 And I had a dream, and I saw a vision of their chastisement, and a voice came to me that I would reprimand (reprove) them.

9 And when I awoke, I came to them, and they were all sitting gathered together, weeping in Abelsjail, which is between Lebanon and Seneser, with their faces covered.

10 And I recounted to them all the visions which I had seen when I was asleep, and I began to speak the words of righteousness, and to reprimand the heavenly Watchers.

[Chapter 14]

1 This is the book of the words of righteousness, and of the reprimand of the eternal Watchers in accordance with the command of the Holy Great One in that vision I saw in my sleep.

2 What I will now say with a tongue of flesh and with the breath of my mouth: which the Great One has given to men to speak with it and to understand with the heart.

3 As He has created and given to man the power of understanding the word of wisdom, so has He created me also and given me the power of reprimanding the Watchers, the children of heaven.

4 I wrote out your petition, and in my vision it appeared that your petition will not be granted to you throughout all the days of eternity, and that judgment has been finally passed on you:

5 Your petition will not be granted. From here on you shall not ascend into heaven again for all eternity, and you will be bound on earth for all eternity.

6 Before this you will see the destruction of your beloved sons and you shall have no pleasure in them, but they shall fall before you by the sword.

7 Your petition shall not be granted on their behalf or on yours, even though you weep and pray and speak all the words contained in my writings.

8 In the vision I saw clouds that invited me and summoned me into a mist, and the course of the stars and the flashes of lightning and hurried me and drove me,

9 And the winds in the vision caused me to fly and lifted me up, and bore me into heaven. And I went in until I drew near to a wall which was built out of crystals and surrounded by tongues of fire, and it began to frighten me.

10 I went into the tongues of fire and drew near a large house which was built of crystals: and the walls of the house were like a mosaic of hailstones and the floor was made of crystals like snow.

Revelation 4: 6 And before the throne there was a sea of glass like unto crystal: and in the midst of the throne, and round about the throne, were four beasts full of eyes before and behind.

Revelation 21:10-12
And he carried me away in the spirit to a great and high mountain, and shewed me that great city, the holy Jerusalem, descending out of heaven from God, [11] Having

the glory of God: and her light was like unto a stone most precious, even like a jasper stone, clear as crystal; [12] And had a wall great and high, and had twelve gates, and at the gates twelve angels, and names written thereon, which are the names of the twelve tribes of the children of Israel:

11 Its ceiling was like the path of the stars and lightning flashes, and between them were fiery cherubim,

12 Their sky was clear as water. A flaming fire surrounded the walls, and its doors blazed with fire.

13 I entered that house, and it was hot as fire and cold as ice; there were no pleasures or life therein: fear covered me, and trembling got hold of me.

14 As I shook and trembled, I fell on my face.

15 And I saw a vision, And lo! there was a second house, greater than the first,

16 And all the doors stood open before me, and it was built of flames of fire. And in every respect it was splendid and magnificent to the extent that I cannot describe it to you.

17 Its floor was of fire, and above it was lightning and the path of the stars, and its ceiling also was flaming fire.

18 And I looked and saw a throne set on high, its appearance was like crystal, and its wheels were like a shining sun, and there was the vision of cherubim.

1Timothy 6:16 Who only hath immortality, dwelling in the light which no man can approach unto; whom no man hath seen, nor can see: to whom be honour and power everlasting. Amen.

19 And from underneath the throne came rivers of fire so that I could not look at it.

3 Enoch: The Holy Chayoth carry the Throne of Glory from below. Each one uses only three fingers. The length of each finger is 800,000 and 700 times one hundred, and 66,000 parasangs. And underneath the feet of the Chayoth there are seven rivers of fire running and flowing

20 And He who is Great in Glory sat on the throne, and His raiment shone more brightly than the sun and was whiter than any snow.

Matthew 25:31 When the Son of man shall come in his glory, and all the holy angels with him, then shall he sit upon the throne of his glory:

21 None of the angels could enter or could behold His face because of the magnificence and glory and no flesh could behold Him.

22 The sea of fire surrounded Him, and a great fire stood in front of Him, and no one could draw close to Him: ten thousand times ten thousand stood before Him, but He needed no holy council.

23 The most Holy Ones who were near to Him did not leave night or day.

24 And until then I had been prostrate on my face, trembling, and the Lord called me with His own mouth, and said to me:

25 'Come here, Enoch, and hear my word.' And one of the Holy Ones came to me, picked me up, and brought me to the door; and I bowed down my face.

[Chapter 15]

1 And He answered and said to me, and I heard His voice: 'Do not be afraid, Enoch, you righteous man and scribe of righteousness.

2 Approach and hear my voice. Go and say to the Watchers of heaven, for whom you have come to intercede: "You should intercede for men, and not men for you."

3 Why and for what cause have you left the high, holy, and eternal heaven, and had sex with women, and defiled yourselves with the daughters of men and taken to yourselves wives, and done like the children of earth, and begotten giants (as your) sons?

4 Though you were holy, spiritual, living the eternal life, you have defiled yourselves with the blood of women, and have begotten children with the blood of flesh, and, as the children of men, you have lusted after flesh and blood like those who die and are killed.

5 This is why I have given men wives, that they might impregnate them, and have children by them, that deeds might continue on the earth.

6 But you were formerly spiritual, living the eternal life, and immortal for all generations of the world.

7 Therefore I have not appointed wives for you; you are spiritual beings of heaven, and in heaven was your dwelling place.

Luke 20:34-36 And Jesus answering said unto them, The children of this world marry, and are given in marriage: 35 But they which shall be accounted worthy to obtain that world, and the resurrection from the dead, neither marry, nor are given in marriage: 36 Neither can they die any more: for they are equal unto the angels; and are the children of God, being the children of the resurrection.

8 And now, the giants, who are produced from the spirits and flesh, shall be called evil spirits on the earth,

9 And shall live on the earth. Evil spirits have come out from their bodies because they are born from men and from the holy Watchers; their beginning is of primal origin;

10 They shall be evil spirits on earth, and evil spirits shall they be called spirits of the evil ones. [As for the spirits of heaven, in heaven shall be their dwelling, but as for the spirits of the earth which were born on the earth, on the earth shall be their dwelling.] And the spirits of the giants afflict, oppress, destroy, attack, war, destroy, and cause trouble on the earth.

11 They take no food, but do not hunger or thirst. They cause offences but are not observed.

12 And these spirits shall rise up against the children of men and against the women, because they have proceeded from them in the days of the slaughter and destruction.'

(Author's note: These are the evil spirits and demons. They are the disembodied spirits of the offspring of angels and humans.)

The Book of Jubilees
Because of these three things came the flood on the earth, namely, the fornication that the Watchers committed against the law of their ordinances when they went whoring after the daughters of men, and took themselves wives of all they chose, and they made the beginning of uncleanness.
And they begat sons, the Naphilim (Naphidim – the fallen), and they were all dissimilar, and they devoured one another, and the Giants killed the Naphil, and the Naphil killed the Eljo, and the Eljo killed mankind, and one man killed another.

Everyone committed himself to crime and injustice and to shed much blood, and the earth was filled with sin.
After this they sinned against the beasts and birds, and all that moved and walked on the earth, and much blood was shed on the earth, and men continually desired only what was useless and evil.
And the Lord destroyed everything from the face of the earth. Because of the wickedness of their deeds, and because of the blood they had shed over all the earth, He destroyed everything. "

[Chapter 16]

1 'And at the death of the giants, spirits will go out and shall destroy without incurring judgment, coming from their bodies their flesh shall be destroyed until the day of the consummation, the great judgment in which the age shall be consummated, over the Watchers and the godless, and shall be wholly consummated.'

Matthew 8:28-29 And when he was come to the other side into the country of the Gergesenes, there met him two possessed with devils, coming out of the tombs, exceeding fierce, so that no man might pass by that way. 29 And, behold, they cried out, saying, What have we to do with thee, Jesus, thou Son of God? art thou come hither to torment us before the time?

2 And now as to the Watchers who have sent you to intercede for them, who had been in heaven before,

3 (Say to them): "You were in heaven, but all the mysteries of heaven had not been revealed to you, and you knew worthless ones, and these in the hardness of your hearts you have made known to the women, and through these mysteries women and men work much evil on earth."

4 Say to them therefore: "You have no peace."

Genesis 6:1-8
1 And it came to pass, when men began to multiply on the face of the earth, and daughters were born unto them, 2 That the sons of God saw the daughters of men that they were fair; and they took them wives of all which they chose. 3 And the LORD said, My spirit shall not always strive with man, for that he also is flesh: yet his days shall be an hundred and twenty years. 4 There were giants in the earth in those days; and also after that, when the sons of God came in unto the daughters of men, and they bare children to them, the same became mighty men which were of old, men of renown.
5 And God saw that the wickedness of man was great in the earth, and that every imagination of the thoughts of his heart was only evil continually. 6 And it repented the LORD that he had made man on the earth, and it grieved him at his heart. 7

And the LORD said, I will destroy man whom I have created from the face of the earth; both man, and beast, and the creeping thing, and the fowls of the air; for it repenteth me that I have made them. [8] But Noah found grace in the eyes of the LORD.

[Chapter 17]

1 And they took me to a place in which those who were there were like flaming fire,

2 And, when they wished, they made themselves appear as men. They brought me to the place of darkness, and to a mountain the point of whose summit reached to heaven.

3 And I saw the lighted places and the treasuries of the stars and of the thunder and in the uttermost depths, where were

4 A fiery bow and arrows and their quiver, and a fiery sword and all the lightning. And they took me to the waters of life, and to the fire of the west, which receives every setting of the sun.

5 And I came to a river of fire in which the fire flows like water into the great sea towards the west.

6 I saw the great rivers and came to the great darkness, and went to the place where no flesh walks.

7 I saw the mountains of the darkness of winter and the place from where all the waters of the deep flow.

8 I saw the mouths of all the rivers of the earth and the mouth of the deep.

[Chapter 18]

1 I saw the storehouse of all the winds: I saw how He had adorned the whole creation with them and the firm foundations of the earth.

2 And I saw the corner-stone of the earth: I saw the four winds which support the earth and the firmament of the heaven.

3 I saw how the winds stretch out the height of heaven, and have their station between heaven and earth; these are the pillars of heaven.

4 I saw the winds of heaven which turn and bring the sky and the sun and all the stars to their setting place.

5 I saw the winds on the earth carrying the clouds: I saw the paths of the angels. I saw at the end of the earth the firmament of heaven above.

6 And I continued south and saw a place which burns day and night, where there are seven mountains of magnificent stones, three towards the east, and three towards the south.

7 And as for those towards the east, they were of colored stone, and one of pearl, and one of jacinth (a stone of healing), and those towards the south of red stone.

8 But the middle one reached to heaven like the throne of God, and was made of alabaster.

9 And the summit of the throne was of sapphire.

Ezekiel 1:22-28 And the likeness of the firmament upon the heads of the living creature was as the colour of the terrible crystal, stretched forth over their heads above.
23 And under the firmament were their wings straight, the one toward the other: every one had two, which covered on this side, and every one had two, which covered on that side, their bodies.
24 And when they went, I heard the noise of their wings, like the noise of great waters, as the voice of the Almighty, the voice of speech, as the noise of an host: when they stood, they let down their wings.
25 And there was a voice from the firmament that was over their heads, when they stood, and had let down their wings.
26 And above the firmament that was over their heads was the likeness of a throne, as the appearance of a sapphire stone: and upon the likeness of the throne was the likeness as the appearance of a man above upon it.
27 And I saw as the colour of amber, as the appearance of fire round about within it, from the appearance of his loins even upward, and from the appearance of his loins even downward, I saw as it were the appearance of fire, and it had brightness round about.
28 As the appearance of the bow that is in the cloud in the day of rain, so was the appearance of the brightness round about. This was the appearance of the likeness of the glory of the LORD. And when I saw it, I fell upon my face, and I heard a voice of one that spake.

10 And I saw a great abyss of the earth, with pillars of heavenly fire, and I saw among them fiery pillars of Heaven, which were falling,

11 And as regards both height and depth, they were immeasurable.

12 And beyond that abyss I saw a place which had no firmament of heaven above, and no firmly founded earth beneath it: there was no water on it, and no birds,

13 But it was a desert and a horrible place. I saw there seven stars like great burning mountains,

14 And an angel questioned me regarding them. The angel said: 'This place is the end of heaven and earth.

15 This has become a prison for the stars and the host of heaven. And the stars which roll over the fire are they which have transgressed the commandment of the Lord in the beginning of their rising, because they did not come out at their proper times.

16 And He was angry with them, and bound them until the time when their guilt should be consummated even for ten thousand years.'

[Chapter 19]

1 And Uriel said to me: 'The angels who have had sex with women shall stand here, and their spirits, having assumed many different forms, are defiling mankind and shall lead them astray into sacrificing to demons as gods, here shall they stand, until the day of the great judgment in which they shall be judged and are made an end of.

1 Timothy 4:1 The Spirit clearly says that in later times some will abandon the faith and follow deceiving spirits and things taught by demons.

Rev 9:20-21 The rest of mankind that were not killed by these plagues still did not repent of the work of their hands; they did not stop worshiping demons, and idols of gold, silver, bronze, stone and wood – idols that cannot see or hear or walk. [21] Nor did they repent of their murders, their magic arts, their sexual immorality or their thefts.

2 And the women also of the angels who went astray shall become sirens (other versions read 'shall become peaceful' also, another version reads, 'shall salute them').'

3 And I, Enoch, alone saw the vision, the ends of all things: and no man shall see as I have seen.

1 Peter 4:7 But the end of all things is at hand: be ye therefore sober, and watch unto prayer.

[Chapter 20]

1 These are the names of the holy angels who watch.

2 Uriel, one of the holy angels, who is over the world, turmoil and terror.

3 Raphael, one of the holy angels, who is over the spirits of men.

4 Raguel, one of the holy angels who takes vengeance on the world of the luminaries.

5 Michael, one of the holy angels, set over the virtues of mankind and over chaos.

6 Saraqael, one of the holy angels, who is set over the spirits, who sin in the spirit.

7 Gabriel, one of the holy angels, who is over Paradise and the serpents and the Cherubim.

8 Remiel, one of the holy angels, whom God set over those who rise.

[Chapter 21]

1 Then, I proceeded to where things were chaotic and void.

2 And I saw there something horrible: I saw neither a heaven above nor a firmly founded earth, but a place chaotic and horrible.

3 And there I saw seven stars of heaven bound together in it, like great mountains and burning with fire.

4 Then I said: 'For what sin are they bound, and on why have they been cast in here?'

5 Then said Uriel, one of the holy angels, who was with me, and was chief over them: 'Enoch, why do you ask, and why are you eager for the truth?

6 These are some of the stars of heaven, which have transgressed the commandment of the Lord, and are bound here until ten thousand years, the time entailed by their sins, are consummated.'

7 And I went out from there to another place, which was still more horrible than the former, and I saw a terrible thing: a great fire there which burned and blazed, and the place was cleft as far as the abyss, full of great falling columns of fire:

8 Neither its width or breadth could I see, nor could I see its source.

9 Then I said: 'I am afraid of this place and cannot stand to look at it.!' Then Uriel, one of the holy angels who was with me, answered and said to me: 'Enoch, why are you so afraid?'

10 And I answered: 'Because of this fearful place, and because of the spectacle of the pain.' And he said to me: 'This place is the prison of the angels, and here they will be imprisoned forever.'

Daniel 7:9-11 As I looked, thrones were set in place, and the Ancient of Days took his seat. His clothing was as white as snow; the hair of his head was white like wool His throne was flaming with fire, and its wheels were all ablaze. [10] A river of fire was flowing, coming out from before him. Thousands upon thousands attended him; ten thousand times ten thousand stood before him. The court was seated and the books were opened. [11] Then I continued to watch because of the boastful words the horn was speaking. I kept looking until the beast was slain and its body destroyed and thrown into the blazing fire.

[Chapter 22]

1 And I went out to another place west where there was a mountain and hard rock.

2 And there was in it four hollow places, deep and wide and very smooth. How smooth are the hollow places and looked deep and dark.

3 Then Raphael answered, one of the holy angels who was with me, and said to me: 'These hollow places have been created for this very purpose, that the spirits of the souls of the dead should be gathered here, that all the souls of the children of men should brought together here. And these places have been made to receive them until the day of their judgment and until the period appointed, until the great judgment comes on them.'

(Author note: The idea of a gathering place of the dead is seen in the doctrine of Purgatory, where the dead are gathered and those who are "redeemable" are kept and purified until such time they might ascend to heaven.)

2 Maccabee 12: 41-45 All men therefore praising the Lord, the righteous Judge, who had opened the things that were hid,
[42] Betook themselves unto prayer, and besought him that the sin committed might wholly be put out of remembrance. Besides, that noble Judas exhorted the people to keep themselves from sin, forsomuch as they saw before their eyes the things that

came to pass for the sins of those that were slain.
43 And when he had made a gathering throughout the company to the sum of two thousand drachms of silver, he sent it to Jerusalem to offer a sin offering, doing therein very well and honestly, in that he was mindful of the resurrection:
44 For if he had not hoped that they that were slain should have risen again; it had been superfluous and vain to pray for the dead.
45 And also in that he perceived that there was great favour laid up for those that died godly, it was an holy and good thought. Whereupon he made a reconciliation for the dead, that they might be delivered from sin.

4 I saw the spirit of a dead man, and his voice went out to heaven and made petitions.

5 And I asked Raphael the angel who was with me, and I said to him: 'This spirit which petitions,

6 Whose is it, whose voice goes up and petitions heaven?'

7 And he answered me saying: 'This is the spirit which went out from Abel, whom his brother Cain slew, and he makes his suit against him until his offspring is destroyed from the face of the earth, and his offspring are annihilated from among the children of men.'

Genesis 4:8-12 And Cain talked with Abel his brother: and it came to pass, when they were in the field that Cain rose up against Abel his brother, and slew him. 9 And the LORD said unto Cain, Where is Abel thy brother? And he said, I know not: Am I my brother's keeper? 10 And he said, What hast thou done? the voice of thy brother's blood crieth unto me from the ground. 11 And now art thou cursed from the earth, which hath opened her mouth to receive thy brother's blood from thy hand; 12 When thou tillest the ground, it shall not henceforth yield unto thee her strength; a fugitive and a vagabond shalt thou be in the earth.

8 Then I asked, regarding all the hollow places: 'Why is one separated from the other?'

9 And he answered me and said to me: 'These three have been made that the spirits of the dead might be separated. Divisions have been made for the spirits of the righteous, in which there is the bright spring of water.

10 And one for sinners when they die and are buried in the earth and judgment has not been executed on them in their lifetime.

11 Here their spirits shall be set apart in this great pain until the great day of judgment and punishment and torment of those who curse forever and retribution for their spirits.

2 Peter 3:7 By the same word the present heavens and earth are reserved for fire, being kept for the day of judgment and destruction of ungodly men.

12 There He shall bind them forever. And such a division has been made for the spirits of those who make their petitions, who make disclosures concerning their destruction, when they were slain in the days of the sinners.

13 Such has been made for the spirits of men who were not righteous but sinners, who were complete in transgression, and of the transgressors they shall be companions, but their spirits shall not be destroyed in the day of judgment nor shall they be raised from here.'

14 Then I blessed the Lord of glory and said: 'Blessed be my Lord, the Lord of righteousness, who rules forever.'

[Chapter 23]

1 From here I went to another place to the west of the ends of the earth.

2 And I saw a burning fire which ran without resting, and never stopped from its course day or night but flowed always in the same way.

3 And I asked saying: 'What is this which never stops?'

4 Then Raguel, one of the holy angels who was with me, answered me and said to me: 'This course of fire which you have seen is the fire in the west and is the fire of all the lights of heaven.'

[Chapter 24]

1 And from here I went to another place on the earth, and he showed me a mountain range of fire which burned day and night.

2 And I went beyond it and saw seven magnificent mountains, all differing from each other, and their stones were magnificent and beautiful, and their form was glorious: three towards the east, one founded on the other, and three towards the south, one on the other, and deep rough ravines, no one of which joined with any other.

3 And the seventh mountain was in the midst of these, and it was higher than them, resembling the seat of a throne.

4 And fragrant trees encircled the throne. And among them was a tree such as I had never smelled, nor was any among them or were others like it; it had a fragrance beyond all fragrance, and its leaves and blooms and wood would not ever wither:

5 And its fruit is beautiful, and its fruit resembles the dates of a palm. Then I said: 'How beautiful is this tree, and fragrant, and its leaves are fair, and its blooms very delightful in appearance.'

6 Then Michael, one of the holy and honored angels who was with me, and was their leader, spoke.

[Chapter 25]

1 And he said to me: 'Enoch, why do you ask me about the fragrance of the tree, and why do you wish to learn the truth?'

2 Then I answered him saying: 'I wish to know about everything, but especially about this tree.'

3 And he answered saying: 'This high mountain which you have seen, whose summit is like the throne of God, is His throne, where the Holy Great One, the Lord of Glory, the Eternal King, will sit, when He shall come down to visit the earth with goodness.

4 And as for this fragrant tree, no mortal is permitted to touch it until the great judgment, when He shall take vengeance on all and bring everything to its completion forever.

Genesis 2:8-17 Now the LORD God had planted a garden in the east, in Eden; and there he put the man he had formed. [9] And the LORD God made all kinds of trees grow out of the ground – trees that were pleasing to the eye and good for food. In the middle of the garden were the tree of life and the tree of the knowledge of good and evil. [10] A river watering the garden flowed from Eden; from there it was separated into four headwaters. [11] The name of the first is the Pishon; it winds through the entire land of Havilah, where there is gold. [12] (The gold of that land is good; aromatic resin and onyx are also there.) [13] The name of the second river is the Gihon; it winds through the entire land of Cush. [14] The name of the third river is the Tigris; it runs along the east side of Asshur. And the fourth river is the Euphrates. [15] The LORD God took the man and put him in the Garden of Eden to work it and take care of it. [16] And the LORD God commanded the man, "You are free to eat from any tree in the garden; [17] but you must not eat from the tree of the knowledge of good and evil, for when you eat of it you will surely die."

5 It shall then be given to the righteous and holy. Its fruit shall be for food to the Elect: it shall be transplanted to the holy place, to the temple of the Lord, the Eternal King.

Revelation 22:1-3 And he shewed me a pure river of water of life, clear as crystal, proceeding out of the throne of God and of the Lamb. 2 In the midst of the street of it, and on either side of the river, was there the tree of life, which bare twelve manner of fruits, and yielded her fruit every month: and the leaves of the tree were for the healing of the nations. 3 And there shall be no more curses: but the throne of God and of the Lamb shall be in it; and his servants shall serve him.

6 Then they shall rejoice and be glad, and enter into the holy place; And its fragrance shall enter into their bones, And they shall live a long life on earth, as your fathers lived. And in their days there will be no sorrow or pain or torment or toil.'

7 Then I blessed the God of Glory, the Eternal King, who has prepared such things for the righteous, and has created them and promised to give to them.

Ezekiel 47:12 (New International Version) Fruit trees of all kinds will grow on both banks of the river. Their leaves will not wither, nor will their fruit fail. Every month they will bear, because the water from the sanctuary flows to them. Their fruit will serve for food and their leaves for healing."

[Chapter 26]

1 And I went from there to the middle of the earth, and I saw a blessed place in which there were trees with branches alive and blooming on a tree that had been cut down.

(Author's note: The "hollow earth theory" has been espoused by various groups throughout history. The theory was used to create the book and movie, *Journey to the Center of the Earth.)*

2 And there I saw a holy mountain,

3 And underneath the mountain to the east there was a stream and it flowed towards the south. And I saw towards the east another mountain higher than this, and between them a deep and narrow valley.

4 In it ran a stream underneath the mountain. And to the west of it there was another mountain, lower than the former and of small elevation, and

a dry, deep valley between them; and another deep and dry valley was at the edge of the three mountains.

5 And all the valleys were deep and narrow, being formed from hard rock, and there were no trees planted on them.

6 And I was very amazed at the rocks in the valleys.

[Chapter 27]

1 Then I said: 'What is the purpose of this blessed land, which is entirely filled with trees, and what is the purpose of this accursed valley between them?'

2 Then Uriel, one of the holy angels who was with me, answered and said: 'This accursed valley is for those who are cursed forever: Here shall all the accursed be gathered together who utter with their lips words against the Lord not befitting His glory or say hard things against Him. Here shall they be gathered together, and here shall be their place of judgment.

3 In the last days there shall be the spectacle of righteous judgment on them in the presence of the righteous forever: here shall the merciful bless the Lord of glory, the Eternal King.

4 In the days of judgment they shall bless Him for the mercy in that He has shown them.'

5 Then I blessed the Lord of Glory and set out His glory and praised Him gloriously.

[Chapter 28]

1 Then, I went towards the east, into the midst of the mountain range in the desert, and I saw a wilderness.

2 And it was solitary, full of trees and plants. And water gushed out from above.

3 Rushing like a torrent which flowed towards the northwest, it caused clouds and dew to fall on every side.

[Chapter 29]

1 Then I went to another place in the desert, and approached to the east of this mountain range.

2 And there I saw aromatic trees exuding the fragrance of frankincense and myrrh, and the trees also were similar to the almond tree.

[Chapter 30]

1 Beyond these, I went far to the east,

2 And I saw another place, a valley full of water like one that would not run dry.

3 And there was a tree, the color of fragrant trees was that of mastic. And on the sides of those valleys I saw fragrant cinnamon. And beyond these I proceeded to the east.

[Chapter 31]

1 And I saw other mountains, and among them were groves of trees, and there was nectar that flowed from them, which is named Sarara and Galbanum.

2 And beyond these mountains I saw another mountain to the east of the ends of the earth, on which there were aloe trees, and all the trees were full of fruit, being like almond trees.

3 And when it was burned it smelled sweeter than any fragrant odor.

[Chapter 32]

1 And after I had smelled these fragrant odors, I looked towards the north over the mountains I saw seven mountains full of fine nard and fragrant trees of cinnamon and pepper.

2 And then I went over the summits of all these mountains, far towards the east of the earth, and passed over the Red Sea and went far from it, and passed over the angel Zotiel.

(Author's note: The angel Zoteil, whose name means, "little one of God," welcomes back those sinners who have gone astray but have repented. Based on the description of the locations, some have suggested the sphinx could be a representation, although most believe this to be unlikely.)

3 And I came to the Garden of Righteousness. I saw far beyond those trees more trees and they were numerous and large. There were two trees there, very large, beautiful, glorious, and magnificent. The tree of knowledge, whose holy fruit they ate and acquired great wisdom.

4 That tree is in height like the fir, and its leaves are like those of the Carob tree,

5 And its fruit is like the clusters of the grapes, very beautiful: and the fragrance of the tree carries far.

Isaiah 60:13 "The glory of Lebanon will come to you, the pine, the fir and the cypress together, to adorn the place of my sanctuary; and I will glorify the place of my feet.

6 Then I said: 'How beautiful is the tree, and how attractive is its look!' Then Raphael the holy angel, who was with me, answered me and said: 'This is the tree of wisdom, of which your father of old and your mother of old, who were your progenitors, have eaten, and they learned wisdom and their eyes were opened, and they knew that they were naked and they were driven out of the garden.'

[Chapter 33]

1 And from there I went to the ends of the earth and saw there large beasts, and each differed from the other; and I saw birds also differing in appearance and beauty and voice, the one differing from the other.

2 And to the east of those beasts I saw the ends of the earth where heaven rests on it, and the doors of heaven open. And I saw how the stars of heaven come out, and I counted the gates from which they came out,
3 And wrote down all their outlets, of each individual star by their number and their names, their courses and their positions, and their times and their months, as Uriel the holy angel who was with me showed me.

4 He showed me all things and wrote them down for me; also their names he wrote for me, and their laws and their functions.

[Chapter 34]

1 From there I went towards the north to the ends of the earth, and there I saw a great and glorious device at the ends of the whole earth.

2 And here I saw three gates of heaven open : through each of them proceed north winds: when they blow there is cold, hail, frost, snow, dew, and rain.

3 And out of one gate they blow for good: but when they blow through the other two gates, it is for violence and torment on the earth, and they blow with force.

[Chapter 35]
1 Then I went towards the west to the ends of the earth, and saw there three gates of heaven open such as I had seen in the east, the same number of gates, and the same number of outlets.

[Chapter 36]
1 And from there I went to the south to the ends of the earth, and saw there three open gates of heaven.

2 And from them come dew, rain, and wind. And from there I went to the east to the ends of heaven, and saw here the three eastern gates of heaven open and small gates above them.

3 Through each of these small gates pass the stars of heaven and they run their course to the west on the path which is shown to them.

4 And as often as I saw I blessed always the Lord of Glory, and I continued to bless the Lord of Glory who has done great and glorious wonders, who has shown the greatness of His work to the angels and to spirits and to men, that they might praise His work and all His creation: that they might see the power of His might and praise the great work of His hands and bless Him forever.

[Chapter 37]
The *Book of Parables* (Chapters 37-71):
1 The second vision which he saw, the vision of wisdom which Enoch the son of Jared, the son of Mahalalel,

2 The son of Cainan, the son of Enos, the son of Seth, the son of Adam, saw. And this is the beginning of the words of wisdom which I lifted up my voice to speak and say to those which dwell on earth: Hear, you men of old time, and see, you that come after, the words of the Holy One which I will speak before the Lord of spirits.

3 The words are for the men of old time, and to those that come after. We will not withhold the beginning of wisdom from this present day. Such wisdom has never been given by the Lord of spirits as I have received according to my insight, according to the good pleasure of the Lord of spirits by whom the lot of eternal life has been given to me.

4 Now three Parables were imparted to me, and I lifted up my voice and recounted them to those that dwell on the earth.

[Chapter 38]

1 The first Parable: When the congregation of the righteous shall appear, and sinners shall be judged for their sins, and shall be driven from the face of the earth;

2 And when the Righteous One shall appear before the eyes of the elect righteous ones, whose works are weighed by the Lord of spirits, light shall appear to the righteous and the elect who dwell on the earth. Where will there be the dwelling for sinners, and where the will there be a resting-place for those who have denied the Lord of spirits? It had been good for them if they had not been born.

John 1:1-5 In the beginning was the Word, and the Word was with God, and the Word was God. [2] The same was in the beginning with God. [3] All things were made by him; and without him was not any thing made that was made. [4] In him was life; and the life was the light of men. [5] And the light shineth in darkness; and the darkness comprehended it not.

3 When the secrets of the righteous shall be revealed and the sinners judged, and the godless driven from the presence of the righteous and elect,

4 From that time those that possess the earth shall no longer be powerful and mighty: And they shall not be able to look at the face of the holy ones, because the Lord of spirits has caused His light to appear on the face of the holy, righteous, and elect.

2 Corinthians 3:18 But we all, with open face beholding as in a glass the glory of the Lord, are changed into the same image from glory to glory, even as by the Spirit of the Lord.

5 Then the kings and the mighty shall be destroyed and be turned over into the hands of the righteous and holy.

6 And from then on none shall seek mercy from the Lord of spirits for themselves for their life is at an end.

[Chapter 39]

1 And it shall come to pass in those days that elect and holy children will descend from the high heaven, and their offspring will become one with the children of men.

(Author's note: Here we have a verse that can be interpreted in various ways. The holy children from the high heaven could be the spirits of the righteous dead. However, other verses seem to suggest those souls are being held until judgment. Enoch 38:1 mentions a judgment and this could be the one we seek to release the souls and make this verse mesh well.

Other theories regarding this verse have been put forward by those who believe God will give his consent to angels that they may finally freely mix with people. This seems unlikely given the previous reaction. Lastly, those involved with "UFO studies" point to this verse as an indication of contact.

Revelation 21:1-5 [1] Then I saw a new heaven and a new earth, for the first heaven and the first earth had passed away, and there was no longer any sea. [2] I saw the Holy City, the new Jerusalem, coming down out of heaven from God, prepared as a bride beautifully dressed for her husband. [3] And I heard a loud voice from the throne saying, "Now the dwelling of God is with men, and he will live with them. They will be his people, and God himself will be with them and be their God. [4] He will wipe every tear from their eyes. There will be no more death or mourning or crying or pain, for the old order of things has passed away." [5] He who was seated on the throne said, "I am making everything new!" Then he said, "Write this down, for these words are trustworthy and true."

2 And in those days Enoch received books of indignation and wrath, and books of turmoil and confusion. There will be no mercy for them, says the Lord of spirits.

3 And in those days a whirlwind carried me off from the earth, And set me down at the end of heaven.

4 There I saw another vision, the dwelling-places of the holy, and the resting-places of the righteous.

5 Here my eyes saw the dwelling places of His righteous angels, and the resting-places of the Holy Ones. And they petitioned and interceded and prayed for the children of men, and righteousness flowed before them like water, and mercy fell like dew on the earth: Thus it is among them forever and ever.

6 And in that place my eyes saw the Elect One of righteousness and of faith,

7 And I saw his dwelling-place under the wings of the Lord of spirits.

8 And righteousness shall prevail in his days, and the righteous and elect shall be innumerable and will be before Him forever and ever.

9 And all the righteous and elect ones before Him shall be as bright as fiery lights, and their mouth shall be full of blessing, and their lips shall praise the name of the Lord of spirits. Righteousness and truth before Him shall never fail.

10 There I wished to dwell, and my spirit longed for that dwelling-place; and thus it was decided and my portion was assigned and established by the Lord of spirits.

11 In those days I praised and exalted the name of the Lord of spirits with blessings and praises, because He had destined me for blessing and glory according to the good pleasure of the Lord of spirits.

12 For a long time my eyes looked at that place, and I blessed Him and praised Him, saying: 'Blessed is He, and may He be blessed from the beginning and forevermore. And in His presence there is no end.

13 He knows before the world was created what is forever and what will be from generation to generation.

14 Those who do not sleep bless you, they stand before your glory and bless, praise, and exalt you, saying: "Holy, holy, holy, is the Lord of spirits: He fills the earth with spirits."'

15 And here my eyes saw all those who do not sleep: they stand before Him and bless Him saying: 'Blessed be you, and blessed be the name of the Lord forever and ever.'

16 And my face was changed; for I could no longer see.

Exodus 34:29 When Moses came down from Mount Sinai with the two tablets of the Testimony in his hands, he was not aware that his face was radiant because he had spoken with the LORD.

[Chapter 40]

1 And after that I saw thousands of thousands and ten thousand times ten thousand,

2 I saw a multitude beyond number and reckoning, who stood before the Lord of spirits. And on the four sides of the Lord of spirits I saw four figures, different from those that did not sleep, and I learned their names;

for the angel that went with me told me their names, and showed me all the hidden things.

3 And I heard the voices of those four presences as they uttered praises before the Lord of glory.

4 The first voice blessed the Lord of spirits forever and ever.

5 The second voice I heard blessing the Elect One and the elect ones who depend on the Lord of spirits.

6 And the third voice I heard pray and intercede for those who live on the earth and pray earnestly in the name of the Lord of spirits.

7 And I heard the fourth voice fending off the Satans (adversary or accusers) and forbidding them to come before the Lord of spirits to accuse them who dwell on the earth.

8 After that I asked the angel of peace who went with me, who showed me everything that is hidden: 'Who are these four figures which I have seen and whose words I have heard and written down?'

9 And he said to me: 'This first is Michael, the merciful and long-suffering; and the second, who is set over all the diseases and all the wounds of the children of men, is Raphael; and the third, who is set over all the powers, is Gabriel' and the fourth, who is set over the repentance and those who hope to inherit eternal life, is named Phanuel.'

10 And these are the four angels of the Lord of spirits and the four voices I heard in those days.

[Chapter 41]

1 And after that I saw all the secrets of heavens, and how the kingdom is divided, and how the actions of men are weighed in the balance.

Daniel 5:27 Thou art weighed in the balances, and art found wanting.

2 And there I saw the mansions of the elect and the mansions of the holy, and my eyes saw all the sinners being driven from there which deny the name of the Lord of spirits, and they were being dragged off; and they could not live because of the punishment which proceeds from the Lord of spirits.

John 14:2-3 In my Father's house are many mansions: if it were not so, I would have told you. I go to prepare a place for you. [3] And if I go and prepare a place for you, I will come again, and receive you unto myself; that where I am, there ye may be also.

3 And there my eyes saw the secrets of the lightning and of the thunder, and the secrets of the winds, how they are divided to blow over the earth, and the secrets of the clouds and dew,

4 And there I saw where they came from and how they saturate the dusty earth.

5 And there I saw closed storehouses out of which the winds are divided, the storehouse of the hail and winds, the storehouse of the mist, and of the clouds, and the cloud thereof hovers over the earth from the beginning of the world.

6 And I saw the storehouses of the sun and moon, where they go and where they come, and their glorious return, and how one is superior to the other, and their stately orbit, and how they do not leave their orbit, and they add nothing to their orbit and they take nothing from it, and they keep faith with each other, in accordance with the oath by which they are bound together.

7 And first the sun goes out and traverses his path according to the commandment of the Lord of spirits, and mighty is His name forever and ever. And after that I saw the invisible and the visible path of the moon, and she accomplishes the course of her path in that place by day and by night - the one holding a position opposite to the other before the Lord of spirits. And they give thanks and praise and rest not; but their thanksgiving is forever and ever.

8 For the sun makes many revolutions for a blessing or a curse, and the course of the path of the moon is light to the righteous and darkness to the sinners in the name of the Lord, who made a separation between the light and the darkness, and divided the spirits of men and strengthened the spirits of the righteous, in the name of His righteousness.

Matthew 5:44-45 But I say unto you, Love your enemies, bless them that curse you, do good to them that hate you, and pray for them which despitefully use you, and persecute you; [45] That ye may be the children of your Father which is in heaven: for he maketh his sun to rise on the evil and on the good, and sendeth rain on the just and on the unjust.

9 For no angel hinders and no power is able to hinder; for He appoints a judge for them all and He judges them all Himself.

[Chapter 42]

1 Wisdom found no place where she might dwell; then a dwelling-place was assigned her in heavens.

2 Wisdom went out to make her dwelling among the children of men, and found no dwelling-place. Wisdom returned to her place, and took her seat among the angels.

3 And unrighteousness went out from her storehouses. She found those she did not seek, and dwelt with them, (she sought no one in particular but found a place...); as rain in a desert and dew on a thirsty land.

[Chapter 43]

1 And I saw other lightning and the stars of heaven, and I saw how He called them all by their names and they obeyed Him.

2 And I saw how they are weighed in a righteous balance according to their proportions of light: I saw the width of their spaces and the day of their appearing, and how their revolution produces lightning:

3 And I saw their revolution according to the number of the angels, and how they keep faith with each other. And I asked the angel who went with me who showed me what was hidden:

4 'What are these?' And he said to me: 'The Lord of spirits has shown you their parable: these are the names of the holy who dwell on the earth and believe in the name of the Lord of spirits forever and ever.'

[Chapter 44]

1 Also another phenomenon I saw in regard to the lightning: how some of the stars arise and become lightning and cannot part with their new form.

[Chapter 45]

1 And this is the second Parable: concerning those who deny the name of the dwelling of the holy ones and the Lord of spirits.

2 They shall not ascend to heaven, and they shall not come on the earth: Such shall be the lot of the sinners who have denied the name of the Lord of spirits, who are preserved for the day of suffering and tribulation.

3 On that day My Elect One shall sit on the throne of glory and shall try the works of the righteous, and their places of rest shall be innumerable. And their souls shall grow strong within them when they see My Elect One, And those who have called on My glorious name:

4 Then will I cause My Elect One to dwell among them. I will transform heaven and make it an eternal blessing and light,

5 And I will transform the earth and make it a blessing, and I will cause My elect ones to dwell on it. But the sinners and evil-doers shall not set foot on it.

6 For I have seen and satisfied My righteous ones with peace and have caused them to dwell before Me, but for the sinners there is judgment impending with Me, so that I shall destroy them from the face of the earth.

[Chapter 46]

1 And there I saw One whose face looked ancient. His head was white like wool, and with Him was another being whose countenance had the appearance of a man, and his face was full of graciousness, like one of the holy angels.

2 And I asked the angel who went with me and showed me all the hidden things, concerning that Son of Man, who he was, and where he came from, and why he went with the Ancient One? And he answered and said to me:

3 "This is the Son of Man who hath righteousness, with whom dwells righteousness, and who reveals all the treasures of that which is hidden, because the Lord of spirits hath chosen him, and whose lot has preeminence before the Lord of spirits in righteousness and is forever.

4 And this Son of Man whom you have seen shall raise up the kings and the mighty from their seats, and the strong from their thrones and shall loosen the reins of the strong, and break the teeth of the sinners.

Matthew 13:41 The Son of man shall send forth his angels, and they shall gather out of his kingdom all things that offend, and them which do iniquity;

5 And he shall put down the kings from their thrones and kingdoms because they do not exalt and praise Him, nor humbly acknowledge who bestowed their kingdom on them.

Matthew 19:28 And Jesus said unto them, Verily I say unto you, That ye which have followed me, in the regeneration when the Son of man shall sit in the throne of his glory, ye also shall sit upon twelve thrones, judging the twelve tribes of Israel.

6 And he shall make the strong hang their heads, and shall fill them with shame. And darkness shall be their dwelling, and worms shall be their bed, and they shall have no hope of rising from their beds, because they do not exalt the name of the Lord of spirits."

7 They raise their hands against the Most High and tread on the earth and dwell on it and all their deeds manifest unrighteousness. Their power rests on their riches, and their faith is in the gods which they have made with their hands. They deny the name of the Lord of spirits,

8 And they persecute the houses of His congregations, and the faithful who depend on the name of the Lord of Spirits.

[Chapter 47]

1 In those days the prayer of the righteous shall have ascended, and the blood of the righteous from the earth shall be before the Lord of spirits.

2 In those days the holy ones who dwell above in heavens shall unite with one voice and supplicate and pray and praise, and give thanks and bless the name of the Lord of spirits on behalf of the blood of the righteous which has been shed, that the prayer of the righteous may not be in vain before the Lord of spirits, that they may have justice, and that they may not have to wait forever.

3 In those days I saw the "Head of Days" when He seated himself on the throne of His glory, and the books of the living were opened before Him; and all His host which is in heaven above and His counselors stood before Him,

4 And the hearts of the holy were filled with joy because the number of the righteous had been offered, and the prayer of the righteous had been heard, and the blood of the righteous not been required before the Lord of spirits.

Revelation 20:11-15 Then I saw a great white throne and him who was seated on it. Earth and sky fled from his presence, and there was no place for them. [12] And I saw the dead, great and small, standing before the throne, and books were opened. Another book was opened, which is the Book of Life. The dead were judged according to what they had done as recorded in the books. [13] The sea gave up the dead that were in it, and death and Hades gave up the dead that were in them, and each person was judged according to what he had done. [14] Then death and Hades were thrown into the lake of fire. The lake of fire is the second death. [15] If anyone's name was not found written in the Book of Life, he was thrown into the lake of fire.

[Chapter 48]

1 And in that place I saw the spring of righteousness which was inexhaustible. And around it were many springs of wisdom. And all the thirsty drank of them, and were filled with wisdom, and their dwellings were with the righteous and holy and elect.

2 And at that hour that Son of Man was named in the presence of the Lord of spirits, And his name was brought before the Head of Days.

3 Even before the sun and the signs were created, before the stars of heaven were made, His name was named before the Lord of spirits.

4 He shall be a staff to the righteous and they shall steady themselves and not fall. And he shall be the light of the Gentiles, and the hope of those who are troubled of heart.

Romans 11: 11-21 I say then, Have they stumbled that they should fall? God forbid: but rather through their fall salvation is come unto the Gentiles, for to provoke them to jealousy.
[12] Now if the fall of them be the riches of the world, and the diminishing of them the riches of the Gentiles; how much more their fulness?
[13] For I speak to you Gentiles, inasmuch as I am the apostle of the Gentiles, I magnify mine office:
[14] If by any means I may provoke to emulation them which are my flesh, and might save some of them.
[15] For if the casting away of them be the reconciling of the world, what shall the receiving of them be, but life from the dead?
[16] For if the firstfruit be holy, the lump is also holy: and if the root be holy, so are the branches.
[17] And if some of the branches be broken off, and thou, being a wild olive tree, wert grafted in among them, and with them partakest of the root and fatness of the olive tree;
[18] Boast not against the branches. But if thou boast, thou bearest not the root, but the root thee.
[19] Thou wilt say then, The branches were broken off, that I might be grafted in.
[20] Well; because of unbelief they were broken off, and thou standest by faith. Be not highminded, but fear:
[21] For if God spared not the natural branches, take heed lest he also spare not thee.

5 All who dwell on earth shall fall down and worship before him, and will praise and bless and sing and celebrate the Lord of spirits.

6 And for this reason he has been chosen and hidden in front of (kept safe by) Him, before the creation of the world and forevermore.

7 And the wisdom of the Lord of spirits has revealed him to the holy and righteous; For he hath preserved the lot of the righteous, because they have hated and rejected this world of unrighteousness, and have hated all its works and ways in the name of the Lord of spirits. For in his name they are saved, and according to his good pleasure and it is He who has regard to their life.

8 In these days the kings of the earth and the strong who possess the land because of the works of their hands will be shamed, because on the day of their anguish and affliction they shall not be able to save themselves. And I will give them over into the hands of My elect.

9 As straw in the fire so shall they burn before the face of the holy; as lead in the water shall they sink before the face of the righteous, and no trace of them shall be found anymore.

Malachi 4:1
For, behold, the day cometh, that shall burn as an oven; and all the proud, yea, and all that do wickedly, shall be stubble: and the day that cometh shall burn them up, saith the LORD of hosts, that it shall leave them neither root nor branch.

10 And on the day of their affliction there shall be rest on the earth (because the evil ones will be destroyed), and before Him they shall fall down and not rise again, and there shall be no one to take them with his hands and raise them up; for they have denied the Lord of spirits and His Anointed. The name of the Lord of spirits be blessed.

[Chapter 49]

1 For wisdom is poured out like water, and glory will not fail before him ever.

2 For he is mighty in all the secrets of righteousness, and unrighteousness shall disappear like a shadow, and will no longer exist; because the Elect One stands before the Lord of spirits, and his glory is forever and ever, and his might for all generations.

3 In him dwells the spirit of wisdom, and the spirit which gives insight, and the spirit of understanding and of might, and the spirit of those who have fallen asleep in righteousness.

4 And he shall judge the secret things, and no one shall be able to utter a lying or idle word before him, for he is the Elect One before the Lord of spirits according to His good pleasure.

[Chapter 50]

1 And in those days a change shall take place for the holy and elect, and the light of days shall abide on them, and glory and honor shall turn to the Holy.

2 On the day of trouble, affliction will be heaped on the evil. And the righteous shall be victorious in the name of the Lord of spirits. For He will tell this to others that they may repent and turn away from the works of their hands.

3 They shall have no honor through the name of the Lord of spirits, but through His name they shall be saved, and the Lord of spirits will have compassion on them, for His mercy is great.

4 He is righteous also in His judgment, and in the presence of His glory unrighteousness also shall not stand: At His judgment the unrepentant shall perish before Him.

5 And from now on I will have no mercy on them, says the Lord of spirits.

[Chapter 51]

1 And in those days shall the earth also give back that which has been entrusted to it, and Sheol (the grave) also shall give back that which it has received, and hell shall give back that which it owes. For in those days the Elect One shall arise,

2 And he shall choose the righteous and holy from among them. For the day has drawn near that they should be saved.

Revelation 20:12-15 And I saw the dead, small and great, stand before God; and the books were opened: and another book was opened, which is the Book of Life: and the dead were judged out of those things which were written in the books, according to their works. [13] And the sea gave up the dead which were in it; and death and hell delivered up the dead which were in them: and they were judged every man according to their works. [14] And death and hell were cast into the lake of fire. This is the second death. [15] And whosoever was not found written in the Book of Life was cast into the lake of fire.

3 And in those days the Elect One shall sit on His throne, and all the secrets of wisdom and counsel shall pour from His mouth, for the Lord of spirits hath given them to Him and has glorified Him.

4 In those days shall the mountains leap like rams, and the hills shall skip like lambs satisfied with milk, and the faces of all the angels in heaven shall be lighted up with joy.

5 And the earth shall rejoice, and the righteous shall dwell on it, and the elect shall walk on it.

[Chapter 52]

1 And after those days in that place where I had seen all the visions of that which is hidden, for I had been carried off in a whirlwind and they had borne me towards the west.

2 There my eyes saw all the secret things of heaven that shall be, a mountain of iron, and a mountain of copper, and a mountain of silver, and a mountain of gold, and a mountain of soft metal, and a mountain of lead.

3 And I asked the angel who went with me, saying, 'What things are these which I have seen in secret?'

4 And he said to me: 'All these things which you have seen shall serve the authority of His Messiah that he may be powerful and mighty on the earth.'

5 The angel of peace answered me saying: 'Wait a little while, and all secret things shall be revealed to you, things which surround the Lord of spirits.

6 And these mountains which your eyes have seen, the mountain of iron, and the mountain of copper, and the mountain of silver, and the mountain of gold, and the mountain of soft metal, and the mountain of lead, all of these shall be like wax before a fire in the presence of the Elect One. Like the water which streams down from above on those mountains, and they shall be weak under his feet.

7 And it shall come to pass in those days that none shall be saved, either by gold or by silver, and none will be able to save themselves or escape.

8 And there shall be no iron for war, nor materials for breastplates. Bronze shall be of no use, tin shall be worthless, and lead shall not be desired.

9 All these things shall be destroyed from the face of the earth, when the Elect One appears before the Lord of spirits.'

[Chapter 53]

1 There my eyes saw a deep valley with its mouth open, and all who dwell on the earth and sea and islands shall bring gifts and presents and tokens of homage to Him, but that deep valley shall not become full.

2 And their hands commit lawless deeds, and everything the righteous work at the sinners devour. The sinners shall be destroyed in front of the face of the Lord of spirits, and they shall be banished from off the face of His earth, and they shall perish forever and ever.

3 For I saw all the angels of punishment abiding there and preparing all the instruments of Satan.

4 And I asked the angel of peace who went with me: 'For whom are they preparing these instruments?'

5 And he said to me: 'They prepare these for the kings and the powerful of this earth, that they may with them be destroyed.

6 After this the Righteous and Elect One shall cause the house of His congregation to appear and from then on they shall hinder no more, in the name of the Lord of spirits.

7 And these mountains shall not stand as solid ground before His righteousness, but the hills shall be like springs of water, and the righteous shall have rest from the oppression of sinners.'

[Chapter 54]

1 And I looked and turned to another part of the earth, and saw there a deep valley with burning fire.

2 And they brought the kings and the powerful, and began to cast them into this deep valley.

Revelation 6:15-17 And the kings of the earth, and the great men, and the rich men, and the chief captains, and the mighty men, and every bondman, and every free man, hid themselves in the dens and in the rocks of the mountains;

[16] And said to the mountains and rocks, Fall on us, and hide us from the face of him that sitteth on the throne, and from the wrath of the Lamb:
[17] For the great day of his wrath is come; and who shall be able to stand?

3 And there my eyes saw how they made their instruments for them, iron chains of immeasurable weight.

4 And I asked the angel of peace who was with me, saying: 'For whom are these chains being prepared ?'

5 And he said to me: 'These are being prepared for the hosts of Azazel, so that they may take them and throw them into the bottom of the pit of hell, and they shall cover their jaws with rough stones as the Lord of spirits commanded.

6 And Michael, and Gabriel, and Raphael, and Phanuel shall take hold of them on that great day, and throw them into the burning furnace on that day, that the Lord of spirits may take vengeance on them for their unrighteousness in becoming servants to Satan and for leading astray those who live on the earth.'

7 And in those days punishment will come from the Lord of spirits, and he will open all the storehouses of waters above heavens, and of the fountains which are under the surface of the earth.

8 And all the waters shall be come together (flow into or be joined) with the waters of heaven (above the sky), that which is above heavens is the masculine, and the water which is beneath the earth is the feminine.

9 And they shall destroy all who live on the dry land and those who live under the ends of heaven.

(Author's note: The previous verse refers to Noah's flood.)

10 And when they have acknowledged the unrighteousness which they have done on the earth, by these they shall perish.

[Chapter 55]

1 And after that the Head of Days repented and said: 'I have destroyed all who dwell on the earth to no avail.'

2 And He swore by His great name: 'From now on I will not do this to all who dwell on the earth again, and I will set a sign in heaven: and this

shall be a covenant of good faith between Me and them forever, so long as heaven is above the earth. And this is in accordance with My command.

(Author's note: The previous verse refers to the rainbow.)

3 When I have desired to take hold of them by the hand of the angels on the day of tribulation, anger, and pain because of this, I will cause My punishment and anger to abide on them, says God, the Lord of spirits.

4 You mighty kings who live on the earth, you shall have to watch My Elect One sit on the throne of glory and judge Azazel, and all his associates, and all his hosts in the name of the Lord of spirits.'

[Chapter 56]

1 And I saw there the hosts of the angels of punishment going, and they held scourges and chains of iron and bronze.

2 And I asked the angel of peace who went with me, saying: 'To whom are these who hold the scourges going?'

3 And he said to me: 'Each one to the ones they have chosen and to their loved ones, that they may be cast into the chasm of the abyss in the valley.

4 And then that valley shall be filled with ones they chose and their loved ones, and the days of their lives shall be at an end, and the days of their leading astray shall no longer be remembered (counted).

5 In those days the angels shall return and gather together and throw themselves to the east on the Parthians and Medes. They shall stir up the kings, so that a spirit of unrest and disturbance will come on them, and they shall drive them from their thrones, that they may rush out like lions from their lairs, and as hungry wolves among their flocks.

(Author's note: The names of certain countries help set the date of the manuscript. Scholars believe, based on the names of the countries mentioned in Enoch, that the book could not have been written prior to 250 B.C. since some countries did not exist before that date. One could add that the particular part of Enoch is the only section dated, since the book consists of several disjointed parts.)

6 And they shall go up and trample the lands of My elect ones, and the land of His elect ones shall be before them a threshing-floor (trampled, barren ground and a highway).

7 But the city of my righteous ones shall be a hindrance to their horses, and they shall begin to fight among themselves, and their own right hand shall be strong against themselves, and a man shall not know his brother, nor a son his father or his mother, until there will be innumerable corpses because of their slaughter, and their punishment shall be not in vain.

8 In those days hell (Sheol) shall open its jaws, and they shall be swallowed up. Their destruction shall be final. Hell (Sheol) shall devour the sinners in the presence of the elect.'

Revelation 20:1-2 And I saw an angel come down from heaven, having the key of the bottomless pit and a great chain in his hand. 2 And he laid hold on the dragon, that old serpent, which is the Devil, and Satan, and bound him a thousand years.

[Chapter 57]

1 And it came to pass after this that I saw another host of chariots, and men riding on them. They were coming on the winds from the east, and from the west to the south.

2 The noise of their chariots was heard, and when this turmoil took place the holy ones from heaven watched it, and the pillars of the earth were shaken and moved, and the sound of it was heard from the one end of heaven to the other, in one day.

3 And all shall fall down and worship the Lord of spirits. This is the end of the second Parable.

[Chapter 58]

1 And I began to speak the third Parable concerning the righteous and elect.

2 Blessed are you, you righteous and elect, for glorious shall be your lot.

3 And the righteous shall be in the light of the sun, and the elect will be in the light of eternal life. The days of their life shall be unending, and the days of the holy will be without number.

4 And they shall seek the light and find righteousness with the Lord of spirits. Peace to the righteous in the name of the Eternal Lord!

5 And after this it shall be said to the holy in heaven that they should seek secrets of righteousness, and the destiny of faith. For it has become bright as the sun on earth, and the darkness is passed away.

6 And there shall be a light that never ends, and to a number of days they shall not come, for the darkness shall first have been destroyed, [And the light established before the Lord of spirits] and the light of righteousness established forever before the Lord of spirits.

[Chapter 59]

1 In those days my eyes saw the secrets of the lightning, and of the lights, and they judge and execute their judgment, and they illuminate for a blessing or a curse as the Lord of spirits wills.

2 And there I saw the secrets of the thunder, and how when it resounds above in heaven, the sound thereof is heard, and he caused me to see the judgments executed on the earth, whether they are for well-being and blessing, or for a curse according to the word of the Lord of spirits.

3 And after that all the secrets of the lights and lightning were shown to me, and they lighten for blessing and for satisfying.

[Chapter 60] - Noah's Vision

1 In the year 500, in the seventh month, on the fourteenth day of the month in the life of Enoch, in that parable I saw how a mighty quaking made the heaven of heavens to quake, and the host of the Most High, and the angels, a thousand thousands and ten thousand times ten thousand, were disquieted with great foreboding.

2 And the Head of Days sat on the throne of His glory, and the angels and the righteous stood around Him.

3 And a great trembling seized me, and fear took hold of me, and my legs gave way, and I melted with weakness and fell on my face.

4 And Michael sent another angel from among the holy ones and he raised me up, and when he had raised me up my spirit returned; for I had not been able to endure the look of this host, and the disturbance and the shaking of heaven.

5 And Michael said to me: 'Why are you upset with such a vision? Until this day, His mercy and long-suffering has lasted toward those who dwell on the earth.'

6 And when the day, and the power, and the punishment, and the judgment come, which the Lord of spirits hath prepared for those who worship not the righteous law, and for those who deny the righteous judgment, and for those who take His name in vain, that day is prepared.

It will be a covenant for the elect, but for sinners an inquisition. When the punishment of the Lord of spirits shall rest on them, it will not come in vain, and it shall slay the children with their mothers and the children with their fathers.

7 And on that day two monsters were separated from one another, a female monster named Leviathan, to dwell in the abyss of the ocean over the fountains of the waters;

8 And the male is named Behemoth, who occupied with his breast a wasted wilderness named Duidain, on the east of the garden where the elect and righteous dwell, where my (great) grandfather was taken up, the seventh from Adam, the first man whom the Lord of spirits created.

9 And I asked the other angel to show me the might of those monsters, how they were separated on one day and thrown, the one into the abyss of the sea, and the other to the earth's desert.

10 And he said to me: ' Son of man, you wish to know what is kept secret.'

11 And the other angel who went with me and showed me what was kept secret; told me what is first and last in heaven in the sky, and beneath the earth in the depth, and at the ends of heaven, and on the foundation of heaven.

12 And the storehouse of the winds, and how the winds are divided, and how they are weighed, and how the doors of the winds are calculated for each according to the power of the wind, and the power of the lights of the moon according to the power that is fitting; and the divisions of the stars according to their names, and how all the divisions are divided.

13 And the thunder according to the places where they fall, and all the divisions that are made among the lightning that it may light, and their host that they may at once obey.

14 For the thunder has places of rest which are assigned while it is waiting for its peal; and the thunder and lightning are inseparable, and although not one and undivided, they both go together in spirit and are not separate.

15 For when the lightning flashes, the thunder utters its voice, and the spirit enforces a pause during the peal, and divides equally between them; for the treasury of their peals is like the sand (of an hourglass), and each one of them as it peals is held in with a bridle, and turned back by

the power of the spirit, and pushed forward according to the many parts of the earth.

16 And the spirit of the sea is masculine and strong, and according to the might of His strength He draws it back with a rein, and in like manner it is driven forward and disperses in the midst of all the mountains of the earth.

17 And the spirit of the hoar-frost is his own angel, and the spirit of the hail is a good angel. And the spirit of the snow has forsaken his storehouse because of his strength.

18 There is a special spirit there, and that which ascends from it is like smoke, and its name is frost. And the spirit of the mist is not united with them in their storehouse, but it has a special storehouse; for its course is glorious both in light and in darkness, and in winter and in summer, and in its storehouse is an angel.

19 And the spirit of the dew has its dwelling at the ends of heaven, and is connected with the storehouse of the rain, and its course is in winter and summer; and its clouds and the clouds of the mist are connected, and the one gives to the other.

20 And when the spirit of the rain goes out from its storehouse, the angels come and open the storehouse and lead it out, and when it is diffused over the whole earth it unites with the water on the earth.

21 And whenever it unites with the water on the earth, (for the waters are for those who live on the earth), they are (become) nourishment for the earth from the Most High who is in heaven.

22 Therefore there is a measurement for the rain, and the angels are in charge of it. And these things I saw towards the Garden of the Righteous.

23 And the Angel of Peace who was with me, said to me:

24 "These two monsters, prepared in accordance with the greatness of the Lord, will feed them the punishment of the Lord. And children will be killed with their mothers, and sons with their fathers.

Job 3:8 May those who curse days curse that day, those who are ready to rouse Leviathan.

Isaiah 27:1
In that day,
the LORD will punish with his sword,
his fierce, great and powerful sword,
Leviathan the gliding serpent,
Leviathan the coiling serpent;
he will slay the monster of the sea.

[Chapter 61]

1 And I saw in those days that long cords were given to those angels, and they took to themselves wings and flew, and they went towards the north.

2 I asked the angel, saying to him: 'Why have those angels who have cords taken flight?' And he said to me: 'They have gone to take measurements.'

(Author's note: There were no tape measures in those days. Measurements were taken by a simple rope or stick. The rope may have knots placed in it. Usual measurement were based on a man's forearm, the length of an arm, or the span of the arms.) In this case, the measurements, based those of the Lord or his appointed angel, encoded secret knowledge.)

3 And the angel who went with me said to me: These shall bring the measurements of the righteous, and the cords of the righteous to the righteous, that they may rely on the name of the Lord of spirits forever and ever.'

4 The elect shall begin to dwell with the elect, and those are the measurements which shall be given to faith and which shall strengthen righteousness.

5 And these measurements shall reveal all the secrets of the depths of the earth, and those who have been destroyed by the desert, and those who have been devoured by the beasts, and those who have been devoured by the fish of the sea, that they may return and rely on the day of the Elect One. For none shall be destroyed before the Lord of spirits, and none can be destroyed.

6 And all who dwell in heaven received a command and power and one voice and one light like to fire.

7 And they blessed Him with their first words and exalted and praised Him in their wisdom. And they were wise in utterance and in the spirit of life.

8 And the Lord of spirits placed the Elect One on the throne of glory. And he shall judge all the works of the holy above in heaven, and in the balance their deeds shall be weighed.

2 Timothy 4:1 I charge thee therefore before God, and the Lord Jesus Christ, who shall judge the quick and the dead at his appearing and his kingdom;

9 And when he shall lift up his face to judge their secret ways according to the word of the name of the Lord of spirits, and their path according to the way of the righteous judgment of the Lord of spirits; then they shall all speak with one voice and bless and glorify and exalt the name of the Lord of spirits.

10 And He will summon all the host of heavens, and all the holy ones above, and the host of God, the cherubim, seraphim and ophannim, and all the angels of power, and all the angels of principalities (angels that rule over other angels), and the Elect One, and the other powers on the earth and over the water. On that day shall raise one voice, and bless and glorify and exalt in the spirit of faith, and in the spirit of wisdom, and in the spirit of patience, and in the spirit of mercy, and in the spirit of judgment and of peace, and in the spirit of goodness, and shall all say with one voice: "Blessed is He, and may the name of the Lord of spirits be blessed forever and ever."

11 All who do not sleep above in heaven shall bless Him. All the holy ones who are in heaven shall bless Him; and all the elect who dwell in the garden of life, and every spirit who is able to bless, and glorify, and exalt, and praise Your blessed name, and to the extent of its ability all flesh shall glorify and bless Your name forever and ever.

12 For great is the mercy of the Lord of spirits. He is long-suffering, and all His works and all that He has created He has revealed to the righteous and elect, in the name of the Lord of spirits.

Numbers 14:18 The LORD is longsuffering, and of great mercy, forgiving iniquity and transgression, and by no means clearing the guilty, visiting the iniquity of the fathers upon the children unto the third and fourth generation.

[Chapter 62]

1 Thus the Lord commanded the kings and the mighty and the exalted, and those who dwell on the earth, and said: 'Open your eyes and lift up your horns if you are able to recognize the Elect One.'

Psalm 24:7 Lift up your heads, O ye gates; and be ye lift up, ye everlasting doors;

and the King of glory shall come in.

2 And the Lord of spirits seated Him on the throne of His glory, and the spirit of righteousness was poured out on Him, and the word of His mouth slays all the sinners, and all the unrighteous are destroyed from in front of His face.

Revelation 19:15-16 And out of his mouth goeth a sharp sword, that with it he should smite the nations: and he shall rule them with a rod of iron: and he treadeth the winepress of the fierceness and wrath of Almighty God. 16 And he hath on his vesture and on his thigh a name written, KING OF KINGS, AND LORD OF LORDS.

3 And in that day all the kings and the mighty, and the exalted and those who hold the earth shall stand up and shall see and recognize that He sits on the throne of His glory, and that righteousness is judged before Him, and no lying word is spoken before Him.

4 Then pain will come on them as on a woman in labor, and she has pain in giving birth when her child enters the mouth of the womb, and she has pain in childbirth.

Micah 4:10 Be in pain, and labour to bring forth, O daughter of Zion, like a woman in travail: for now shalt thou go forth out of the city, and thou shalt dwell in the field, and thou shalt go even to Babylon; there shalt thou be delivered; there the LORD shall redeem thee from the hand of thine enemies.

5 And one portion of them shall look at the other, and they shall be terrified, and they shall look downcast, and pain shall seize them, when they see that Son of Man sitting on the throne of His glory.

Matthew 25:31 When the Son of Man shall come in His glory, and all the holy angels with Him, then shall He sit upon the throne of His glory:

6 And the kings and the mighty and all who possess the earth shall bless and glorify and exalt Him who rules over all, who was hidden.

7 For from the beginning the Son of Man was hidden, and the Most High preserved Him in the presence of His might, and revealed Him to the elect.

8 And the congregation of the elect and holy shall be sown, and all the elect shall stand before Him on that day.

9 And all the kings and the mighty and the exalted and those who rule the earth shall fall down before Him on their faces, and worship and set their hope on that Son of Man, and petition Him and supplicate for mercy at His hands.

10 Nevertheless that Lord of spirits will so press them that they shall heavily go out from His presence, and their faces shall be filled with shame, and the darkness grows deeper on their faces.

11 And He will deliver them to the angels for punishment, to execute vengeance on them because they have oppressed His children and His elect.

12 And they shall be a spectacle for the righteous and for His elect. They shall rejoice over them, because the wrath of the Lord of spirits rests on them, and His sword is drunk with their blood.

13 The righteous and elect shall be saved on that day, and they shall never again see the face of the sinners and unrighteous.

14 And the Lord of spirits will abide over them, and they shall eat, lie down and rise up with the Son of Man forever and ever.

Revelation 21:3-4 Now the dwelling of God is with men, and he will live with them. They will be his people, and God himself will be with them and be their God. [4] He will wipe every tear from their eyes. There will be no more death or mourning or crying or pain, for the old order of things has passed away."

15 The righteous and elect shall have risen from the earth, and ceased to be downcast and they will have been clothed with garments of life.

16 And these shall be the garments of life from the Lord of spirits; they shall not wear out nor will your glory pass away from before the Lord of spirits.

[Chapter 63]

1 In those days shall the mighty and the kings who possess the earth beg Him to grant them a little respite from His angels of punishment to whom they were delivered, that they might fall down and worship before the Lord of spirits, and confess their sins before Him.

Romans 14:11-12 For it is written, As I live, saith the Lord, every knee shall bow to me, and every tongue shall confess to God. [12] So then every one of us shall give account of himself to God.

2 And they shall bless and glorify the Lord of spirits, and say: 'Blessed is the Lord of spirits and the Lord of kings, and the Lord of the mighty and the Lord of the rich, and the Lord of glory and the Lord of wisdom,

3 And every secret is revealed in front of you. Your power is from generation to generation, and your glory forever and ever. Deep and innumerable are all your secrets, and your righteousness is beyond reckoning.

4 We have now learned that we should glorify and bless the Lord of kings and He who is King over all kings.'

5 And they shall say: 'Would that we had a respite to glorify and give thanks and confess our faith before His glory!

6 And now we long for a little respite but find it not. We are driven away and obtain it not: And light has vanished from before us, and darkness is our dwelling-place forever and ever;

7 Because we have not believed in Him nor glorified the name of the Lord of spirits, but our hope was in the scepter of our kingdom, and in our own glory.

8 In the day of our suffering and tribulation He does not save and we find no respite for confession that our Lord is true in all His works, and in His judgments and His justice, and His judgments have no respect of persons.

Romans 2: 7-13 To them who by patient continuance in well doing seek for glory and honour and immortality, eternal life:
8 But unto them that are contentious, and do not obey the truth, but obey unrighteousness, indignation and wrath,
9 Tribulation and anguish, upon every soul of man that doeth evil, of the Jew first, and also of the Gentile;
10 But glory, honour, and peace, to every man that worketh good, to the Jew first, and also to the Gentile:
11 For there is no respect of persons with God.
12 For as many as have sinned without law shall also perish without law: and as many as have sinned in the law shall be judged by the law;
13 For not the hearers of the law are just before God, but the doers of the law shall be justified.

9 We pass away from before His face on account of our works, and all our sins are judged in (comparison to) righteousness.'

10 Now they shall say to themselves: 'Our souls are full of unrighteous gain, but what we have gained does not prevent us from descending from the midst of our worldly gain into the torment (burden) of Hell (Sheol).'

11 And after that their faces shall be filled with darkness and shame before that Son of Man, and they shall be driven from His presence, and the sword shall abide before His face in their midst.

12 Thus spoke the Lord of spirits: 'This is the ordinance and judgment with respect to the mighty and the kings and the exalted and those who possess the earth before the Lord of spirits.'

[Chapter 64]

1 And other forms I saw hidden in that place.

2 I heard the voice of the angel saying: 'These are the angels who descended to the earth, and revealed what was hidden to the children of men and seduced the children of men into committing sin.'

Jude 1:6 And the angels which kept not their first estate, but left their own habitation, he hath reserved in everlasting chains under darkness unto the judgment of the great day.

[Chapter 65]

1 And in those days Noah saw the earth that it had sunk down and its destruction was near.

2 And he arose from there and went to the ends of the earth, and cried aloud to his grandfather, Enoch.

3 And Noah said three times with an embittered voice: "Hear me, hear me, hear me." And I said to him: 'Tell me what it is that is falling out on the earth that the earth is in such evil plight and shaken, lest perchance I shall perish with it?'

4 And there was a great disturbance on the earth, and a voice was heard from heaven, and I fell on my face. And Enoch my grandfather came and stood by me, and said to me: 'Why have you cried to me with a bitter cry and weeping?'

5 A command has gone out from the presence of the Lord concerning those who dwell on the earth that their ruin is accomplished because they

have learned all the secrets of the angels, and all the violence of the Satans (deceivers, accusers);

(Author's note: There are many meanings of the word "satan" but all indicate great negativity. It can mean one who opposes, accuses, or deceives. In this case there is some confusion as to who the satans are. We are told the fallen angels taught men to war, but we are also told that it was the children of the angels that were so destructive. We are told that the angels taught men sorcery and spells, but it was the spirits of the nephilim that went out from their bodies to destroy.)

6 And all their powers - the most secret ones - and all the power of those who practice sorcery, and the power of witchcraft, and the power of those who make molten images for the whole earth.

7 And how silver is produced from the dust of the earth, and how soft metal originates in the earth.

8 For lead and tin are not produced from the earth like the first; it is a fountain that produces them;

9 And an angel stands in it, and that angel is preeminent.' And after that my grandfather Enoch took hold of me by my hand and lifted me up, and said to me:

10 'Go, for I have asked the Lord of spirits about this disturbance on the earth. And He said to me: "Because of their unrighteousness their judgment has been determined and shall not be withheld by Me forever. Because of the sorceries which they have searched out and learned, the earth and those who dwell on it shall be destroyed."

(Author's note: Flesh and blood will drown under the waters of the flood. All those who knew the fallen angels and all those who had given birth to their children would be killed, but the angels cannot die and the spirits of the nephilim do not need a body to survive. The text indicates the spirits need no food or water and go about unseen.)

11 And from these, they have no place of repentance forever, because they have shown them what was hidden, and they are the damned. But as for you, my son, the Lord of spirits knows that you are pure and guiltless of this reproach concerning the secrets.

12 And He has destined your name to be among the holy, and will preserve you among those who dwell on the earth; and has destined your

righteous seed both for kingship and for great honors, and from your seed shall proceed a fountain of the righteous and holy without number forever.

[Chapter 66]

1 And after that he showed me the angels of punishment who are prepared to come and let loose all the powers of the waters which are beneath in the earth in order to bring judgment and destruction on all who dwell on the earth.

2 Kings 19:35 And it came to pass that night, that the angel of the LORD went out, and smote in the camp of the Assyrians an hundred fourscore and five thousand: and when they arose early in the morning, behold, they were all dead corpses.

Revelation 14:15-19 And another angel came out of the temple, crying with a loud voice to him that sat on the cloud, Thrust in thy sickle, and reap: for the time is come for thee to reap; for the harvest of the earth is ripe. [16] And he that sat on the cloud thrust in his sickle on the earth; and the earth was reaped. [17] And another angel came out of the temple which is in heaven, he also having a sharp sickle.
[18] And another angel came out from the altar, which had power over fire; and cried with a loud cry to him that had the sharp sickle, saying, Thrust in thy sharp sickle, and gather the clusters of the vine of the earth; for her grapes are fully ripe.
[19] And the angel thrust in his sickle into the earth, and gathered the vine of the earth, and cast it into the great winepress of the wrath of God.

2 And the Lord of spirits gave commandment to the angels who were going out, that they should not cause the waters to rise but should hold them in check; for those angels were in charge of the forces of the waters.

3 And I went away from the presence of Enoch.

[Chapter 67]

1 And in those days the word of God came to me, and He said to me: 'Noah, your lot has come up before Me, a lot without blame, a lot of love and righteousness.

2 And now the angels are making a wooden structure, and when they have completed that task I will place My hand on it and preserve it (keep it safe), and there shall come out of it the seed of life, and a change shall set in so that the earth will not remain without inhabitants.

3 And I will establish your seed before me forever and ever, and I will spread abroad those who dwell with you; and the face of the earth will be

fruitful. They shall be blessed and multiply on the earth in the name of the Lord.'

4 And He will imprison those angels, who have shown unrighteousness, in that burning valley which my grandfather Enoch had formerly shown to me in the west among the mountains of gold and silver and iron and soft metal and tin.

5 And I saw that valley in which there was a great earth quake and a tidal waves of the waters.

6 And when all this took place, from that fiery molten metal and from the convulsion thereof in that place, there was a smell of sulfur produced, and it was connected with those waters, and that valley of the angels who had led mankind astray burned beneath that ground.

7 And there were streams of fire throughout the valley, where these angels are punished who had led astray those who dwell on the earth.

8 But those waters shall in those days serve for the kings and the mighty and the exalted, and those who dwell on the earth, for the healing of the body, but for the punishment of the spirit. Their spirit is full of lust, that they will be punished in their body, for they have denied the Lord of spirits. They will see their punishment daily, and yet, they believe not in His name.

9 There will be a relationship between the punishment and change. As their bodies burn, a change will take place in their spirit forever and ever; for before the Lord of spirits none shall utter an idle word.

10 For the judgment shall come on them, because they believe in the lust of their body and deny the Spirit of the Lord.

1 John 2:16-17 (New International Version) [16] Foreverything in the world – the cravings of sinful man, the lust of his eyes and the boasting of what he has and does – comes not from the Father but from the world. [17] And the world passeth away, and the lust thereof: but he that doeth the will of God abideth forever.

11 And the waters will change in those days; for when those angels are punished in these waters, the springs shall change, and when the angels ascend, this water of the springs shall change their temperature and become cold.

12 And I heard Michael answering and saying: 'This judgment in which the angels are judged is a testimony for the kings and the mighty who possess the earth.'

13 Because these waters of judgment minister to the healing of the body of the kings and the lust of their bodies; therefore they will not see and will not believe that those waters will change and become a fire which burns forever.

[Chapter 68]

1 And after that my grandfather Enoch gave me the explanations of all the secrets in the Book of the Parables which had been given to him, and he put them together for me in the words of the Book of the Parables.

2 And on that day Michael answered Raphael and said: 'The power of the spirit grips me and makes me tremble because of the severity of the judgment of the secrets, and the judgment of the angels. Who can endure the severe judgment which has been executed, and before which they melt away?'

3 And Michael answered again, and said to Raphael: 'Who would not have a softened heart concerning it, and whose mind would not be troubled by this judgment against them because of those who have led them out?'

4 And it came to pass when he stood before the Lord of spirits, Michael said thus to Raphael: 'I will not defend them under the eye of the Lord; for the Lord of spirits has been angry with them because they act as if they were the Lord.

5 Therefore all that is hidden shall come on them forever and ever; for no other angel or man shall have his portion in this judgment, but they alone have received their judgment forever and ever.

Psalm 82
1 God standeth in the congregation of the mighty; he judgeth among the gods.
2 How long will ye judge unjustly, and accept the persons of the wicked? Selah.
3 Defend the poor and fatherless: do justice to the afflicted and needy.
4 Deliver the poor and needy: rid them out of the hand of the wicked.
5 They know not, neither will they understand; they walk on in darkness: all the foundations of the earth are out of course.
6 I have said, Ye are gods; and all of you are children of the most High.

7 But ye shall die like men, and fall like one of the princes.
8 Arise, O God, judge the earth: for thou shalt inherit all nations.

(Author's note: The above Bible verse is in bold because it may play one of the pivotal roles in understanding the connections between the book of Enoch and the Bible.

God stands in the congregation of the mighty; He judgeth among the gods. KJV

Another version reads:
God has taken His place in the divine council. In the midst of the gods He holds judgment. RSV

The Septuagint reads:
God stands in the assembly of gods; and in the midst of them will judge gods. How long will ye judge unrighteous, and accept the persons of sinners?

In verse one we read that God (Elohiym) is standing in the congregation of the mighty; that He ("El" or God) is judging (Shaphat: governing) the gods (elohiym). One way to easily understand this is to look at a supreme God (capital "G") judging and governing a group of "godlings."

In an early study on Psalm 82, J. A. Emerton argued that in the Targum (Aramaic translation of the Old Testament) to the Psalms, as well as in the the Peshitta (Syriac Bible), and according to the Fathers, elohim (gods) in Psalm 82 was understood by all to refer to "angels." Emerton suggests that elohim refers to superhuman beings to whom the nations were allotted, whom the Jews regarded as angels but whom the Gentiles called gods (see 1 Cor 10:20). Jesus quotes the verse in John 10:34-36.

To stand in a court setting and judge indicates there was some transgression. This adds weight to the fact that some angels committed transgressions while others did not. Thus, it is this verse that points to the fall of some angels and the judgment handed down. It also articulates the position of angels as gods. It is assumed the point of view is that of men and not God.
In our mythology we see some "gods" were evil and violent, while other "gods" were kind and gentle. There were giants, Cyclops, monsters, and those, such as Hercules, Achilles who fought alongside men. These could be various angels, but it could point back to the three types of beings coming from the union of angels and women; Giants, Nephilim, and Eljo.

With their great height and six fingers per hand, it has been speculated that Goliath, his mother (the giant of Gath), and their family were descendants of the angel-woman union. We have also speculated that the Eljo could be the "men of renown" mentioned in Genesis.

Genesis 6:4 There were giants in the earth in those days; and also after that, when the sons of God came in unto the daughters of men, and they bare children to them, the same became mighty men which were of old, men of renown.

The term, "eljo or elyo" indicates a type of godlike being. The term indicates these were humanoids with special powers or abilities, to the extent they would be remembered and placed in mythic stories so that they should not be forgotten. This leaves the Nephilim, which could be the monsters such as Cyclops, Medusa, and other creatures memorialized in mythology.

It is not suggested that these stories are totally accurate, but only that they indicate the existence of some vastly unusual being with powers or abilities that spawned stories of monsters. Together these three types of angelic offspring make up the corpus of mythology, containing gods, giants, and monsters.)

To add additional fuel to the fire of controversy over Psalm 82, Jesus quotes the verse in John 10:34-35.

John 10:31 (New International Version) Again the Jews picked up stones to stone him, 32 but Jesus said to them, "I have shown you many great miracles from the Father. For which of these do you stone me?" 33 "We are not stoning you for any of these," replied the Jews, "but for blasphemy, because you, a mere man, claim to be God." 34 Jesus answered them, "Is it not written in your Law, 'I have said you are gods'? 35 If he called them 'gods,' to whom the word of God came – and the Scripture cannot be broken –

Does the word of God, if we accept and understand it, makes us gods? What power or authority does the knowledge, secrets, and words brought to us from heaven by fallen angels give us?

[Chapter 69]

1 And after this judgment I will terrify and make them tremble because they have shown this to those who dwell on the earth.

2 And behold the names of those angels: the first of them is Samjaza; the second Artaqifa; and the third Armen, the fourth Kokabe, the fifth Turael; the sixth Rumjal; the seventh Danjal; the eighth Neqael; the ninth Baraqel; the tenth Azazel; the eleventh Armaros; the twelfth Batarjal; the

thirteenth Busasejal; the fourteenth Hananel; the fifteenth Turel; and the sixteenth Simapesiel; the seventeenth Jetrel; the eighteenth Tumael; the nineteenth Turel; the twentieth Rumael; the twenty-first Azazyel;

(Author's note: For more information on the heavenly names, such as the various names of the "Presence of the Lord," see the Third Book of Enoch, also called the "Hebrew Book of Enoch" or "3 Enoch."

The leader of the Watchers was Samjaza, also spelled Shemhazai. Two hundred angels made the descent to earth, at Mount Hermon. Two hundred angels were divided into group of ten, each under the leadership of chieftain or captain.

They defiled themselves with women, producing children. Their children were giants of three-thousand ells tall, which some sources say is approximately 3,420 meters in height (11,250 feet tall).

According to the Haggada (book 1, chapter 4: Punishment of the Fallen Angels), the angel Shemhazai lusted after a maiden named Istehar, however, she tricked him to reveal the Ineffable Name of God. Istehar used the name to ascend to heaven and escaped her violation by Shemhazai. God rewarded Istehar for her by commemorating her as the seven-star constellation Pleides.

In Genesis 4:22, Naamah was a daughter of Lamech and Zillah, and sister of Tubal-Cain. She was a descendant of Cain, hence a Cainite. According to the Haggada, Naamah was the opposite of Istehar, because the angel Shamdon had succeeded in sexual union with Naamah. Naamah's offspring was Asmodeus, a demon, instead of a giant. Asmodeus appeared in the apocrypha Tobit.

According to the introduction of the Zohar, it was Naamah who first deceived and seduced the angels, rather than the angel seducing Naamah. Zohar 3 mentioned the angels Aza and Azael, instead of Shamdon; they were victims of her beauty. She became mother of an unknown number of demons.

Our vampire lore may have begun with the 1 Enoch, since it states the giants consumed all the food men could produce and then began devouring people and sucking their blood, like vampires.)

3 And these are the chiefs of their angels and their names, and their leaders over hundreds, and leaders over fifties, and leaders over tens.

4 The name of the first Jeqon, that is, the one who led astray the sons of God, and brought them down to the earth, and led them astray through the daughters of men.

5 And the second was named Asbeel; he imparted to the holy sons of God evil counsel, and led them astray so that they defiled their bodies with the daughters of men.

6 And the third was named Gadreel; it is he who showed the children of men all the blows of death, and he led astray Eve, and showed the weapons of death to the sons of men; the shield and the coat of mail, and the sword for battle, and all the weapons of death to the children of men.

7 And from his hand they have proceeded against those who dwell on the earth from that day and forevermore.

8 And the fourth was named Penemue; he taught the children of men the bitter and the sweet, and he taught them all the secrets of their wisdom.

9 And he instructed mankind in writing with ink and paper, and thereby many sinned from eternity to eternity and until this day.

10 For men were not created for the purpose of confirming their good faith with pen and ink.

(Author's note: Reading and writing are considered grievous sins because they allow knowledge, and thus sin, to be propagated from generation to generation. It should be pointed out that God himself wrote the Ten Commandments on stone. It is possible that this verse may refer to the Enochian alphabet, thought to convey the original teachings of the fallen angels.

The Enochian alphabet was thought to be lost with the flood, but "re-discovered" by John Dee.

John Dee (13 July 1527–1608 or 1609) was a noted mathematician, astrologer, navigator, occultist, and a consultant to Queen Elizabeth I. According to Tobias Churton in his book *The Golden Builders*, the concept of an Angelic or pre-deluge language was common during Dee's time. If one could speak with angels, it was believed one could directly interact with them.

In 1581, Dee mentioned in his personal journals that God had sent "good angels" to communicate directly with prophets. In 1582, Dee teamed up with the seer Edward Kelley, although Dee had used several other seers previously. With Kelley's help as a scryer, Dee set out to establish lasting contact with the angels, which resulted, among other things, in the reception of the Enochian or Angelical language.

According to Dee's journals, Angelical was supposed to have been the language God used to create the world, and which was later used by Adam to speak with God and the angels, and to name all things into existence.

The alphabet codified the phonetics of the language Dee claimed could be used to summon various angels, who would dispatch knowledge or assistance. The chants used complex phonetic streams named "Angelic Calls" to name and call forth angels.

THE ENOCHIAN ALPHABET

Family of Pa — Family of Tal — Family of Pal

Table of Enochian Letters, Print, and Script

11 For men were created exactly like the angels, to the intent that they should continue pure and righteous; and death, which destroys

everything, should not have taken hold of them, but through this their knowledge they are perishing, and through this power consumes them.

Romans 5:12 (King James Version) Wherefore, as by one man sin entered into the world, and death by sin; and so death passed upon all men, for that all have sinned:

12 And the fifth was named Kasdeja; this is he who showed the children of men all the wicked smitings (blows) of spirits and demons, and the smitings (blows) of the embryo in the womb, that it may pass away, and the smitings (blows) of the soul, the bites of the serpent, and the smitings (blows) which befall through the midday heat, the son of the serpent named Taba'et.

13 And this is the task of Kasbeel, the chief of the oath which he showed to the holy ones when he dwelt high above in glory, and its name is Biqa.

14 This (angel) requested Michael to show him the hidden name, that he might enunciate it in the oath,

15 So that those might quake before that name and oath who revealed all that was in secret to the children of men. And this is the power of this oath, for it is powerful and strong, and he placed this oath Akae in the hand of (under the control of) Michael.

(Author's note: The ineffable name of God holds the power to create, bind, and destroy. In the Lillith myth, it is said she spoke this name when she argued against God and Adam. By speaking the name she flew off and became a demon.)

16 And these are the secrets of this oath (God's promise, word) that heaven was suspended before the world was created, and forever, and they are strong through his oath (word, promise).

17 And through it the earth was founded on the water, and from the secret recesses of the mountains come beautiful waters, from the creation of the world and to eternity.

18 And through that oath the sea was created, and as its foundation He set for it the sand against the time of its anger (rage) that it dare not pass beyond it from the creation of the world to eternity.

19 And through that oath are the depths made fast (strong), and abide and stir not from their place from eternity to eternity.

20 And through that oath the sun and moon complete their course, and deviate not from their ordinance from eternity to eternity.

21 And through that oath the stars complete their course, and He calls them by their names, and they answer Him from eternity to eternity.

22 [And in like manner the spirits of the water, and of the winds, and of all kinds of spirits, and (their) paths from all the quarters of the winds respond to His command.]

(Author's note: Verse 22 is not complete in some translations.)

23 And there are preserved the voices of the thunder and the light of the lightning: and there are preserved the storehouses of the hail and the storehouses of the hoarfrost,

24 And the storehouses of the mist, and the storehouses of the rain and the dew. And all these believe and give thanks before the Lord of spirits, and glorify (Him) with all their power, and their food is in every act of thanksgiving; they thank and glorify and exalt the name of the Lord of spirits forever and ever.

25 And this oath is mighty over them and through it they are preserved and their paths are preserved, and their course is not destroyed.

26 And there was great joy among them, and they blessed and glorified and exalted because the name of that Son of Man had been revealed to them.

(Author's note: The name of a person reveals their personality and power. There remains a ceremony to this day that if a person is on his deathbed a rabbi may change the person's name to trick the Angel of Death so the person might escape his reaping, suggesting the Angel seeks by name.)

27 And he sat on the throne of his glory, and the sum of judgment was given to the Son of Man. And he caused the sinners and all those who led the world astray to pass away and be destroyed from off the face of the earth.

28 They shall be bound with chains, and shut up and imprisoned in their place of assembly, and all their works vanish from the face of the earth.

29 And from that time forward, there shall be nothing corruptible; for that Son of Man has appeared, and has seated himself on the throne of his

glory. And all evil shall pass away before his face, and the word of that Son of Man shall go out and be strong before the Lord of spirits.

[Chapter 70]

1 And it came to pass after this that during His lifetime His name was raised up to the Son of Man, and to the Lord of spirits from among those who dwell on the earth.

2 And He was raised aloft on the chariots of the spirit and His name vanished among them. And from that day I was no longer numbered among them; and He placed me between the two winds, between the North and the West, where the angels took the cords to measure the place for the elect and righteous for me.

3 And there I saw the first fathers and the righteous who dwell in that place from the beginning.

[Chapter 71]

1 And it came to pass after this that my spirit was translated (carried off) and it ascended into heaven; and I saw the sons of the holy angels (sons) of God. They were walking on flames of fire; their garments were white, and their faces shone like snow.

2 And I saw two rivers of fire, and the light of that fire shone like hyacinth, and I fell on my face before the Lord of spirits.

3 And the angel Michael, one of the archangels, seized me by my right hand, and lifted me up and led me out into all the secrets, and he showed me all the secrets of righteousness.

4 And he showed me all the secrets of the ends of heaven, and all the storehouses of all the stars, and all the lights, from where they proceed before the face of the holy ones.

5 And he translated (carried) my spirit into heaven of heavens, and I saw there as it were built of crystals, and between those crystals tongues of living fire.

Revelation 21:10-11 And he carried me away in the spirit to a great and high mountain, and shewed me that great city, the holy Jerusalem, descending out of heaven from God, 11 Having the glory of God: and her light was like unto a stone most precious, even like a jasper stone, clear as crystal.

6 My spirit saw circle of fire binding around the house of fire, and on its four sides were rivers full of living fire, and they encircled that house.

7 And round about were seraphim, cherubim, and ophannim; and these are they who never sleep and they guard the throne of His glory.

8 And I saw angels who could not be counted, a thousand thousands, and ten thousand times ten thousand, encircling that house. And Michael, and Raphael, and Gabriel, and Phanuel, and the holy angels who are in heaven above, go in and out of that house.

9 And they came out from that house, and Michael and Gabriel, Raphael and Phanuel, and many holy angels without number.

10 And with them the Head of Days, His head white and pure as wool, and His raiment indescribable.

11 And I fell on my face, and my whole body melted, and my spirit was (transformed) transfigured. And I cried with a loud voice in the spirit of power, and I blessed and glorified and exalted.

Psalm 22:14-15 I am poured out like water, and all my bones are out of joint: my heart is like wax; it is melted in the midst of my bowels.
15 My strength is dried up like a potsherd; and my tongue cleaveth to my jaws; and thou hast brought me into the dust of death.

12 And these blessings which came from my mouth were very pleasing before that Head of Days.

13 And the Head of Days came with Michael and Gabriel, Raphael and Phanuel, and thousands and ten thousands of angels without number.

14 And the angel came to me and greeted me with his voice, and said to me 'This is the Son of Man who is born to righteousness, and righteousness abides over him, and the righteousness of the Head of Days forsakes him not.'

15 And he said to me: 'He proclaims to you peace in the name of the world to come; for from there peace has proceeded since the creation of the world, and it shall be with you forever and forever and ever.

John 17:24 Father, I will that they also, whom thou hast given me, be with me where I am; that they may behold my glory, which thou hast given me: for thou lovest me before the foundation of the world.

16 And all shall walk in His ways since righteousness never forsook Him. Their dwelling-place shall be with Him and it will be their heritage, and they shall not be separated from Him forever and ever and ever.

17 And so there shall be length of days with the Son of Man, and the righteous shall have peace and an upright way in the name of the Lord of spirits forever and ever.'

Hebrews 4:3 For we which have believed do enter into rest, as he said, As I have sworn in my wrath, if they shall enter into my rest: although the works were finished from the foundation of the world.

[Chapter 72]

The Book of *Astronomy and Calendar* (Chapters 72-82):

(Author's note: Full description of the calendar and its application in prophecy are discussed in the section, "The Calendar of Enoch's and Daniel's Prophecies, starting on page 158.)

1 The book of the courses of the luminaries of heaven, the relations of each, according to their name, origin, and months (dominion and seasons) which Uriel, the holy angel who was with me, who is their guide, showed me; and he showed me all their laws (regulations) exactly as they are, and how it is with each of the years of the world and to eternity, until the new creation is accomplished which endures until eternity.

2 And this is the first law of the luminaries: the luminary the Sun has its rising in the eastern doors of heaven, and its setting in the western doors of heaven.

3 And I saw six doors in which the sun rises, and six doors in which the sun sets and the moon rises and sets in these doors, and the leaders of the stars and those whom they lead: six in the east and six in the west, and all following each other in accurately corresponding order.

4 There were also many windows to the right and left of these doors. And first there goes out the great luminary, named the Sun, and his sphere (orbit, disc) is like the sphere (orbit, disc) of heaven, and he is quite filled with illuminating and heating fire.

5 The chariot on which he ascends, the wind drives, and the sun goes down from heaven and returns through the north in order to reach the east, and is so guided that he comes to the appropriate door and shines in the face of heaven.

6 In this way he rises in the first month in the great door, which is the fourth.

7 And in that fourth door from which the sun rises in the first month are twelve windows, from which proceed a flame when they are opened in their season.

8 When the sun rises in heaven, he comes out through that fourth door, thirty mornings in succession, and sets accurately in the fourth door in the west of the heaven.

9 And during this period the day becomes daily longer and nights grow shorter to the thirtieth morning.

10 On that day the day is longer than the night by a ninth part, and the day amounts exactly to ten parts and the night to eight parts.

11 And the sun rises from that fourth door, and sets in the fourth and returns to the fifth door of the east thirty mornings, and rises from it and sets in the fifth door.

12 And then the day becomes longer by two parts and amounts to eleven parts, and the night becomes shorter and amounts to seven parts.

13 And it returns to the east and enters into the sixth door, and rises and sets in the sixth door one-and-thirty mornings on account of its sign.

14 On that day the day becomes longer than the night, and the day becomes double the night, and the day becomes twelve parts, and the night is shortened and becomes six parts.

15 And the sun mounts up to make the day shorter and the night longer, and the sun returns to the east and enters into the sixth door, and rises from it and sets thirty mornings.

16 And when thirty mornings are accomplished, the day decreases by exactly one part, and becomes eleven parts, and the night seven.

17 And the sun goes out from that sixth door in the west, and goes to the east and rises in the fifth door for thirty mornings, and sets in the west again in the fifth western door.

18 On that day the day decreases by two parts, and amounts to ten parts and the night to eight parts.

19 And the sun goes out from that fifth door and sets in the fifth door of the west, and rises in the fourth door for one-and-thirty mornings on account of its sign, and sets in the west.

20 On that day the day becomes equal with the night in length, and the night amounts to nine parts and the day to nine parts.

21 And the sun rises from that door and sets in the west, and returns to the east and rises thirty mornings in the third door and sets in the west in the third door.

22 And on that day the night becomes longer than the day, and night becomes longer than night, and day shorter than day until the thirtieth morning, and the night amounts exactly to ten parts and the day to eight parts.

23 And the sun rises from that third door and sets in the third door in the west and returns to the east, and for thirty mornings rises in the second door in the east, and in like manner sets in the second door in the west of heaven.

24 And on that day the night amounts to eleven parts and the day to seven parts.

25 And the sun rises on that day from that second door and sets in the west in the second door, and returns to the east into the first door for one-and-thirty mornings, and sets in the first door in the west of heaven.

26 And on that day the night becomes longer and amounts to the double of the day: and the night amounts exactly to twelve parts and the day to six.

(Author's note: If the night is 12 parts and the day is six parts, the entire 24 hour day is divided into 18 sections of 80 minutes each.)

27 And the sun has traversed the divisions of his orbit and turns again on those divisions of his orbit, and enters that door thirty mornings and sets also in the west opposite to it.

28 And on that night has the night decreased in length by a ninth part, and the night has become eleven parts and the day seven parts.

29 And the sun has returned and entered into the second door in the east, and returns on those his divisions of his orbit for thirty mornings, rising and setting.

30 And on that day the night decreases in length, and the night amounts to ten parts and the day to eight.

31 And on that day the sun rises from that door, and sets in the west, and returns to the east, and rises in the third door for one-and-thirty mornings, and sets in the west of heaven.

32 On that day the night decreases and amounts to nine parts, and the day to nine parts, and the night is equal to the day and the year is exactly as to its days three hundred and sixty-four.

33 And the length of the day and of the night, and the shortness of the day and of the night arise through the course of the sun these distinctions are separated'.

34 So it comes that its course becomes daily longer, and its course nightly shorter.

35 And this is the law and the course of the great luminary which is named the sun, and his return as often as he returns sixty times and rises, forever and ever.

36 And that which rises is the great luminary, and is so named according to its appearance, according as the Lord commanded.

37 As he rises, so he sets and decreases not, and rests not, but runs day and night, and his light is sevenfold brighter than that of the moon; but in regard to size, they are both equal.

[Chapter 73]

1 And after this law I saw another law dealing with the smaller luminary, which is named the Moon.

2 And her orbit is like the sphere (orbit, disc) of heaven, and her chariot in which she rides is driven by the wind, and light is given to her in measurement.

3 And her rising and setting change every month and her days are like the days of the sun, and when her light is uniformly (completely) full it amounts to the seventh part of the light of the sun.

4 And thus she rises. And her first phase in the east comes out on the thirtieth morning and on that day she becomes visible, and constitutes for you the first phase of the moon on the thirtieth day together with the sun in the door where the sun rises.

5 And the one half of her goes out by a seventh part, and her whole disc is empty, without light, with the exception of one-seventh part of it, and the fourteenth part of her light.

6 And when she receives one-seventh part of the half of her light, her light amounts to one-seventh part and the half thereof.

7 And she sets with the sun, and when the sun rises the moon rises with him and receives the half of one part of light, and in that night in the beginning of her morning in the beginning of the lunar day the moon sets with the sun, and is invisible that night with the fourteen parts and the half of one of them.

8 And she rises on that day with exactly a seventh part, and comes out and recedes from the rising of the sun, and in her remaining days she becomes bright in the remaining thirteen parts.

[Chapter 74]

1 And I saw another course, a law for her, and how according to that law she performs her monthly revolution.

2 And all these Uriel, the holy angel who is the leader of them all, showed to me, and their positions, and I wrote down their positions as he showed them to me, and I wrote down their months as they were, and the appearance of their lights until fifteen days were accomplished.

3 In single seventh parts she accomplishes all her light in the east, and in single seventh parts accomplishes all her darkness in the west.

4 And in certain months she alters her settings, and in certain months she pursues her own peculiar course.

5 In two months the moon sets with the sun: in those two middle doors the third and the fourth.

6 She goes out for seven days, and turns about and returns again through the door where the sun rises, and all her light is full; and she recedes from the sun, and in eight days enters the sixth door from which the sun goes out.

7 And when the sun goes out from the fourth door she goes out seven days, until she goes out from the fifth and turns back again in seven days into the fourth door and accomplishes all her light; and she recedes and enters into the first door in eight days.

8 And she returns again in seven days into the fourth door from which the sun goes out.

9 Thus I saw their positions, how the moons rose and the sun set in those days.

10 And if five years are added together the sun has an excess of thirty days, and all the days which accrue to it for one of those five years, when they are full, amount to 364 days.

11 And an excess of the sun and of the stars amounts to six days; in five years six days every year come to 30 days, and the moon falls behind the sun and stars to the number of 30 days.

12 And the sun and the stars bring in all the years exactly, so that they do not advance or delay their position by a single day to eternity; but complete the years with perfect justice in 364 days.

13 In three years there are 1,092 days, and in five years 1,820 days, so that in eight years there are 2,912 days.

(Author's note: At the end of five years a week may be added to bring the year back in line. Compare 1826.25 days of the solar year in five years to 1820 days of the Enochian calendar after five years. This leaves 6.25 days difference. Adding a week to the Enochian calendar leaves a difference of only .75 of a day. The years is adjusted in this way so that the alignment is kept very close.)

14 For the moon alone the days amount in three years to 1,062 days, and in five years she falls 50 days behind to the sum of 1,770 there is five to be added 1,000 and 62 days.

15 And in five years there are 1,770 days, so that for the moon the days six in eight years amount to 21,832 days.

16 For in eight years she falls behind to the amount of 80 days, all the days she falls behind in eight years are 80.

17 And the year is accurately completed in conformity with their world-stations and the stations of the sun, which rise from the doors through which the sun rises and sets 30 days.

[Chapter 75]

1 And the leaders of the heads of the (ten) thousands, who are in charge of the whole creation and over all the stars, have also to do with the four days of the year which are not counted in the yearly calendar, being not separated from their office, according to the reckoning of the year, and these render service on the four days which are not counted in the reckoning of the year.

2 And because of them men go wrong in them, for those luminaries truly render service to the stations of the world, one in the first door, one on the third door of heaven, one in the fourth door, and one in the sixth door, and the exactness of the year is accomplished through its separate three hundred and sixty-four stations.

3 For the signs and the times and the years and the days the angel Uriel showed to me, whom the Lord of glory hath set forever over all the luminaries of heaven, in heaven and in the world, that they should rule on the face of heaven and be seen on the earth, and be leaders for the day via the sun and the night via the moon, and stars, and all the ministering creatures which make their revolution in all the chariots of heaven.

4 In like manner, twelve doors Uriel showed me, open in the sphere (disc) of the sun's chariot in heaven, through which the rays of the sun break out; and from them is warmth diffused over the earth, when they are opened at their appointed seasons.

5 And there are openings for the wind and the spirit of dew that when they are opened, stand open in heaven at the ends of the earth.

6 As for the twelve doors in the heaven, at the ends of the earth, out of which go out the sun, moon, and stars, and all the works of heaven in the east and in the west; there are many windows open to the left and right of them,

7 And one window at its appointed season produces warmth, corresponding to the doors from which the stars come out as He has commanded them; and in which they are set, corresponding to their number.

8 And I saw chariots in heaven, running in the world, above those doors in which the stars that never set.

9 And one is larger than all the rest, and it is that that makes its course through the entire world.

[Chapter 76]

1 At the ends of the earth I saw twelve doors open to all quarters of heaven, from which the winds go out and blow over the earth.

2 Three of them are open on the face of heaven, and three in the west; and three on the right of heaven, and three on the left.

3 And the three first are those of the east, and three are of the north, and three, after those on the left, of the south, and three of the west.

4 Through four of these come winds of blessing and prosperity (peace), and from those eight come hurtful winds; when they are sent, they bring destruction on all the earth and the water on it, and on all who dwell on it, and on everything which is in the water and on the land.

5 And the first wind from those doors, called the east wind, comes out through the first door which is in the east, inclining towards the south; from it desolation, drought, heat, and destruction come out .

6 And through the second door in the middle comes what is fitting (right, correct), and there come rain and fruitfulness and prosperity and dew. And through the third door which lies toward the north comes cold and drought.

7 And after these, comes out the south winds through three doors; through the first door of them inclining to the east comes out a hot wind.

8 And through the middle door next to it there comes out fragrant smells, and dew and rain, and prosperity and health.

9 And through the third door which lies to the west dew comes out and also rain, locusts and desolation.

10 And from the seventh door in the east comes the north winds, and dew, rain, locusts and desolation.

11 And from the center door come health and rain and dew and prosperity; and through the third door in the west come cloud and hoar-frost, and snow and rain, and dew and locusts.

12 And after these came the four west winds; through the first door adjoining the north come out dew and hoar-frost, and cold and snow and frost.

13 And from the center door come out dew and rain, and prosperity and blessing.

14 And through the last door which adjoins the south, come drought and desolation, and burning and destruction. And the twelve doors of the four quarters of heaven are therewith completed, and all their laws and all their plagues and all their benefactions have I shown to you, my son Methuselah.

[Chapter 77]

1 And the first quarter is called the east, because it is the first; and the second, the south, because the Most High will descend there. From there will He who is blessed forever descend.

2 And the west quarter is named the diminished, because there all the luminaries of the heaven wane and go down.

3 And the fourth quarter, named the north, is divided into three parts: the first of them is for the dwelling of men; and the second contains seas of water, and the abyss (deep) and forests and rivers, and darkness and clouds; and the third part contains the garden of righteousness.

4 I saw seven high mountains, higher than all the mountains which are on the earth: and from here comes hoar-frost, and days, seasons, and years pass away.

5 I saw seven rivers on the earth larger than all the rivers. One of them coming from the west pours its waters into the Great Sea.

6 And these two come from the north to the sea and pour their waters into the Erythraean Sea in the east.

7 And the remaining four come out on the side of the north to their own sea, two of them to the Erythraean Sea, and two into the Great Sea and some say they discharge themselves there into the desert.

8 I saw seven great islands in the sea and in the mainland, two in the mainland and five in the Great Sea.

[Chapter 78]

1 And the names of the sun are the following: the first Orjares, and the second Tomas.

2 And the moon has four names: the first name is Asonja, the second Ebla, the third Benase, and the fourth Erae.

3 These are the two great luminaries; their spheres (disc) are like the sphere (disc) of the heaven, and the size of the spheres (disc) of both is alike.

4 In the sphere (disc) of the sun there are seven portions of light which are added to it more than to the moon, and in fixed measurements it is transferred until the seventh portion of the sun is exhausted.

5 And they set and enter the doors of the west, and make their revolution by the north, and come out through the eastern doors on the face of heaven.

6 And when the moon rises one-fourteenth part appears in heaven, and on the fourteenth day the moon's light becomes full.

7 And fifteen parts of light are transferred to her until the fifteenth day when her light is full, according to the sign of the year, and she becomes fifteen parts, and the moon grows by an additional fourteenth parts.

8 And as the moon's waning decreases on the first day to fourteen parts of her light, on the second to thirteen parts of light, on the third to twelve, on the fourth to eleven, on the fifth to ten, on the sixth to nine, on the seventh to eight, on the eighth to seven, on the ninth to six, on the tenth to five, on the eleventh to four, on the twelfth to three, on the thirteenth to two, on the fourteenth to the half of a seventh, and all her remaining light disappears wholly on the fifteenth.

9 And in certain months the month has twenty-nine days and once twenty-eight.

10 And Uriel showed me another law: when light is transferred to the moon, and on which side it is transferred to her by the sun.

11 During all the period during which the moon is growing in her light, she is transferring it to herself when opposite to the sun during fourteen days her light is full in heaven, and when she is ablaze throughout, her light is full in heaven.

12 And on the first day she is called the new moon, for on that day the light rises on her.

13 She becomes the full moon exactly on the day when the sun sets in the west, and from the east she rises at night, and the moon shines the whole night through until the sun rises over against her and the moon is seen over against the sun.

14 On the side whence the light of the moon comes out, there again she wanes until all the light vanishes and all the days of the month are at an end, and her sphere (disc) is empty, void of light.

15 And three months she makes of thirty days, and at her time she makes three months of twenty-nine days each, in which she accomplishes her waning in the first period of time, and in the first door for one hundred and seventy-seven days.

16 And in the time of her going out she appears for three months consisting of thirty days each, and she appears for three months consisting of twenty-nine each.

17 By night she looks like a man for twenty days each time, and by day she appears like heaven, and there is nothing else in her save her light.

[Chapter 79]

1 And now, my son Methuselah, I have shown you everything, and the law of all the stars of heaven is completed.

2 And he showed me all the laws of these for every day, and for every season of every rule, and for every year, and for its going out, and for the order prescribed to it every month and every week.

3 And the waning of the moon which takes place in the sixth door, for in this sixth door her light is accomplished, and after that there is the beginning of the waning.

4 And the waning which takes place in the first door in its season, until one hundred and seventy-seven days are accomplished, calculated according to weeks, twenty-five weeks and two days.

5 She falls behind the sun and the order of the stars exactly five days in the course of one period, and when this place which you see has been traversed.

6 Such is the picture and sketch of every luminary which Uriel the archangel, who is their leader, showed to me.

(Author's note: For more information on the storehouses of heaven, the starts, gates, and luminaries, see 2 Enoch.)

[Chapter 80]

1 And in those days the angel Uriel answered and said to me: 'Behold, I have shown you everything, Enoch, and I have revealed everything to you that you should see this sun and this moon, and the leaders of the stars of heaven and all those who turn them, their tasks and times and departures.

2 And in the days of the sinners the years shall be shortened, and their seed shall be tardy on their lands and fields, and all things on the earth shall alter, and shall not appear in their time. And the rain shall be kept back, and heaven shall withhold it.

3 And in those times the fruits of the earth shall be backward, and shall not grow in their time, and the fruits of the trees shall be withheld in their time.

4 And the moon shall alter her customs, and not appear at her time.

5 And in those days the sun shall be seen and he shall journey in the evening on the extremity of the great chariot in the west and shall shine more brightly than accords with the order of light.

6 And many rulers of the stars shall transgress their customary order. And these shall alter their orbits and tasks, and not appear at the seasons prescribed to them.

7 And the whole order of the stars shall be concealed from the sinners, and the thoughts of those on the earth shall err concerning them, and they shall be altered from all their ways, they shall err and take them to be gods.

Romans 1:18-27 The wrath of God is being revealed from heaven against all the godlessness and wickedness of men who suppress the truth by their wickedness, [19] since what may be known about God is plain to them, because God has made it plain to them. [20] For since the creation of the world God's invisible qualities – his eternal power and divine nature – have been clearly seen, being understood from what has been made, so that men are without excuse.
[21] For although they knew God, they neither glorified him as God nor gave thanks to him, but their thinking became futile and their foolish hearts were darkened. [22] Although they claimed to be wise, they became fools [23] and exchanged the glory of the immortal God for images made to look like mortal man and birds and animals and reptiles.
[24] Therefore God gave them over in the sinful desires of their hearts to sexual impurity for the degrading of their bodies with one another. [25] They exchanged the truth of God for a lie, and worshiped and served created things rather than the Creator – who is forever praised. Amen.
[26] Because of this, God gave them over to shameful lusts. Even their women exchanged natural relations for unnatural ones. [27] In the same way the men also abandoned natural relations with women and were inflamed with lust for one another. Men committed indecent acts with other men, and received in themselves the due penalty for their perversion.

(Author's note: Recall that many people of the time believed the stars to be angels. They worshipped the stars, believing them to have power to control fate. The scripture above tells us that God was angry because men had taken to the worship of the things God created and had forsaken the worship of Him who created those things. As an added note, we are told in other ancient texts that angels had begun taking men as lovers as well as females. Angels are always considered males in these texts.)

8 And evil shall be multiplied on them, and punishment shall come on them so as to destroy all.'

[Chapter 81]

1 And he said to me: 'Enoch, look at these heavenly tablets and read what is written on them, and mark every individual fact.'

2 And I looked at the heavenly tablets, and read everything which was written on it and understood everything, and read the book of all the deeds of mankind, and of all the children of flesh; that shall be on the earth to the end of generations.

3 And I blessed the great Lord the King of glory forever, in that He has made all the works of the world, and I exalted the Lord because of His

patience, and blessed Him because of the children of men (sons of Abraham).

4 And then I said: 'Blessed is the man who dies in righteousness and goodness, concerning whom there is no book of unrighteousness written, and against whom no day of judgment shall be found.'

5 And the seven holy ones brought me and placed me on the earth before the door of my house, and said to me: 'Declare everything to your son Methuselah, and show to all your children that no flesh is righteous in the sight of the Lord, for He is their Creator.

6 For one year we will leave you with your son, until you give your last commands, that you may teach your children and record it for them, and testify to all your children; and in the second year they shall take you from their midst.

7 Let your heart be strong, for the good shall proclaim righteousness to the good; the righteous shall rejoice with the righteous, and shall wish one another well.

8 But the sinners shall die with the sinners, and the apostate shall go down with the apostate.

9 And those who practice righteousness shall die on account of the deeds of men, and be taken away on account of the deeds of the godless.'

10 And in those days they finished speaking to me, and I came to my people, blessing the Lord of the world.

[Chapter 82]

1 And now, my son Methuselah, all these things I am recounting to you and writing down for you! And I have revealed to you everything, and given you books concerning all these; so, my son Methuselah, preserve the books from your father's hand, and see that you deliver them to the generations of the world.

2 I have given wisdom to you and to your children, and those children to come, that they may give it to their children for generations. This wisdom namely that passes their understanding.

3 And those who understand it shall not sleep, but shall listen that they may learn this wisdom, and it shall please those that eat thereof better than good food.

4 Blessed are all the righteous, blessed are all those who walk in the way of righteousness and sin not as the sinners, in the numbering of all their days in which the sun traverses heaven, entering into and departing from the doors for thirty days with the heads of thousands of the order of the stars, together with the four which are within the calendar which divide the four portions of the year, which lead them and enter with them four days.

(Author's note: It is verse 4 that leads some to believe the week should begin on a Wednesday, the fourth day of the week.. The verse is unclear and seems to point more to the fact that there are four seasons and the divisions of time were created on the fourth day. All Hebrew calendars had the same week and began on Sunday, the first day of the week, no matter what the name of the day was at that time in that tongue.)

Genesis 1:14-19 And God said, "Let there be lights in the expanse of the sky to separate the day from the night, and let them serve as signs to mark seasons and days and years, [15] and let them be lights in the expanse of the sky to give light on the earth." And it was so. [16] God made two great lights – the greater light to govern the day and the lesser light to govern the night. He also made the stars. [17] God set them in the expanse of the sky to give light on the earth, [18] to govern the day and the night, and to separate light from darkness. And God saw that it was good. [19] And there was evening, and there was morning – the fourth day.

5 Owing to them men shall be at fault and not count them in the whole number of days of the year. Men shall be at fault, and not recognize them accurately.

6 For they belong to the calculations of the year and are truly recorded therein forever, one in the first door and one in the third, and one in the fourth and one in the sixth, and the year is completed in three hundred and sixty-four days.

7 And the account of it is accurate and the recorded counting thereof is exact; for the luminaries, and months and festivals, and years and days, has Uriel shown and revealed to me, to whom the Lord of the whole creation of the world hath subjected the host of heaven.

8 And he has power over night and day in heaven to cause the light to shine on men via the sun, moon, and stars, and all the powers of the heaven which revolve in their circular chariots. And these are the orders of the stars, which set in their places, and in their seasons and festivals and months.

9 And these are the names of those who lead them, who watch that they enter at their times, in their orders, in their seasons, in their months, in their periods of dominion, and in their positions.

10 Their four leaders who divide the four parts of the year enter first; and after them the twelve leaders of the orders who divide the months; and for the three hundred and sixty days there are heads over thousands who divide the days; and for the four days in the calendar there are the leaders which divide the four parts of the year.

11 And these heads over thousands are interspersed between leader and leader, each behind a station, but their leaders make the division.

12 And these are the names of the leaders who divide the four parts of the year which are ordained:

13 Milki'el, Hel'emmelek, and Mel'ejal, and Narel. And the names of those who lead them: Adnar'el, and Ijasusa'el, and 'Elome'el.

14 These three follow the leaders of the orders, and there is one that follows the three leaders of the orders which follow those leaders of stations that divide the four parts of the year. In the beginning of the year Melkejal rises first and rules, who is named Tam'aini and sun, and all the days of his dominion while he bears rule are ninety-one days.

15 And these are the signs of the days which are to be seen on earth in the days of his dominion: sweat, and heat; and calms; and all the trees bear fruit, and leaves are produced on all the trees, and the harvest of wheat, and the rose-flowers, and all the flowers which come out in the field, but the trees of the winter season become withered.

16 And these are the names of the leaders which are under them: Berka'el, Zelebs'el, and another who is added a head of a thousand, called Hilujaseph: and the days of the dominion of this leader are at an end.

17 The next leader after him is Hel'emmelek, whom one names the shining sun, and all the days of his light are ninety-one days.

18 And these are the signs of his days on the earth: glowing heat and dryness, and the trees ripen their fruits and produce all their fruits ripe and ready, and the sheep pair and become pregnant, and all the fruits of the earth are gathered in, and everything that is in the fields, and the winepress: these things take place in the days of his dominion.

19 These are the names, and the orders, and the leaders of those heads of thousands: Gida'ljal, Ke'el, and He'el, and the name of the head of a thousand which is added to them, Asfa'el: and the days of his dominion are at an end.

(Author's note: The seasons are 91 days each. There are four seasons. The years is 91 x 4 or 364 days. We are warned to calculate the years correctly in order to celebrate the holy days on the days they were meant to be honored. Descriptions of the seasons are given along with the angels who control them.)

[Chapter 83]

The *Book of Visions* (Chapters 83-90):

1 And now, my son Methuselah, I will show you all my visions which I have seen, recounting them before you.

2 I saw two visions before I got married (took a wife), and the one was quite unlike the other: the first when I was learning to write: the second before I married (took) your mother, was when I saw a terrible vision.

3 And regarding them I prayed to the Lord. I had laid down in the house of my grandfather Mahalalel, when I saw in a vision how heaven collapsed and was carried off (removed, torn down) and fell to the earth.

4 And when it fell to the earth I saw how the earth was swallowed up in a great abyss, and mountains were suspended on mountains, and hills sank down on hills, and high trees were ripped from their stems, and hurled down and sunk in the abyss.

5 And then a word fell into my mouth, and I lifted up my voice to cry aloud, and said:

6 'The earth is destroyed.' And my grandfather Mahalalel woke me as I lay near him, and said to me: 'Why do you cry so, my son, and why do you make such moaning (lamentation)?'

7 And I recounted to him the whole vision which I had seen, and he said to me: 'You have seen a terrible thing, my son. Your dream (vision) is of a grave time and concerns the secrets of all the sin of the earth: it must sink into the abyss and be totally destroyed.

8 And now, my son, arise and pray to the Lord of glory, since you are a believer, that a remnant may remain on the earth, and that He may not destroy the whole earth.

9 My son, from heaven all this will come on the earth, and on the earth there will be great destruction.

10 After that I arose and prayed and implored and besought (God), and wrote down my prayer for the generations of the world, and I will show everything to you, my son Methuselah.

11 And when I had gone out below and seen the heaven, and the sun rising in the east, and the moon setting in the west, and a few stars, and the whole earth, and everything as He had known it in the beginning, then I blessed the Lord of judgment and exalted Him because He had made the sun to go out from the windows of the east, and he ascended and rose on the face of heaven, and set out and kept traversing the path shown to it.

(Author's note: This first vision would seem to foreshadow the flood, but since the vision was of a piece of heaven breaking off and falling to earth with destructive force, it may be an end time prophecy of a meteor strike. Another, more timely interpretation is that of Satan falling to earth, which is the beginnings of sorrow.)

[Chapter 84]

1 And I lifted up my hands in righteousness and blessed the Holy and Great One, and spoke with the breath of my mouth, and with the tongue of flesh, which God has made for the children of the flesh of men, that they should speak therewith, and He gave them breath and a tongue and a mouth that they should speak therewith:

2 Blessed be you, O Lord, King, Great and mighty in your greatness, Lord of the whole creation of heaven, King of kings and God of the whole world. And your power and kingship and greatness abide forever and ever, and throughout all generations your dominion and all heavens are your throne forever, and the whole earth your footstool forever and ever.

3 For you have made and you rule all things, and nothing is too hard for you, wisdom never departs from the place of your throne, nor turns away from your presence. You know and see and hear everything, and there is nothing hidden from you for you see everything.

4 And now the angels of your heavens are guilty of trespass, and on the flesh of men abide your wrath until the great day of judgment.

5 And now, O God and Lord and Great King, I implore and beseech you to fulfill my prayer, to leave me a posterity on earth, and not destroy all the flesh of man, and make the earth without inhabitant, so that there should be an eternal destruction.

6 And now, my Lord, destroy from the earth the flesh which has aroused your wrath, but the flesh of righteousness and uprightness establish as an eternal plant bearing seed forever, and hide not your face from the prayer of your servant, O Lord.'

(Author's note: In chapter 85 and following, a series of animals is mentioned. These seem to refer to nations or ethnicities. For example, the eagles may refer to the Roman empire; the Islamic nation is represented by the asses; Egyptians are wolves; the Assyrians are lions, and so on. See Daniel 10 for other like imagery.

Other writers have attempted to be more specific. Starting with Adam and Eve, the story begins. Abraham may be a white bull, Ishmael the wild ass; Isaac the white bull, Jacob a white sheep, Esau the wild boar. There is the concept that Noah's three sons, Shem, Ham and Japheth, give rise to all the various animals or nations. The small lambs with open eyes are the Essenes; Jesus is the "sheep with the big horn," and in 90.17, the final 12 shepherds represent the Christian era and the 12 Apostles.

Notes are included within the chapters and at the end of the section. They suggest possible interpretations. As with any prophecy written in such imagery, it is impossible to know exactly what the author was trying to convey. Prophecy tends to be interpreted according to one's viewpoint. When one looks at the prophecies from a purely Jewish viewpoint it is likely that the savior of the people, represented by the sheep with a large horn, is not the Messiah at all, but a historical military figure such as Judas Maccabaeus, who led the great Maccabean revolt of 167 B.C. - 160 B.C. against Rome.

Judas Maccabeus is also described as a great horn among six others on the head of a lamb. This possibly pertains to his five brothers and Mattathias. If you take this in context of the history from Maccabeus time, the explanation of the verse may be found in 1 Maccabees 3:7 and 6:52, 2 Maccabees 6:8-14, and 1 Maccabees 7:41-42.

[Chapter 85]

1 And after this I saw another dream, and I will show the whole dream to you, my son.

2 And Enoch lifted up his voice and spoke to his son Methuselah: 'I will speak to you, my son, hear my words. Incline your ear to the dream (vision) of your father.

3 Before I married (took) your mother Edna, I saw in a vision on my bed, and behold a bull came out from the earth, and that bull was white.

4 And after it came out a heifer, and along with this later came out two bulls, one of them black and the other red.

5 And that black bull gored the red one and pursued him over the earth, and then I could no longer see that red bull. But that black bull grew and that heifer went with him, and I saw that many oxen proceeded from him which resembled and followed him.

6 And that cow, that first one, went from the presence of that first bull in order to seek that red one, but found him not, and mourned with a great lamentation and sought him.

7 And I looked until that first bull came to her and quieted (calmed) her, and from that time onward she cried no more.

8 And after that she bore another white bull, and after him she bore many bulls and black cows.

9 And I saw in my sleep that white bull likewise grew and became a great white bull, and from him proceeded many white bulls, and they resembled him. And they began to father many white bulls, which resembled them, one following another.

(Author's note: Many believe verses 1-9 represent the story of Adam, Eve, Cain, and Abel. The first white bull mentioned is Adam. The heifer is Eve. The two bulls born to them are a black one [Cain] and a red one [Abel]. Eve leaves to seek Abel and finds him. She laments his death. Adam comforts her. Cain goes on to produce many oxen. Eve produces another son and thus produces many more bulls and cows.)

[Chapter 86]

1 And again I looked with my eyes as I slept, and I saw the heaven above, and behold a star fell from heaven, and it arose and ate and pastured among those oxen (bulls).

2 And after that I saw the large and the black oxen (bulls), and behold they all changed their stalls and pastures and their heifers (cattle) , and began to live with each other.

(Author's note: The first star to fall was Satan. Then other stars fell, and these are the Watchers.. They caused the heifers, who are the women, to begin living with and having sex with the angels. Based on the previous verses it would appear that Satan and the fallen angels picked the descendents of Cain with whom to have sex.)

Second Book of Adam and Eve, Chapter 20
29 Enoch was already grown up at that time, and in his zeal for God, he stood and said, "Hear me, you large and small (young and old) sons of Seth! When you transgress the commandment of our fathers and go down from this holy mountain, you shall not come up here again forever."
30 But they rose up against Enoch and would not listen to his words, but they went down from the Holy Mountain.
31 And when they looked at the daughters of Cain, at their beautiful figures, and at their hands and feet dyed with color, and the tattoos on their faces that ornamented them, the fire of sin was set ablaze in them.
32 Then Satan made them look most beautiful before the sons of Seth, as he also made the sons of Seth appear the most handsome in the eyes of the daughters of Cain, so that the daughters of Cain lusted after the sons of Seth like ravenous beasts, and the sons of Seth lusted after the daughters of Cain until they committed disgusting and disgraceful acts with them.)

3 And again I saw in the vision, and looked towards heaven, and behold I saw many stars descend and cast themselves down from heaven to that first star, and they became bulls among those cattle and pastured with them.

4 And I looked at them and saw they all let out their private (sexual) members, like horses, and began to mount the cows of the bulls (oxen), and they all became pregnant and bore elephants, camels, and asses.

Author's note: The Book of Jubilees indicates that the offspring of the angels and women were somehow different, and they are divided into categories of the Naphidim (or Naphilim, depending or the transliteration), the Giants, and the Eljo. (Naphil are mentioned but this is the singular of Naphilim.)

The word "Naphil" means "The Fallen." There is no indication as to the meaning of "Eljo *(Elyo)*," but the word would indicate these are "godlings" and are likely those referred to in the Book of Genesis as "men of renown."

5 And all the bulls (oxen) feared them and were frightened of them, and began to bite with their teeth and to devour, and to gore with their horns.

6 And, moreover, they began to devour those oxen; and behold all the children of the earth began to tremble and shake before them and to flee from them.

[Chapter 87]

1 And again I saw how they began to gore each other and to devour each other, and the earth began to cry aloud.

2 And I raised my eyes again to heaven, and I saw in the vision, and behold there came out from heaven beings who were like white men, and four went out from that place and three others with them.

3 And those three that had come out last grasped me by my hand and took me up, away from the generations of the earth, and raised me up to a high place, and showed me a tower raised high above the earth, and all the hills were lower.

4 And one said to me: 'Remain here until you see everything that befalls those elephants, camels, and asses, and the stars and the oxen, and all of them.'

[Chapter 88]

1 And I saw one of those four who had come out first, and he seized that first star which had fallen from heaven, and bound it hand and foot and cast it into an abyss; now that abyss was narrow and deep, and horrible and dark.

2 Peter 2:4 For if God spared not the angels that sinned, but cast them down to hell, and delivered them into chains of darkness, to be reserved unto judgment…

2 And one of them drew a sword, and gave it to those elephants and camels and asses then they began to smite each other, and the whole earth shook because of them.

3 And as I was beholding in the vision one of those four who had come out stoned them from heaven, and gathered and took all the great stars

whose private (sexual) members were like those of horses, and bound them all hand and foot, and threw them in an abyss of the earth.

(Author's note: One must smile at the idea of the angels having penises the size of horses. In the ancient mind, this was one reason some of the women gave in so easily. If a spiritual creature is determined to become corporeal, why not create a body that will fulfill the lust that drives one to incarnate in the first place?)

[Chapter 89]

1 And one of those four went to that white bull and instructed him in a secret, and he was terrified: he was born a bull and became a man, and built for himself a great vessel and dwelt on it.

2 And three bulls dwelt with him in the vessel and they were covered over. And again I raised my eyes towards heaven and saw a high roof, with seven water torrents on it, and those torrents flowed with much water into an enclosure. And I looked again, and behold fountains were opened on the surface of that great enclosure, and the water began to bubble and swell and rise on the surface, and I saw that enclosure until all its surface was covered with water.

3 And the water, the darkness, and mist increased on it; and as I looked at the height of that water, the water had risen above the height of the enclosure, and was streaming over the enclosure, and it stood on the earth.

4 And all the cattle of the enclosure were gathered together until I saw how they sank and were swallowed up and perished in that water.

5 But that vessel floated on the water, while all the oxen (bulls) and elephants and camels and asses sank to the bottom with all the animals, so that I could no longer see them, and they were not able to escape, but perished and sank into the depths.

6 And again I watched in the vision until those water torrents were removed from that high roof, and the chasms of the earth were leveled up and other abysses were opened.

7 Then the water began to run down into these abysses, until the earth became visible; but that vessel settled on the earth, and the darkness retired and light appeared.

8 But that white bull which had become a man came out of that vessel, and the three bulls with him, and one of those three was white like that bull, and one of them was red as blood, and one black; and that white bull departed from them.

(Author's note: Here we have the story of Noah and the flood. The flood came because of the sins of the Watchers and their offspring, who began killing everything. The flood cleansed the earth and left only the sons of Noah and their wives to repopulate. The story seems to indicate that the various races of the world (white, red, and black, began with the sons of Noah.)

9 And they began to bring out beasts of the field and birds, so that there arose different genera: lions, tigers, wolves, dogs, hyenas, wild boars, foxes, squirrels, swine, falcons, vultures, kites, eagles, and ravens; and among them was born a white bull.

10 And they began to bite one another; but that white bull which was born among them fathered a wild ass and a white bull with it, and the wild asses multiplied.

11 But that bull which was born from him fathered a black wild boar and a white sheep; and the former fathered many boars, but the sheep gave birth to twelve sheep.

(Author's note: Abraham gave birth to Ishmael (the wild ass) and Isaac (the white bull). Isaac fathered a boar (Esau) and a sheep (Jacob.) Jacob had 12 sheep, who are the 12 patriarchs and the beginning of the 12 tribes.)

12 And when those twelve sheep had grown, they gave up one of them to the asses, and the asses again gave up that sheep to the wolves, and that sheep grew up among the wolves.

(Author's note: Joseph was sold to the Midiantes or Ishaelites as a slave. They, in turn, sold him to the Egyptians. See Genesis 37:25-39.)

13 And the Lord brought the eleven sheep to live with it and to pasture with it among the wolves and they multiplied and became many flocks of sheep.

(Author's note: This begins the story of Moses and how the Egyptians oppressed the Israelites until he led them out of captivity.)

14 And the wolves began to fear them, and they oppressed them until they destroyed their little ones, and they threw their young into a deep river, but those sheep began to cry aloud on account of their little ones, and to complain to their Lord.

15 And a sheep which had been saved from the wolves fled and escaped to the wild asses; and I saw the sheep how they lamented and cried, and besought their Lord with all their might, until that Lord of the sheep descended at the voice of the sheep from a high abode, and came to them and pastured them.

16 And He called that sheep which had escaped the wolves, and spoke with it concerning the wolves that it should admonish them not to touch the sheep.

17 And the sheep went to the wolves according to the word of the Lord, and another sheep met it and went with it, and the two went and entered together into the assembly of those wolves, and spoke with them and admonished them not to touch the sheep from then on.

18 And on it I saw the wolves, and how they more harshly oppressed the sheep with all their power; and the sheep cried aloud.

19 And the Lord came to the sheep and they began to beat those wolves, and the wolves began to make lamentation; but the sheep became quiet and ceased to cry out.

20 And I saw the sheep until they departed from among the wolves; but the eyes of the wolves were blinded, and the wolves departed in pursuit of the sheep with all their power.

21 And the Lord of the sheep went with them, as their leader, and all His sheep followed Him.

22 And his face was dazzling and glorious and terrible to behold. But the wolves began to pursue those sheep until they reached a sea of water.

23 And that sea was divided, and the water stood on this side and on that before their face, and their Lord led them and placed Himself between them and the wolves.

24 And as those wolves had not yet seen the sheep, they proceeded into the midst of that sea, and the wolves followed the sheep, and those wolves ran after them into that sea.

25 And when they saw the Lord of the sheep, they turned to flee before His face, but that sea gathered itself together, and became as it had been created, and the water swelled and rose until it covered the wolves.

26 And I watched until all the wolves who pursued those sheep perished and were drowned.

27 But the sheep escaped from that water and went out into a wilderness, where there was no water and no grass; and they began to open their eyes and to see;

28 And I saw the Lord of the sheep pasturing them and giving them water and grass, and that sheep going and leading them.

(Author's note: The Israelites escaped. They passed through the divided sea, but the Egyptians were covered by the water and drowned. Now, we begin the story of Moses and the ascent up the mountain, where God gave him the Ten Commandments.)

29 And the sheep ascended to the summit of that high rock, and the Lord of the sheep sent it to them. And after that I saw the Lord of the sheep who stood before them, and His appearance was great and terrible and majestic, and all those sheep saw Him and were afraid before His face.

30 And they all feared and trembled because of Him, and they cried to that sheep which was among them:

31 'We are not able to stand before our Lord or to behold Him.' And that sheep which led them again ascended to the summit of that rock, but the sheep began to be blinded and to wander from the way which he had showed them, but that sheep did not realize it.

(Author's note: When Moses came down from the mountain he discovered a large group of the Israelites had made a golden calf idol and were worshipping it.)

32 And the Lord of the sheep was very angry with them, and that sheep discovered it, and went down from the summit of the rock, and came to the sheep, and found the greatest part of them blinded and fallen away.

33 And when they saw it they feared and trembled at its presence, and desired to return to their folds. And that sheep took other sheep with it, and came to those sheep which had fallen away, and began to slay them;

and the sheep feared its presence, and thus that sheep brought back those sheep that had fallen away, and they returned to their folds.

34 And I saw in this vision until that sheep became a man and built a house for the Lord of the sheep, and placed all the sheep in that house.

35 And I saw until this sheep which had met that sheep which led them fell asleep (died); and I saw until all the great sheep perished and little ones arose in their place, and they came to a pasture, and approached a stream of water.

36 Then that sheep, their leader which had become a man, withdrew from them and fell asleep (died), and all the sheep looked for it (sought it) and cried over it with a great crying.

37 And I saw until they left off crying for that sheep and crossed that stream of water, and there arose the two sheep as leaders in the place of those which had led them and fallen asleep.

38 And I saw until the sheep came to a good place, and a pleasant and glorious land, and I saw until those sheep were satisfied; and that house stood among them in the (green) pleasant land.

(Author's note: After Moses died and the two spies were sent into the Promised Land to bring back a report, Joshua took over and led the Israelites into the Promised Land.)

39 And sometimes their eyes were opened, and sometimes blinded, until another sheep arose and led them and brought them all back, and their eyes were opened.

40 And the dogs and the foxes and the wild boars began to devour those sheep until the Lord of the sheep raised up another sheep, a ram from their midst, which led them.

41 And that ram began to butt on either side those dogs, foxes, and wild boars until he had destroyed them all.

(Author's note: This is the succession of judges and kings leading up to David. All of them had to fight the surrounding nations.)

42 And that sheep whose eyes were opened saw that ram, which was among the sheep, until it forsook its glory and began to butt those sheep, and trampled on them, and behaved itself unseemly.

43 And the Lord of the sheep sent the lamb to another lamb and raised it to being a ram and leader of the sheep instead of that ram which had forsaken its glory.

44 And it went to it and spoke to it alone, and raised it to being a ram, and made it the prince and leader of the sheep; but during all these things those dogs oppressed the sheep.

45 And the first ram pursued the second ram, and the second ram arose and fled before it; and I saw until those dogs pulled down the first ram.

46 And that second ram arose and led the little sheep. And those sheep grew and multiplied; but all the dogs, and foxes, and wild boars feared and fled before it, and that ram butted and killed the wild beasts, and those wild beasts had no longer any power among the sheep and robbed them no more of anything.

47 And that ram fathered many sheep and fell asleep; and a little sheep became ram in its place, and became prince and leader of those sheep.

48 And that house became great and broad, and it was built for those sheep: and a high and great tower was built on the house for the Lord of the sheep, and that house was low, but the tower was elevated and high, and the Lord of the sheep stood on that tower and they offered a full table before him.

49 And again I saw those sheep that they again erred and went many ways, and forsook that their house, and the Lord of the sheep called some from among the sheep and sent them to the sheep, but the sheep began to slay them.

50 And one of them was saved and was not slain, and it sped away and cried aloud over the sheep; and they sought to slay it, but the Lord of the sheep saved it from the sheep, and brought it up to me, and caused it to live there.

(Author's note: Verse 50 could be a reference to Elijah.)

51 And many other sheep He sent to those sheep to testify to them and lament over them.

52 And after that I saw that when they forsook the house of the Lord and His tower they fell away entirely, and their eyes were blinded; and I saw

the Lord of the sheep how He worked much slaughter among them in their herds until those sheep invited that slaughter and betrayed His place.

53 And He gave them over into the hands of the lions and tigers, and wolves and hyenas, and into the hand of the foxes, and to all the wild beasts, and those wild beasts began to tear in pieces those sheep.

54 And I saw that He forsook their house and their tower and gave them all into the hand of the lions, to tear and devour them, into the hand of all the wild beasts.

55 And I began to cry aloud with all my power, and to appeal to the Lord of the sheep, because the sheep were being devoured by all the wild beasts.

56 But He remained unmoved, though He saw it, and rejoiced that they were devoured and swallowed and robbed, and left them to be devoured in the hand of all the beasts.

57 And He called seventy shepherds, and gave those sheep to them that they might pasture them, and He spoke to the shepherds and their companions: 'Let each individual of you pasture the sheep from now on, and everything that I shall command you that do you.

(Author's note: The 70 are religious leaders of that time frame. In the 3 Enoch God mentions 70 nations, leading one to believe that from God's viewpoint there are only 70 true nations. All other divisions are man made and false.)

58 And I will deliver them over to you duly numbered, and tell you which of them are to be destroyed-and them you will destroy.' And He gave over to them those sheep.

59 And He called another and spoke to him: 'Observe and mark everything that the shepherds will do to those sheep; for they will destroy more of them than I have commanded them.

60 And every excess and the destruction which will be done through the shepherds, record how many they destroy according to my command, and how many according to their own caprice; record against every individual shepherd all the destruction he effects.

61 And read out before me by number how many they destroy, and how many they deliver over for destruction, that I may have this as a testimony against them, and know every deed of the shepherds, that I may comprehend and see what they do, whether or not they abide by my command which I have commanded them.

62 But they shall not know it, and you shall not declare it to them, nor admonish them, but only record against each individual all the destruction which the shepherds effect each in his time and lay it all before me.'

63 And I saw until those shepherds pastured in their season, and they began to slay and to destroy more than they were bidden, and they delivered those sheep into the hand of the lions.

64 And the lions and tigers ate and devoured the greater part of those sheep, and the wild boars ate along with them; and they burned that tower and demolished that house.

65 And I became very sorrowful over that tower because that house of the sheep was demolished, and afterwards I was unable to see if those sheep entered that house.

66 And the shepherds and their associates delivered over those sheep to all the wild beasts, to devour them, and each one of them received in his time a definite number, it was written by the other in a book how many each one of them destroyed of them.

67 And each one slew and destroyed many more than was prescribed; and I began to weep and lament on account of those sheep.

68 And thus in the vision I saw that one who wrote, how he wrote down every one that was destroyed by those shepherds, day by day, and carried up and laid down and showed actually the whole book to the Lord of the sheep - everything that they had done, and all that each one of them had made away with, and all that they had given over to destruction.

69 And the book was read before the Lord of the sheep, and He took the book from his hand and read it and sealed it and laid it down.

(Author's note: Verses 65–69 refer to the first temple being destroyed. Verse 72 begins the story of Ezra and the return to Jerusalem to rebuild the city and temple.)

70 And I saw how the shepherds pastured for twelve hours, and behold three of those sheep turned back and came and entered and began to build up all that had fallen down of that house; but the wild boars tried to hinder them, but they were not able.

71 And they began again to build as before, and they raised up that tower, and it was named the high tower; and they began again to place a table before the tower, but all the bread on it was polluted and not pure.

72 And as touching all this the eyes of those sheep were blinded so that they saw not, and the eyes of their shepherds likewise were blinded; and they delivered them in large numbers to their shepherds for destruction, and they trampled the sheep with their feet and devoured them.

73 And the Lord of the sheep remained unmoved until all the sheep were dispersed over the field and mingled with the beasts, and the shepherds did not save them out of the hand of the beasts.

74 And this one who wrote the book carried it up, and showed it and read it before the Lord of the sheep, and implored Him on their account, and besought Him on their account as he showed Him all the doings of the shepherds, and gave testimony before Him against all the shepherds.

(Author's note: Ezra, Haggai, and Zechariah returned and wrote books of the Old Testament.)

75 And he took the actual book and laid it down beside Him and departed.

[Chapter 90]

1 And I saw until that in this manner thirty-five shepherds undertook the pasturing of the sheep, and they completed their periods as did the first; and others received them into their hands, to pasture them for their period, each shepherd in his own period.

2 And after that I saw in my vision all the birds of heaven coming, the eagles, the vultures, the kites, the ravens; but the eagles led all the birds; and they began to devour those sheep, and to pick out their eyes and to devour their flesh.

(Author's note: Now the Eagle, which is Roman, appears from among the nations.)

3 And the sheep cried out because their flesh was being devoured by the birds, and as for me I looked and lamented in my sleep over that shepherd who pastured the sheep.

4 And I saw until those sheep were devoured by the dogs and eagles and kites, and they left neither flesh nor skin nor sinew remaining on them until only their bones stood there; and their bones too fell to the earth and the sheep became few.

5 And I saw until that twenty-three had undertaken the pasturing and completed in their many periods fifty-eight times.

(Author's note: Of the 70 appointed religious leaders throughout time, 58vhave passed. Verse 6 introduces the Essenes. Verse 8 probably refers to John The Baptist.)

6 But behold lambs were borne by those white sheep, and they began to open their eyes and to see, and to cry to the sheep.

7 They cried to them, but they did not hearken to what they said to them, but were very deaf, and their eyes were very blinded.

8 And I saw in the vision how the ravens flew on those lambs and took one of those lambs, and dashed the sheep in pieces and devoured them.

9 And I saw until horns grew on those lambs, and the ravens cast down their horns; and I saw until there sprouted a great horn of one of those sheep, and their eyes were opened.

(Author's note: According to the way in which verse 9 is interpreted, it begins the story of Jesus. The story seems to end at verse 16. The sheep with the great horn is never said to be killed. It only states that he was stopped. Another interpretation points to Judas Maccabaeus.)

10 And it looked at them and their eyes opened, and it cried to the sheep, and the rams saw it and all ran to it.

11 And notwithstanding all this, those eagles and vultures and ravens and kites kept on tearing the sheep and swooping down on them and devouring them until the sheep remained silent, but the rams lamented and cried out.

12 And those ravens fought and battled with it and sought to lay low its horn, but they had no power over it.

13 All the eagles and vultures and ravens and kites were gathered together, and there came with them all the sheep of the field, they all came together, and helped each other to break that horn of the ram.

14 And I saw that man, who wrote down the names of the shepherds and brought them up before the Lord of the sheep, came, and he helped that ram and showed it everything; its help was coming down.

15 And I looked until that Lord of the sheep came to them angry, all those who saw him ran, and they all fell into the shadow in front of Him.

16 All the eagles and vultures and ravens and kites, gathered together and brought with them all the wild sheep, and they all came together and helped one another in order to dash that horn of the ram in pieces.

17 And I looked at that man, who wrote the book at the command of the Lord, until he opened that book of the destruction that those last twelve shepherds had done. And he showed, in front of the Lord of the sheep, that they had destroyed even more than those before them had.

(Author's note: The 12 shepherds are either the Apostles, if one interprets the sheep with the large horn as Jesus, or the 12 shepherds are the leaders of the Jews joining themselves in the revolt led by Judas Maccabeus. If one goes with the apostle theory, the books refer to the New Testament, but more specifically it refers to the path of "enlightenment." I use this word since the text itself uses the terms "to be blinded" and "to have the eyes opened." It should be noted that there are books attributed to most of the Apostles, but many are not included in the Bible. This ends past events. What remains from verse 17 on is prophetic. Following the idea that Enoch is one of the first apocalyptic books, we will see in figurative language a great battle and the judgment. The stars are judged. This is the judgment of the fallen angels. The 70 Jewish religious leaders, representing the Pharisee mind set and the religious oppression of the Jewish people are judged. Then the eyes of the faithful are opened and they are brought into the Lord's house. The number of believers is so great the house overflows.)

18 And I looked and the Lord of the sheep came to them and took the Staff of His Anger and struck the Earth. And the Earth was split. And all the animals, and the birds of the sky, fell from those sheep and sank in the earth, and it closed over them.

19 And I saw until a great sword was given to the sheep, and the sheep proceeded against all the beasts of the field to slay them, and all the

beasts and the birds of the heaven fled before their face. And I saw that man, who wrote the book according to the command of the Lord, until he opened that book concerning the destruction which those twelve last shepherds had wrought, and showed that they had destroyed much more than their predecessors, before the Lord of the sheep. And I saw until the Lord of the sheep came to them and took in His hand the staff of His wrath, and smote the earth, and the earth clave asunder, and all the beasts and all the birds of heaven fell from among those sheep, and were swallowed up in the earth and it covered them.

20 And I saw until a throne was erected in the pleasant land, and the Lord of the sheep sat Himself on it, and the other took the sealed books and opened those books before the Lord of the sheep.

21 And the Lord called those men, the seven first white ones, and commanded that they should bring before Him, beginning with the first star which led the way, all the stars whose private members were like those of horses, and they brought them all before Him.

22 And He said to that man who wrote before Him, being one of those seven white ones, and said to him: 'Take those seventy shepherds to whom I delivered the sheep, and who taking them on their own authority slew more than I commanded them.'

23 And behold they were all bound, I saw, and they all stood before Him.

24 And the judgment was held first over the stars, and they were judged and found guilty, and went to the place of condemnation, and they were cast into an abyss, full of fire and flaming, and full of pillars of fire.

25 And those seventy shepherds were judged and found guilty, and they were cast into that fiery abyss.

26 And I saw at that time how a like abyss was opened in the midst of the earth, full of fire, and they brought those blinded sheep, and they were all judged and found guilty and cast into this fiery abyss, and they burned; now this abyss was to the right of that house.

27 And I saw those sheep burning and their bones burning.

28 And I stood up to see until they folded up that old house; and carried off all the pillars, and all the beams and ornaments of the house were at the same time folded up with it, and they carried it off and laid it in a place in the south of the land.

29 And I saw until the Lord of the sheep brought a new house greater and loftier than that first, and set it up in the place of the first which had been folded up; all its pillars were new, and its ornaments were new and larger than those of the first, the old one which He had taken away, and all the sheep were within it.

Hebrews 13:14 For here have we no continuing city, but we seek one to come.

30 And I saw all the sheep which had been left, and all the beasts on the earth, and all the birds of heaven, falling down and doing homage to those sheep and making petition to and obeying them in every thing.

31 And thereafter those three who were clothed in white and had seized me by my hand [who had taken me up before], and the hand of that ram also seizing hold of me, they took me up and set me down in the midst of those sheep before the judgment took place.

32 And those sheep were all white, and their wool was abundant and clean.

33 And all that had been destroyed and dispersed, and all the beasts of the field, and all the birds of heaven, assembled in that house, and the Lord of the sheep rejoiced with great joy because they were all good and had returned to His house.

34 And I saw until they laid down that sword, which had been given to the sheep, and they brought it back into the house, and it was sealed before the presence of the Lord, and all the sheep were invited into that house, but it held them not.

35 And the eyes of them all were opened, and they saw the good, and there was not one among them that did not see.

36 And I saw that the house was large and broad and very full.

37 And I saw that a white bull was born, with large horns and all the beasts of the field and all the birds of the air feared him and made petition to him all the time.

(Author's note: If one assumes the previous "sheep with a large horn" was Judas Maccabaeus, then verse 37 is the birth of the Messiah.)

38 And I saw until all their generations were transformed, and they all became white bulls; and the first among them became a lamb, and that lamb became a great animal and had great black horns on its head; and the Lord of the sheep rejoiced over it and over all the oxen.

39 And I slept in their midst: And I awoke and saw everything.

40 This is the vision which I saw while I slept, and I awoke and blessed the Lord of righteousness and gave Him glory.

41 Then I wept greatly and my tears ceased not until I could no longer endure it; when I saw, they flowed on account of what I had seen; for everything shall come and be fulfilled, and all the deeds of men in their order were shown to me.

42 On that night I remembered the first dream, and because of it I wept and was troubled-because I had seen that vision.

[Author's note: At this point, the time frame and text flow becomes non sequitur. It appears the codex was not kept in sequence here. Thus, the translated pages are out of sequence. The flow of time and occurrences seems to follow the pattern listed:

91:6 to 92.1 through 92:5 then jumps to 93:1. The flow then continues from 93:1 to 93:10 and then jumps to 91:7. From 91:7 the text continues to 91:19. It then picks up again at 93:11 and continues.

If one were to attempt to put this section into a timeline, the interval would link together in some fashion resembling the following:

Ten Weeks of Judgment

WEEK 1 Antediluvian	Judgment & righteousness 93.3 Enoch's time (Ice-age - 16,000 B.C.)
WEEK 2 flood	Judgment & cleansing 93.4 Noah's time and the great The first judgment of the world (16,000 - 10,000 B.C)
WEEK 3	Righteousness is planted 93.5 Abraham's time (10,000 - 2000 B.C.)
WEEK 4 WEEK 4	Law for all generations 93.6 Moses' time 2000 - 1400 B.C.
WEEK 5	House of Glory 93.7 Solomon's time 1400 - 900 B.C.

WEEK 6	Jesus ascends, temple burned, elect scattered 93.8 Jesus' time 900 B.C - 100 A.D.
WEEK 7	Apostate generation Judgment of Fire 93.9 - 91.11 Our time The second judgment of earth. 100 A.D. - ?
WEEK 8	A sword 91.12–13 New house, new heaven & earth Future time
WEEK 9	The righteous judgment revealed 91.14 The judgment time
WEEK 10	God's power is forever 91.15-16 Eternal time

When reading the text from this point to the end of chapter 93, one should keep this flow in mind.]

[Chapter 91]

The Book of Warnings and Blessings of Enoch **(Chapters 91-104):**

1 And now, my son Methuselah, call to me all your brothers and gather together to me all the sons of your mother; for the word calls me, and the spirit is poured out on me, that I may show you everything that shall befall you forever.'

2 And thereon Methuselah went and summoned to him all his brothers and assembled his relatives.

3 And he spoke to all the children of righteousness and said: 'Hear, you sons of Enoch, all the words of your father, and hearken, as you should, to the voice of my mouth; for I exhort you and say to you, beloved:

4 Love righteousness and walk in it, and draw near to righteousness without a double heart, and do not associate with those of a double heart, but walk in righteousness, my sons. And it shall guide you on good paths. And righteousness shall be your companion.'

James 1:6-8 But let him ask in faith, nothing wavering. For he that wavereth is like a wave of the sea driven with the wind and tossed. [7] For let not that man think that he shall receive any thing of the Lord. [8] A double-minded man is unstable in all his ways.

5 'For I know that violence must increase on the earth, and a great punishment will be executed on the earth, it shall be cut off from its roots, and its whole construct will be destroyed.

6 And unrighteousness shall again be complete on the earth, and all the deeds of unrighteousness and of violence and sin shall prevail a second time.

7 And when sin and unrighteousness and blasphemy and violence in all kinds of deeds increase, and apostasy and transgression and uncleanness increase; a great chastisement shall come from heaven on all these, and the holy Lord will come out with wrath and chastisement to execute judgment on earth.

2 Thessalonians 2:3 Let no man deceive you by any means: for that day shall not come, except there come a falling away first, and that man of sin be revealed, the son of perdition.

8 In those days violence shall be cut off from its roots, and the roots of unrighteousness together with deceit, and they shall be destroyed from under heaven.

9 And all the idols of the heathen shall be abandoned. And the temples burned with fire, and they shall remove them from the whole earth; and the heathen shall be cast into the judgment of fire, and shall perish in wrath and in grievous judgment forever.

10 And the righteous shall arise from their sleep, and wisdom shall arise and be given to them.

11 And after that the roots of unrighteousness and those who plan violence and those who commit blasphemy shall be cut off, and the sinners shall be destroyed by the sword.

12 And after this there will be another week; the eighth, that of righteousness, and a sword will be given to it so that the Righteous Judgment may be executed on those who do wrong, and the sinners will be handed over into the hands of the righteous.

13 And, at its end, they will acquire Houses because of their righteousness, and a House will be built for the Great King in Glory, forever.

14 And after this, in the ninth week, the Righteous Judgment will be revealed to the whole world. And all the deeds of the impious will vanish from the whole Earth. And the world will be written down for destruction and all men will look to the Path of Uprightness.

15 And, after this, in the tenth week, in the seventh part, there will be an Eternal Judgment that will be executed on the Watchers and the Great Eternal Heaven that will spring from the midst of the Angels.

16 And the First Heaven will vanish and pass away and a New Heaven will appear, and all the Powers of Heaven will shine forever, with light seven times as bright.

17 And after this, there will be many weeks without number, forever, in goodness and in righteousness. And from then on sin will never again be mentioned.

18 And now I tell you, my sons, and show you, the paths of righteousness and the paths of violence. I will show them to you again that you may know what will come to pass.

19 And now, hearken to me, my sons, and walk in the paths of righteousness, and walk not in the paths of violence; for all who walk in the paths of unrighteousness shall perish forever.'

[Chapter 92]

1 The book written by Enoch (Enoch indeed wrote this complete doctrine of wisdom, [which is] praised of all men and a judge of all the earth) for all my children who shall live on the earth. And for the future generations who shall observe righteousness and peace.

2 Let not your spirit be troubled on account of the times; for the Holy and Great One has appointed days for all things.

3 And the righteous one shall arise from sleep, (shall arise) and walk in the paths of righteousness, and all his path and conversation shall be in eternal goodness and grace.

4 He will be gracious to the righteous and give him eternal righteousness, and He will give him power so that he shall be (endowed) with goodness and righteousness. And he shall walk in eternal light.

5 And sin shall perish in darkness forever, and shall no more be seen from that day forevermore.

[Chapter 93]

(Author's note: Chapters 91-93 recount and expand on the events listed in the following weeks of prophecy. The explanations of the events are scattered in chapters 91-93; however, the list of events are stated clearly in the following list of weeks in Chapter 93.)

1 And after that Enoch both gave and began to recount from the books. And Enoch said:

2 'Concerning the children of righteousness and concerning the elect of the world, and concerning the plant of righteousness, I will speak these things. I Enoch will declare (them) to you, my sons, according to that which appeared to me in heavenly vision, and which I have known through the word of the holy angels, and have learned from heavenly tablets.'

3 And Enoch began to recount from the books and said: 'I was born the seventh in the first week, able judgment and righteousness still endured.

(Author's note: Enoch was the seventh son. He was born in the beginning of the timeline he is laying out.)

4 And after me there shall arise in the second week great wickedness, and deceit shall have sprung up; and in it there shall be the first end.

(Author's note: This is the rise of evil. The angels have fallen.)

5 And in it a man shall be saved; and after it is ended unrighteousness shall grow up, and a law shall be made for the sinners. And after that in the third week at its close a man shall be elected as the plant of righteous judgment, and his posterity shall become the plant of righteousness forevermore.

(Author's note: This is the time of Moses and the establishment of the Ten Commandments, the beginning of the law.)

6 And after that in the fourth week, at its close, visions of the holy and righteous shall be seen, and a law for all generations and an enclosure shall be made for them.

(Author's note: This is the time of David and the wars that defined the Holy Land.)

7 And after that in the fifth week, at its close, the house of glory and dominion shall be built forever.

(Author's note: This concerns the time of Solomon and the first temple.)

8 And after that in the sixth week, all who live in it shall be blinded, and the hearts of all of them shall godlessly forsake wisdom. And in it a man shall ascend; and at its close the house of dominion shall be burned with fire, and the whole race of the chosen root shall be dispersed.

(Author's note: In the sixth week Christ came to the chosen ones, but they were blinded. He ascended and the Jewish nation was scattered. In the holocaust innumerable Jews were burned. The diaspora remains scattered but has begun to gather into the new nation of Israel.)

9 And after that in the seventh week shall an apostate generation arise, and many shall be its deeds, and all its deeds shall be apostate.

(Author's note: It is assumed that we are in the seventh week of Enoch's prophecy. This aligns in a very general way to the prophecies of the churches in Revelation. At the end of the seventh week there will be a "great falling away.")

2 Thessalonians 2:3 Let no man deceive you by any means: for that day shall not come, except there come a falling away first, and that man of sin be revealed, the son of perdition;

Revelation 2
1 Unto the angel of the church of Ephesus write; These things saith he that holdeth the seven stars in his right hand, who walketh in the midst of the seven golden candlesticks;
2 I know thy works, and thy labour, and thy patience, and how thou canst not bear them which are evil: and thou hast tried them which say they are apostles, and are not, and hast found them liars:
3 And hast borne, and hast patience, and for my name's sake hast laboured, and hast not fainted.
4 Nevertheless I have somewhat against thee, because thou hast left thy first love.
5 Remember therefore from whence thou art fallen, and repent, and do the first works; or else I will come unto thee quickly, and will remove thy candlestick out of his place, except thou repent.
6 But this thou hast, that thou hatest the deeds of the Nicolaitanes, which I also hate.
7 He that hath an ear, let him hear what the Spirit saith unto the churches; To him that overcometh will I give to eat of the tree of life, which is in the midst of the paradise of God.
8 And unto the angel of the church in Smyrna write; These things saith the first and the last, which was dead, and is alive;
9 I know thy works, and tribulation, and poverty, (but thou art rich) and I know the blasphemy of them which say they are Jews, and are not, but are the synagogue of

Satan.
10 Fear none of those things which thou shalt suffer: behold, the devil shall cast some of you into prison, that ye may be tried; and ye shall have tribulation ten days: be thou faithful unto death, and I will give thee a crown of life.
11 He that hath an ear, let him hear what the Spirit saith unto the churches; He that overcometh shall not be hurt of the second death.
12 And to the angel of the church in Pergamos write; These things saith he which hath the sharp sword with two edges;
13 I know thy works, and where thou dwellest, even where Satan's seat is: and thou holdest fast my name, and hast not denied my faith, even in those days wherein Antipas was my faithful martyr, who was slain among you, where Satan dwelleth.
14 But I have a few things against thee, because thou hast there them that hold the doctrine of Balaam, who taught Balac to cast a stumblingblock before the children of Israel, to eat things sacrificed unto idols, and to commit fornication.
15 So hast thou also them that hold the doctrine of the Nicolaitanes, which thing I hate.
16 Repent; or else I will come unto thee quickly, and will fight against them with the sword of my mouth.
17 He that hath an ear, let him hear what the Spirit saith unto the churches; To him that overcometh will I give to eat of the hidden manna, and will give him a white stone, and in the stone a new name written, which no man knoweth saving he that receiveth it.
18 And unto the angel of the church in Thyatira write; These things saith the Son of God, who hath his eyes like unto a flame of fire, and his feet are like fine brass;
19 I know thy works, and charity, and service, and faith, and thy patience, and thy works; and the last to be more than the first.
20 Notwithstanding I have a few things against thee, because thou sufferest that woman Jezebel, which calleth herself a prophetess, to teach and to seduce my servants to commit fornication, and to eat things sacrificed unto idols.
21 And I gave her space to repent of her fornication; and she repented not.
22 Behold, I will cast her into a bed, and them that commit adultery with her into great tribulation, except they repent of their deeds.
23 And I will kill her children with death; and all the churches shall know that I am he which searcheth the reins and hearts: and I will give unto every one of you according to your works.
24 But unto you I say, and unto the rest in Thyatira, as many as have not this doctrine, and which have not known the depths of Satan, as they speak; I will put upon you none other burden.
25 But that which ye have already hold fast till I come.
26 And he that overcometh, and keepeth my works unto the end, to him will I give power over the nations:
27 And he shall rule them with a rod of iron; as the vessels of a potter shall they be broken to shivers: even as I received of my Father.
28 And I will give him the morning star.

29 He that hath an ear, let him hear what the Spirit saith unto the churches.

Revelation 3
1 And unto the angel of the church in Sardis write; These things saith he that hath the seven Spirits of God, and the seven stars; I know thy works, that thou hast a name that thou livest, and art dead.
2 Be watchful, and strengthen the things which remain, that are ready to die: for I have not found thy works perfect before God.
3 Remember therefore how thou hast received and heard, and hold fast, and repent. If therefore thou shalt not watch, I will come on thee as a thief, and thou shalt not know what hour I will come upon thee.
4 Thou hast a few names even in Sardis which have not defiled their garments; and they shall walk with me in white: for they are worthy.
5 He that overcometh, the same shall be clothed in white raiment; and I will not blot out his name out of the Book of Life, but I will confess his name before my Father, and before his angels.
6 He that hath an ear, let him hear what the Spirit saith unto the churches.
7And to the angel of the church in Philadelphia write; These things saith he that is holy, he that is true, he that hath the key of David, he that openeth, and no man shutteth; and shutteth, and no man openeth;
8 I know thy works: behold, I have set before thee an open door, and no man can shut it: for thou hast a little strength, and hast kept my word, and hast not denied my name.
9 Behold, I will make them of the synagogue of Satan, which say they are Jews, and are not, but do lie; behold, I will make them to come and worship before thy feet, and to know that I have loved thee.
10 Because thou hast kept the word of my patience, I also will keep thee from the hour of temptation, which shall come upon all the world, to try them that dwell upon the earth.
11 Behold, I come quickly: hold that fast which thou hast, that no man take thy crown.
12 Him that overcometh will I make a pillar in the temple of my God, and he shall go no more out: and I will write upon him the name of my God, and the name of the city of my God, which is new Jerusalem, which cometh down out of heaven from my God: and I will write upon him my new name.

(Author's note: Most scholars agree that we are in the age of Laodicea)

13 He that hath an ear, let him hear what the Spirit saith unto the churches.
14 And unto the angel of the church of the Laodiceans write; These things saith the Amen, the faithful and true witness, the beginning of the creation of God;
15 I know thy works, that thou art neither cold nor hot: I would thou wert cold or hot.
16 So then because thou art lukewarm, and neither cold nor hot, I will spue thee out

of my mouth.
17 Because thou sayest, I am rich, and increased with goods, and have need of nothing; and knowest not that thou art wretched, and miserable, and poor, and blind, and naked:
18 I counsel thee to buy of me gold tried in the fire, that thou mayest be rich; and white raiment, that thou mayest be clothed, and that the shame of thy nakedness do not appear; and anoint thine eyes with eyesalve, that thou mayest see.
19 As many as I love, I rebuke and chasten: be zealous therefore, and repent.
20 Behold, I stand at the door, and knock: if any man hear my voice, and open the door, I will come in to him, and will sup with him, and he with me.
21 To him that overcometh will I grant to sit with me in my throne, even as I also overcame, and am set down with my Father in his throne.
22 He that hath an ear, let him hear what the Spirit saith unto the churches.

10 And at its end shall be elected, the elect righteous of the eternal plant of righteousness shall be chosen to receive sevenfold instruction concerning all His creation.

11 For who is there of all the children of men that is able to hear the voice of the Holy One without being troubled? And who can think His thoughts? Who is there that can behold all the works of heaven?

12 And how should there be one who could behold heaven, and who is there that could understand the things of heaven and see a soul or a spirit and could tell of it, or ascend and see all their ends and think them or do like them?

13 And who is there of all men that could know what is the breadth and the length of the earth, and to whom has the measurement been shown of all of them?

14 Or is there any one who could discern the length of the heaven and how great is its height, and on what it is founded, and how great is the number of the stars, and where all the luminaries rest?

(Author's note: In this age of space travel, we have indeed beheld the heavens and measured and numbered the stars. These are the end times.)

[Chapter 94]

1 And now I say to you, my sons, love righteousness and walk in it; because the paths of righteousness are worthy of acceptation, but the paths of unrighteousness shall suddenly be destroyed and vanish.

2 And to certain men of a generation shall the paths of violence and of death be revealed, and they shall hold themselves afar from them, and shall not follow them.

3 And now I say to you, the righteous, walk not in the paths of wickedness, nor in the paths of death, and draw not near to them, lest you be destroyed.

4 But seek and choose for yourselves righteousness and an elect life, and walk in the paths of peace, and you shall live and prosper.

5 And hold (keep) my words in the thoughts of your hearts, and permit them not to be erased from your hearts; for I know that sinners will tempt men to evilly entreat wisdom, so that no place may be found for her, and temptation will increase.

Ecclesiastes 12:13 Now all has been heard; here is the conclusion of the matter: Fear God and keep his commandments, for this is the whole duty of man. 14 For God will bring every deed into judgment, including every hidden thing, whether it is good or evil.

6 Woe to those who build unrighteousness and oppression and lay deceit as a foundation; for they shall be suddenly overthrown, and they shall have no peace.

7 Woe to those who build their houses with sin; for from all their foundations shall they be overthrown, and by the sword shall they fall. And those who acquire gold and silver shall suddenly perish in the judgment.

8 Woe to you, you rich, for you have trusted in your riches, and from your riches shall you depart, because you have not remembered the Most High in the days of your riches.

Isaiah 5:19-23 Woe to those who rise early in the morning to run after their drinks, who stay up late at night till they are inflamed with wine.
20 Woe to those who call evil good and good evil, who put darkness for light and light for darkness, who put bitter for sweet and sweet for bitter.
21 Woe to those who are wise in their own eyes and clever in their own sight.
22 Woe to those who are heroes at drinking wine and champions at mixing drinks,
23 who acquit the guilty for a bribe, but deny justice to the innocent.

9 You have committed blasphemy and unrighteousness, and have become ready for the day of slaughter, and the day of darkness and the day of the great judgment.

10 Thus I speak and tell you: He who hath created you will overthrow you, and for your fall there shall be no compassion, and your Creator will rejoice at your destruction.

11 And your righteousness shall be a reproach to the sinners and the godless in those days.

James 5:1-6 Go to now, ye rich men, weep and howl for your miseries that shall come upon you. [2] Your riches are corrupted, and your garments are moth-eaten. [3] Your gold and silver is cankered; and the rust of them shall be a witness against you, and shall eat your flesh as if it were fire. Ye have heaped treasure together for the last days. [4] Behold, the hire of the labourers who have reaped down your fields, which is of you kept back by fraud, crieth: and the cries of them which have reaped are entered into the ears of the Lord of sabaoth. [5] Ye have lived in pleasure on the earth, and been wanton; ye have nourished your hearts, as in a day of slaughter. [6] Ye have condemned and killed the just; and he doth not resist you.

(Author's note: In the above biblical verses from James, "sabaoth" is from the Hebrew, plural form of "host" or "army." The word is used almost exclusively in conjunction with the Divine name as a title of majesty: "the Lord of Hosts," or "the Lord God of Hosts.")

[Chapter 95]

1 Would that my eyes were rain clouds of water that I might weep over you, and pour down my tears as a cloud of water, that I might rest from my trouble of heart!

2 Who has permitted you to practice reproaches and wickedness? And so judgment shall overtake you, sinners.

3 You, righteous! Fear not the sinners, for again the Lord will deliver them into your hands, that you may execute judgment on them according to your desires.

4 Woe to you who speak against God (fulminate anathemas) which cannot be removed (reversed) - healing shall be far from you because of your sins.

5 Woe to you who repay your neighbor with evil; for you shall be repaid according to your works.

6 Woe to you, lying witnesses, and to those who weigh out injustice, for you shall suddenly perish.

7 Woe to you, sinners, for you persecute the righteous; for you shall be delivered up and persecuted because of injustice, and your yoke shall be heavy on you.

Luke 6:24-31 "But woe to you who are rich, for you have already received your comfort. [25] Woe to you who are well fed now, for you will go hungry. Woe to you who laugh now, for you will mourn and weep. [26] Woe to you when all men speak well of you, for that is how their fathers treated the false prophets. [27] "But I tell you who hear me: Love your enemies, do good to those who hate you, [28] bless those who curse you, pray for those who mistreat you. [29] If someone strikes you on one cheek, turn to him the other also. If someone takes your cloak, do not stop him from taking your tunic. [30] Give to everyone who asks you, and if anyone takes what belongs to you, do not demand it back. [31] Do to others as you would have them do to you.

[Chapter 96]

1 Be hopeful, you righteous; for suddenly shall the sinners perish before you, and you shall have lordship over them, according to your desires.

2 And in the day of the tribulation of the sinners, your children shall mount and rise as eagles, and your nests shall be higher than the vultures'. You shall ascend as badgers and enter the crevices of the earth, and the clefts of the rock forever before the unrighteous. And the satyrs (sirens) shall sigh and weep because of you.

3 Wherefore fear not, you that have suffered, for healing shall be your portion, and a bright light shall enlighten you, and the voice of rest you shall hear from heaven.

4 Woe to you, you sinners, for your riches make you appear like the righteous, but your hearts convict you of being sinners, and this fact shall be a testimony against you for a memorial of your evil deeds.

5 Woe to you who devour the finest of the wheat, and drink wine in large bowls (the best of waters), and tread under foot the lowly (humble) with your might.

6 Woe to you who drink water from every fountain (drink water all the time), for suddenly shall you be consumed and wither away, because you have forsaken the fountain of life.

(Author's note: The above reference is a euphemism for promiscuity.)

7 Woe to you who work unrighteousness and deceit and blasphemy; it shall be a memorial against you for evil.

8 Woe to you, you mighty, who with might oppress the righteous; for the day of your destruction is coming. Many and good days shall come to the righteous in those days - in the day of your judgment.

[Chapter 97]

1 Believe, you righteous, that the sinners will become a shame and perish in the day of unrighteousness.

2 Be it known to you, you sinners, that the Most High is mindful of your destruction, and the angels of heaven rejoice over your destruction.

3 What will you do, you sinners, and where shall you flee on that day of judgment, when you hear the voice of the prayer of the righteous?

4 You shall fare like to them, against whom these words shall be a testimony: "You have been companions of sinners."

5 And in those days the prayer of the righteous shall reach to the Lord, and for you the days of your judgment shall come.

6 And all the words of your unrighteousness shall be read out before the Great Holy One, and your faces shall be covered with shame, and He will reject every work which is grounded on unrighteousness.

7 Woe to you, you sinners, who live on the middle of the ocean and on the dry land, whose remembrance is evil against you.

8 Woe to you who acquire silver and gold in unrighteousness and say: "We have become rich with riches and have possessions; and have acquired everything we have desired.

9 And now let us do what we purposed, for we have gathered silver, and many are the servants in our houses and our granaries are full to the brim as if with water."

10 Yea, and like water your lies shall flow away; for your riches shall not abide but quickly depart (go up) from you, for you have acquired it all in unrighteousness, and you shall be given over to a great curse.

[Chapter 98]

1 And now I swear to you, to the wise and to the foolish, that you shall see (have) many experiences on the earth.

2 For you men shall put on more adornments than a woman, and colored garments more than a young woman, like royalty and in grandeur and in power, and in silver and in gold and in purple, and in splendor and in food they shall be poured out as water.

3 Therefore they shall have neither knowledge nor wisdom, and because of this they shall die together with their possessions; and with all their glory and their splendor, and in shame and in slaughter and in great destitution, their spirits shall be thrown into the furnace of fire.

4 I have sworn to you, you sinners, as a mountain has not become a slave, and a hill does not become the servant of a woman, even so sin has not been sent on the earth, but man of himself has created it, and they that commit it shall fall under a great curse.

5 And barrenness has not been given to the woman, but on account of the deeds of her own hands she dies without children.

6 I have sworn to you, you sinners, by the Holy Great One, that all your evil deeds are revealed in heaven, and that none of your wrong deeds (of oppression) are covered and hidden.

7 And do not think in your spirit nor say in your heart that you do not know and that you do not see that every sin is recorded every day in heaven in the presence of the Most High.

8 From now on, you know that all your wrongdoing that you do will be written down every day, until the day of your judgment.

9 Woe to you, you fools, for through your folly you shall perish; and you do not listen to the wise so no good will come to you against the wise,

10 And so and now, know you that you are prepared for the day of destruction. Therefore do not hope to live, you sinners, but you shall depart and die; for there will be no ransom for you; because you are prepared for the day of the great judgment, for the day of tribulation and great shame for your spirits.

11 Woe to you, you obstinate of heart, who work wickedness and eat blood. Where do you have good things to eat and to drink and to be

filled? From all the good things which the Lord the Most High has placed in abundance on the earth; therefore you shall have no peace.

(Author's note: The above reference to eating blood may indicate cannibalism. As a side note, The Book of Jubilees tells us that the offspring of the fallen angels drank blood.)

Genesis 9:3-6 Every moving thing that liveth shall be meat for you; even as the green herb have I given you all things. [4] But flesh with the life thereof, which is the blood thereof, shall ye not eat. [5] And surely your blood of your lives will I require; at the hand of every beast will I require it, and at the hand of man; at the hand of every man's brother will I require the life of man. [6] Whoso sheddeth man's blood, by man shall his blood be shed: for in the image of God made he man.

12 Woe to you who love the deeds of unrighteousness; wherefore do you hope for good for yourselves? You know that you shall be delivered into the hands of the righteous, and they shall cut off your necks and slay you, and have no mercy on you.

13 Woe to you who rejoice in the distress of the righteous; for no grave shall be dug for you.

14 Woe to you who say the words of the wise are empty; for you shall have no hope of life.

15 Woe to you who write down lying and godless words; for they write down their lies so that men may hear them and act godlessly towards their neighbor. Therefore they shall have no peace but die a sudden death.

[Chapter 99]

1 Woe to you who do godless acts, and praise and honor lies; you shall perish, and no happy life shall be yours.

2 Woe to them who pervert the words of righteousness, and transgress the eternal law, and count themselves as sinless. They shall be trodden under foot on the earth.

3 In those days make ready, you righteous, to raise your prayers as a memorial, and place them as a testimony before the angels, that they may place the sin of the sinners for a reminder before the Most High.

4 In those days the nations shall be stirred up, and the families of the nations shall arise on the day of destruction.

5 And in those days the destitute shall go and throw their children out, and they shall abandon them, so that their children shall perish because of them. They shall abandon their children that are still babies (sucklings), and not return to them, and shall have no pity on their loved ones.

6 Again, I swear to you, you sinners, that sin is prepared for a day of unceasing bloodshed.

Matthew 24:6-8 And ye shall hear of wars and rumours of wars: see that ye be not troubled: for all these things must come to pass, but the end is not yet. [7] For nation shall rise against nation, and kingdom against kingdom: and there shall be famines, and pestilences, and earthquakes, in diverse places. [8] All these are the beginning of sorrows.

7 And they who worship stones, and carved images of gold and silver and wood and stone and clay, and those who worship impure spirits and demons, and all kinds of idols not according to knowledge, shall get no manner of help from them.

8 And they shall become godless by reason of the folly of their hearts, and their eyes shall be blinded through the fear of their hearts and through visions in their ambitions (dreams).

Colossians 2:16-19 Let no man therefore judge you in meat, or in drink, or in respect of an holyday, or of the new moon, or of the sabbath days:
[17] Which are a shadow of things to come; but the body is of Christ.
[18] Let no man beguile you of your reward in a voluntary humility and worshipping of angels, intruding into those things which he hath not seen, vainly puffed up by his fleshly mind,
[19] And not holding the Head, from which all the body by joints and bands having nourishment ministered, and knit together, increaseth with the increase of God.

9 Through these they shall become godless and fearful; for they shall have done all their work with lies, and shall have worshiped a stone, therefore in an instant shall they perish.

Revelation 9:19-21 For their power is in their mouth, and in their tails: for their tails were like unto serpents, and had heads, and with them they do hurt.
[20] And the rest of the men which were not killed by these plagues yet repented not of the works of their hands, that they should not worship devils, and idols of gold, and silver, and brass, and stone, and of wood: which neither can see, nor hear, nor walk:
[21] Neither repented they of their murders, nor of their sorceries, nor of their

fornication, nor of their thefts.

10 But in those days blessed are all they who accept the words of wisdom, and understand them, and observe the paths of the Most High, and walk in the path of His righteousness, and become not godless with the godless, for they shall be saved.

11 Woe to you who spread evil to your neighbors, for you shall be slain in Hell.

12 Woe to you who make your foundation that of deceitful (sin) and lies, and who cause bitterness on the earth; for they shall thereby be utterly consumed.

13 Woe to you who build your houses through the hard labor of others, and all their building materials are the bricks and stones of sin; I tell you, you shall have no peace.

14 Woe to them who reject the measure and eternal inheritance of their fathers and whose souls follow after idols; for they shall have no rest.

15 Woe to them who do unrighteous acts and help oppression, and kill their neighbors until the day of the great judgment, for He will throw down your glory.

16 For He shall throw down your glory, and bring affliction on your hearts, and shall arouse His fierce anger, and destroy you all with the sword; and all the holy and righteous shall remember your sins.

[Chapter 100]

1 And in those days in one place the fathers together with their sons shall kill one another and brothers shall fall in death together until the streams flow with their blood.

2 For a man shall not withhold his hand from killing his sons and his sons' sons, and the sinner shall not withhold his hand from his honored brother, from dawn until sunset they shall kill one another.

Mark 13:12 Now the brother shall betray the brother to death, and the father the son; and children shall rise up against their parents, and shall cause them to be put to death.

3 And the horse shall walk up to the breast in the blood of sinners, and the chariot shall be submerged to its height.

Revelation 14:20 And the winepress was trodden without the city, and blood came out of the winepress, even unto the horse bridles, by the space of a thousand and six hundred furlongs.

4 In those days the angels shall descend into the secret places and gather together into one place all those who brought down sin and the Most High will arise on that day of judgment to execute great judgment among sinners.

5 And over all the righteous and holy He will appoint guardians from among the holy angels to guard them as the apple of an eye, until He makes an end of all wickedness and all sin, and even if the righteous sleep a long sleep, they have nothing to fear.

6 And the wise men will seek the truth and they and their sons will understand the words of this book, and recognize that their riches shall not be able to save them or overcome their sins.

7 Woe to you sinners, on the day of strong anguish, you who afflict the righteous and burn them with fire; you shall be requited according to your works.

8 Woe to you, you obstinate of heart, who watch in order to devise wickedness; therefore shall fear come on you and there shall be none to help you.

9 Woe to you, you sinners, on account of the words of your mouth, and on account of the deeds of your hands which your godlessness has caused, in blazing flames burning worse than fire shall you burn.

2 Thessalonians 1:7-9 And to you who are troubled rest with us, when the Lord Jesus shall be revealed from heaven with his mighty angels, [8] In flaming fire taking vengeance on them that know not God, and that obey not the gospel of our Lord Jesus Christ: [9] Who shall be punished with everlasting destruction from the presence of the Lord, and from the glory of his power?

10 And now, know that the angels will ask Him in heaven about your deeds and from the sun and from the moon and from the stars they will ask about your sins because on the earth you execute judgment on the righteous.

11 And He will summon to testify against you every cloud and mist and dew and rain; for they shall all be withheld from falling on you, and they shall be mindful of your sins.

12 And now give gifts to the rain that it cease not from falling on you, nor the dew, when it has received gold and silver from you that it may fall. When the hoar-frost and snow with their chilliness, and all the snow storms with all their plagues fall on you, in those days you shall not be able to stand before them.

[Chapter 101]

1 Observe heaven, you children of heaven, and every work of the Most High, and fear Him and work no evil in His presence.

2 If He closes the windows of heaven, and withholds the rain and the dew from falling on the earth on your account, what will you do then?

3 And if He sends His anger on you because of your deeds, you cannot petition Him; for you spoke proud and arrogant words against His righteousness, therefore you shall have no peace.

4 Don't you see the sailors of the ships, how their ships are tossed back and forth by the waves, and are shaken by the winds, and are in great trouble?

5 And therefore they are afraid because all their nice possessions go on the sea with them, and they have bad feelings in their heart that the sea will swallow them and they will perish therein.

6 Are not the entire sea and all its waters, and all its movements, the work of the Most High, and has He not set limits to its actions, and confined it throughout by the sand?

7 And at His reproof it fears and dries up, and all its fish die and all that is in it; but you sinners that are on the earth fear Him not.

8 Has He not made heaven and the earth, and all that is in it? Who has given understanding and wisdom to everything that moves on the earth and in the sea?

9 Do not the sailors of the ships fear the sea? Yet you sinners do not fear the Most High.

[Chapter 102]

1 In those days if He sent a horrible fire on you, where will you flee, and where will you find deliverance? And when He launches out His Word against you will you not be shaken and afraid?

2 And all the luminaries shall be shaken with great fear, and all the earth shall be afraid and tremble and be alarmed.

3 And all the angels shall execute their commands and shall seek to hide themselves from the presence of He who is Great in Glory, and the children of earth shall tremble and shake; and you sinners shall be cursed forever, and you shall have no peace.

2 Peter 3:8-13 But, beloved, be not ignorant of this one thing, that one day is with the Lord as a thousand years, and a thousand years as one day.
9 The Lord is not slack concerning his promise, as some men count slackness; but is longsuffering to us-ward, not willing that any should perish, but that all should come to repentance.
10 But the day of the Lord will come as a thief in the night; in which the heavens shall pass away with a great noise, and the elements shall melt with fervent heat, the earth also and the works that are therein shall be burned up.
11 Seeing then that all these things shall be dissolved, what manner of persons ought ye to be in all holy conversation and godliness,
12 Looking for and hasting unto the coming of the day of God, wherein the heavens being on fire shall be dissolved, and the elements shall melt with fervent heat?
13 Nevertheless we, according to his promise, look for new heavens and a new earth, wherein dwelleth righteousness.

4 Fear you not, you souls of the righteous, and fear not you who have died in righteousness.

5 And don't grieve if your soul has descended in to the grave in grief, and that in your life you were not rewarded according to your goodness, but wait for the day of the judgment of sinners and for the day of cursing and chastisement.

6 And when you die the sinners will say about you: "As we die, so die the righteous, and what benefit do they reap for their deeds?

7 See, even as we, so do they die in grief and darkness, and what have they more than we? From now on we are equal.

8 And what will they receive and what will they see forever? Look, they too have died, and from now on forever shall they see no light."

9 I tell you, you sinners, you are content to eat and drink, and rob and sin, and strip men naked, and acquire wealth and see good days.

10 Have you seen the righteous how their end was peace, that no violence is found in them until their death?

11 Nevertheless they died and became as though they had not been, and their spirits descended into Hell in tribulation.

Matthew 10:28 Do not be afraid of those who kill the body but cannot kill the soul. Rather, be afraid of the One who can destroy both soul and body in hell.

[Chapter 103]

1 Now, therefore, I swear to the righteous, by the glory of the Great and Honored and Mighty One who reigns, I swear to you, I know this mystery.

2 I have read the heavenly tablets, and have seen the holy books, and have found written in it and inscribed regarding them.

3 That all goodness and joy and glory are prepared for them, and written down for the spirits of those who have died in righteousness, and that much good shall be given to you in reward for your labors, and that your lot is abundant beyond the lot of the living.

4 And the spirits of you who have died in righteousness shall live and rejoice, and your spirits shall not perish, nor shall your memory from before the face of the Great One to all the generations of the world, therefore no longer fear their abuse.

5 Woe to you, you sinners, when you have died, if you die in the abundance of your sins, and woe to those who are like you and say regarding you: "Blessed are the sinners, they have seen all their days.

6 And how they have died in prosperity and in wealth, and have not seen tribulation or murder in their life; and they have died in honor, and judgment has not been executed on them during their life."

7 You know that their souls will be made to descend into Hell and they shall be wracked in great tribulation.

8 And into darkness and chains and a burning flame where there is harsh judgment your spirits shall enter, and the great judgment shall be for all the generations of the world. Woe to you, for you shall have no peace.

9 The righteous and good who are alive, do not say: "In our troubled days we have worked hard and experienced every trouble, and met with much evil and been afflicted, and have become few and our spirit small.

10 And we have been destroyed and have not found any to help us even with a word. We have been tortured and destroyed, and not expect to live from day to day.

11 We hoped to be the head and have become the tail. We have worked hard and had no satisfaction in our labor; and we have become the food of the sinners and the unrighteous, and they have laid their yoke heavily on us.

12 They have ruled over us and hated us and hit us, and to those that hated us we have bowed our necks but they pitied us not.

13 We desired to get away from them that we might escape and be at rest, but found no place where we should flee and be safe from them.

14 We complained to the rulers in our tribulation, and cried out against those who devoured us, but they did not pay attention to our cries and would not listen to our voice.

15 And they helped those who robbed us and devoured us and those who made us few; and they concealed their oppression (wrongdoing), and they did not remove from us the yoke of those that devoured us and dispersed us and murdered us, and they concealed their murder, and did not remember that they had lifted up their hands against us."

Jeremiah 30:15-19 Why do you cry out over your wound, your pain that has no cure? Because of your great guilt and many sins I have done these things to you.
[16] But all who devour you will be devoured; all your enemies will go into exile. Those who plunder you will be plundered; all who make spoil of you I will despoil.
[17] But I will restore you to health and heal your wounds, declares the LORD,'because you are called an outcast, Zion for whom no one cares.
[18] This is what the LORD says: "I will restore the fortunes of Jacob's tents and have compassion on his dwellings; the city will be rebuilt on her ruins, and the palace will stand in its proper place.
[19] From them will come songs of thanksgiving and the sound of rejoicing. I will add to their numbers, and they will not be decreased; I will bring them honor, and they

will not be disdained."

[Chapter 104]

1 I swear to you, that in heaven the angels remember you for good before the glory of the Great One.

2 And your names are written before the glory of the Great One. Be hopeful; for before you were put to shame through sickness and affliction; but now you shall shine as the lights of heaven,

3 You shall shine and you shall be seen, and the doors of heaven shall be opened to you. And in your cry, cry for judgment, and it shall appear to you; for all your tribulation shall be visited on the rulers, and on all who helped those who plundered you.

4 Be hopeful, and do not throw away your hopes for you shall have great joy as the angels of heaven.

5 What will you have to do ? You shall not have to hide on the day of the great judgment and you shall not be found as sinners, and the eternal judgment shall not come to you for all the generations, eternally.

6 And now fear not, you righteous, when you see the sinners growing strong and prospering in their ways; do not be their companions, but keep away from their violence.

7 For you shall become companions of the hosts of heaven. And, although you sinners say, "All our sins shall not be found out and be written down," nevertheless they shall write down all your sins every day.

8 And now I show to you that light and darkness, day and night, see all your sins.

9 Do not be godless in your hearts, and do not lie and do not change the words of righteousness, nor say that the words of the Holy Great One are lies, nor praise or rely on your idols; for all your lying and all your godlessness come not from (or lead not to) righteousness but from (or lead to) great sin.

10 And now I know this mystery, that sinners will alter and pervert the words of righteousness in many ways, and will speak wicked words, and lie, and practice great deceits, and write books concerning their words.

11 But when they write down all my words truthfully in their languages, and do not change or omit any of my words but write them all down truthfully - all that I first testified concerning them.

12 Then, I know another mystery, that books will be given to the righteous and the wise to produce joy and righteousness and much wisdom.

13 And to them the books shall be given, and they shall believe them and rejoice over them, and then all the righteous who have learned from them all the paths of righteousness shall be paid back.'

[Chapter 105]

Later Additions to the Text – Book of Noah **(Chapters 105-108):**

1 In those days the Lord called them (the wise and righteous) to testify to the children of earth concerning their wisdom: Show it to them; for you are their guides, and a recompense over the whole earth.

2 For I and my son will be united with them forever in the paths of righteousness in their lives; and you shall have peace: rejoice, you children of righteousness. Amen.

[Chapter 106]

This section of Enoch was not originally attached. It is a fragment from the Book of Noah.

Though this book has not come down to us independently, it has in large measure been incorporated in the Ethiopic Book of Enoch, and can in part be reconstructed from it.

The Book of Noah is mentioned several times in the Book of Jubilees. The editor simply changed the name Noah in the context before him into Enoch, for the statement is based on Gen. 5: 32, and Enoch lived only 365 years. Chapters 6-11 are from the same source. They make no reference to Enoch, but bring forward Noah and mention the sin of the angels that led to the flood, and of their temporal and eternal punishment. This section is a repeat of the Semjaza and Azazel myths.

Other pieces of the Book of Noah can be found scattered throughout Enoch in chapters 6-11, 39:1-2a, 54:7-55:2, 60, 65:1-69:25, and 106-107. The fragments seem to have been written earlier than the Book of Jubilees and thus was likely written around 200 B.C.

Fragment from the Book of Noah.

1 And after some days my son Methuselah took a wife for his son, Lamech, and she became pregnant by him and bore a son. And his body was white as snow and red as the blooming of a rose, and the hair of his head and his long curls were white as wool, and his eyes beautiful.

2 And when he opened his eyes, he lit up the whole house like the sun, and the whole house was very bright.

3 And on it he levitated (arose) in the hands of the midwife, opened his mouth, and conversed with the Lord of righteousness.

4 And his father, Lamech, was afraid of him and fled, and came to his father Methuselah. And he said to him: 'I have begotten a strange son, different and unlike man, and resembling the sons of the God of heaven; and his nature is different and he is not like us, and his eyes are as the rays of the sun, and his face is glorious.

5 And it seems to me that he did not spring from me but from the angels, and I fear that in his days a wonder may be performed on the earth.

6 And now, my father, I am here to ask you and beg you that you may go to Enoch, our father, and learn from him the truth, for his dwelling-place is among the angels."

7 And when Methuselah heard the words of his son, he came to me to the ends of the earth; for he had heard that I was there, and he cried aloud, and I heard his voice and I came to him. And I said to him: 'Behold, here am I, my son, why have you come to me? '

8 And he answered and said: 'Because of a great cause of anxiety have I come to you, and because of a disturbing vision have I approached.

9 And now, my father, hear me. To Lamech, my son, there has been born a son, the like of whom there is none other, and his nature is not like man's nature, and the color of his body is whiter than snow and redder than the bloom of a rose, and the hair of his head is whiter than white wool, and his eyes are like the rays of the sun, and he opened his eyes and the whole house lit up.

10 And he levitated (arose) in the hands of the midwife, and opened his mouth and blessed the Lord of heaven.

11 And his father Lamech became afraid and fled to me, and did not believe that he was sprung from him, but that he was in the likeness of

the angels of heaven; and now I have come to you that you may make known to me the truth.'

12 And I, Enoch, answered and said to him: 'The Lord will do a new thing on the earth, and this I have already seen in a vision, and make known to you that in the generation of my father Jared some of the angels of heaven violated the word of the Lord. And they commit sin and broke the law, and have had sex (united themselves) with women and committed sin with them, and have married some of them, and have had children by them.

13 And they shall produce on the earth giants not according to the spirit, but according to the flesh, and there shall be a great punishment on the earth, and the earth shall be cleansed from all impurity.

14 There shall come a great destruction over the whole earth, and there shall be a flood (deluge) and a great destruction for one year.

15 And this son who has been born to you shall be left on the earth, and his three children shall be saved with him: when all mankind that are on the earth shall die, he and his sons shall be saved.

16 And now make known to your son, Lamech, that he who has been born is in truth his son, and call his name Noah; for he shall be left to you, and he and his sons shall be saved from the destruction, which shall come on the earth on account of all the sin and all the unrighteousness, which shall be full (completed) on the earth in his days.

17 And after that (flood) there shall be more unrighteousness than that which was done before on the earth; for I know the mysteries of the holy ones; for He, the Lord, has showed me and informed me, and I have read (them) in heavenly tablets.

[Chapter 107]

1 And I saw written about them that generation after generation shall transgress, until a generation of righteousness arises, and transgression is destroyed and sin passes away from the earth, and all manner of good comes on it.

2 And now, my son, go and make known to your son Lamech that this son, which has been born, is in truth his son, and this is no lie.'

3 And when Methuselah had heard the words of his father Enoch, for he had shown to him everything in secret, he returned and showed those

things to him and called the name of that son Noah; for he will comfort the earth after all the destruction.

[Chapter 108]

(Author's note: Chapter 108 was added later and was not part of the original text.)

1 Another book which Enoch wrote for his son Methuselah and for those who will come after him, and keep the law in the last days.

2 You who have done good shall wait for those days until an end is made of those who work evil; and an end of the power of the wrongdoers.

3 And wait until sin has passed away indeed, for their names shall be blotted out of the Book of Life and out of the holy books, and their (children) seed shall be destroyed forever, and their spirits shall be killed, and they shall cry and lament in a place that is a chaotic desert, and they shall be burned in the fire; for there is no earth there.

4 I saw something there like an invisible cloud; because it was so deep I could not look over it, and I saw a flame of fire blazing brightly, and things like shining mountains circling and sweeping back and forth.

5 And I asked one of the holy angels who was with me and said to him: 'What is this bright thing (shining)? For it is not heaven but there was only the flame of a blazing fire, and the voice of weeping and crying and moaning, lamenting, and agony.'

6 And he said to me: 'This place which you see are where the spirits of sinners and blasphemers, and of those who work wickedness, are cast and the spirits of those who pervert everything that the Lord hath spoken through the mouth of the prophets and even the prophecies (things that shall be).

7 For some of them are written and inscribed above in heaven, in order that the angels may read them and know that which shall befall the sinners, and the spirits of the humble, and of those who have afflicted their bodies, and been recompensed by God; and of those who have been abused (put to shame) by wicked men:

8 Who love God and loved neither gold nor silver nor any of the good things which are in the world, but gave over their bodies to torture.

9 Who, since they were born, longed not after earthly food, but regarded everything as a passing breath, and lived accordingly, and the Lord tried them much, and their spirits were found pure so that they should bless His name.

10 And all the blessings destined for them I have recounted in the books. And he has assigned them their reward, because they have been found to love heaven more than their life in the world, and though they were trodden under foot by wicked men, and experienced abuse and reviling from them and were put to shame, they blessed Me.

11 And now I will summon the spirits of the good who belong to the generation of light, and I will transform those who were born in darkness, who in the flesh were not rewarded with such honor as their faithfulness deserved.

12 And I will bring out in shining light those who have loved My holy name, and I will seat each on the throne of his honor.

Matthew 19:28 And Jesus said unto them, Verily I say unto you, That ye which have followed me, in the regeneration when the Son of Man shall sit in the throne of his glory, ye also shall sit upon twelve thrones, judging the twelve tribes of Israel.

13 And they shall shine for time without end; for righteousness is the judgment of God; because to the faithful He will give faithfulness in the habitation of upright paths.

14 And they shall see those who were born in darkness led into darkness, while the righteous shall shine. And the sinners shall cry aloud and see them shining, and they indeed will go where days and seasons are written down (prescribed) for them.'

The Calendar of Enoch's and Daniel's Prophecies

Before we proceed, let us state the obvious. As scholars, as rational people, we must understand and acknowledge the propensity of our minds. The human brain is made in such a way as to recognize patterns. This was a survival mechanism at one time. We would see movement, shape, and various patterns in such a way as to predict the object, direction, and action We also attributed patterns to sequences, shapes, and markings in an attempt to determine of an object was food, or predator. The human brain tends to look for patterns and attribute them to items or circumstances, imposing a pattern at times even if in one time occurrences or if no clear pattern exists. This is why one may see a face, animal, bird, bat, or butterfly in a cloud, or even an ink blot.

Such may be the case with the prophecy we are about to investigate. Admittedly, the Enochian calendar seems to make the prophecy of Daniel's 70 weeks fit a timeline exactly. On the other hand, we may have looked at all possible timelines and calendars until we found one that happened to fit. You, the reader, should decide for yourself if Enoch holds the key to Biblical prophecy, or if we are simply looking at a singular, amazing coincidence without an established pattern. It is my task to attempt only a clear presentation of the facts.

John Pratt and Sir Isaac Newton

I first ran across the idea of taking the Enochian Calendar and applying it to the Prophecy in the Book of Daniel after reading the work of John Pratt. He had been spurred into the project after reading the calculations of Sir Isaac Newton regarding Biblical prophecies. After combing through the math and scriptural references, I concluded there was enough coincidence to give the theory weight. It is my hope that the language and references makes this complicated study understandable.

To review: When a prophecy is uttered that is relative to a space of time, the mode of measurement must be specified. Daniel's prophecy is spoken of as 70 weeks, but it is understood that the weeks are actually years. Thus, the week of 70 years is a time span of 490 years. Now, the question becomes, "What kind of years?" Are these lunar years, solar years, or another type of year? Each type of year has a different length and over a period of 490 years the accumulative differences become significant.

There have been thousands of attempts to explain Daniel's "Weeks of Years." All seem to be rather contrived to force a predetermined solution. Most deal with future prophecies, which is always a safe way to go, seeing as how the interpreter would usually be dead before his or her theory was proven incorrect.

A new solution to Daniel's "Weeks of Years"

What if we interpret this passage differently? If we assume Daniel is speaking of a time period that begins with a ruler making peace with the Jews and ending with the bringing of everlasting righteousness?

What would happen if we applied the Enochian year, based on weeks, to solve Daniel's "Week of Years?"

The portion of 1 Enoch referred to as the Book of Astronomy is dated in the fourth to third century B.C. according to many western scholars.

This book contains descriptions of the movement of heavenly bodies as revealed to Enoch in his trips to Heaven. The book describes a solar calendar that was later described in The Book of Jubilees. The most Jews of that time used a lunar-based calendar. The use of this calendar made it impossible to celebrate the festivals simultaneously with those in the temple of Jerusalem.

The year was composed of 364 days, divided in four seasons of 91 days each. Each season was composed of three equal months of 30 days, plus an extra day at the end of the third month. The whole year was thus composed of exactly 52 weeks, and every calendar day occurred always on the same day of the week. There is some controversy as to which day of the year the calendar started on each year. Some say each year and each season started always on Wednesday, which was the fourth day of creation and the day when the lights in the sky, the seasons, the days and the years were created. Others claim the calendar began on Sunday, the first day of the week. To reconcile this calendar with the exact 365.24219 days they added a week every few years, in order to have the year always to start on Wednesday or Sunday, according to which scholar one believes.

For this exercise in Daniel, we will assume the calendar begins on a Sunday. Since the calendar of Enoch is based on weeks, it begins every year on a Sunday, and adds a week of days when needed to keep the first day of the year as near the spring equinox (usually 21 or 22 March) as possible.

Artaxerxes and Ezra Pact

Artaxerxes, king of Persia, and Ezra the prophet made a pact. The king agreed to release the Jews and permit them to return to Jerusalem and rebuild the city.

Daniel 9 (King James Version)
1 In the first year of Darius the son of Ahasuerus, of the seed of the Medes, which was made king over the realm of the Chaldeans;
2 In the first year of his reign I Daniel understood by books the number of the years, whereof the word of the LORD came to Jeremiah the prophet, that he would

accomplish seventy years in the desolations of Jerusalem.
3 And I set my face unto the Lord God, to seek by prayer and supplications, with
fasting, and sackcloth, and ashes:
4 And I prayed unto the LORD my God, and made my confession, and said, O
Lord, the great and dreadful God, keeping the covenant and mercy to them that love
him, and to them that keep his commandments;
5 We have sinned, and have committed iniquity, and have done wickedly, and have
rebelled, even by departing from thy precepts and from thy judgments:
6 Neither have we hearkened unto thy servants the prophets, which spake in thy
name to our kings, our princes, and our fathers, and to all the people of the land.
7 O LORD, righteousness belongeth unto thee, but unto us confusion of faces, as at
this day; to the men of Judah, and to the inhabitants of Jerusalem, and unto all
Israel, that are near, and that are far off, through all the countries whither thou hast
driven them, because of their trespass that they have trespassed against thee.
8 O Lord, to us belongeth confusion of face, to our kings, to our princes, and to our
fathers, because we have sinned against thee.
9 To the Lord our God belong mercies and forgivenesses, though we have rebelled
against him;
10 Neither have we obeyed the voice of the LORD our God, to walk in his laws,
which he set before us by his servants the prophets.
11 Yea, all Israel have transgressed thy law, even by departing, that they might not
obey thy voice; therefore the curse is poured upon us, and the oath that is written in
the law of Moses the servant of God, because we have sinned against him.
12 And he hath confirmed his words, which he spake against us, and against our
judges that judged us, by bringing upon us a great evil: for under the whole heaven
hath not been done as hath been done upon Jerusalem.
13 As it is written in the law of Moses, all this evil is come upon us: yet made we
not our prayer before the LORD our God, that we might turn from our iniquities,
and understand thy truth.
14 Therefore hath the LORD watched upon the evil, and brought it upon us: for the
LORD our God is righteous in all his works which he doeth: for we obeyed not his
voice.
15 And now, O Lord our God, that hast brought thy people forth out of the land of
Egypt with a mighty hand, and hast gotten thee renown, as at this day; we have
sinned, we have done wickedly.
16 O LORD, according to all thy righteousness, I beseech thee, let thine anger and
thy fury be turned away from thy city Jerusalem, thy holy mountain: because for
our sins, and for the iniquities of our fathers, Jerusalem and thy people are become a
reproach to all that are about us.
17 Now therefore, O our God, hear the prayer of thy servant, and his supplications,
and cause thy face to shine upon thy sanctuary that is desolate, for the Lord's sake.
18 O my God, incline thine ear, and hear; open thine eyes, and behold our
desolations, and the city which is called by thy name: for we do not present our
supplications before thee for our righteousnesses, but for thy great mercies.

19 O Lord, hear; O Lord, forgive; O Lord, hearken and do; defer not, for thine own sake, O my God: for thy city and thy people are called by thy name.
20 And whiles I was speaking, and praying, and confessing my sin and the sin of my people Israel, and presenting my supplication before the LORD my God for the holy mountain of my God;
21 Yea, whiles I was speaking in prayer, even the man Gabriel, whom I had seen in the vision at the beginning, being caused to fly swiftly, touched me about the time of the evening oblation.
22 And he informed me, and talked with me, and said, O Daniel, I am now come forth to give thee skill and understanding.
23 At the beginning of thy supplications the commandment came forth, and I am come to shew thee; for thou art greatly beloved: therefore understand the matter, and consider the vision.
24 Seventy weeks are determined upon thy people and upon thy holy city, to finish the transgression, and to make an end of sins, and to make reconciliation for iniquity, and to bring in everlasting righteousness, and to seal up the vision and prophecy, and to anoint the most Holy.
25 Know therefore and understand, that from the going forth of the commandment to restore and to build Jerusalem unto the Messiah the Prince shall be seven weeks, and threescore and two weeks: the street shall be built again, and the wall, even in troublous times.
26 And after threescore and two weeks shall Messiah be cut off, but not for himself: and the people of the prince that shall come shall destroy the city and the sanctuary; and the end thereof shall be with a flood, and unto the end of the war desolations are determined.
27 And he shall confirm the covenant with many for one week: and in the midst of the week he shall cause the sacrifice and the oblation to cease, and for the overspreading of abominations he shall make it desolate, even until the consummation, and that determined shall be poured upon the desolate.

In the year 458 B.C. the first day of the Enochian year fell on Sunday, March 21st, which was the spring equinox. On Saturday, April 3, 458 B.C., the 14th day of the first month (14 Spring), which is Passover on that calendar, Ezra and the Jews departed Babylon and headed for the Holy City of Jerusalem.

Ezra 7
1 Now after these things, in the reign of Artaxerxes king of Persia, Ezra the son of Seraiah, the son of Azariah, the son of Hilkiah,
2 The son of Shallum, the son of Zadok, the son of Ahitub,
3 The son of Amariah, the son of Azariah, the son of Meraioth,
4 The son of Zerahiah, the son of Uzzi, the son of Bukki,
5 The son of Abishua, the son of Phinehas, the son of Eleazar, the son of Aaron the chief priest:

6 This Ezra went up from Babylon; and he was a ready scribe in the law of Moses, which the LORD God of Israel had given: and the king granted him all his request, according to the hand of the LORD his God upon him.
7 And there went up some of the children of Israel, and of the priests, and the Levites, and the singers, and the porters, and the Nethinims, unto Jerusalem, in the seventh year of Artaxerxes the king.
8 And he came to Jerusalem in the fifth month, which was in the seventh year of the king.
9 For upon the first day of the first month began he to go up from Babylon, and on the first day of the fifth month came he to Jerusalem, according to the good hand of his God upon him.
10 For Ezra had prepared his heart to seek the law of the LORD, and to do it, and to teach in Israel statutes and judgments.

Using Enoch's calendar: ***the exact day?***

The day of the crucifixion, Friday, April 1, A.D. 33, was the day preceding Passover on the Enochian calendar. Passover always falls on a Saturday on the Enochian calendar. The Friday crucifixion completed exactly 490 years to the very day on the Enoch calendar, because the 491st year would have begun on Passover, April 2, A.D. 33. Remember, there is no year zero. The calendar goes from 1 B.C. to 1 A.D.

Thus, the interval from Ezra's departure to rebuild Jerusalem to the date Christ died was 7 x 70 or 490 years according to the Calendar of Enoch.

How do we know it was the exact day? Passover lasts seven days according to the Hebrew calendar and eight days according to the Gregorian and Enochian calendar, because the Hebrew Calendar begins the day at sundown. Out of these eight days, how do we know which day Jesus died?

Luke 22:7 Now the day of Unleavened Bread came, during which it was necessary to sacrifice the Passover lamb. And he sent out Peter and Johannes, saying, 'Go and prepare the Passover for us, so that we may eat.'....Now they went and found it just as he had told them, and they prepared the Passover.

This was the evening which began Nisan 14. Luke 22:1 indicates that the entire feast (Nisan 14-20) was called "Passover." We know that only one day is actually the specific day of Passover. Matthew uses this term indicating the week-long observance. In a while, we will examine Jesus' timeline in more detail and will see that this is the case.

Matthew 26:17 tells us that it was the evening which began the first day of the Feast of Unleavened Bread, it was the beginning of Nisan 14. Their lamb had already been slaughtered. This was done on the afternoon of the 13th of Nisan.

According to Luke 22:15, on the evening of the 14th, they were going to prepare and eat the lamb--one day earlier than normal. The accounts give no reason, but it may have been simply that Jesus wanted to eat the feast one more time before he was crucified.

Luke 22 (King James Version)
1 Now the feast of unleavened bread drew nigh, which is called the Passover.
2 And the chief priests and scribes sought how they might kill him; for they feared the people.
3 Then entered Satan into Judas surnamed Iscariot, being of the number of the twelve.
4 And he went his way, and communed with the chief priests and captains, how he might betray him unto them.
5 And they were glad, and covenanted to give him money.
6 And he promised, and sought opportunity to betray him unto them in the absence of the multitude.
7 Then came the day of unleavened bread, when the passover must be killed.
8 And he sent Peter and John, saying, Go and prepare us the passover, that we may eat.
9 And they said unto him, Where wilt thou that we prepare?
10 And he said unto them, Behold, when ye are entered into the city, there shall a man meet you, bearing a pitcher of water; follow him into the house where he entereth in.
11 And ye shall say unto the goodman of the house, The Master saith unto thee, Where is the guestchamber, where I shall eat the passover with my disciples?
12 And he shall shew you a large upper room furnished: there make ready.
13 And they went, and found as he had said unto them: and they made ready the passover.
14 And when the hour was come, he sat down, and the twelve apostles with him.
15 And he said unto them, With desire I have desired to eat this passover with you before I suffer:
16 For I say unto you, I will not any more eat thereof, until it be fulfilled in the kingdom of God.
17 And he took the cup, and gave thanks, and said, Take this, and divide it among yourselves:
18 For I say unto you, I will not drink of the fruit of the vine, until the kingdom of God shall come.
19 And he took bread, and gave thanks, and brake it, and gave unto them, saying, This is my body which is given for you: this do in remembrance of me.
20 Likewise also the cup after supper, saying, This cup is the new testament in my blood, which is shed for you.
21 But, behold, the hand of him that betrayeth me is with me on the table.
22 And truly the Son of man goeth, as it was determined: but woe unto that man by whom he is betrayed!

John tells us that it was not yet the day of the Passover when Jesus and his students had their meal. Since the term "day" is used, it points to the specific day. However, it was the day before the feast that Jesus and his students ate the meal. Both John and Luke refer to this as the "Day of Preparation." This is when the lambs were sacrificed.

Both John and Luke indicate that the day of Jesus' crucifixion preceded a Sabbath, with John providing the further detail that this was a "Great Sabbath." The Great Sabbath was the Sabbath that occurred on the feast day. In this case it was Nisan 15. *(Jn 19:14, 31, 42; Lk 23:54).*

John 19
1 Then Pilate therefore took Jesus, and scourged him.
2 And the soldiers platted a crown of thorns, and put it on his head, and they put on him a purple robe,
3 And said, Hail, King of the Jews! and they smote him with their hands.
4 Pilate therefore went forth again, and saith unto them, Behold, I bring him forth to you, that ye may know that I find no fault in him.
5 Then came Jesus forth, wearing the crown of thorns, and the purple robe. And Pilate saith unto them, Behold the man!
6 When the chief priests therefore and officers saw him, they cried out, saying, Crucify him, crucify him. Pilate saith unto them, Take ye him, and crucify him: for I find no fault in him.
7 The Jews answered him, We have a law, and by our law he ought to die, because he made himself the Son of God.
8 When Pilate therefore heard that saying, he was the more afraid;
9 And went again into the judgment hall, and saith unto Jesus, Whence art thou? But Jesus gave him no answer.
10 Then saith Pilate unto him, Speakest thou not unto me? knowest thou not that I have power to crucify thee, and have power to release thee?
11 Jesus answered, Thou couldest have no power at all against me, except it were given thee from above: therefore he that delivered me unto thee hath the greater sin.
12 And from thenceforth Pilate sought to release him: but the Jews cried out, saying, If thou let this man go, thou art not Caesar's friend: whosoever maketh himself a king speaketh against Caesar.
13 When Pilate therefore heard that saying, he brought Jesus forth, and sat down in the judgment seat in a place that is called the Pavement, but in the Hebrew, Gabbatha.
14 And it was the preparation of the passover, and about the sixth hour: and he saith unto the Jews, Behold your King!
15 But they cried out, Away with him, away with him, crucify him. Pilate saith unto them, Shall I crucify your King? The chief priests answered, We have no king but Caesar.
16 Then delivered he him therefore unto them to be crucified. And they took Jesus, and led him away.

Matthew agrees with Mark

Matthew's account does not indicate that it was the Day of Preparation during which Jesus was slain, but he does say that the next day, Sabbath/Passover, was "after the preparation" (27:62), implying that the day of Jesus' death was the same Day of Preparation mentioned by the others. Mark 14:12 tells us that the Passover lamb was killed during the first day of the Feast of Unleavened Bread.

Mark 14:10 And Judas Iscariot, one of the twelve, went unto the chief priests, to betray him unto them.
11 And when they heard it, they were glad, and promised to give him money. And he sought how he might conveniently betray him.
12 And the first day of unleavened bread, when they killed the passover, his disciples said unto him, Where wilt thou that we go and prepare that thou mayest eat the passover?
13 And he sendeth forth two of his disciples, and saith unto them, Go ye into the city, and there shall meet you a man bearing a pitcher of water: follow him.
14 And wheresoever he shall go in, say ye to the goodman of the house, The Master saith, Where is the guestchamber, where I shall eat the passover with my disciples?

Mark 15:42 tells us it was this evening during which Jesus ate his dinner one day early. Mark further mentions that Jesus died on the Day of Preparation.

Mark 15:42-44
42 And now when the even was come, because it was the preparation, that is, the day before the sabbath,
43 Joseph of Arimathaea, an honourable counsellor, which also waited for the kingdom of God, came, and went in boldly unto Pilate, and craved the body of Jesus.
44 And Pilate marvelled if he were already dead: and calling unto him the centurion, he asked him whether he had been any while dead.
We are told that the Jewish rulers wanted to kill Jesus before the feast, because they feared the people would become upset at the brutality and work attributed to the death.

Mark 14:1-2
1 After two days was the feast of the passover, and of unleavened bread: and the chief priests and the scribes sought how they might take him by craft, and put him to death.
2 But they said, Not on the feast day, lest there be an uproar of the people.

This means it was the day before Nisan 15 when Jesus died. Thus, Jesus died in the afternoon of Nisan 14.

He was captured in the night (after the day started upon sundown.)

The trial of Jesus lasted less than one day, with his crucifixion beginning on the cross around noon of Nisan 14 and his death occurring before sundown of the same day.

Now we are presented with a problem. Having established the pattern of 490 years, we should be able to track back to pinpoint the exact date of the birth of Jesus. However, that does not seem to work. What does jump out of the calendar is the exact length of time between the dedication to the Lord in the temple after his birth, as described in Leviticus 12, to the day of the resurrection.

Leviticus 12
1 And the LORD spake unto Moses, saying,
2 Speak unto the children of Israel, saying, If a woman have conceived seed, and born a man child: then she shall be unclean seven days; according to the days of the separation for her infirmity shall she be unclean.
3 And in the eighth day the flesh of his foreskin shall be circumcised.
4 And she shall then continue in the blood of her purifying three and thirty days; she shall touch no hallowed thing, nor come into the sanctuary, until the days of her purifying be fulfilled.
5 But if she bear a maid child, then she shall be unclean two weeks, as in her separation: and she shall continue in the blood of her purifying threescore and six days.
6 And when the days of her purifying are fulfilled, for a son, or for a daughter, she shall bring a lamb of the first year for a burnt offering, and a young pigeon, or a turtledove, for a sin offering, unto the door of the tabernacle of the congregation, unto the priest:
7 Who shall offer it before the LORD, and make an atonement for her; and she shall be cleansed from the issue of her blood. This is the law for her that hath born a male or a female.
8 And if she be not able to bring a lamb, then she shall bring two turtles, or two young pigeons; the one for the burnt offering, and the other for a sin offering: and the priest shall make an atonement for her, and she shall be clean.

An astonishing solution

The law of Moses required that the mother should present the son on the fortieth day after his birth, with an offering to the priest at the temple. The day of the birth was counted as day one, so the offering was made on his 39th day of life. That means that the day of presentation at the temple fell on Sunday, May 14, 1 B.C.. Because the Savior lived 33 years, that means the time from the presentation at the temple to his death was very close to 33 Enoch-fixed years. But, there is an exact match between his dedication and resurrection. It is exactly 33 years of 364 days from his presentation at the temple to his resurrection. That was an astounding amount of information, but it can be broken down and restated as follows:

The time period being looked at begins in 458 B.C. and ends in 33 A.D. There is no year zero, so we must subtract for that. 458 + 33 = 491. 491 - 1 = 490. Now we are down to the days within the proper year. The Enochian calendar is adjusted so that each year begins around the Equinox in March.

The month of Abib should always start in the spring. Spring begin at the equinox, when the sun (apparently) crosses the equator, between 3/19 and 3/22, as reckoned by the Roman Calendar. Scriptures indicate the first month should always start in the same season of the year, which is spring. Please compare the King James Version with the Revised Standard Version.

"It seems to have been understood all over the world, from ancient times until now, that the vernal equinox signals the arrival of spring and the autumnal equinox signals the arrival of fall. ... Wait until the sun signals the arrival of spring at the equinox, then select the first visible new crescent for the beginning of months: ... the first month of the year to you."

The Jewish calendar was changed to keep Passover at the beginning of spring by looking to the first new moon after the spring equinox and start the year. This will always keep Passover in spring and Tabernacles in fall. The Enochian calendar was set to being on the Sunday closest to the Equinox. In the years each are examining, these events were in sync.

Design or Coincidence?

The calendar of Enoch is the only calendar that fits the prophecy of Daniel without any manipulations. Now, we must decide if it is by design or by coincidence.

Bibliography

Laurence, The Book of Enoch (Oxford, 1821) Translations & Commentaries;

Dillmann, Das Buch Henoch (1853);

Schodde, The Book of Enoch (1882);

Charles, The Book of Enoch (1893);

Cyrus Gordon and Gary Rendsburg, The Bible And The Ancient Near East (1997)

Various articles and research

Conclusion of 1 Enoch:

Thoughts from the Author

Both men and angels were given the highest gift in the universe, that of free will. We have the power of choice. Evil resides within the problem of choice. It is free will that convicts us. We are guilty of being evil because we can choose good. Free will is the very foundation of love, and the cornerstone of evil.

It is free will which allows us to decide whether we will seek the glories of heaven or torment of hell. Whether one believes in a physical hell or not is beside the point. We, like Enoch, have the ability to transcend ourselves and become more than we now are. We, like the Grigori, can be trapped within our selfish choices and grieve the outcome for all eternity. Whether or not our judgment comes from the Lord, or from within, it is coming to each of us.

2 Peter 3:9-12 The Lord is not slack concerning his promise, as some men count slackness; but is longsuffering to us-ward, not willing that any should perish, but that all should come to repentance. [10] But the day of the Lord will come as a thief in the night; in which the heavens shall pass away with a great noise, and the elements shall melt with fervent heat, the earth also and the works that are therein shall be burned up. [11] Seeing then that all these things shall be dissolved, what manner of persons ought ye to be in all holy conversation and godliness, [12] Looking for and hasting unto the coming of the day of God, wherein the heavens being on fire shall be dissolved, and the elements shall melt with fervent heat?

1 Enoch- And wait until sin has passed away indeed, for their names shall be blotted out of the Book of Life and out of the holy books, and their (children) seed shall be destroyed forever, and their spirits shall be killed, and they shall cry and lament in a place that is a chaotic desert, and they shall be burned in the fire; for there is no earth there.

4 I saw something there like an invisible cloud; because it was so deep I could not look over it, and I saw a flame of fire blazing brightly, and things like shining mountains circling and sweeping back and forth.

The Second Book of Enoch

2 Enoch

The Slavic Book of Enoch

Introduction to 2 Enoch: Slavonic Enoch

As part of the Enochian literature, 2 Enoch is included in the *pseudepigraphal corpus*.

Also known as *pseudepigrapha arespurious,* or pseudonymous writings, these are essentially Jewish writings ascribed to various biblical patriarchs and prophets. As well, they are composed within approximately 200 years of the birth of Jesus Christ.

How 2 Enoch was found and preserved

In 1773, rumors of a surviving copy of an ancient book drew Scottish explorer James Bruce to distant Ethiopia. There, he found 1 Enoch. Later, another "Book of Enoch" surfaced. The text, which is known as 2 Enoch, was discovered in 1886 by Professor Sokolov in the archives of the Belgrade Public Library.

2 Enoch was written in the latter half of the first century A.D. The text was preserved only in Slavonic and consequently bears the designation, "Slavonic Enoch." The text has also been known by the titles of "The Second Book of Enoch," and "The Secrets of Enoch."

Contents of 2 Enoch

2 Enoch is basically an expansion of Genesis 5:21-32, taking the reader from the time of Enoch to the onset of the great flood of Noah's day.

The main theme of the book is the ascension of Enoch progressively through multiple heavens. During the ascension Enoch is transfigured into an angel and granted access to the secrets of creation. Enoch is then given a 30-day grace period to return to earth and instruct his sons and all the members of his household regarding everything God had revealed to him. The text reports that after a period of grace an angel will then come to retrieve him to take him from the earth.

Many credible versions end with chapter 68, however there is a longer version of 2 Enoch, which we will examine. In this version the wisdom and insights given to the family of Enoch are passed from family members to Melchizedek, whom God raises up as an archpriest. Melchizedek then fulfills the function of a prophet-priest. To pave the way to Melchizedek, Methuselah functions as a priest for ten years and then passes his station on to Nir, Noah's younger brother. Nir's wife, Sopanim, miraculously conceives without human intercourse while about to die and posthumously gives birth to Melchizedek, who is born with the appearance and maturity of a three-year old child and the symbol of the priesthood on his chest.

The world is doomed to suffer the flood but Michael the Archangel promises Melchizedek salvation. This establishes his priesthood for all of eternity. The text goes on to report that in the last generation, there will be another Melchizedek who will be "the head of all, a great archpriest, the Word and Power of God, who will perform miracles, greater and more glorious than all the previous ones."

The manuscripts, which contain and preserve this document, exist only in Old Slavonic. Of the 20 or more manuscripts dating from the 13th century A.D. no single one contains the complete text of 2 Enoch. When pieced together there appear to be two versions. These we will refer to as the long and short version.

The difference in length between the two is due to two quite different features. There are blocks of text found only in the longer manuscripts; but even when the passages are parallel, the longer manuscripts tend to be more full and detailed. At the same time there is so much verbal similarity when the passages correspond that a common source must be supposed.

Versions of 2 Enoch

The form of 2 Enoch is what one finds in Jewish wisdom literature and Jewish apocalyptic literature. It has been suggested that the longer version is characterized by editorial expansions and Christian interpolations. Hence, the shorter version contains fewer Christian elements. The author of 2 Enoch speaks much of the Creator and final judgment, but he speaks very little about redemption, which seems to be absent from the thoughts of the author. Indeed, there seems to be a total lack of a Savior or Redeemer in 2 Enoch. What is noteworthy is that 2 Enoch has no reference to the mercy of God.

In the long version presented here, it appears that the last portion of the text was added as an afterthought. It contains the rise of Melchizedek. The appearance of Melchizedek ties 2 Enoch to several other texts forming a Melchizedkian tradition. The author of 2 Enoch follows a tradition in which an aged mother, who had been barren up to her deathbed, miraculously conceived Melchizedek without human intervention. Before she was able to give birth to the baby she died. The baby then emerged from her dead body with the maturity of a three-year-old boy. His priesthood will be perpetuated throughout the generations until "another Melchizedek" appears. If the last Melchizedek serves as the archpriest for the last generation, it indicates that in the mind of this Jewish writer, the temple was to be rebuilt and would be the place were God would meet His people when the heathen nations were destroyed. The continuation and victory of the Jews as the selected and blessed people of God is implied. In this vein, 2

Enoch follows certain apocalyptic writings. *(For more information on apocalyptic writings see* End of Days, *by Joseph Lumpkin.)*

The Slavonic version is translated from a Greek source. Most scholars agree that there was either a Hebrew or Aramaic original lying behind the Greek source from which the Slavonic manuscripts were produced. The Hebrew origins are indicated by "Semitisms" in the work, but there are also Greek words and expressions, such as the names of the planets in chapter 30.

Proof that The Slavonic Enoch was first written in Greek is shown by the derivation of Adam's name, and by several coincidences with the Septuagint. The origin of the story is perhaps based on Hebrew traditions, and certain Semitic turns of language show up in the text. This tends to indicate that there was at one time a Hebrew or Aramaic text that preceded the Greek. From the Greek it was translated into Slavonic. Of this version there are five manuscripts or pieces thereof found.

The short version or the Slavonic Enoch was probably written by a single author in an attempt to bring all the current traditions about Enoch of his time into a central storyline and system. The schema to accomplish the unity of traditions implements Enoch's ascension through multiple heavens. This author was probably a Jew living in Egypt. There are several elements in the book, which indicate Egyptian origin. The longer version of 2 Enoch was seeded with Christian elements and appended with an ending that does not fit well, illuminating the fact that there were several authors involved in the longer version.

2 Enoch dated

Parts of the book was probably written in the late first century A.D. The first date is a limit set by the fact that Ethiopic Enoch, Ecclesiasticus, and Wisdom of Solomon are used as sources or references within the text; the second date is a limit set by the fact that the destruction of the Temple is not mentioned at all. However, it must be added that apocalyptic literature bloomed after the destruction of the temple, especially between late first century and throughout the second century A.D.

Relevance to today of 2 Enoch

The Slavonic Enoch furnishes new material for the study of religious thought in the beginning of the Common Era. The ideas of the millennium and of the multiple heavens are the most important in this connection. Another very interesting feature is the presence of evil in heaven, the fallen angels in the second heaven, and hell in the third. The idea of evil in heaven may be a nod to the book of Job and the dialog between God and Satan, who was coming and going between heaven and earth. The idea of hell in the third heaven may have been derived from ideas expressed in the Old

Testament book of Isaiah, which mentions that the sufferings of the wicked will be witnessed by the righteous in paradise.

Chapter 21 and forward for several chapters shows a heavy influence of Greek mythology. The Zodiac is mentioned along with celestial bodies with names such as Zeus, Cronus, Aphrodite, and others. The part of the text containing names and astrological descriptions could have been tampered with as late as the seventh century A.D.

2 Enoch embraces gnostic concepts

By far, the most interesting and confusing section begins around chapter 25 and runs for several chapters. Here the text takes a turn toward Gnostic theology and cosmology. The Gnostics were a Christian sect, which formed and grew in the first century A.D. and thrived in the second century A.D.

Although Gnosticism borrowed from Plato's (428 B.C. - 348 B.C.) creation myth, the maturity and construction of the story shows it to be of Gnostic Christian origin, placing it no earlier than the last part of the first century A.D. and no later than the end of the second century. Add to the dating question the fact that the destruction of the temple in Jerusalem is not mentioned, which leads to a date just before 70 A.D., if one assumes the Gnostic flavor was not added later.

The history of the text is obviously long and varied. It probably began as a Jewish oral tradition with pieces taken from several Enochian stories. Although the foundation of the story was first penned in Hebrew or Aramaic around the first or second centuries A.D. the date of the version of the text here is unknown. Later, the story was expanded and embellished by Greek influences. Lastly, Christians and Gnostics commandeered the book and added their own matter. Thus 2 Enoch exhibits a kaleidoscope of cultural and religious contributions over a great scope of time from the first century B.C. (assuming it came after 1 Enoch) and ending as late as the seventh century A.D. These additions would allow any serious student insight into how ancient texts evolve.

Charles and Morfill translation

2 Enoch was rediscovered and published in the early 19th century A.D The text before you uses the R. H. Charles and W. R. Morfill translation of 1896 with additions from other sources. Archaic terms and sentence structure were revised or explained to convey a more modern rendering for the 21st century readers.

2 Enoch

Slavonic Enoch

The Book of the Secrets of Enoch

Chapter 1

1 There was a wise man and a great craftsman, and the Lord formed a love for him and received him, so that he should see the highest dwellings and be an eye-witness of the wise and great and inconceivable and unchanging realm of God Almighty, and of the very wonderful and glorious and bright and manifold vision of the position of the Lord's servants, and of the inaccessible throne of the Lord, and of the degrees and manifestations of the spiritual (non-physical) hosts, and of the unspeakable ministration of the multitude of the elements, and of the various apparition and singing of the host of Cherubim which is beyond description, and of the limitless light.
2 At that time, he said, when my one hundred and sixty-fifth year was completed, I begat my son Methuselah.
3 After this I lived two hundred years and finished of all the years of my life three hundred and sixty-five years.
4 On the first day of the month I was in my house alone and was resting on my bed and slept.
5 And when I was asleep, great distress came up into my heart, and I was weeping with my eyes in sleep, and I could not understand what this distress was, or what was happening to me.
6 And there appeared to me two very large men, so big that I never saw such on earth. Their faces were shining like the sun, their eyes were like a burning light, and from their lips fire was coming out. They were singing. Their clothing was of various kinds in appearance and was purple. Their wings were brighter than gold, and their hands whiter than snow.
7 They were standing at the head of my bed and began to call me by my name.
8 And I arose from my sleep and clearly saw the two men standing in front of me.
9 And I greeted them and was seized with fear and the appearance of my face was changed to terror, and those men said to me:
10 Enoch, have courage and do not fear. The eternal God sent us to you, and you shall ascend today with us into heaven, and you shall tell your sons and all your household all that they shall do without you on earth in your house, and let no one seek you until the Lord returns you to them.
11 And I hurried to obey them and went out of my house, and went to the doors, as I was ordered, and I summoned my sons Methuselah and Regim and Gaidad and explained to them all the marvels the men had told me.

Chapter 2

1 Listen to me, my children, I do not know where I will go, or what will befall me. So now, my children, I tell you, do not turn from God in the face of that which is empty or prideful, which did not make heaven and earth, for these shall perish along with those who worship them, and may the Lord make your hearts confident in the fear (respect) of him. And now, my children, let no one consider seeking me, until the Lord returns me to you.

Chapter 3

1 (It came to pass, when Enoch had finished speaking to his sons, that the angels took him on to their wings and lifted him up on to the first heaven and placed him on the clouds.)

And there I (Enoch) looked, and again I looked higher, and saw the ether, and they placed me on the first heaven and showed me a very large sea, bigger than the earthly sea. (See 2 Cor 12:2)

Chapter 4

1 They brought the elders and rulers of the stellar orders in front of me, and showed me two hundred angels, who rule the stars and services of the stars to the heavens, and fly with their wings and come round all those who sail.

Chapter 5

1 And here I looked down and saw the storehouses of snow, and the angels who keep their amazing storehouses, and the clouds where they come out of and into which they go.

Chapter 6

1 They showed me the storehouse of the dew, like olive oil in its appearance and its form, as of all the flowers of the earth. And they also showed me many angels guarding the storehouses of these things, and how they are made to shut and open.

Chapter 7

1 And those men took me and led me up on to the second heaven, and showed me darkness, greater than earthly darkness, and there I saw prisoners hanging, watched, (guarded), awaiting the great and limitless judgment, and the spirits were dark in appearance, more than earthly darkness, and perpetually weeping through all hours.
2 And I said to the men who were with me: Why are these being unceasingly tortured? They answered me: These are God's apostates, who did not obey God's commands, but took counsel with their own will, and turned away with their prince, who is also held captive in the fifth heaven.

3 And I felt great pity for them, and they greeted me, and said to me: Man of God, pray to the Lord for us. And I answered them: I am just a mortal man. Who am I that I should pray for spirits? Who knows where I go or what will become of me? Or who will pray for me?

Chapter 8

1 And those men took me from there and led me up on to the third heaven, and placed me there. I looked down and saw what this place produces and that it was so good that such as has never been known.
2 And I saw all the sweet, flowering trees and I saw their fruits, which were sweet smelling, and I saw all the foods that came from them and that the food was bubbling with fragrant vapors.
3 And in the middle of the trees was the tree of life, in that place where the Lord rests when he goes up into paradise. And this tree is of indescribable goodness and fragrance, and adorned more than anything existing. And all sides of its form were golden and brilliant red and fire-like and it was completely covered, and it produced all fruits. *(See Revelation 22:2)*
4 Its root is in the garden at the earth's end.
5 And paradise resides between spiritual and physical.
6 And two springs come out which send forth honey and milk, and their springs send forth oil and wine, and they separate into four parts, and flow quietly around, and go down into the paradise of Eden, between the mutable and the eternal. *(See Gen. 2:11-14)*
7 And there they go forth along the earth, and have a circular flow even as other elements.
8 And there is no unfruitful tree here, and every place is blessed.
9 Three hundred angels, which are very bright, are there to keep the garden, and with incessant sweet singing with voices, which are never silent, serve the Lord throughout all the hours of days.
10 And I said: How very sweet is this place, and those men said to me:

Chapter 9

1 This place, O Enoch, is prepared for the righteous, who endure all manner of offence from those that exasperate their souls, who avert their eyes from iniquity, and make righteous judgment, and give bread to the hungering, and cover the naked with clothing, and raise up the fallen, and help injured orphans, and who walk without fault before the face of the Lord, and serve him alone, and for them is prepared this place for eternal inheritance.

Chapter 10

1 And those two men led me up on to the Northern side, and showed me there a very terrible place, and there were every kind of tortures in that place: cruel darkness and gloom, and there was absolutely no light at all

there, but murky fire constantly flaming above, and there is a fiery river coming out, and everywhere in that entire place is fire, and everywhere there is frost and ice, thirst and shivering, while the physical restraints are very cruel, and the spirits were fearsome and merciless, bearing angry weapons, torturing without mercy.
2 And I said: Woe, woe! This place is so terrible.
3 And those men said to me: This place, O Enoch, is prepared for those who dishonor God, who on earth practice sin against nature, which is sodomy of a child, corruption of children, performing magic, enchantments and devilish witchcrafts, and who boast of their wicked deeds, stealing, lying, slander, envy, resentment, fornication, murder, and who are accursed and steal the souls of men, and those who see the poor and still take away their goods so they grow rich, and injure them for other men's goods. And this is reserved for those who, to satisfy their own emptiness made the hungering die; those who clothe themselves by stripping the naked; and who did not know their creator, but instead bowed to lifeless gods who have no soul who cannot see nor hear, who are empty, and who built carved images and bow down to unclean fashioning of useless gods, this place is prepared for these as an eternal inheritance.

Chapter 11

1 Those men took me, and led me up on to the fourth heaven, and showed me the entire succession of activities, and all the rays of the light of sun and moon.
2 And I measured their progression, and compared their light, and saw that the sun's light is greater than the moon's.
3 Its circle and the wheels on which it goes always is like the wind passing with very amazing speed with no rest day or night.
4 Its egress and ingress are accompanied by four huge stars, and each star has a thousand stars under it, to the right of the sun's wheel there are four thousand stars and to the left are four thousand, altogether eight thousand, going out with the sun continually.
5 And by day fifteen groups of ten thousand angels attend it, and by night there were a thousand.
6 And six-winged ones go fourth with the angels before the sun's wheel into the fiery flames, and a hundred angels kindle the sun and set it alight.

Chapter 12

1 And I looked and saw other flying elements of the sun, whose names are Phoenixes and Chalkydri, which are marvelous and wonderful, with feet and tails of a lion, and a crocodile's head, they appear to be purple in color like that in the rainbow; their size is nine hundred measures, their wings are like those of angels, each has twelve wings, and they attend and accompany the sun, bearing heat and dew, as it is ordered them from God.

(Note: The word CHALKYDRI means "serpents." It appears that the Slavonic translators rendered the Hebrew word SERAPHIM differently in various places in the text. The word was translated "serpent" in some places and SERAPHIM in others. Seraph means, "to burn.")

2 This is how the sun revolves and goes, and rises under the heaven, and its course goes under the earth with the light of its rays continually.

Chapter 13

1 Then those men carried me away to the east, and placed me at the sun's gates, where the sun has egress according to the seasons circuit and regulation of the months of the whole year, and the number of the hours day and night.
2 And I saw six gates open, each gate having sixty-one stadia (185 meters) and a quarter of one stadium (46.25 meters), and I measured them accurately, and knew their size. Through the gates the sun goes out, and goes to the west, and is made even, and rises throughout all the months, and turns back again from the six gates according to the succession of the seasons. In this way the period of the entire year is finished after the return of the four seasons.

(Note: 6 X 61=366 With the quarter day added, this is the length of the leap year.)

Chapter 14

1 And again those men led me away to the western parts, and showed me six great open gates corresponding to the eastern gates, opposite to where the sun sets, according to the number of the days three hundred and sixty-five and a quarter.

(Note that this is a solar calendar of the same length as our modern calendar.)

2 Again it goes down to the western gates, and diminishes (pulls away) its light with the prominent brightness, under the earth. The crown of its glory is in heaven with the Lord, and it is guarded by four hundred angels while the sun goes round on wheel under the earth. And it stands seven great hours in night, and spends half its course under the earth. And when it comes to the eastern approach in the eighth hour of the night it brings its lights and the crown of glory, and the sun burns (flames) outwardly more than fire.

Chapter 15

1 Then the elements of the sun, called Phoenixes and Chalkydri (Seraphim) break into song, therefore every bird flutters its wings, rejoicing at the giver

of light, and they brake into song at the command of the Lord. *(The Kadosh – Holy, Holy, Holy)*
2 The giver of light comes to illuminate the entire world, and the morning guard takes shape, which is the rays of the sun, and the sun of the earth goes out, and receives its luminance to light up the entire face of the earth, and they showed me this calculation of the sun's going.
3 And the great gates, which it enters into, are for the calculation of the hours of the year. For this reason the sun is a great creation, whose circuit lasts twenty-eight years, and begins again from the beginning.

(Note: For February 29, which is the leap year day, to fall on a particular weekday, there is a 28-year (2 x-14 year) cycle. This forms a type of perpetual calendar.)

Chapter 16

1 Those men showed me the great course of the moon. There are twelve great gates that are crowned from west to east, by which the moon comes and goes in its customary times.
2 It goes in at the first gate to the western places of the sun, by the first gates with thirty-one days exactly, by the second gates with thirty-one days exactly, by the third with thirty days exactly, by the fourth with thirty days exactly, by the fifth with thirty-one days exactly, by the sixth with thirty-one days exactly, by the seventh with thirty days exactly, by the eighth with thirty-one days perfectly, by the ninth with thirty-one days exactly, by the tenth with thirty days perfectly, by the eleventh with thirty-one days exactly, by the twelfth with twenty-eight days exactly.

(Note: The sum of the days total 365 with the year beginning in March.)

3 And it goes through the western gates in the order and number of the eastern, and accomplishes the three hundred and sixty-five and a quarter days of the solar year, while the lunar year has three hundred fifty-four, and there twelve days lacking of the solar circle, which are the lunar epacts of the whole year.

(Note: Epact *is the number of days by which the solar year differs from the lunar year. It is also the number of days into the moon's phase cycle at the beginning of the solar or calendar year. The word originated in the mid-16th century and denotes the age of the moon in days at the beginning of the calendar year. It is from the French* épacte, *via late Latin from Greek* epakta, *meaning intercalated.*

4 The great circle also contains five hundred and thirty-two years.

(Note: The 532-year cycle is calculated from the creation of Adam, which took place on Friday, March 1, 5508 B.C., according to some of the founding documents of the

Orthodox Church which are still in use. It is the base date on which the entire calendar system of the Orthodox Church is founded. The cycles are laid out in the final sections of the Typikon, which is the book that dictates the services, and are the Paschalion Calendar sections. There are tables reflecting the 532-year cycle of the church services, which consists of 19-year solar cycles multiplied by 28-day lunar cycles. There is a table that consists of 19 columns by 28 rows, giving the Paschal Key number or letter for each of the years of the 532-year cycle. Once you know the Paschal Key, you look up the details in the following section, which consists of 35 brief calendar synopses, one for each possible day that Pascha can fall. Each of these synopses actually consists of two services; one for regular years, and one for leap years.

5 The quarter (of a day) is omitted for three years, the fourth fulfills it exactly.
6 Because of this, they are taken outside of heaven for three years and are not added to the number of days, because they change the time of the years to two new months toward completion, to two others toward the decrease.
7 And when the course through the western gates is finished, it returns and goes to the eastern to the lights, and goes this way day and night in its heavenly circles, below all circles, swifter than the heavenly winds, and spirits and elements and flying angels. Each angel has six wings.
8 In nineteen years it travels the course seven times.

Chapter 17

1 In the midst of the heavens I saw armed soldiers, serving the Lord, with drums and organs, with constant voice, with sweet voice, with sweet and unceasing voice and various singing, which it is impossible to describe, and which astonishes every mind, so wonderful and marvelous is the singing of those angels, and I was delighted listening to it.

Chapter 18

1 The men took me on to the fifth heaven and placed me, and there I saw many and countless soldiers, called Grigori, of human appearance, and their size (was) greater than that of great giants and their faces withered, and the silence of their mouths perpetual, and their was no service on the fifth heaven, and I said to the men who were with me:

(Note: The Greek transliteration egegoroi *are the Watchers; a group of fallen angels who mated with mortal women and produced the Nephilim mentioned in the books of Jubilees, 1 Enoch, and Genesis 6:4.)*

2 Why are they so very withered and their faces melancholy, and their mouths silent, and why is there no service in this heaven?

3 And they said to me: These are the Grigori, who with their prince Satanail (Satan) rejected the Lord of Light. After them are those who are held in great darkness in the second heaven, and three of them went down on to earth from the Lord's throne, to the place Ermon, and broke through their vows on the shoulder of the hill Ermon and saw the daughters of men how good they are, and took to themselves wives, and fouled the earth with their deeds, who broke the law and mixing (with the women), giants are born and amazingly large men with great hatred.

(Note: The Hill of Ermon could be Mount Hermon, which is mentioned over a dozen times in the Bible.

4 And therefore God judged them with great judgment, and they weep for their brethren and they will be punished on the Lord's great day.
5 And I said to the Grigori: I saw your brethren and their works, and their great torments, and I prayed for them, but the Lord has condemned them to be under earth until this heaven and this earth shall end forever.
6 And I said: Why do you stand there, brethren, and do not serve before the Lord's face, and have not put your services before the Lord's face? You could anger your Lord completely.
7 And they listened to my advice, and spoke to the four ranks in heaven. As I stood with those two men four trumpets sounded together with a loud voice, and the Grigori broke into song with one voice, and their voice went up before the Lord pitifully and touchingly.

Chapter 19

1 From there, those men took me and lifted me up on to the sixth heaven, and there I saw seven bands of angels, very bright and very glorious, and their faces shining more than the sun's shining, glistening, and there is no difference in their faces, or behavior, or manner of dress; and these make the orders, and learn the goings of the stars, and the alteration of the moon, or revolution of the sun, and the good administration of the world.
2 And when they see evildoing they make commandments and instruction, and make sweet and loud singing, and all (songs) of praise.
3 These are the archangels who are above angels, and they measure all life in heaven and on earth, and the angels who are (appointed) over seasons and years, the angels who are over rivers and sea, and who are over the fruits of the earth, and the angels who are over every grass, giving food to every and all living things, and the angels who write down all the souls of men, and all their deeds, and their lives before the Lord's face. In their midst are six Phoenixes and six Cherubim and six six-winged ones continually singing with one voice, and it is not possible to describe their singing, and they rejoice before the Lord at his footstool.

Chapter 20

1 And those two men lifted me up from there on to the seventh heaven, and I saw there a very great light, and fiery troops of great archangels, incorporeal forces, and dominions, orders and governments, Cherubim and Seraphim, thrones and many-eyed ones, nine regiments, the Ioanit stations of light, and I became afraid, and began to tremble with great terror, and those men took me, and led me after them, and said to me:
2 Have courage, Enoch, do not fear, and showed me the Lord from afar, sitting on His very high throne. For what is there on the tenth heaven, since the Lord dwells there?
3 On the tenth heaven is God, in the Hebrew tongue he is called Aravat.

(Note: The meaning of Ioanit *is not clear. However, it may be derived from the transliteration of the name John. John means, "The Lord is Gracious." The meaning of* Aravat *is equally unclear but seems to mean, "Father of Creation." Each level of heaven represents or demonstrates a personality or part of the Godhead. One of the highest demonstrations of God's power and divinity is the power of Creation. It is found on the tenth level of heaven.)*

4 And all the heavenly soldiers would come and stand on the ten steps according to their rank, and would bow down to the Lord, and would then return to their places in joy and bliss, singing songs in the unlimited light with soft and gentle voices, gloriously serving him.

(Note: Strong and fierce soldiers sing with soft, gentle voices, bowing and serving in bliss.)

Chapter 21

1 And the Cherubim and Seraphim standing around the throne, and the six-winged and many-eyed ones do not depart, standing before the Lord's face doing his will, and cover his whole throne, singing with gentle voice before the Lord's face: Holy, holy, holy, Lord Ruler of Sabaoth (host/army), heavens and earth are full of Your glory.
2 When I saw all these things, the men said to me: Enoch, thus far we were commanded to journey with you, and those men went away from me and after that I did not see them.
3 And I remained alone at the end of the seventh heaven and became afraid, and fell on my face and said to myself: Woe is me. What has befallen me?
4 And the Lord sent one of his glorious ones, the archangel Gabriel, and he said to me: "Have courage, Enoch, do not fear, arise before the Lord's face into eternity, arise and come with me."
5 And I answered him, and said within myself: My Lord, my soul has departed from me due to terror and trembling, and I called to the men who

led me up to this place. I relied on them, and it is with them that I can go before the Lord's face.

(Note: When speaking to God, Enoch "said within himself." He did not have to speak aloud.)

6 And Gabriel lifted me up like a leaf caught up by the wind, and he placed me before the Lord's face.
7 And I saw the eighth heaven, which is called in the Hebrew tongue Muzaloth (Zodiac), the changer of the seasons, of drought, and of wet, and of the twelve constellations of the circle of the firmament, which are above the seventh heaven.
8 And I saw the ninth heaven, which is called in Hebrew Kuchavim, where are the heavenly homes of the twelve constellations of the circle of the firmament.

Chapter 22

1 On the tenth heaven, which is called Aravoth, I saw the appearance of the Lord's face, like iron made to glow in fire, and it shone forth and casted out, emitting sparks, and it burned.

(Note: One possible meaning of Aravoth *is "three times holy" or "holy, holy, holy.")*

2 In a moment of eternity I saw the Lord's face, but the Lord's face is indescribable, marvelous and very amazing, and very, very terrible.
3 And who am I to tell of the Lord's unspeakable being, and of his very wonderful face? I cannot tell the amount of his instructions, and the variety of voices. The Lord's throne is very great and not made with hands, and I cannot tell the number of those standing around him. There were troops of Cherubim and Seraphim, and they sang unceasingly. I cannot tell of his unchanging beauty. Who shall tell of the unpronounceable greatness of his glory?
4 And I fell prone and bowed down to the Lord, and the Lord with his lips said to me:
5 Have courage, Enoch, do not fear, arise and stand before my face into eternity (stand before my face eternally/stand before my eternal face.)

(Note: Enoch is out of and above time-space. Eternity is now and he can feel the timelessness of where he is. The language struggles to convey this fact.)

6 And the archangel Michael lifted me up, and led me to the Lord's face.

7 And the Lord said to his servants, testing them: Let Enoch stand before my
face into eternity, and the glorious ones bowed down to the Lord, and said:
Let Enoch go according to Your word.
8 And the Lord said to Michael: Go and take Enoch and remove his earthly
garments, and anoint him with my sweet ointment, and put him into the
garments of My glory.
9 And Michael did as the Lord told him. He anointed me, and dressed me,
and the appearance of that ointment is more than the great light, and his
ointment is like sweet dew, and its smell mild, shining like the sun's ray,
and I looked at myself, and I was transformed into one of his glorious ones.

(Note: The number symbolism of ten is that of new starts at a higher level, new beginnings, and re-creation.)

10 And the Lord summoned one of his archangels, whose name is Pravuil,
whose knowledge was quicker in wisdom than the other archangels, who
wrote all the deeds of the Lord; and the Lord said to Pravuil: Bring out the
books from my store-houses, and a reed of quick-writing, and give it to
Enoch, and deliver to him the best and comforting books out of your hand.

(Note: Enoch is now an angel. He now has access to the heavenly records and the understanding to use the knowledge. A reed was used in writing much like a quill was used.)

Chapter 23

1 And he was explaining to me all the works of heaven, earth and sea, and
all the elements, their passages and goings, and the sounding of the
thunders, the sun and moon, the progression and changes of the stars, the
seasons, years, days, and hours, as well as the risings of the wind, the
numbers of the angels, and the formation of their songs, and all human
things, the tongue of every human song and life, the commandments,
instructions, and sweet-voiced singings, and all things that are fitting to
learn.
2 And Pravuil told me: All the things that I have told you, we have written.
Sit and write all the souls of mankind, however many of them are born, and
the places prepared for them to eternity. And he said, all souls are prepared
for eternity, before the formation of the world.
3 And for both thirty days and thirty nights, and I wrote out all things
exactly, and wrote three hundred and sixty-six books.

(Note: If all things were created in six days, then the souls of all people were created at that time. In Jewish mythology, the place that the souls were housed until birth was called the Guf (Guph). Each soul was created for a certain place, time, and destiny. According to one version of the myth, when the Guf (Gup) is emptied of

souls, time ceases. In another version, when the last soul dies and returns to God, time will end. Enoch wrote 366 books in a 720-hour period containing information on all things, including, "all souls who are prepared for eternity, before the formation of the world.")

Chapter 24

1 And the Lord summoned me, and said to me: Enoch, sit down on my left with Gabriel.
2 And I bowed down to the Lord, and the Lord spoke to me: Enoch, beloved, all that you see, all things that are standing finished, I tell you even before the very beginning, I created all things from non-being. I created the visible, physical things from the invisible, spiritual (world).
3 Hear, Enoch, and take in my words, for I have not told My angels My secret, and I have not told them their rise (beginnings), nor My endless realm, nor have they understood my creating, which I tell you today.
4 For before all things were visible (physical), I alone used to go about in the invisible, spiritual things, like the sun from east to west, and from west to east.
5 But even the sun has peace in itself, while I found no peace, because I was creating all things, and I conceived the thought of placing foundations, and of creating the visible, physical creation.

(Note: Overview of the heavens:
First heaven: Enoch arrives on angel's wings. There are storehouses of snow and dew.
Second heaven: Enoch finds a group of fallen angels. There is darkness and torture.
Third heaven: There are sweet flowers, trees, and fruit.
Fourth heaven: There are soldiers, heaven's army, and the progression of sun and moon.
Fifth heaven: The leaders of the fallen angels, the Grigori *(Greek* Gregoroi, *translated* Mearim, *the Hebrew word for Watchers.) A company of them went down and had intercourse with the daughters of men, yielding giants, who became the source of enmity on earth.*
Sixth heaven: Seven bands of angels and the ordering of the stars.
Seventh heaven: Shows something unusual happening to Enoch when Gabriel puts Enoch in front of the throne of the Lord.
The Eighth, Ninth, and Tenth Heavens: Thought to be later additions and not part of the original text.
Eighth heaven: Known in Hebrew as Muzaloth, *or Zodiac*
Ninth heaven: Known in Hebrew as Kuchavim, *or heavenly bodies or stars.*
Tenth heaven: Aravoth; *God's face was revealed like that of iron made to glow in fire. Enoch sees the "appearance of the Lord's face," but calls it indescribable. Pravuil, the archangel, is commanded to write down secret information about astronomy, climate, and language and give it over to Enoch. In other Enochian*

writings the same angel, also spelled Penemue, *is criticized for teaching humans to write.*

Chapter 25

1 I commanded in the very lowest parts, that the visible, physical things should come down from the invisible, spiritual (realm), and Adoil came down very great, and I beheld him, and he had a belly of great light.
2 And I said to him: Become undone, Adoil, and let the visible, physical (universe) come out of you.
3 And he came undone, and a great light came out. And I was in the midst of the great light, and as there is born light from light, there came forth a great age (eon/space of time), and showed all creation, which I had thought to create.
4 And I saw that it was good.
5 And I placed for myself a throne, and took my seat on it, and said to the light: Go up higher from here and station yourself high above the throne, and be a foundation to the highest things.
6 And above the light there is nothing else, and then I rose up and looked up from my throne.

(Note: Beginning with chapters 25 and 26, the book of 2 Enoch takes a rather Gnostic diversion. The Gnostics were a Christian sect that flourished around the 3rd century A.D. The Gnostic view of the Godhead borrowed heavily from the creation saga preached by Plato [circa 428 B.C. to 348 B.C.] The story of Adoil and the emanation of pure light from God, which brings about creation of the physical world, is similar to other Gnostic works. Gnosticism teaches that in the beginning a Supreme Being called The Father, The Divine All, The Origin, The Supreme God, or The Fullness, emanated the element of existence, both visible and invisible. His intent was not to create but, just as light emanates from a flame, so did creation shine forth from God. This manifested the primal element needed for creation.

This was the creation of Barbelo, who is the "Thought of God." The Father's thought performed a deed and she was created from it. It is she who had appeared before him in the shining of his light. This is the first power which was before all of them and which was created from his mind. She is the Thought of the All and her light shines like his light. It is the perfect power, which is the visage of the invisible. She is the pure, undefiled Spirit who is perfect. She is the first power. Adoil has that place in this myth.

It could be said that Barbelo was the creative emanation and, like the Divine All, is both male and female. It was the "agreement" of Barbelo and the Divine All, representing the union of male and female,that created the Christ Spirit and all the Aeons. In some renderings the word "Aeon" is used to designate an ethereal realm or kingdom. In other versions "Aeon" indicates the ruler of the realm. The Aeons of this world are merely reflections of the Aeons of the eternal realm. The reflection is always inferior to real.

In several Gnostic cosmologies the "living" world is under the control of entities called Aeons, of which Sophia is head. This means the Aeons influence or control the soul, life force, intelligence, thought, and mind. Control of the mechanical or inorganic world is given to the archons.

The archons were created by Sophia. Sophia, probably out of pride, tried to emulate the creative force of God by created an image of herself, meaning that she wanted to produce an offspring, without either consort or the approval of her Father, God. As an aeon, she did have the power to do so, but she wasn't perfect like the Great Spirit, or like the other two perfect aeons, Barbelo and the Autogenes. Nevertheless, in her arrogance, she attempted to create and failed. She was horrified when she saw her creation, imperfect, bruthish creature with a lion-faced serpent with eyes of fire, whom she called Yaldabaoth.

Sophia cast her offspring out of pleroma (heaven), and hid her child within a thick cloud from the other aeons, because of her embarrassment and shame.

Yaldabaoth was the first of the archon (ruler) and he stole his mother's power, so that she wasn't able to escape from the cloud. Despite gaining Sophia's aeonic power, he was weak, but prideful, ambitious and power hungry.

Since the archons, including Yaldabaoth, were androgynous beings, Yaldabaoth fathered twelve archons, giving each a bit of his power. They were named Athoth, Harmas, Kalila-Oumbri, Yabel, Adonaiou (or Sabaoth), Cain, Abel, Abrisene, Yobel, Armoupieel, Melceir-Adonein and Belias. Seven archons would rule seven heavens and five in the abyss, which Yaldabaoth and the archons created. Each archon would rule a heaven (or the abyss), and created 365 angels to help them.

The archons rule the physical aspects of systems, regulation, limits, and order in the world. Both the ineptitude and cruelty of the archons are reflected in the chaos and pain of the material realm.

(See the book, The Gnostic Scriptures, *by Joseph Lumpkin, published by Fifth Estate.)*

Although the above may be a digression from the text of 2 Enoch, it adds insight into the time frame and origins of its production. Gnostic influences were felt from the late first century to the early fourth century A.D. If the writer of this section of 2 Enoch was exposed to the Gnostic sect, it would conclusively make 2 Enoch a text with Christian influences.)

Chapter 26

1 And I summoned the very lowest a second time, and said: Let Archas come forth hard, and he came forth hard from the invisible, spiritual.
2 And Archas came forth, hard, heavy, and very red.
3 And I said: Be opened, Archas, and let there be born from you, and he came apart, and an age came forth, very great and very dark, bearing the creation of all lower things, and I saw that it was good and said to him:
4 Go down below, and make yourself solid, and be a foundation for the lower things, and it happened and he went down and stationed himself, and became the foundation for the lower things, and below the darkness there is nothing else.

(Note: Hard and heavy could be terms for "gravid" or pregnant, with birth being imminent. Archas could equate to the archons.

Chapter 27

1 And I commanded that there should be taken from light and darkness, and I said: Be thick, and it became thick, and I spread it out with the light, and it became water, and I spread it out over the darkness, below the light, and then I made firm the waters, that is to say the bottomless (abyss), and I made foundation of light around the water, and created seven circles from inside, and made the water look like crystal, wet and dry, so it was like glass, and the circles were around the waters and the other elements, and I showed each one of them its path, and the seven stars each one of them in its heaven, that they go the correct way, and I saw that it was good.
2 And I made separations between light and darkness in the midst of the water here and there, and I said to the light, that it should be the day, and to the darkness, that it should be the night, and there was evening and there was morning on the first day.

(Note: The foundation of light around the water that is like crystal is likely a reference to the sky. One belief at the time of writing was that the sky was an expanse of water like an endless sea.)

Chapter 28

1 And then I made firm the heavenly circle, and made that the lower water which is under heaven collect itself together into one whole (piece), and that the chaos become dry, and it became so.
2 Out of the waves I created hard and large rock, and from the rock I piled up the dry (land), and the dry (land) I called earth, and the middle of the earth I called the abyss, or the bottomless. I collected the sea in one place and bound it together with a yoke.

(Note: This is the bank or shoreline.)

3 And I said to the sea: Behold I give you eternal limits, and you shall not break loose from your integral parts.
4 Thus I made the firmament hold together. This day I called the first-created, Sunday. (This, I call the first day of creation.)

Chapter 29

1 And for all the heavenly soldiers I made them the image and essence of fire, and my eye looked at the very hard, firm rock, and from the gleam of my eye the lightning received its wonderful nature, (which) is both fire in water and water in fire, and one does not put out the other, nor does the one dry up the other, therefore the lightning is brighter than the sun, softer than water and firmer than hard rock.

(Note: If the sky is made of water and lightning, which is fire, issues from the sky, then water and fire must exist together in a heavenly form.)

2 And from the rock I cut off a great fire, and from the fire I created the orders of the incorporeal (spiritual/non-physical) ten troops of angels, and their weapons are fiery and their raiment a burning flame, and I commanded that each one should stand in his order.
3 And one from out the order of angels, having violated the command he was given, conceived an impossible thought, to place his throne higher than the clouds above the earth so that he might become equal in rank to my power.
4 And I threw him out from the height with his angels, and he was flying in the air continuously above the bottomless (abyss).

(Note: We assume this ends the second day, although it is not mentioned.)

Chapter 30

1 On the third day I commanded the earth to make and grow great and fruitful trees, and hills, and seeds to sow, and I planted Paradise, and enclosed it, and placed armed guards in the form of my flaming angels, and in this way I created renewal.
2 Then came evening, and morning came of the fourth day.
3 On Wednesday, the fourth day, I commanded that there should be great lights on the heavenly circles.
4 On the first uppermost circle I placed the stars, Cronus, and on the second Aphrodite, on the third Ares, on the fifth Zeus, on the sixth Ermis (Hermes), on the seventh lesser the moon, and adorned it with the lesser stars.

(Note: The fourth heavenly circle is vacant. The Greek names for the heavenly bodies leave no doubt as to the influence of Greek words and ideas within this section of the text.)

5 And on the lower (parts) I placed the sun for the illumination of day, and
the moon and stars for the illumination of night.
6 (And I set) the sun that it should go according to each of the twelve
constellations , and I appointed the succession of the months and their
names and lives, their thundering, and how they mark the hours, and how
they should proceed.
7 Then evening came and morning came of the fifth day.
8 On Thursday, the fifth day, I commanded the sea, that it should bring
forth fishes, and feathered birds of many varieties, and all animals creeping
over the earth, going forth over the earth on four legs, and soaring in the air,
of male and female sex, and every soul breathing the spirit of life.

(Note: Verse eight proclaims the creation of all souls breathing (inspired by) the spirit of life. The next verse proclaims the creation of man. This day filled the Guf and incarnation begins in the next.)

9 And there came evening, and there came morning of the sixth day.
10 On Friday, the sixth day, I commanded my wisdom to create man from
seven consistent applications: one, his flesh from the earth; two, his blood
from the dew; three, his eyes from the sun; four, his bones from stone; five,
his intelligence from the swiftness of the angels and cloud; six, his veins and
his hair from the grass of the earth; seven, his soul from my breath and from
the wind.
11 And I gave him seven natures: to the flesh - hearing, the eyes for sight, to
the soul- smell, the veins for touch, the blood for taste, the bones for
endurance, to the intelligence - enjoyment.
12 I created a saying (speech) from knowing. I created man from spiritual
and from physical nature, from both come his death and life and
appearance. He knows speech like some created thing. He is small in
greatness and great in smallness, and I placed him on earth, like a second
angel, to be honorable, great and glorious. And I appointed him as ruler to
rule on earth and to have my wisdom, and there was none like him on earth
of all my existing creatures.
13 And I appointed him a name made from the four components, from east,
from west, from south, and from north. And I appointed for him four
special stars, and I called his name Adam, and showed him the two ways,
the light and the darkness, and I told him:
14 This is good, and that bad, so that I should learn whether he has love
towards me, or hatred, and so that it would be clear who in his race loves
me.

(Note: The Hebrew name of Adam means man.)

15 For I have seen his nature, but he has not seen his own nature, and therefore by not seeing it he will sin worse, and I said, "After sin is there nothing but death?"
16 And I put sleep into him and he fell asleep. And I took from him a rib, and created him a wife, so that death should come to him by his wife, and I took his last word and called her name Mother, that is to say, Eve.

Chapter 31

1 Adam has life on earth, and I created a garden in Eden in the east, so that he should observe the testament and keep the command.
2 I made the heavens open to him, so that he would see the angels singing the song of victory, and the light without shadow.
3 And he was continuously in paradise, and the devil understood that I wanted to create another world, because Adam was lord on earth, to rule and control it.
4 The devil is the evil spirit of the lower places, he made himself a fugitive from the heavens as the devil and his name was Satan. Thus he became different from the angels, but his nature did not change his intelligence as it applied to his understanding of righteous and sinful things.
5 And he understood his condemnation and the sin that he had committed before. Therefore he devised a thought against Adam, in which he entered and seduced Eve, but did not touch Adam.
6 But I cursed ignorance. However, what I had blessed before I did not curse. I did not curse man, nor the earth, nor other creatures. But I cursed man's evil results, and his works.

Chapter 32

1 I said to him: You are earth (dirt), and into the earth from where I took you, you shall go, and I will not destroy you, but send you back from where I took you.
2 Then I can again receive you at My second presence.
3 And I blessed all my creatures, both physical and spiritual. And Adam was five and half hours in paradise.
4 And I blessed the seventh day, which is the Sabbath, on which he rested from all his works.

(Note: The five and a half hours is tied to the 5500 years of punishment mentioned in the Books of Adam and Eve. See The First and Second Books of Adam and Eve, *by Joseph Lumpkin.)*

Chapter 33

1 And I appointed the eighth day also, that the eighth day should be the first-created after my work, and that the first seven revolve in the form of the seventh thousand, and that at the beginning of the eighth thousand there should be a time of not-counting, endless, with neither years nor months nor weeks nor days nor hours.

(Note: A day is as a thousand years. This prophecy seems to indicate that after six thousand years there will be a thousand years of rest, then there will be timelessness.)

2 And now, Enoch, all that I have told you, all that you have understood, all that you have seen of heavenly things, all that you have seen on earth, all that I have written in books by my great wisdom, and all these things I have devised and created from the uppermost foundation to the lower and to the end, and there is no counselor nor inheritor to my creations.
3 I am eternal unto myself, not made with hands, and without change.
4 My thought is my own counselor, my wisdom and my word creates, and my eyes observe how all things stand here and tremble with terror.
5 If I turn away my face, then all things will be destroyed.
6 Apply your mind, Enoch, and know him who is speaking to you, and take the books there, which you yourself have written.
7 I give you Samuil and Raguil, who led you upward with the books, and go down to earth, and tell your sons all that I have told you, and all that you have seen, from the lower heaven up to my throne, and all the troops.
8 For I created all forces, and there is none that resists me and none that does not subject himself to me. For all subject themselves to my kingdom, and labor for my complete rule.
9 Give them the books of the handwriting, and they will read them and will know that I am the creator of all things, and will understand how there is no other God but me.
10 And let them distribute the books of your handwriting from children to children, generation to generation, nation to nation.
11 And Enoch, I will give you, my intercessor, the archangel Michael, for the writings of your fathers Adam, Seth, Enos, Cainan, Mahaleleel, and Jared your father.

Chapter 34

1 They have rejected my commandments and my yoke, therefore worthless seed has come up, not fearing God, and they would not bow down to me, but have begun to bow down to empty gods, and rejected my unity (oneness/sovereignty), and have piled the whole earth up with lies, offences, abominable lust with one another, and all manner of other unclean wickedness, which are disgusting to even mention.

2 And therefore I will bring down a deluge upon the earth and will destroy all men, and the whole earth will crumble together into great darkness.

Chapter 35

1 You will see that from their seed shall arise another generation, long afterward, but of them many will be full of very strong desires that are never satisfied.
2 He who raises that generation shall reveal the books of your writing of your fathers to them. And He must point out the guardianship of the world to the faithful men and workers of my pleasure, who do not acknowledge my name in empty words.
3 And they shall tell another generation, and those others who, having read, shall afterward be glorified more than the first.

Chapter 36

1 Now, Enoch, I give you a period of thirty days to spend in your house, and tell your sons and all your household, so that all may hear from you what was spoken by my face, so that they may read and understand that there is no other God but me.
2 And that they may always keep my commandments, and begin to read and absorb the books of your writing.
3 And after thirty days I shall send my angel for you, and he will take you from earth and from your sons and bring you to me.

Chapter 37

1 And the Lord called upon one of the older angels who was terrible and menacing, and He placed him by me. He appeared white as snow, and his hands were like ice, having the appearance of great frost, and he froze my face, because I could not endure the terror of the Lord, just as it is not possible to endure a stove's fire or the sun's heat, or the frost of the air.
2 And the Lord said to me: Enoch, if your face is not frozen here, no man will be able to look at your face.

Chapter 38

1 And the Lord said to those men who first led me up: "Let Enoch go down on to earth with you, and await him until the determined day."
2 And by night they placed me on my bed.
3 But Methuselah was expecting my return and was keeping watch at my bed by day and night. And he was filled with awe when he heard my return, and I told him, "Let all my household come together, so that I may tell them everything."

Chapter 39

1 Oh my children, my loved ones, hear the advice of your father, as much as is according to the Lord's will.
2 I have been allowed to come to you today, and preach to you, not from my lips, but from the Lord's lips, all that is now, and was, and all that will be until judgment day.
3 For the Lord has allowed me to come to you so that you could hear the words of my lips, a man who made great for you. But I am one who has seen the Lord's face, and it was like iron made to glow from fire it sends forth sparks and burns.
4 You look upon my eyes now. They are the eyes of a man enlarged with meaning for you, but I have seen the Lord's eyes, shining like the sun's rays and filling the eyes of man with awe.
5 You see now, my children, the right hand of a man that helps you, but I have seen the Lord's right hand filling heaven as he helped me.
6 You see the scope of my work is like your own, but I have seen the Lord's limitless and perfect scope, which has no end.
7 You hear the words of my lips, as I heard the words of the Lord, and they are like constant and great thunder with hurling of clouds.
8 And now, my children, hear the lecture of the father of the earth. I will tell you how fearful and awful it is to come before the face of the ruler of the earth, and how much more terrible and awful it is to come before the face of the ruler of heaven, who is the judge of the quick and the dead, and of the controller of the heavenly troops. Who (of us) can endure that endless pain?

Chapter 40

1 And now, my children, I know all things, for this is from the Lord's lips, and my eyes have seen this, from beginning to end.
2 I know all things, and have written all things in the books, the heavens and their end, and their abundance, and all the armies and their marching.
3 I have measured and described the stars, the great innumerable multitude of them.
4 What man has seen their revolutions and their entrances? For not even the angels see their number, but I have written all their names.
5 And I measured the sun's circumference, and measured its rays, and counted the hours. I also wrote down all things that go over the earth. I have written down the things that are nourished, and all seed sown and unsown, which the earth produces, and all plants, and every grass and every flower, and their sweet smells, and their names, and the dwelling-places of the clouds, and their composition, and their wings, and how they carry rain and raindrops.
6 And I investigated all things, and described the road of the thunder and of the lightning, and they showed me the keys and their guardians, their rise, and the way they precede. They are let out gradually, in measure, by a

chain. If they were not let out at a measured rate by a heavy chain their violence would hurl down the angry clouds and destroy all things on earth.
7 I described the treasure houses of the snow, and the storehouses of the cold and the frosty airs, and I observed the key-holders of the seasons. He fills the clouds with them, and it does not exhaust the treasure houses.
8 And I wrote down the resting places of the winds and observed and saw how their key-holders bear weighing-scales and measures. First, they put them in one side of the weighing-scale, then in the other side they place the weights and let them out according to measure skillfully, over the whole earth, to keep the heavy winds from making the earth rock. (The wind blows and makes the earth hard and rock.)
9 And I measured out the whole earth, its mountains, and all hills, fields, trees, stones, rivers, all existing things I wrote down, the height from earth to the seventh heaven, and downwards to the very lowest hell, and the judgment-place, and the very great, open and weeping (gaping) hell.
10 And I saw how the prisoners are in pain, expecting the limitless judgment.
11 And I wrote down all those being judged by the judge, and all their judgment and sentences and all their works.

Chapter 41

1 And I saw throughout all time all the forefathers from Adam and Eve, and I sighed and broke into tears and spoke of the ruin and their dishonor.
2 And I sad, "Woe is me for my infirmity and for that of my forefathers," and thought in my heart and said:
3 "Blessed is the man who has not been born or who has been born and shall not sin before the Lord's face, because he will not come into this place, nor bear the yoke of this place on himself.

Chapter 42

1 I saw the key-holders and guards of the gates of hell standing like great serpents. And their faces were glowing like extinguishing lamps, and I saw their eyes of fire, and their sharp teeth. And I saw all of the Lord's works, how they are right, while some of the works of man are of limited good, and others bad, and in their works are those who are known to speak evil lies.

Chapter 43

1 My children, I measured and wrote out every work and every measure and every righteous judgment.
2 As one year is more honorable than another, so is one man more honorable than another. Some men are honored for great possessions, some for wisdom of heart, some for particular intellect, some for skillfulness, one for silence of lip, another for cleanliness, one for strength, another for beauty, one for youth, another for sharp wit, one for shape of body, another

for sensibility, but let it be heard everywhere: There is none better than he who fears God. He shall be more glorious in time to come.

Chapter 44

1 The Lord created man with his hands in the likeness of his own face. The Lord made him small and great.
2 Whoever reviles the ruler's face hates the Lord's face, and has contempt for the Lord's face, and he who vents anger on any man without having been injured by him, the Lord's great anger will cut him down, he who spits on the face of man reproachfully will be cut down at the Lord's great judgment.
3 Blessed is the man who does not direct his heart with malice against any man, and helps the injured and condemned, and raises up the broken down, and does charity to the needy, because on the day of the great judgment every weight, every measure and every makeweight will be as in the market, so they are hung on scales and stand in the market, and every one shall learn his own measure, and according to his measure shall take his reward.

(Note: Makeweight is something put on a scale to make up the required weight for a more precise measurement.)

Chapter 45

1 Whoever hurries to make offerings before the Lord's face, the Lord will hasten that offering by giving of His work.
2 But whoever increases his lamp before the Lord's face and makes a judgment that is not true, the Lord will not increase his treasure in the realm of the highest.

(Note: Whoever makes himself out to be more than he is and whoever judges others without truth or cause, the Lord will not reward in heaven.)

3 When the Lord demands bread, or candles, or the flesh of beasts, or any other sacrifice, it is nothing; but God demands pure hearts, and with all He does it is only the tests of man's heart.

Chapter 46

1 Hear, my people, and take in the words of my lips.
2 If any one brings any gifts to an earthly ruler, and has disloyal thoughts in his heart, and the ruler know this, will the ruler not be angry with him, and refuse his gifts, and give him over to judgment?
3 Or if one man makes himself appear good to another by deceit of the tongue, but has evil in his heart, then will the other person not understand the treachery of his heart, and condemned him, since his lie was plain to all?

4 And when the Lord shall send a great light, then there will be judgment for the just and the unjust, and no one shall escape notice.

Chapter 47

1 And now, my children, with your minds and your hearts, mark well the words of your father, which all have come to you from the Lord's lips.
2 Take these books of your father's writing and read them.
3 For there are many books, and in them you will learn all the Lord's works, all that has been from the beginning of creation, and will be until the end of time.
4 And if you will observe my writing, you will not sin against the Lord; because there is no other except the Lord in heaven, nor in earth, nor in the very lowest places, nor in the foundation.
5 The Lord has placed the foundations in the unknown, and has spread out heavens, both physical and spiritual; he anchored the earth on the waters, and created countless creatures. Who has counted the water and the foundation of the mutable (changeable, corruptible), or the dust of the earth, or the sand of the sea, or the drops of the rain, or the morning dew, or the wind's blowing (breathing)? Who has filled earth and sea, and the indestructible winter?
6 I (The Lord) cut the stars out of fire, and decorated heaven, and put it in their midst.

Chapter 48

1 The sun goes along the seven heavenly circles, which are the appointment of one hundred and eighty-two thrones. It goes down on a short day, and again one hundred and eighty-two. It goes down on a long day, and he has two thrones on which he rests, revolving here and there above the thrones of the months, from the seventeenth day of the month Tsivan it goes down to the month Thevan, from the seventeenth of Thevan it goes up.

(Note: The words Tsivan *and* Thevan *refer to the summer and winter solstice, dividing the lengthening and shortening of days.*
The sun goes in a sinusoidal wave, decreasing daylight time for 182 days and growing longer in daylight hours for 182 days, with an extra day, which is a long day. The total is 365 days.)

2 When it goes close to the earth, then the earth is glad and makes its fruits grow, and when it goes away, then the earth is sad, and trees and all fruits will not flower.
3 All this He measured, with good measurement of hours, and predetermined a measure by his wisdom, of the physical and the spiritual (realms).

4 From the spiritual realm he made all things that are physical, himself being spiritual.
5 So I teach you, my children, and tell you to distribute the books to your children, into all your generations, and among the nations who shall have the sense to fear God. Let them receive them, and may they come to love them more than any food or earthly sweets, and read them and apply themselves to them.
6 And those who do not understand the Lord, who do not fear God, who do not accept, but reject, who do not receive the books, a terrible judgment awaits these.
7 Blessed is the man who shall bear their yoke and shall drag them along, for he shall be released on the day of the great judgment.

Chapter 49

1 I swear to you, my children, but I do not swear by any oath, neither by heaven nor by earth, nor by any other creature created by God.
2 The Lord said: "There is no oath in Me, nor injustice, but only truth."
3 But there is no truth in men, so let them swear by the words, Yea, yea, or else, Nay, nay.
4 And I swear to you, yea, yea, that every man that has been in his mother's womb has had a place prepared for the repose of that soul, and a measure predetermined of how much it is intended that a man be tried (tested) in this world.
5 Yea, children, do not deceive yourselves, for there has been a place previously prepared for the soul of every man. *(A statement of predestination.)*

Chapter 50

1 I have put every man's work in writing and none born on earth can remain hidden nor his works remain concealed.
2 I see all things.
3 Therefore, my children, spend the number of your days in patience and meekness so that you may inherit eternal life.
4 For the sake of the Lord, endure every wound, every injury, every evil word, and every attack.
5 If your good deeds are not rewarded but returned for ill to you, do not repay them to neither neighbor nor enemy, because the Lord will return them for you and be your avenger on the day of great judgment, so that there should be no vengeance here among men.
6 Whoever of you spends gold or silver for his brother's sake, he will receive ample treasure in the world to come.
7 Do not injure widows or orphans or strangers, for if you do God's wrath will come upon you.

Chapter 51

1 Stretch out your hands to the poor according to your strength.
2 Do not hide your silver in the earth.
3 Help the faithful man in affliction, and affliction will not find you in the time of your trouble.
4 And bear every grievous and cruel yoke that comes upon you, for the sake of the Lord, and thus you will find your reward in the Day of Judgment.
5 It is good to go morning, midday, and evening into the Lord's house, for the glory of your creator.
6 Because every breathing thing glorifies him, and every creature, both physical and spiritual, gives him praise. (Gives His praise back to Him.)

Chapter 52

1 Blessed is the man who opens his lips in praise of God of Sabaoth (Host/army) and praises the Lord with his heart.
2 Cursed is every man who opens his lips for the purpose of bringing contempt and slander to (of) his neighbor, because he brings God into contempt.
3 Blessed is he who opens his lips blessing and praising God.
4 Cursed before the Lord all the days of his life, is he who opens his lips to curse and abuse.
5 Blessed is he who blesses all the Lord's works.
6 Cursed is he who brings the Lord's creation into contempt.
7 Blessed is he who looks down and raises the fallen.
8 Cursed is he who looks to and is eager for the destruction of what is not his.
9 Blessed is he who keeps the foundations of his fathers that were made firm from the beginning.
10 Cursed is he who corrupts the doctrine of his forefathers.
11 Blessed is he who imparts peace and love.
12 Cursed is he who disturbs those that love their neighbors.
13 Blessed is he who speaks with humble tongue and heart to all.
14 Cursed is he who speaks peace with his tongue, while in his heart there is no peace but a sword.
15 For all these things will be laid bare in the scales of balance and in the books, on the day of the great judgment.

Chapter 53

1 And now, my children, do not say: "Our father is standing before God, and is praying for our sins. For there is there no helper for any man who has sinned.
2 You see how I wrote down all of the works of every man, before his creation, all that is done among all men for all time, and none can tell or relate my writing, because the Lord sees all imaginings of man, and how

they are empty and prideful, where they lie in the treasure houses of the heart.
3 And now, my children, mark well all the words of your father that I tell you, or you will be regretful, saying: Why did our father not tell us?

(Note: Although chapters 51 and 52 seem similar to the Sermon on the Mount, Chapter 53 offers no balance between mercy and justice. "There is no helper for any man who has sinned," is a statement excluding a savior. Scholars point to this verse to conclude 2 Enoch is a Jewish text. As stated before, 2 Enoch seems to be a Jewish text that was Christianized by additions and embellishment of the core text. Chapter 53 is part of the core Jewish text, likely written before the Christian sect. Verse 2 is a statement of predestination or foreknowledge.)

Chapter 54

1 Let these books, which I have given you, be for an inheritance of your peace in that time that you do not understand things.
2 Hand them to all who want them, and instruct them, that they may see the Lord's very great and marvelous works.

Chapter 55

1 My children, behold, the day of my determined period (term and time) has approached.
2 For the angels who shall go with me are standing before me and urge me to my departure from you. They are standing here on earth, awaiting what has been told them.
3 For tomorrow I shall go up to heaven, to the uppermost Jerusalem, to my eternal inheritance.
4 Therefore I bid you to do the Lord's good pleasure before his face at all times.

(Note: The Jerusalem spoken of here is the spiritual Jerusalem, spoken of by John, coming down from heaven. The name, Jerusalem refers to the components of the actual name, which break down to mean "provision" and "peace.")

Chapter 56

1 Methuselah answered his father Enoch, and said: What (food) is agreeable to your eyes, father, that I may prepare before your face, that you may bless our houses, and your sons, and that your people may be made glorious through you, and then that you may depart, as the Lord said?"
2 Enoch answered his son Methuselah and said: "Hear me, my child. From the time when the Lord anointed me with the ointment of his glory, there has been no food in me, and my soul remembers not earthly enjoyment, neither do I want anything earthly."

Chapter 57
1 My child Methuselah, summon all your brethren and all of your household and the elders of the people, that I may talk to them and depart, as is planned for me.
2 And Methuselah hurried, and summoned his brethren, Regim, Riman, Uchan, Chermion, Gaidad, and all the elders of the people before the face of his father Enoch; and he blessed them, and said to them:

Chapter 58
1 "Listen to me, my children, today.
2 In those days when the Lord came down to earth for Adam's sake, and visited all his creatures, which he created himself, after all these he created Adam, and the Lord called all the beasts of the earth, all the reptiles, and all the birds that soar in the air, and brought them all before the face of our father Adam.
3 And Adam gave names to all things living on earth.
4 And the Lord appointed him ruler over all, and subjected all things to him under his hands, and made them dumb and made them dull that they would be commanded by man, and be in subjection and obedience to him.
5 The Lord also created every man lord over all his possessions.
6 The Lord will not judge a single soul of beast for man's sake, but He judges the souls of men through their beasts in this world, for men have a special place.
7 And as every soul of man is according to number, similarly beasts will not perish, nor all souls of beasts which the Lord created, until the great judgment, and they will accuse man, if he did not feed them well.

Chapter 59
1 Whoever defiles the soul of beasts, defiles his own soul.
2 For man brings clean animals to make sacrifice for sin, that he may have cure for his soul.
3 And if they bring clean animals and birds for sacrifice, man has a cure. He cures his soul.
4 All is given you for food, bind it by the four feet, to make good the cure.
5 But whoever kills beast without wounds, kills his own souls and defiles his own flesh.
6 And he who does any beast any injury whatsoever, in secret, it is an evil practice, and he defiles his own soul.

(Note: To kill without a wound is to inflict blunt force trauma--to beat them to death.)

Chapter 60

1 He who works the killing of a man's soul (he who murders), kills his own soul, and kills his own body, and there is no cure for him for all time.
2 He who puts a man in any snare (moral entrapment), shall stick himself in it, and there is no cure for him for all time.
3 He who puts a man in any vessel, his retribution will not be wanting at the great judgment for all time.
4 He who works dishonestly or speaks evil against any soul, will not make justice for himself for all time.

Chapter 61

1 And now, my children, keep your hearts from every injustice, which the Lord hates. Just as a man asks something for his own soul from God, so let him do the same to every living soul, because I know all things, how in the great time to come there is a great inheritance prepared for men, good for the good, and bad for the bad, no matter the number.
2 Blessed are those who enter the good houses, for in the bad houses there is no peace or return from them.
3 Hear, my children, small and great! When man puts a good thought in his heart, it brings gifts from his labors before the Lord's face. But if his hands did not make them, then the Lord will turn away his face from the labor of his hand, and (that) man cannot find the labor of his hands.
4 And if his hands made it, but his heart murmurs (complains), and his heart does not stop murmurs incessantly, he does not have (gain) any advantage.

Chapter 62

1 Blessed is the man who, in his patience, brings his gifts with faith before the Lord's face, because he will find forgiveness of sins.
2 But if he takes back his words before the time, there is no repentance for him; and if the time passes and he does not of his own will perform what is promised, there is no repentance after death.
3 Because every work which man does before the time (outside the time he has promised it), is all deceit before men, and sin before God.

Chapter 63

1 When man clothes the naked and fills the hungry, he will find reward from God.
2 But if his heart complains, he commits a double evil; ruin of himself and of that which he gives; and for him there will be no finding of reward because of that.
3 And if his own heart is filled with his food and his own flesh is clothed with his own clothing, he commits contempt, and will forfeit all his

endurance of poverty, and will not find reward of his good deeds. (If he is selfish and does not add to the economy of others…)
4 Every proud and pontificating man is hateful to the Lord, and every false speech is clothed in lies. It will be cut with the blade of the sword of death, and thrown into the fire, and shall burn for all time.

Chapter 64

1 When Enoch had spoken these words to his sons, all people far and near heard how the Lord was calling Enoch. They took counsel together:
2 Let us go and kiss Enoch, and two thousand men came together and came to the place called Achuzan, where Enoch was with his sons.
3 And the elders of the people with the entire assembly came and bowed down and began to kiss Enoch and said to him:
4 "Our father Enoch, may you be blessed by the Lord, the eternal ruler, and now bless your sons and all the people, that we may be glorified today before your face.
5 For you shall be glorified before the Lord's face for eternity, since the Lord chose you from among all men on earth, and designated you as the writer of all his creation, both physical and spiritual, and you are redeemed from the sins of man, and are the helper of your household."

Chapter 65

1 And Enoch said to all his people: "Hear me, my children. Before all creatures were created, the Lord created the physical and spiritual things.
2 And then a long term passed. Then after all of that he created man in the likeness of his own form, and put eyes into him to see, and ears into him to hear, and a heart to reflect, and intellect to enable him to deliberate.
3 And the Lord saw all the works of man, and created all his creatures, and divided time. From time he determined the years, and from the years he appointed the months, and from the months he appointed the days, and of days he appointed seven.
4 And in those he appointed the hours, measured them out exactly, that man might reflect on time and count years, months, and hours, as they alternate from beginning to end, so that he might count his own life from the beginning until death, and reflect on his sin and write his works, both bad and good. No work is hidden from the Lord, so that every man might know his works and never transgress all his commandments, and keep my writing from generation to generation.
5 When all creation, both physical and spiritual, as the Lord created it, shall end, then every man goes to the great judgment, and then all time shall be destroyed along with the years. And from then on there will be neither months nor days nor hours. They will run together and will not be counted.
6 There will be one eon (age), and all the righteous who shall escape the Lord's great judgment, shall be collected in the great eon (age). For the

righteous the great eon will begin, and they will live eternally, and there will be no labor, nor sickness, nor humiliation, nor anxiety, nor need, nor brutality, nor night, nor darkness, but great light among them.
7 And they shall have a great indestructible wall, and a paradise that is bright and eternal, for all mortal things shall pass away, and there will be eternal life.

(Note: An eon is one billion years but is used to mean a very long but indefinite period of time. The word "eternal" means "unchanging, incorruptible, immortal." The word used for "mortal" is the opposite of "eternal," thus, "mortal, corruptible, changing.")

Chapter 66

1 And now, my children, keep your souls from all injustice the Lord hates.
2 Walk before his face with great fear (respect) and trembling and serve him only.
3 Bow down to the true God, not to dumb idols, but bow down to his likeness, and bring all just offerings before the Lord's face. The Lord hates what is unjust.

(Note: This is an odd command issued by Enoch, that the people are not to bow to dumb idols but are to bow to the likeness or similitude of God. This was likely added by Christians around the third or fourth centuries A.D.)

4 For the Lord sees all things; when man takes thought in his heart, then he counsels the intellects, and every thought is always before the Lord, who made firm the earth and put all creatures on it.
5 If you look to heaven, the Lord is there; if you take thought of the sea's depth and all under the earth, the Lord is there.
6 For the Lord created all things. Bow not down to things made by man, leaving the Lord of all creation, because no work can remain hidden before the Lord's face.
7 Walk, my children, in long-suffering, in meekness, honesty, in thoughtfulness, in grief, in faith and in truth. Walk in (rely on) promises, in (times of) illness, in abuse, in wounds, in temptation, in nakedness, in privation, loving one another, until you go out from this age of ills, that you become inheritors of endless time.
8 Blessed are the just who shall escape the great judgment, for they shall shine forth more than the sun sevenfold, for in this world the seventh part is taken off from all, light, darkness, food, enjoyment, sorrow, paradise, torture, fire, frost, and other things; he put all down in writing, that you might read and understand.

Chapter 67

1 When Enoch had talked to the people, the Lord sent out darkness on to the earth, and there was darkness, and it covered those men standing with Enoch, and they took Enoch up on to the highest heaven, where the Lord is. And there God received him and placed him before His face, and the darkness went off from the earth, and light came again.
2 And the people saw and did not understand how Enoch had been taken, and they glorified God, and found a scroll in which was written "The God of the Spiritual." Then all went to their dwelling places.

Chapter 68

1 Enoch was born on the sixth day of the month Tsivan (the first month of the year), and lived three hundred and sixty-five years.
2 He was taken up to heaven on the first day of the month Tsivan and remained in heaven sixty days.
3 He wrote all these signs of all creation, which the Lord created, and wrote three hundred and sixty-six books, and handed them over to his sons and remained on earth thirty days, and was again taken up to heaven on the sixth day of the month Tsivan, on the very day and hour when he was born.
4 As every man's nature in this life is dark, so are also his conception, birth, and departure from this life.
5 At what hour he was conceived, at that hour he was born, and at that hour also he died.
6 Methuselah and his brethren, all the sons of Enoch, made haste, and erected an altar at that place called Achuzan, where Enoch had been taken up to heaven.
7 And they took sacrificial oxen and summoned all people and sacrificed the sacrifice before the Lord's face.
8 All people, the elders of the people and the whole assembly came to the feast and brought gifts to the sons of Enoch.
9 And they made a great feast, rejoicing and making merry three days, praising God, who had given them such a sign through Enoch, who had found favor with him, and that they should hand it on to their sons from generation to generation, from age to age. Amen.

(Note: Enoch was born on the sixth day of Tsivan. Tsivan is the first month of the year. The sum is seven, one of the holy numbers. He lived 365 years. One year of years. He remained in heaven 60 days. Six is the number of man, which always falls short of God.)

The Short Version Ends Here

The wife of Nir was Sopanim. She was sterile and never had at any time given birth to a child by Nir. Sopanim was in her old age and in the last days (time) of her death. She conceived in her womb, but Nir the priest had not slept with her from the day that that the Lord had appointed him to conduct the liturgy in front of the face of the people.

When Sopanim saw her pregnancy, she was ashamed and embarrassed, and she hid herself during all the days until she gave birth. Not one of the people knew about it. When 282 days had been completed, and the day of birth had begun to approach, Nir thought about his wife, and he called her to come to him in his house, so that he might converse with her. *(282 days is 9.4 of 30-day months.)*

Sopanim came to Nir, her husband; and, behold, she was pregnant, and the day appointed for giving birth was drawing near. Nir saw her and became very ashamed. He said to her, "What is this that you have done, O wife? Why have you disgraced me in front of the face of these people? Now, depart from me and go back to where you began this disgrace of your womb, so that I might not defile my hands in front of The Face of The Lord on account of you and sin."

Sopanim spoke to her husband, Nir, saying, "O my lord! Look at me. It is the time of my old age, the day of my death has arrived. I do not understand how my menopause and the barrenness of my womb have been reversed." But Nir did not believe his wife, and for the second time he said to her, "Depart from me, or else I might assault you, and commit a sin in front of the face of The Lord."

And after Nir had spoken to his wife, Sopanim, she fell down at Nir's feet and died. Nir was extremely distressed and said to himself, "Could this have happened because of my words? And now, merciful is The Eternal Lord, because my hand was not upon her."

The archangel Gabriel appeared to Nir, and said to him, "Do not think that your wife Sopanim has died due to your error. This child, which is to be born from her, is a righteous fruit, and one whom I shall receive into paradise so that you will not be the father of a gift of God."

Nir hurried and shut the door of his house. He went to Noah, his brother, and he reported to him everything that had happened in connection with his wife. Noah hurried to the room of his brother. The appearance of his brother's wife was as if she were dead but her womb was at the same time giving birth.

Noah said to Nir, "Don't let yourself be sorrowful, Nir, my brother! Today the Lord has covered up our scandal, because nobody from the people knows this. Now let us go quickly and bury her, and the Lord will cover up the scandal of our shame." They placed Sopanim on the bed, wrapped her around with black garments, and shut the door. They dug a grave in secret.

When they had gone out toward the grave, a child came out from Sopanim's dead body and sat on the bed at her side. Noah and Nir came in to bury Sopanim and they saw the child sitting beside Sopanim's dead body and he was wiping his clothing. Noah and Nir were very terrified with a great fear, because the child was physically fully developed. The child spoke with his lips and blessed The Lord.

Noah and Nir looked at him closely, saying, "This is from the Lord, my brother." The badge of priesthood is on his chest, and it is glorious in appearance. Noah said to Nir, "God is renewing the priesthood from blood related to us, just as He pleases."

Noah and Nir hurried and washed the child, they dressed him in the garments of the priesthood, and they gave him bread to eat and he ate it. And they called him Melchizedek.

Noah and Nir lifted up the body of Sopanim, and took the black garment off of her and washed her. They clothed her in exceptionally bright garments and built a grave for her. Noah, Nir, and Melchizedek came and they buried her publicly. Then Noah said to his brother Nir, "Take care of this child in secret until the proper time comes, because all of the people on earth will become treacherous and they will begin to turn away from God. Having become completely ignorant (of God), when they see him, they will put him to death in some way."

Then Noah went away to his own place, and there came great lawlessness that began to become abundant over all the earth in the days of Nir. And Nir began to worry greatly about the child saying, "What will I do with him?" And stretching out his hands toward heaven, Nir called out to The Lord, saying, " It is miserable for me, Eternal Lord, that all of this lawlessness has begun to become abundant over all the earth in my lifetime! I realize how much nearer our end is because of the lawlessness of the people. And now, Lord, what is the vision about this child, and what is his destiny, or what will I do for him, so that he will not be joined along with us in this destruction?"

The Lord took notice of Nir and appeared to him in a night vision. And He said to him, "Nir, the great lawlessness which has come about on the earth I shall not tolerate anymore. I plan to send down a great destruction onto the earth. But do not worry about the child, Nir. In a short while I will send My archangel Gabriel and he will take the child and put him in the paradise of

Edem. He will not perish along with those who must perish. As I have revealed it, Melchizedek will be My priest to all holy priests, I will sanctify him and I will establish him so that he will be the head of the priests of the future."

(Note: Edem means "God will save." It is assumed Edem is Eden.)

Then Nir arose from his sleep and blessed The Lord, who had appeared to him saying: "Blessed be The Lord, The God of my fathers, who has approved of my priesthood and the priesthood of my fathers, because by His Word, He has created a great priest in the womb of Sopanim, my wife. For I have no descendants. So let this child take the place of my descendants and become as my own son. You will count him in the number of your servants."

"Therefore honor him together with your servants and great priests and me your servant, Nir. And behold, Melchizedek will be the head of priests in another generation. I know that great confusion has come and in confusion this generation will come to an end, and everyone will perish, except that Noah, my brother, will be preserved for procreation. From his tribe, there will arise numerous people, and Melchizedek will become the head of priests reigning over a royal people who will serve you, O Lord."

It happened when the child had completed 40 days in Nir's tent, The Lord said to the archangel Gabriel, "Go down to the earth to Nir the priest, and take the child Melchizedek, who is with him. Place him in the paradise of Edem for preservation. For the time is already approaching, and I will pour out all the water onto the earth, and everything that is on the earth will perish. And I will raise it up again, and Melchizedek will be the head of the priests in that generation." And Gabriel hurried, and came flying down when it was night when Nir was sleeping on his bed that night.

Gabriel appeared to him and said to him, "The Lord says: "Nir! Restore the child to me whom I entrusted to you." But Nir did not realize who was speaking to him and he was confused. And he said, "When the people find out about the child, they will seize him and kill him, because the heart of these people are deceitful before The Lord." And he answered Gabriel and said, "The child is not with me, and I don't know who is speaking to me."

Gabriel answered him, " Nir, do not be afraid. I am the archangel Gabriel. The Lord sent me to take your child today. I will go with him and I will place him in the paradise of Edem." Then Nir remembered the first dream and believed it. He answered Gabriel, "Blessed be The Lord, who has sent you to me today! Now bless your servant Nir! Take the child and do to him all that has been said to you." And Gabriel took the child, Melchizedek on his wings in that same night, and he placed him in the paradise of Edem. Nir got up in the morning, and he went into his tent and did not find the child. There was great joy and grief for Nir because he felt the child had the place of a son.

The Lord said to Noah, "Make an ark that is 300 cubits in length, 50 cubits in width and in 30 cubits height. Put the entrance to the ark in its side; and make it with two stories in the middle" The Lord God opened the doors of heaven. Rain came onto the earth and all flesh died.

Noah fathered 3 sons: Shem, Ham and Japheth. He went into the ark in his six hundredth year. After the flood, he lived 350 years. He lived in all 950 years, according to The Lord our God.
To our God be Glory always, now and eternally. AMEN.

The Third Book of Enoch

3 Enoch

The Hebrew Book of Enoch

Introduction of 3 Enoch

The Hebrew Book of Enoch, or 3 Enoch, was very difficult to find in its entirety. It was likely written by a highly educated rabbi around 300 to 400 A.D. and preserved only in fragments, here and there. Then, in 1928 Dr. Hugo Odeberg Ph.D. gathered the various fragmentary sources and published the first full translation along with copious scholarly notes and the source Hebrew material. The University Press at Cambridge in the United Kingdom published his work. A photocopy of the book made its way to the United States and into the University of Chicago library, where it was kept for many years. It was from this body of work and from this photocopied and preserved manuscript that some of the Hebrew language source material was compiled. The Hebrew source from the work at Cambridge was compared to and supplemented with various articles, fragments, quotes, and commentaries from dozens of other sources and references to produce the work before you.

Origins of 3 Enoch

3 Enoch purports to have been written around 100 A.D., but its origins can only be traced to the late fourth or early fifth centuries. Other names for 3 Enoch include "The Third Book of Enoch" and "The Book of the Palaces."

The book is rife with Hebrew words, which have no single English equivalent. Even though care was taken to define the majority of these words when first they appear in the text, the reader should expect only keywords to replace or augment meanings thereafter. To do otherwise would either leave the reader to remember the meanings of all Hebrew words or bloat the book to the point of making it difficult for the reader to follow.

Modern scholars describe this book as belonging to a body of work called the *Pseudepigraphia*. 3 Enoch claims to be written by a rabbi, who became a 'high priest' after he had visions of an ascension to heaven, 90 A.D. - 135 A.D. Rabbi Ishmael is a leading figure of Merkabah literature; however, a number of scholars suggest that it was in fact written by a number of people over a prolonged period of time.

Merkabah writings had to do with the theme of ascension into heaven. The name is derived from a Hebrew word meaning "chariot," referring to Ezekiel's vision beginning in Ezekiel 1:4. Enoch's contents and ideas are unique and newer than those shown in other Merkabah texts, suggesting the book may be among the first in the Merkabah movement or that it is derived through unique influences.

Merkabah and 3 Enoch

As the book's other name, The Book of the Palaces, implies, 3 Enoch is part of the Temple or Hekalot body of literature in which the "Palace" or "Temple" of heaven is described.

As with 1 Enoch, the exact dating of this book is a difficult task, but some scholars believe it was completed around the time of the Babylonian Talmud, which was around the early 5th century A.D.

3 Enoch was originally written in Hebrew, although it contains a number of words from both Greek and Latin. Parts of the book seem to have been influenced by 1 Enoch, showing the author was familiar with the mystical Enochian tradition.

1 Enoch vs. 3 Enoch

Similar points appearing in 1 Enoch and 3 Enoch are

- Enoch ascends to Heaven in a storm chariot (3 Enoch 6:1; 7:1)
- Enoch is translated into an angel (3 Enoch 9:1-5; 15:1-2)
- Enoch, as an angel, is given authority in Heaven (3 Enoch 10:1-3; 16:1)
- Enoch receives an explanation or vision of creation and cosmology (3 Enoch 13:1-2)
- Enoch sees a hostile angel named Azazel (3 Enoch 4:6; 5:9)

3 Enoch and Metatron

The main theme throughout the book is the "transubstantiation" of Enoch into the angel Metatron.

Metatron appears in various Jewish, Christian, and Islamic works but was a central focus in medieval Jewish mystical texts and occult sources. Rabbinical texts point to Metatron as the angel who stilled the hand of Abraham, preventing him from sacrificing Isaac.

The place and authority of Metatron has been hotly debated, as is seen even within the book. He is seen as sitting in heaven. This is only permitted if one is a deity. He is referred to in the text as "The Lesser YHWH."

YHWH makes up the Tetragrammaton forming the name we pronounce as *Yahweh* or *Jehovah.* The four letters making up the divine name are *Yodh, He Waw, He,* having the sounds of *Y, H, W, O, U* or a place holder, and *H.* When *He* ends a word it is often silent. Due to the fact that German theologians were heavily involved in theological research and study, one may also find the Tetragrammaton rendered as YHVH, since the V in German has a *W* sound.

A curse for dualism

There is a very personal attack within the text, which should be explained. A curse is placed on a man known only as Acher. In Hebrew the name means, "the other," and is used as a term of alienation from the rabbinic community. The Talmud tells us that Elisha be Abuyah entered Paradise in a vision and saw Metatron sitting down (an action that in heaven is permitted only to God himself). Elishah ben Abuyah therefore looked to Metatron as a deity and proclaimed, "There are indeed two powers in heaven!" The other rabbis explain that Metatron was allowed to sit because he was the Heavenly Scribe, writing down the deeds of Israel (Babylonian Talmud, Hagiga 15a).

The intense hatred for any idea hinting at dualism or polytheism, as opposed to monotheism, caused such a reaction within the Rabbinical community that they labeled Elisha be Abuyah a heretic. In 3 Enoch this point is driven home when the entire nation of Israel is to be reconciled to God, except for Acher, whose name is blotted out.

Who is Metatron?

In spite of the disagreements within the ancient Jewish community, the reader is still left to wonder what position Metatron occupies in heaven. Metatron is described in two ways: as a primordial angel (9:2–13:2) and as the transformation of Enoch after he was assumed into Heaven, and he is called "The Lesser YHWH."

According to Genesis 5:24, Enoch walked with God; then he was no more, because God took him away. This Enoch, whose flesh was turned to flame, his veins to fire, his eyelashes to flashes of lightning, his eyeballs to flaming torches, and whom God placed on a throne next to the throne of glory, received after this heavenly transformation the name Metatron

A Christian perspective

As the Christian community came in contact with the Jewish book of 3 Enoch, they had little trouble reconciling the names and position of Metatron. To those Christians a person who may sit in heaven, who judges, and who is called by the same name taken by God must be *Yeshua* (Jesus.) It may be of help if the meaning of the name, Metatron, could be ascertained, but it is not clear. Suggestions are that the name originated from the root words of such phrases as, "keeper of the watch," "guard," "to protect," "one who serves behind the throne," "one who occupies the throne next to the throne of glory," "to lead," or "to measure." None of these suggestions can be proven. From the text itself we know only that Metatron is referred to as "the youth," likely because he would be the newest and youngest angel. He is also called, "the prince of the presence (of God)." His purpose in heaven was to be a witness against mankind.

Numerology in 3 Enoch

A type of numerology is used and referred to within the text. Temurah is one of the three ancient methods used by Cabbalist to rearrange words and sentences in the Torah, in the belief that by this method they can derive the deeper, hidden spiritual meaning of the words. Temurah may be used to change letters in certain words to create a new meaning for a Biblical statement. Another method is called Gematria. In this method letters are substituted for numbers and the meaning of words with the same value are compared along with the numerical meaning of the words.

Metatron is Enoch

A preparatory summary of the first section of the book may be framed as a revelation from Metatron, or the Prince of the Presence, to Rabbi Ishmael. Metatron, as it turns out, is Enoch and this is why the title of this book has come to be called, 3 Enoch. Any question as to who Metatron may be is answered clearly in CHAPTER IV, where it is written, "Rabbi Ishmael said: I asked Metatron and said to him: "Why are you called by the name of your Creator, by seventy names? You are greater than all the princes, higher than all the angels, beloved more than all the servants, honored above all the mighty ones in kingship, greatness and glory: Why do they call you 'Youth' in the high heavens?" He answered and said to me: "Because I am Enoch, the son of Jared. For when the generation of the flood sinned and were confounded in their deeds, saying unto God: Depart from us, for we desire not the knowledge of your ways (Job 21:14), then the Holy One, blessed be He, removed me from their midst to be a witness against them in the high heavens to all the inhabitants of the world, that they may not say, "The Merciful One is cruel."

The following text begins the book of 3 Enoch. Notes and explanations are italicized. Words placed in parentheses are alternate renderings of a word or phrase.

3 Enoch

The Hebrew Book of Enoch

By Rabbi ISHMAEL BEN ELISHA
THE HIGH PRIEST

CHAPTER I

INTRODUCTION: Rabbi Ishmael ascends to heaven to witness the vision of the Merkaba (chariot). He is given to Metatron

AND ENOCH WALKED WITH GOD: AND HE WAS NOT; FOR GOD TOOK HIM.

(1) I ascended on high to witness the vision of the Merkaba (the divine chariot) and I had entered the six halls, which were situated within one another.

The halls were in concentric circles, one within the other.

(2) As soon as I reached the door of the seventh hall I stood still in prayer before the Holy One, blessed be He. I lifted up my eyes on high towards the Divine Majesty and I said: (3) "Lord of the Universe, I pray you, that the worthiness of Aaron, the son of Amram, who loves and pursues peace, and who received the crown of priesthood from Your Glory on Mount Sinai, be upon me in this hour, so that Khafsiel, (Qafsiel) the prince, and the angels with him may not overcome (overpower) me nor cast me down from the heavens."

Qafsiel or Qaphsiel is an angel of a high order set to guard the Seventh Hall Of Heaven

(4) At that moment the Holy One, blessed be He, sent Metatron, his Servant, also called Ebed, to me. He is the angel, the Prince of the Presence. With great joy he spread his wings as he came to meet me in order to save me from their hand. (5) And by his hand he took me so that they could see us, and he said to me: "Enter in peace before the high and exalted King and see the picture of Merkaba (chariot)."

Merkaba *means chariot, or in this case chariot of fire or chariot of light . It is pulled by four* Chayot *or living creatures, each of which has four wings and the four faces of a man, lion, ox, and eagle… See Ezekiel 1:4-26. The Bible makes mention of three types of angel found in the Merkaba. The first is the Seraphim (lit.*

"burning") angels. These angels appear like flashes of fire continuously ascending and descending. These Seraphim angels powered the movement of the chariot. In the hierarchy of these angels, Seraphim are the highest, that is, closest to God, followed by the Chayot, *which are followed by the* Ophanim. *The chariot is in a constant state of motion, and the energy behind this movement runs according to this hierarchy. The movement of the* Ophanim *is controlled by the* Chayot *while the movement of the* Chayot *is controlled by the Seraphim. The movement of all the angels of the chariot are controlled by the "Likeness of a Man" on the Throne.*

(6) Then I entered the seventh hall, and he led me to the camps of *Shekina* (understanding) and stood me in front of the Holy One, blessed be He, to see the Merkaba.

Shekina, *or* Shekhinah, *is derived from a Hebrew verb literally meaning "to settle, inhabit, or dwell." See Exodus 40:35 ("Moses could not enter the Tent of Meeting, for the cloud rested [shakhan] upon it, and the glory of the Lord filled the Tabernacle.) See also Genesis 9:27, 14:13, Psalms 37:3, Jeremiah 33:16, as well as the weekly Shabbat blessing recited in the temple ("May He who causes His name to dwell [shochan] in this House, cause to dwell among you love and brotherliness, peace and friendship"). Also see Talmud Ketubot 85b.* Shekina *can also mean royalty or royal residence.* Shekina *has come to mean the effect or manifestation caused by the presence or inhabitation of God. The manifestation is glory, creativity, and understanding. These words may be used to explain* Shekina.

(7) As soon as the princes of the Merkaba (chariot) and the flaming Seraphim knew I was there, they fixed their gaze on me. Trembling and shuddering seized me at once and I fell down and was numbed by the brightness of the vision of their faces; until the Holy One, blessed be He, chastised them, saying: (8) "My servants, my Seraphim, my Cherubim and my Ophannim! Cover your eyes before Ishmael, my son, my friend, my beloved one and (my) glory, so that he ceases trembling and shaking! "

The root of Seraphim comes either from the Hebrew verb saraph *(to burn) or the Hebrew noun* saraph *(a fiery, flying serpent). Because the term appears several times with reference to the serpents encountered in the wilderness* (Num. 21.8, Deut. 8.15; Isa. 14.29; 30.6), *it has often been understood to refer to "fiery serpents." From this it has also often been proposed that the seraphim were serpentine in form and in some sense "fiery" creatures or associated with fire. It is said that whoever lays eyes on a Seraph, he would instantly be incinerated due to its the immense brightness.*

Cherubs are described as winged beings. The prophet Ezekiel describes the Cherubim as a tetrad of living creatures, each having four faces: that of a lion, an ox, an eagle, and a man. They are said to have the stature and hands of a man, the feet of a calf, and four wings. Two of the wings extended upward, meeting above and sustaining the throne of God, while the other two stretched downward and covered the creatures themselves.

Ophanim *are described in 1 Enoch as never sleeping. They watch and guard the throne of God.The word* ophan *means "wheel" in Hebrew. For this reason the Ophanim have been associated with the chariots in Ezekiel and Daniel. They are mentioned as* gagal, *traditionally "the wheels of* gagallin,*" in "fiery flame" and "burning fire" of the four eye-covered wheels, each composed of two nested wheels, that move next to the winged Cherubim, beneath the throne of God. The four wheels move with the Cherubim because the spirit of the Cherubim is in them. These are also referred to as the "many-eyed ones" in 2 Enoch. The Ophanim are also equated as the "Thrones," and associated with the "Wheels," in the vision of Daniel 7:9. They carry the throne of God, hence the name.*

This may be a good time to explain the singular and plural in Hebrew. Whereas in English we add an "s" to denote a plural, in Hebrew an "im" is added. Thus, there is one Cherub but many Cherubim. There is one Seraph but many Seraphim. Knowing this fact may make the text easier to follow.

(9) Then Metatron, the Prince of the Presence, came and placed my spirit in me again and he stood me up on my feet. (10) After that (moment) for an hour I did not have enough strength to sing a song before the Throne of Glory of the Glorious King, the mightiest of all kings, the most excellent of all princes. (11) After an hour had passed the Holy One, blessed be He, opened the gates of Shekina (understanding) to me. These are the gates of Peace, and of Wisdom, and of Strength, and of Power, and of Speech (Dibbur), and of Song, and of Kedushah (Sacred Salutation of Holy, Holy, Holy), and the gates of Chanting. (12) And he opened and shined His light in my eyes and my heart by words of psalm, song, praise, exaltation, thanksgiving, extolment, glorification, hymn and eulogy (to speak well of). And as I opened my mouth, singing a song before the Holy One, blessed be He the Holy Chayoth beneath and above the Throne of Glory answered and said (chanted the prayer): "HOLY!" "BLESSED BE THE GLORY OF YHWH FROM HIS PLACE!."

The Chayot *(or* Chayyot*) are a class of Merkabah, or Jewish mystical angels, reported in Ezekeil's vision of the Merkabah and its surrounding angels as recorded in the first chapter of the Book of Ezekiel describing his vision by the river Chebar.*

Kedushah *(Sacred Salutation of Holy, Holy, Holy) is a call to greet and glorify God.* KODOISH, KODOISH, KODOISH ADONAI 'TSEBAYOTH: Holy, Holy, Holy, is the Lord God of Hosts. *This is the Sacred Salutation, the Kedushah (Sacred Salutation of Holy, Holy, Holy) which is used by all the heavenly hosts to worship The Father before His Throne.*

CHAPTER 2

The highest classes of angels make inquiries about Rabbi Ishmael, which are answered by Metatron

Rabbi Ishmael said:
(1) Within the hour the eagles of The Chariot (Merkaba), the flaming Ophannim and the Seraphim of consuming fire asked Metatron: (2) "Youth! Why do you permit one born of woman to enter and see the chariot (Merkaba)? From which nation and from which tribe is this one? What is his nature?" (3) Metatron answered and said to them: "From the nation of Israel whom the Holy One, blessed be He, chose for his people from among seventy tongues (nations of the world). He is from the tribe of Levi, whom He set aside as a contribution to his name. He is from the seed of Aaron whom the Holy One, blessed be He, chose for his servant and He put upon him the crown of priesthood on Sinai." (4) Then they spoke and said: "Happy is the people (nation) that is in that position!" (Ps. 144:15).

CHAPTER 3

Metatron has 70 names, but God calls him 'Youth'

Rabbi Ishmael said:
(1) In that hour I asked Metatron, the angel, the Prince of the Presence: "What is your name?" (2) He answered me: "I have seventy names, corresponding to the seventy nations of the world and all of them are based upon the name Metatron, angel of the Presence; but my King calls me 'Youth' (Naar)."

Seventy tongues represent the 70 nations or the entirety of the known world. It is likely the word "youth" is used because Metatron is the newest and youngest being in heaven.

The 70 names are derived from the divine name or the Tetragrammaton - YHWH. Yah is a shortened version of this, meaning "God."

CHAPTER 4

Metatron is Enoch who was translated to heaven at the time of the flood.

Rabbi Ishmael said:
(1) I asked Metatron and said to him: "why does your Creator call you by seventy names? You are greater than all the princes, higher than all the angels, beloved more than all the servants, honored above all the mighty ones in kingship, greatness and glory, so why do they in the high heavens call you 'Youth'? (2) He answered and said to me: "Because I am Enoch, the son of Jared. (3) When the generation of the flood sinned and were twisted and contorted in their deeds, saying unto God: "Depart from us! We do not

want the knowledge of your ways," *(Job 21:14)*, then the Holy One, blessed be He, removed me from their midst so that I could be a witness against them in the high heavens to all the inhabitants of the world, so that they can not say: 'The Merciful One is cruel.' (4) "What sin did all those throngs of their wives, their sons and their daughters, their horses, their mules and their cattle and their property, and all the birds of the world commit so that the Holy One, blessed be He, destroyed the world, together with them in the waters of the flood?" They cannot say: "What in the generation of the flood sinned and what sin did they do so that the beasts and the birds should perish with them?" (5) Then the Holy One, blessed be He, lifted me up in their lifetime in their sight to be a witness against them to the future world. And the Holy One, blessed be He, assigned me to be a prince and a ruler among the ministering angels.

This chapter lays out the purpose of 3 Enoch and why it is so named. Metatron confirms that he is indeed Enoch, who was taken to heaven, translated into the being, Metatron. His primary purpose was to be a witness against man's sin on earth. When man or angel asked what sin was committed that all on earth should be destroyed, Enoch, now known as Metatron, would be a witness.

(6) In that hour three of the ministering angels, UZZA, 'AZZA and AZZAEL came out and accused me in the high heavens in front of the Holy One, blessed be He: And they said, "The Progenitors, The Ancient Ones, said before You with justification: Do not create man! The Holy One, blessed be He, answered and said unto them: "I have made and I will bear, and yes, I will carry and will deliver." (7) As soon as they saw me, they said before Him: "Lord of the Universe! What is this one that he should ascend to the highest heights? Is he not one from among the sons of those who perished in the days of the Flood? What is he doing in the Raqia (firmament/heavens)." What business does he have being in heaven?

Some sources have the names of the angels include Mal'aki *or* Mamlaketi. Azzael *is one of the ten heads of the heavenly Sanhedrin. Rabbinical sources have Azza and Azzael as giants. All three are said to be agents of evil who accuse man of sins. These are the fallen angels. Another theory is that* Azza *and Azzael are not individual angels but are orders of angels.*

Raquia *is a key Hebrew word in Genesis 1:6–8a. It is translated "firmament" in the King James Version and "expanse" in most Hebrew dictionaries and modern translations.* Raqa *means to spread out, beat out, or hammer as one would a malleable metal. It can also mean "plate." The Greek Septuagint translated* raqia 16 *out of 17 times with the Greek word* stereoma, *which means "a firm or solid structure." The Latin Vulgate (A.D. 382) used the Latin term "firmamentum," which also denotes solidness and firmness. The King James translators coined the word "firmament" because there was no single word equivalent in English. Today, "firmament" is usually used poetically to mean sky, atmosphere, or heavens. In modern Hebrew,* raqia *means sky or heavens. However, originally it probably meant something solid or firm that was spread out.*

Azzael is likely the same being as Azazel, the accuser angel who was the leader of the fallen ones. Etymology connects the word with the mythological Uza *and* Azael, *the fallen angels, to whom a reference is believed to be found in Gen. 6:2,4. In accordance with this etymology, the sacrifice of the goat atones for the sin of fornication of which those angels were guilty. (See 1 Enoch.) Leviticus 16:8-10: "and Aaron shall cast lots upon the two goats, one lot for the Lord and the other lot for Azazel. And Aaron shall present the goat on which the lot fell for the Lord, and offer it as a sin offering; but the goat on which the lot fell for Azazel shall be presented alive before the Lord to make atonement over it, that it may be sent away into the wilderness to Azazel."*

(8) Again, the Holy One, blessed be He, answered and said to them: "What are you, that you enter and speak in my presence? I delight more in this one than in all of you put together, and therefore he will be a prince and a ruler over you in the high heavens." (9) Then they all stood up and went out to meet me, and bowed themselves down before me and said: "Happy are you and happy is your father for your Creator favors you." (10) And because I am small and a youth among them in days, months and years, therefore they call me "Youth" (Na'ar).

CHAPTER 5
The idolatry of the generation of Enosh causes God to remove the Shekina from earth.
Idolatry was inspired by Azza, Uzza and Azzael

Rabbi Ishmael said: Metatron, the Prince of the Presence, said to me:
(1) From the day when the Holy One, blessed be He, evicted the first Adam from the Garden of Eden, and continuing from that day, the Shekina (glory) was dwelling upon a Cherub under the Tree of Life. (2) And the ministering angels were gathering together and going down from heaven in groups. From the Raqia (heaven) they went in companies from the heavens in camps to perform His will in the entire world. (3) And the first man and his children were sitting outside the gate of the Garden to see the glowing, bright appearance of the Shekina (glory). (4) For the splendor of the Shekina (glory) enfolds the world from end to end with its splendor 365,000 times that of the orb of the sun. And everyone who made use of the splendor of the Shekina, on him no flies and no gnats lit, and he was not ill and he suffered no pain. No demons could overpower him, neither were they able to injure him. (5) When the Holy One, blessed be He, went out and went in from the Garden to Eden, from Eden to the Garden, from the Garden to

Raqia (heaven) and from Raqia (heaven) to the Garden of Eden then everything and everyone saw His magnificent Shekina and they were not injured; (6) until the time of the generation of Enosh who was the head of all idol worshippers of the world.

The Shekina *was an energy or substance that was protecting those who used it from illness, demons, and even bugs.*

(7) And what did the generation of Enosh do? They went from one end of the world to the other, and each person brought silver, gold, precious stones and pearls in heaps the size of mountains and hills to make idols out of them throughout the entire world. And they erected the idols in every corner of the world: the size of each idol was 1,000 parasangs.

The generations of Enoch are as follows: Adam, Seth, Enosh, Kenan, Mahalalel, Jared, Enoch.

The highest (worst) sins, according to rabbis, are idolatry, adultery, bloodshed, and sorcery and calling God's name in vain.

A parasang is a length or measurement of distance used in what is now Iran. It varied according to the region. The north-eastern parasang was about 15,000 paces; the north-western parasang was 18,000 paces, and the one of the southwest was merely 6,000 paces. The measurement called the "true parasang" was about 9,000 paces.

(8) And they brought down the sun, the moon, planets and constellations, and placed them in front of the idols on the right side and on the left side of the idols, to attend to them just like they attend the Holy One, blessed be He, for it is written *(I Kings 22:19):* "And all the hosts of heaven were standing by him on his right hand and on his left." (9) What power was in them to enable to bring them down? They would not have been able to bring them down, if it had not been for the fact that UZZA, and AZZIEL (other sources have Azzael) taught them sorceries by which they brought them down and enslaved them.

It is obvious that the actual sun and stars were not brought down, but the angelic powers controlling them were summoned. Also, keep in mind that some cultures thought stars to be evil angels who flew across the sky. These agents were summoned and used.

(10) In that time the ministering angels accused them before the Holy One, blessed be He, saying: "Master of the World! Why do you bother with the children of men? As it is written *(Ps. 8:4)* 'What is man (Adam) that you are

mindful of him?' But it was not about Adam that this was written but about Enosh, for he is the head of the idol worshippers. (11) Why have you left the highest of the high heavens which are filled with the majesty of your glory and are high, lifted up, and exalted on the high and exalted throne in the Raqia (heaven) of Araboth (highest heaven) and are gone and dwell with the children of men who worship idols and equate you to (place you on the same level as) the idols.

The word Araboth *(highest heaven) occurs in Psalm 68:4 (Extol him who rides upon the Araboth), in which it is usually translated simply as the highest heaven. In the case of 3 Enoch, this would be the throne of God. In the Zoharic commentary on Exodus it is referred to thus:* Be glad in the presence of him who rides upon that concealed heaven which is supported by the Chayoth. *The Zohar also interprets the word to mean "mixture" because, it says, this heaven is a mixture of fire and water. This is a mystical statement of a place containing opposites, and thus everything.*

(12) Now you are on earth just like the idols. What have you to do with the inhabitants of the earth who worship idols? (13) Then the Holy One, blessed be He, lifted up His Shekina from the earth, from their midst (14) In that moment the ministering angels came. They are troops of the host and the armies of Araboth (highest heaven) in thousand camps and ten thousand host. They brought trumpets and took the horns in their hands and surrounded the Shekina with all kinds of songs. And He ascended to the high heavens, for it is written *(Ps. 47:5)*, "God is gone up with a shout, the Lord with the sound of a trumpet."

Here the presence and dwelling of God is the Shekina. *When the* Shekina *was taken, God himself left them and took his glory because of idolatry.*

CHAPTER 6

Enoch is lifted up to heaven together with the Shekina.

Rabbi Ishmael said: Metatron, the Angel, the Prince of the Presence, said to me:

(1) When the Holy One, blessed be He, wanted to lift me up on high, He first sent Anaphiel YHWH, the Prince, and he took me from their company out of their sight and carried me away in great glory on a chariot of fire pulled by horses of fire, and servants of glory. And he lifted me up to the high heavens together with the Shekina. (2) As soon as I reached the high heavens, the Holy Chayoth, the Ophannim, the Seraphim, the Cherubim, the Wheels of the Merkaba (chariot) (the Galgallim), and the ministers of the consuming fire, all smelled my scent from a distance of 365,000 myriads of parasangs, and said: "What smells like one born woman and what tastes

like a white drop? Who is this that ascends on high. He is merely a gnat among those who can divide flames of fire?"

Chayot are considered angels of fire, who hold up the throne of God and the earth itself. The angel smells the scent of a human, which he finds revolting. He can taste it in the air. The white drop refers to semen. This is an extremely hateful and distasteful statement for the angel to make.

The Holy One, blessed be He, answered and spoke to them: "My servants, my host, my Cherubim, my Ophannim, my Seraphim! Do not be displeased on account of this! Since all the children of men have denied me and my great Kingdom and have all gone worshipping idols, I have removed my Shekina from among them and have lifted it up on high. But this one whom I have taken from among them is an Elect One among (the inhabitants of) the world and he is equal to all of them (put together) in his faith, righteousness and perfection of deed and I have taken him as a tribute from my world under all the heavens.

The statement of "taking a tribute" can be better understood if one looks at Enoch as the best mankind has to offer and God took him as a an act of admiration, indicating the intended worth of mankind, had they not turned away from him. The term "Elect One" is very important. It occurs in 1 Enoch and in certain scripture regarding Christ.

CHAPTER 7
Enoch is raised upon the wings of Shekina to the place of the Throne

Rabbi Ishmael said: Metatron, the Angel, the Prince of the Presence, said to me: When the Holy One, blessed be He, took me away from the generation of the Flood, he lifted me on the wings of the wind of Shekina (his glory/understanding) to the highest heaven and brought me to the great palaces of the Araboth (highest heaven) in Raqia (heaven), where the glorious Throne of Shekina, the Merkaba (chariot), the troops of anger, the armies of vehemence, the fiery Shin'anim (accusers), and the flaming Cherubim, the burning Ophanim, the flaming servants, the flashing Chashmallin, the lightning Seraphim live. And he placed me (there) to attend daily to the Throne of Glory.

In some Jewish mystical writings the attributes of Elijah and those of Enoch are interchangeable. Here Enoch takes the same trip to heaven on a fiery chariot. Here we have various classes of angels, on which we have little information. The Chashmallin *are one of the ten classes, which are sometimes silent for a time in heaven. They cease speaking or singing when "The Word" emanates from the throne.*

Shin'anim *are a class of angel seen in lists of angelic orders. Their name seems to come from a word for "accuser" and thus could be the satans in heaven.*

CHAPTER 8

The gates of heaven opened to Metatron

Rabbi Ishmael said: Metatron, the Prince of the presence, said to me:
(1) Before he appointed me to attend the Throne of Glory, the Holy One, blessed be He, opened to me
three hundred thousand gates of Understanding
three hundred thousand gates of Wisdom
three hundred thousand gates of Life
three hundred thousand gates of Grace and Loving-kindness
three hundred thousand gates of Love
three hundred thousand gates of The Torah
three hundred thousand gates of Meekness
three hundred thousand gates of Steadfastness
three hundred thousand gates of Mercy
three hundred thousand gates of Respect for heaven

Other readings add three hundred thousand gates of Shekina,
three hundred thousand gates of fear of sin,
three hundred thousand gates of power.
The gates of steadfastness is also rendered as maintenance and refers to the sustenance to maintain life. All of man's needs come from heaven. Subtlety is rendered as wisdom but includes diplomacy and craftiness.

(2) Within the hour the Holy One, blessed be He, gave me additional wisdom and to wisdom He added understanding unto understanding, cunning unto cunning, knowledge unto knowledge, mercy unto mercy, instruction unto instruction, love unto love, loving-kindness unto loving-kindness, goodness unto goodness, meekness unto meekness, power unto power, strength unto strength, might unto might, brightness unto brightness, beauty unto beauty, splendor unto splendor, and I was honored and adorned with all these good praiseworthy things more than all the children of heaven.

Enoch has become more blessed or equipped than "all the children of heaven." Lovingkindness equates to "grace" of the New Testament.

CHAPTER 9

Enoch receives blessings from the Most High and is adorned with angelic attributes

Rabbi Ishmael said: Metatron, the Prince of the Presence, said to me: (1) After all these things the Holy One, blessed be He, put His hand on me and blessed me with 5,360 blessings. (2) And I was raised up and grew to the size of the length and width of the world. (3) And he caused 72 wings to grow on me, 36 on each side. And each wing covered the entire world. (4) And He attached to me 365 eyes: each eye was as the great luminary (moon?). (5) And He left no kind of splendor, brilliance, radiance, beauty of all the lights of the universe that He did not affix to me.

There is no direct correlation for the number 5,360. It is not evenly divisible by any other number in the chapter, but it is thought to reflect the number 365, the number of days in a solar year. The number 72 is used to reflect the number of the nations of the world and represents the known world. This is backed up by the phrase stating the wings cover the world.

CHAPTER 10

God places Metatron on a throne as ruler in the seventh hall.

Rabbi Ishmael said: Metatron, the Prince of the Presence, said to me: (1) All these things the Holy One, blessed be He, made for me. He made me a Throne, similar in form and substance to the Throne of Glory. And He spread a curtain of magnificently bright appearance over me. And it was of beauty, grace, and mercy, similar to the curtain of the Throne of the Glory; and on it were affixed all kinds of lights in the universe.

The idea of a curtain could represent the divine secrets and processes unknown and not available to others.

(2) And He placed the curtain at the door of the seventh hall and sat me down on it. (3) And the announcement went forth into every heaven, saying: "This is Metatron, my servant. I have made him a prince and ruler over all the princes of my kingdoms and over all the children of heaven, except the eight great, honored, and revered princes who are the ones called YHWH, by the name of their King."

The eight beings who are called YHWH may refer to those angels who have the Tetragrammaton as part of their name. These are highly ranked angels that are outside the normal system of authority. They are the ones God uses as his counsel.

(4) "And every angel and prince who has a word to speak to me shall now go before him and they shall speak to him instead of Me. (5) And every

command that he speaks to you in my name, you will obey, carry out, and fulfill. (Some sources add "Beware of him and do not provoke him.") For the Prince of Wisdom and the Prince of Understanding have I committed to him to instruct him in the wisdom of heavenly things and earthly things, in the wisdom of this world and of the world to come. (6) Moreover, I have set him over all the storehouses of the palaces of Araboth (highest heaven) and over all the storehouses (reserves) of life that I have in the high heavens."

CHAPTER 11
God reveals all of the great mysteries to Metatron

Rabbi Ishmael said: Metatron, the angel, the Prince of the Presence, said to me:
(1) The Holy One, blessed be He, began revealing to me all the mysteries of Torah and all the secrets of wisdom and the deep mysteries of the Perfect Law. He revealed the thoughts of all living beings and their feelings and all the secrets of the universe and all the secrets of creation. All these were revealed to me just as they are known to the Maker of Creation. (2) And I watched intently to see and understand the secrets and depths of the wonderful mystery. Before a man thought a thought in secret, I saw it and before a man made a thing I watched it. (3) And there was nothing on high or in the depth of the world that was hidden from me.

Here Metatron is given the omniscient power of God.

CHAPTER 12
God puts a crown on him and calls him "the Lesser YHWH"

Rabbi Ishmael said: Metatron, the Prince of the Presence, said to me: (1) Because of the love that the Holy One, blessed be He, loved me with, was more than all the children of heaven, He made me a garment of glory on which were affixed lights of all varieties, and He clothed me in it. (2) And He made me a robe of honor on which were affixed beauty, magnificent brilliance and majesty of all sorts. (3) And he made me a crown of royalty on which were affixed 49 stones of worth, which were like the light of the orb of the sun.

Forty-nine is a mystical number of seven sevens. The number seven represents spiritual perfection.

(4) Its splendor went out into the four coners of the Araboth (highest heaven) of Raqia (heaven), and through the seven heavens, and throughout the four corners of the world. He placed it on my head. (5) And He called

me THE LESSER YHWH in the presence of all His heavenly household; for it is written *(Ex. 22: 21):* " For my name is in him."

Without delving too deeply into Jewish mysticism, it should be pointed out that the numerical value (gematria) *of the name Metatron and that of* Shahhdai *are the same.*

CHAPTER 13
God writes with a flaming pen on Metatron's crown the letters by which heaven and earth were created

Rabbi Ishmael said: Metatron, the angel, the Glory of all heavens and the Prince of the Presence, , said to me: (1) Holy One, blessed be He, loved and cherished me with great love and mercy, more than all the children of heaven. Thus, He wrote with his finger with a flaming pen on the crown upon my head the letter by which heaven and earth, the seas and rivers, the mountains and hills, the planets and constellations, the lightning, winds, earthquakes and thunders, the snow and hail, the wind of the storm and the tempest were created. These are the letters by which all the needs of the world and all the orders of Creation were created. (2) And every single letter flashed out time after time like lightning, and time after time like lanterns, time after time like flames of fire, time after time rays like those of the rising of the sun and the moon and the planets.

There are 22 letters in the Hebrew alphabet. It is thought that all things were created when God spoke the words in the Hebrew tongue. These words are symbolized by the combinations of the 22 letters.

CHAPTER 14
All the highest of the princes and lowest angels fear and tremble at the sight of Metatron crowned.

Rabbi Ishmael said: Metatron, the Angel, the Prince of the Presence, said to me: (1) When the Holy One, blessed be He, put this crown on my head, all the Princes of Nations who are in the height of Araboth (highest heaven) of Raqia (heaven) and all the host of every heaven and even the prince of the Elim, the princes of the 'Er'ellim and the princes of the Tafsarim, who are greater than all the ministering angels who minister before the Throne of Glory, trembled before me. They shook, feared and trembled before me when they looked at me.

This is a very interesting list of angels and princes. According to Jewish mystical sources, such as the Zohar, there are ten classes of angels under Mikael (Michael). The Er'ellim *denotes a general class of angels, while the* Elim *minster before God in the high heavens. The* Tafsarim *are the princes of the* Elim.

(2) Even Sammael, the Prince of the Accusers, who is greater than all the princes of Nations on high, feared me and shook before me.

Sammael is the head of the satans or accusers. He is also the ruling angel over Rome, the archenemy of Israel.

(3) And even the angel of fire, and the angel of hail, and the angel of wind, and the angel of the lightning, and the angel of wrath, and the angel of the thunder, and the angel of the snow, and the angel of the rain; and the angel of the day, and the angel of the night, and the angel of the sun, and the angel of the moon, and the angel of the planets, and the angel of the constellations whose hands rule the world, all of them feared and shook and were frightened when they looked at me. (4) These are the names of the rulers of the world: Gabriel, the angel of fire, Baradi-el, the angel who controls hail, Ruchi-el who controls the wind, Baraqi-el who controls the lighting, Zahafi-el who controls the winds of the storm, Rahami-el who controls the thunders, Rahashi-el who controls the earthquake, Shalgiel who controls the snow, Matari-el who controls the rain, Shimshi-el who controls the planets, Rahati-el who controls the constellations. (5) And they all fell to the ground and bowed, when they saw me. And they were not able to look at me because of the majestic glory of the crown on my head.

CHAPTER 15
Metatron is transformed into fire

Rabbi Ishmael said: Metatron, the angel, the Prince of the Presence, and the Glory of all heavens, said to me: (1) As soon as the Holy One, blessed be He, took me into (His) service to attend the Throne of Glory and the Wheels (Galgallim) of the Merkaba (chariot) and the service of Shekina, suddenly my flesh was changed into flames, my muscles into flaming fire, my bones into coals of juniper wood, the light of my eye-lids into hot flames, and all of my limbs into wings of burning fire and my entire body into glowing fire.

Galgallim *(sometimes spelled* Galgalim*) are a high-ranking order of angels, the equivalent of Seraphim. They are metaphorically called "the wheels of the Merkabah" (the 'divine chariot' used to connect people to the divine) and are considered the equivalent of the* Orphanim *(Cherubim).* Galgalim *is Hebrew for "wheels."*

(2) And on my right flames were burning and dividing, on my left staves of wood (burning staves) were burning, around me the winds of storms and tempests were blowing and in front of me and behind me was roaring thunder accompanied by earthquakes.

CHAPTER 15B
(This chapter does not occur in all manuscripts. It seems to be a later addition.)

Rabbi Ishmael said me: Metatron, the Prince of the Presence and the prince ruling over all the princes, stands before Him who is greater than all the Elohim. And he enters in under the Throne of Glory. And he has a great dwelling of light on high. And he brings into existence the fire of deafness and places it in the ears of the Holy Chayoth, so that they cannot hear the voice of the Word that sounds from the mouth of the Divine Majesty.

This may indicate that he goes into the Holy of Holies where he worships and has his own sanctuary.

The idea of more than one Elohim is not new. It is addressed in Psalm 82, a Psalm of Asaph: 1 God stands in the council of the gods; he judges among the gods. 2 How long will you judge unjustly, and show preference to the wicked? Selah. 3 Judge the poor and the orphans; do righteousness to the afflicted and dispossessed. 4 Deliver the poor and oppressed; save them from the hand of the evil. 5 They do not know and they have no understanding; they walk about in darkness. All the foundations of the earth are shaken. 6 I said, "You are gods, and children of Elyon, every one of you." 7 But you will die like mortals, and fall like one of the princes. 8 Rise up, O God, and judge the earth, for you have inherited all the nations.

This section seems to preserve a fragment of a book called, "The Ascension of Moses." The chashmal *is the highest point of heaven. It is like a zenith line out of which a window opens.*

(2) And when Moses ascended on high, he fasted 121 fasts, until the places where the chashmal live were opened to him; and he saw that the place was as white as a Lion's heart and he saw the companies of the host round about him, which could not be counted. And they wished to burn him. But Moses prayed for mercy, first for Israel and then for himself: and He who was sitting on the Merkaba (chariot) opened the windows above the heads of the Cherubim. And a host of 1800 helpers along with the Prince of the Presence, Metatron, all went out to meet Moses. They took the prayers of Israel and placed them like a crown on the head of the Holy One, blessed be He.
(3) The they said *(Deut. 6:4):* "Hear, O Israel; the Lord our God is one Lord." And their face were shining and they rejoiced over Shekina and they said to Metatron: "What are these? And to whom do they give all honor and glory?" And they answered: "To the Glorious Lord of Israel." And they spoke: Hear, O Israel: the Lord, our God is one Lord. To Who else shall be given this abundance of honor and majesty but to You YHWH, the Divine Majesty, the King, the living and eternal one." (4) In that moment Akatriel Ya Yehod Sebaoth (a name of the most high) spoke and said to Metatron,

the Prince of the Presence and said, "Let no prayer that he prays before me return to him empty (not done). Hear his prayer and fulfill his desire whether it is great or small (5) Then Metatron, the Prince of the presence, said to Moses, "Son of Amram! Do not be afraid. God delights in you. He asks you what you desire from the Glory and Majesty. Your face shines from one end of the world to the other." But Moses answered him: "I fear that I should bring guiltiness upon myself." Metatron said to him, "Receive the letters of the oath, which makes a covenant that cannot be broken."

Metatron is moving through time to and from the time of Moses. The letters make up the divine names, which are eternal.

CHAPTER 16

This continues the additional material.

His privilege of presiding on a Throne are taken.

Rabbi Ishmael said: Metatron, the Angel, the Prince of the Presence, the Glory of all heaven, said to me: (1) At first I was sitting on a large Throne at the door of the seventh hall. There, by authority of the Holy One, blessed be He, I was judging the children of heaven and the servants on high. And I judged Greatness, Kingship, Dignity, Rulership, Honor and Praise, and the Diadem and Crown of Glory for all the princes of kingdoms. While I was presiding in the Court of the Sky (Yeshiba), the princes of nations were standing before me, on my right and on my left, by authority of the Holy One, blessed be He. (2) But when Acher came to see the vision of the Merkaba (chariot) and locked his eyes on me, he was afraid and shook before me so much that his soul was departing from him, because of fear, horror and dread of me, when he saw me sitting upon a throne like a king with all the ministering angels standing by my side serving me and all the princes of kingdoms adorned with crowns all around me. (3) At that moment he opened his mouth and said, "Surely there are two Divine Powers in heaven!" (4) Then the Divine Voice went out from heaven from the Shekina and said: "Return, you backsliding children (Jer.3:22), except for Acher!" (5) Then Anieyel came (Other sources have "Anaphiel YHWH), the Prince, the honored, glorified, beloved, wonderful, revered and fearful one, as ordered by the Holy One, blessed be He and beat me sixty times with whips of fire and made me stand to my feet.

Anieyel , *or* Anaphiel YHWH *is higher in status than Metatron. It is possible the* Anieyel *is the angel who punishes. The purpose of this chapter is to refute the heresy of the Rabbi called Acher, who believed that there were now two deities in heaven, God and Metatron. To show Metatron is not a deity, God sends in a higher angel to take him off his throne and beat him, proving Metatron is not God, nor is he a god. The chapter goes on to call all of Israel to return to God, except for Acher, who has committed an unforgivable sin against the monotheists and against God.*

CHAPTER 17
The princes of the seven heavens, and of the sun, moon, planets and constellations

Rabbi Ishmael said: Metatron, the angel, the Prince of the Presence, the glory of all heavens, said to me: (1) The number of princes are seven. They are the great, beautiful, wonderful, honored, and revered ones. They are assigned over the seven heavens, And these are they: MIKAEL (Michael), GABRIEL, SHATQIEL, BAKARIEL, BADARIEL, PACHRIEL. *(Some sources omit Parchriel and add Sidriel.)* (2) And every one of them is the prince of the host of one heaven. And each one of them is accompanied by 496,000 groups of ten-thousand ministering angels.

496 is the numerical value of the word Malkut *(kingdom). These 496,000 angels are the ones who sing of the glory of God, singing "Holy, Holy. Holy."*

(3) MIKAEL is the great prince assigned to ruler over the seventh heaven, the highest one, which is in the Araboth (highest heaven). Gabriel is the prince of the host assigned to rule over the sixth heaven which is in Makon. SHATAQIEL is the prince of the host assigned to rule over the fifth heaven which is in Makon. SHAHAQIEL is the prince of the host assigned to rule over the fourth heaven which is in Zebul. BADARIEL is the prince of the host assigned to rule over the third heaven which is in Shehaqim. BARAKIEL is the prince of the host assigned to rule over the second heaven which is in the height of Raqia (heaven). PAZRIEL is the prince of the host assigned to rule over the first heaven which is in Wilon (or Velum, as the first heaven is called), which is in Shamayim. (4) Under them in GALGALLIEL, the prince who is assigned as ruler over the orb (galgal) of the sun, and with him are 96 great and revered angels who moves the sun in Raqia (heaven) a distance of 365,000 parasangs each day. (5) Under them is OPHANNIEL, the prince who is set the globe (Ophan) of the moon. And with him are 88 (some have it as 68) angels who move the globe of the moon 354 thousand parasangs every night at the time when the moon stands in the East at its turning point. And the moon is situated in the East at its turning point in the fifteenth day of every month. (6) Under them is RAHATIEL, the prince who is appointed to rule over the constellations. He is accompanied by 72 great and revered angels. And why is he called RAHATIEL? Because he makes the stars run (marhit) in their orbits and courses, which is 339 thousand parasangs every night from the East to West, and from West to East. The Holy One, blessed be He, has made a tent for all of them, for the sun, the moon, the planets and the stars, and they travel in it at night from the West to the East. (7) Under them is KOKBIEL, the prince who is assigned to rule over all the planets. And with him are 365,000 groups of ten-thousand ministering angels, great and revered ones who

move the planets from city to city and from province to province in Raqia (the heaven) of heavens. (8) And ruling over them are seventy-two princes of nations (kingdoms) on high corresponding to the seventy-two nations of the world. And all of them are crowned with crowns of royalty and clothed in royal clothes and wrapped in royal robes. And all of them are riding on royal horses and holding royal scepters in their hands. In front of each of them when he is traveling in Raqia (heaven), royal servants are running with great glory and majesty just as on earth the Princes are traveling in chariots with horsemen and great armies and in glory and greatness with praise, song and honor.

CHAPTER 18
The order of ranks of the angels is established by the homage

Rabbi Ishmael said: Metatron, the Angel, the Prince of the Presence, the glory of all heaven, said to me: (1) THE ANGELS OF THE FIRST HEAVEN, when (ever) they see their prince, they dismount from their horses and bow themselves. And THE PRINCE OF THE FIRST HEAVEN, when he sees the prince of the second heaven, he dismounts, removes the glorious crown from his head and bows himself to the ground. AND THE PRINCE OF THE SECOND HEAVEN, when he sees the prince of the third heaven, he removes the glorious crown form his head and bows himself to the ground. AND THE PRINCE OF THE THIRD HEAVEN, when he sees the prince of the fourth heaven, he removes the glorious crown form his head and bows himself to the ground. AND THE PRINCE OF THE FOURTH HEAVEN, when he sees the prince of the fifth heaven, he removes the glorious crown form his head and bows himself to the ground. AND THE PRINCE OF THE FIFTH HEAVEN, when he sees the prince of the sixth heaven, he removes the glorious crown from his head and bows himself to the ground. AND THE PRINCE OF THE SIXTH HEAVEN, when he sees the prince of the seventh heaven he removes the glorious crown from his head and bows himself to the ground. (2) AND THE PRINCE OF THE SEVENTH HEAVEN, when he sees THE SEVENTY-TWO PRINCES OF KINGDOMS, he removes the glorious crown from his head and bows himself to the ground.

The number 70 appears as does the number 72. It is possible the difference can be explained by the 70 angels along with two leaders, such as Mikael (Michael) and Sammael. In the following section the names of the angels do not follow their function, as in the prior portion of the book. The names are obscure, and it is difficult to understand their meanings. The expression "bows himself to the ground" and "bow themselves" likely indicates a complete kneeling position with the head touching the earth.

(3) And the seventy two princes of kingdoms, when they see The door keepers of the first hall in the ARABOTH RAQIA in the highest heaven, they remove the royal crown from their head and bow themselves. And The door keepers of the first hall, when they see the doorkeepers of the second hall, they remove the glorious crown form their head and bow themselves. The door keepers of the second hall, when they see the door keepers of the third hall, they remove the glorious crown from their head and bow themselves. The door keepers of the third hall, when they see the door keepers of the fourth hall, they remove the crown from their head and bow themselves. The door keepers of the fourth hall, when they see the door keepers of the fifth hall, they remove the glorious crown from their head and bow themselves. The door keepers of the fifth hall, when they see the doorkeepers of the sixth hall, they remove the crown from their head and fall to their face. The door keepers of the sixth hall, when they see the The door keepers of the seventh hall, they remove the glorious crown from their head and bow themselves. (4) And the door keepers of the seventh hall, when they see The Four Great Princes, the honored ones, who are appointed over the four Camps Of SHEKINA, they remove the crowns of glory from their head and bow themselves. (5) And the four great prince, when they see TAGHAS, the prince, great and honored with song (and) praise, at the head of all the children of heaven, they remove the glorious crown from their head and bow themselves. (6) And Taghas, the great and honored prince, when he sees BARATTIEL, the great prince of three fingers in the height of Araboth, the highest heaven, he removes the glorious crown from his head and bows himself to the ground.

To derive three fingers in height, hold your hand out at arm's length with three fingers held out horizontally in front of your eyes. This is the measurement.

(7) And Barattiel, the great prince, when he sees HAMON, the great prince, the fearful and honored, beautiful and terrible, he who makes all the children of heaven to shake, when the time draws near that is set for the saying of the 'Thrice Holy', he removes the glorious crown form his head and bows himself to the ground. For it is written *(Isa.33:3)*, "At noise of the confusion at the anxious preparation of the salutation of "Holy, Holy, Holy" the people are fled; at the lifting up of yourself the nations are scattered," (8) And Hamon, the great prince, when he sees TUTRESSIEL, the great prince he removes the glorious crown from his head and bows himself to the ground. (9) And Tutresiel YHWH, the great prince, when he sees ATRUGIEL, the great prince, he removes the glorious crown from his head and bows himself to the ground. (10) And Aatrugiel the great prince, when he sees NA'ARIRIEL YHWH, the great prince, he removes the glorious crown from his head and bows himself to the ground. (11) And Na'aririel YHWH, the great prince when he see SAANIGIEL, the great prince, he

removes the glorious crown from his head and bows himself to the ground. (12) And Sasnigiel YHWH, when he sees ZAZRIEL YHWH, the great prince, he removes the glorious crown from his head and bows himself to the ground. (13) And Zazriel YHWH, the prince, when he sees GEBURATIEL YHWH, the prince, he removes the glorious crown from his head and bows himself to the ground. (14) And Geburatiel YHWH, the prince, when he sees ARAPHIEL YHWH, the prince, he removes the glorious crown from his head and bows himself to the ground. (15) And Araphiel YHWH, the prince, when he sees ASHRUYLU, the prince, who presides in all the sessions of the children of heaven, he removes the glorious crown from his head and bows himself to the ground. (16) And Ashruylu YHWH, the prince, when he sees GALLISUR YHWH, THE PRINCE, WHO REVEALS ALL THE SECRETS OF THE LAW (Torah), he removes the glorious crown from his head and bows himself to the ground. (17) And Gallisur YHWH, the prince, when he sees ZAKZAKIEL YHWH , the prince who is appointed to write down the merits of Israel on the Throne of Glory, he removes the glorious crown form his head and bows himself to the ground. (18) And Zakzakiel YHWH, the great prince, when he sees ANAPHIEL YHWH, the prince who keeps the keys of the heavenly halls, he removes the glorious crown from his head and bows himself to the ground. Why is he called by the name of Anaphiel? Because the shoulders of his honor and majesty and his crown and his splendor and his brilliance overshadows all the chambers of Araboth (highest heaven) of Raqia (heaven) on high even as the Maker of the World overshadows them. Regarding the Maker of the world, it is written that His glory covered the heavens, and the earth was full of His praise. The honor and majesty of Anaphiel cover all the glories of Araboth (highest heaven) the highest.

Araphiel *means "neck or strength of God."* Ashruylu *means "to cause to rest/dwell." It is one of the names of the Godhead.* Gallisur *means "reveal the secrets of the Law." He reveals the reasons and secrets of the Creator.* Raziel *means "secrets of God." He hears the divine decrees.* Anaphiel *means "branch of God."* Zakzakiel *means "merit of God." The glorious crowns signify honor and status.*

(19) And when he sees SOTHER ASHIEL YHWH, the prince, the great, fearful and honored one, he removes the glorious crown from his head and bows himself to the ground. Why is he called Sother Ashiel? Because he is assigned to rule over the four heads of the river of fire, which are beside the Throne of Glory; and every single prince who goes out or enters before the Shekina, goes out or enters only by his permission. For the seals of the river of fire are entrusted to him. And furthermore, his height is 7000 groups of ten-thousand parasangs. And he stirs up the fire of the river; and he goes out and enters before the Shekina to expound what is recorded concerning the inhabitants of the world. According for it is written *(Dan. 7:10):* "the

judgment was set, and the books were opened." (20) And Sother Ashiel the prince, when he sees SHOQED CHOZI, the great prince, the mighty, terrible and honored one, he removes the glorious crown from his head and falls upon his face. And why is he called Shoqed Chozi? Because he weighs all the merits of man on a scale in the presence of the Holy One, blessed be He. (21) And when he sees ZEHANPURYU YHWH, the great prince, the mighty and terrible one, honored, glorified and feared in the entire heavenly household, he removes the glorious crown from his head and bows himself to the ground. Why is he called Zehanpuryu? Because he commands the river of fire and pushes it back to its place. (22) And when he sees AZBUGA YHWH, the great prince, glorified, revered, honored, adorned, wonderful, exalted, loved and feared among all the great princes who know the mystery of the Throne of Glory, he removes the glorious crown from his head and bows himself to the ground. Why is he called Azbuga? Because in the future he will clothe the righteous and pious of the world with garments of life and wrap them in the cloak of life, so that they can live an eternal life in them. (23) And when he sees the two great princes, the strong one and the glorified one who are standing above him, he removes the glorious crown from his head and bows himself to the ground. And these are the names of the two princes: SOPHERIEL YHWH (Sopheriel YHWH the Killer), the great prince, the honored, glorified, blameless, venerable, ancient and mighty one. (24) Why is he called Sopheriel YHWH who kills (Sopheriel YHWH the Killer)? Because he is assigned to control the books of the dead, so that everyone, when the day of his death draws near, is written by him in the books of the dead. Why is he called Sopheriel YHWH who makes alive (Sopheriel YHWH the Lifegiver)? Because he is assigned control over the books of life, so that every one whom the Holy One, blessed be He, will bring into life, he writes him in the Book of Life, by authority of The Divine Majesty. Perhaps he might say: "Since the Holy One, blessed be He, is sitting on a throne, they are also sitting when writing." The Scripture teaches us *(I Kings 22:19, 2 Chron. 28:18)*, "And all the host of heaven are standing by him." They are called "The host of heaven" in order to show us that even the Great Princes and all like them in the high heavens, fulfill the requests of the Shekina in no other way than standing. But how is it possible that they are able to write, when they are standing?

This section is very important to Jewish mystics and Cabbalists in that it sets the balance within the act of judgment between mercy and justice. If one were to strip down to the barest essentials the spiritual life of a person some may conclude it is to find balance between mercy and justice. The books of life and death are records of the birth and death of individuals. This is not the same as the Book of Life referred to in the Bible, which contains the names of the righteous.

(25) It is done thusly. One is standing on the wheels of the tempest and the other is standing on the wheels of the wind of the storm. The one is clothed in kingly garments, the other is clothed in kingly garments. The one is wrapped in a mantle of majesty and the other is wrapped in a mantle of majesty. One is crowned with a royal crown, and the other is crowned with a royal crown. The one's body is full of eyes, and the other's body is full of eyes. One looks like lightning, and the other looks like lightning. The eyes of the one are like the sun in its power, and the eyes of the other are like the sun in its power. The one's height is the height of the seven heavens, and the other's height is the height of the seven heavens. The wings of the one are as many as the days of the year, and the wings of the other are as many as the days of the year. The wings of one reach over the width of Raqia (heaven), and the wings of the other reach over the width of Raqia (heaven). The lips of one look like the gates of the East, and the lips of the other look like the gates of the East. The tongue of the one is as high as the waves of the sea, and the tongue of the other is as high as the waves of the sea. From the mouth of the one a flame proceeds, and from the mouth of the other a flame proceeds. From the mouth of the one lightning is emitted and from the mouth of the other lightning is emitted. From the sweat of one fire is kindled, and from the sweat of the other fire is kindled. From the one's tongue a torch is burning, and from the tongue of the other a torch is burning. On the head of the one there is a sapphire stone, and upon the head of the other there is a sapphire stone. On the shoulders of the one there is a wheel of a swift Cherubim, and on the shoulders of the other there is a wheel of a swift Cherubim. One has in his hand a burning scroll; the other has in his hand a burning scroll. The length of the scroll is 3,000 times ten-thousand parasangs; the size of the pen is 3000 times ten-thousand of parasangs; the size of every single letter that they write is 365 parasangs.

Sopheriel *is the prince appointed over the Book of Life. The name means "scribe of God."* Azbuga *is a messenger. The name denoted strength, as many angelic names do.* Zehanpuryu *means "the face of fear." To be full of eyes is a symbol of omniscience. Eastern gates were large, tall structures. The two symbolic uses of fire are destruction and purification.*

CHAPTER 19
Rikbiel, the prince of the wheels of the Merkaba (chariot)
The Sacred Salutation of Holy, Holy, Holy

Rabbi Ishmael said: Metatron, the Angel, the Prince of the Presence, said to me: (1) Above these three angels, who are these great princes, there is one Prince, distinguished, revered, noble, glorified, adorned, fearful, fearless, mighty, great, uplifted, glorious, crowned, wonderful, exalted, blameless, loved, like a ruler, he is high and lofty, ancient and mighty, there is none among the princes like him. His name is RIKBIEL YHWH, the great and revered prince who is standing by Merkaba (chariot). (2) And why is he called RIKBIEL? Because he is assigned to rule over the wheels of the Merkaba (chariot), and they are given to his authority. (3) And how many are the wheels? Eight; two in each direction. And there are four winds compassing them round about. And these are their names: "the Winds of the Storm," "the Tempest," "the Strong Wind," and "the Wind of Earthquake." (4) And under them four rivers of fire are constantly running and there is one river of fire on each side. And around them, between the rivers, four clouds are affixed. They are "clouds of fire," "clouds of torches," "clouds of coal," "clouds of brimstone" and they are standing by their wheels.

There is much number symbolism here. Some Eastern cultures believe there are only eight possible directions of movement. They could be looked at as north, south, east, west, up, down, in, out. Anything else must be a combination of these. Four is the number of limits and testing. Two is the number of assistance, witness, or duplicity.

(5) And the feet of the Chayoth are resting on the wheels. And between two wheels an earthquake is roaring and thunder is sounding. (6) And when the time draws near for the recital of the Song, numerous wheels are moved, the numerous clouds tremble, all the chieftains (shallishim) become afraid, and all the horsemen (parashim) become angry, and all the mighty ones (gibborim) are excited, all the host (seba'im) are frightened, and all the troops (gedudim) are fearful, all the appointed ones (memunnim) hurry away, all the princes (sarim) and armies (chayelim) are confused, all the servants (mesharetim) faint and all the angels (mal'akim) and divisions (degalim) suffer with pain. (7) And one wheel makes a sound to be heard by the other and one Cherub speaks to another, one Chayya to another, one Seraph to another (saying) *(Ps. 68:5)*, "Extol to him that rides in Araboth (highest heaven), by his name Jah (Yah) and rejoice before him!"

The name Jah (Yah) is a shortened and "speakable" version of YHWH or Jehovah.

CHAPTER 20
CHAYYLIEL, the prince of the Chayoth

Rabbi Ishmael said: Metatron, the angel, the Prince of the Presence, said to me: (1) Above these there is one great and mighty prince. His name is CHAYYLIEL YHWH, a noble and honorable prince, a prince before whom all the children of heaven tremble, a prince who is able to swallow up the entire earth in one moment at a single mouthful. (2) And why is he called CHAYYLIEL YHWH? Because he is assigned to rule over the Holy Chayoth and he strikes the Chayoth with lashes of fire: and glorifies them, when they give praise and glory and rejoicing and he causes them to hurry and say

"Holy" "Blessed be the Glory of YHWH from His place!" (The Kedushah - Sacred Salutation of Holy, Holy, Holy).

CHAPTER 21
The Chayoth

Rabbi Ishmael said: Metatron, the angel, the Prince of the Presence, said to me: (1) The Four Chayoth correspond to the four winds. Each Chayya is as big as the space of the entire world. And each one has four faces; and each face is like the face of the East (sunrise). (2) Each one has four wings and each wing is like the tent (ceiling) of the universe. (3) And each one has faces in the middle of faces and wings in the middle of wings. The size of the faces is 248 faces, and the size of the wings is 365 wings. (4) And every one is crowned with 2000 crowns on his head. And each crown is like the rainbow in the cloud. And its splendor is like the magnificence of the circle of the sun. And the sparks that go out from every one are like the glory of the morning star (planet Venus) in the East.

CHAPTER 22
KERUBIEL, the Prince of the Cherubim.
Description of the Cherubim

Rabbi Ishmael said: Metatron, the angel, the Prince of the Presence, said to me: (1) Above these there is one prince, noble, wonderful, strong, and praised with all kinds of praise. His name is CHERUBIEL YHWH, a mighty prince, full of power and strength, a prince of highness, and Highness (is) with him, a righteous Prince, and Righteousness (is) with him, a holy prince, and holiness (is) with him, a prince of glorified in (by) thousand host, exalted by ten thousand armies (2) At his anger the earth trembles, at his anger the camps (of armies) are moved, from fear of him the foundations are shaken, at his chastisement the Araboth (highest heaven) trembles. (3) His stature is full of (burning) coals. The height is that of the seven heavens and the breadth of his stature is like the sea. (4) The opening of his mouth is like a lamp of fire. His tongue is a consuming fire. His eyebrows are like the splendor of the lightning. His eyes are like sparks of bright light. His face is like a burning fire. (5) And there is a crown of holiness upon his head on which the Explicit Name is graven, and lightning proceeds from it. And the bow of the Shekina is between his shoulders. And his sword is like lightning; and on his thighs there are arrows like flames, and upon his armor and shield there is a consuming fire, and on his neck there are coals of burning juniper wood and (also) around him (there are coals of burning juniper).

The bow can represent a rainbow but it is certainly a weapon of great power. Juniper is a symbol of strength and longevity. It was said to shelter the prophet Elijah from Queen Jezebel's pursuit. Tales in the apocryphal books tell of how the infant Jesus and his parents were hidden from King Herod's soldiers by a juniper during their flight into Egypt.

(7) And the splendor of Shekina is on his face; and the horns of the majesty on his wheels; and a royal diadem upon his head. (8) And his body is full of eyes. And wings are covering the entire of his high stature (lit. the height of his stature is all wings). (9) On his right hand a flame is burning, and on his left a fire is glowing; and coals are burning from it. And burning staves go forth from his body. And lightning is projected from his face. With him there is always thunder within thunder, and by his side there is a never ending earthquake within an earthquake. (10) And the two princes of the Merkaba (chariot) are together with him. (11) Why is he called CHERUBIEL YHWH, the Prince. Because he is assigned to rule over the chariot of the Cherubim. And the mighty Cherubim are subject to his authority. And he adorns the crowns on their heads and polishes the diadem upon their heads (skulls). (12) He increases the glory of their appearance. And he glorifies the beauty of their majesty. And he expands the greatness of their honor. He makes their songs of praise to be sung. He makes the strength of their beauty increase. He causes the brightness of their glory to shine forth. He makes their goodness, mercy, and lovingkindess to grow. He separates their radiance so it show even more. He makes the beauty of their mercy even more beautiful. He glorifies their upright majesty. He sings the order of their praise to establish the dwelling place of Him who dwells on the Cherubim. (13) And the Cherumim are standing by the Holy Chayoth, and their wings are raised up to their heads (are as the height of their heads) and Shekina is (resting) upon them and the bright Glory is upon their faces and songs of praise are in their mouth and their hands are under their wings and their feet are covered by their wings and horns of glory are upon their heads and the splendor of Shekina on their face and Shekina is resting on them and sapphire stones surround them and columns of fire are on their four sides and columns of burning staves are beside them. (14) There is one sapphire on one side and another sapphire on the other side and under the sapphires there are coals of burning juniper wood. (15) And a Cherub is standing in each direction but the wings of the Cherubim surround each other above their heads in glory; and they spread them to sing with them a song to him that inhabits the clouds and to praise the fearful majesty of the king of kings with their wings.

The sound coming from their wings is heard as a song. This hearkens back to a description of Lucifer, before the fall. It was said that his body had instruments made within it, which made beautiful music.

(16) And CHERUBIEL YHWH, is the prince who is assigned to rule over them. He arrays them in proper, beautiful and pleasant orders and he exalts

them in all manner of exaltation, dignity and glory. And he hurries them in glory and might to do the will of their Creator every moment. Above their high heads continually dwells the glory of the high king "who dwells on the Cherubim."

Names in this section are related to the station of the angels. Chayyliel *is the prince of the Chayyoth;* Cherubiel *or* Kerubiel *is the prince of the* Kerubim *or* Cherubim, *and so on.*

CHAPTER 22-B

Rabbi Ishmael said to me: Metatron, the angel, the Prince of the Presence, said to me: (1) How are the angels standing on high? He said: A bridge is placed from the beginning of the doorway to the end, like a bridge that is placed over a river for every one to pass over it. And three ministering angels surround it and sing a song before YHWH, the God of Israel. And standing before it are the lords of dread and captains of fear, numbering a thousand times a thousand and ten thousand times ten thousand, and they sing praises and hymns before YHWH, the God of Israel. (3) Many bridges are there. There are bridges of fire and many bridges of hail. Also many rivers of hail, numerous storehouses of snow, and many wheels of fire. (4) And how many are the ministering angels are there? Twelve thousand times ten-thousand: six-thousand time ten-thousand above and six (thousand times ten-thousand) below. And twelve thousand are the storehouses of snow, six above and six below. And 24 times ten thousand wheels of fire, 12 times ten-thousand above and 12 times ten thousand below. And they surround the bridges and the rivers of fire and the rivers of hail. And there are numerous ministering angels, forming entries, for all the creatures that are standing in the midst thereof, over against the paths of Raqia (heaven) Shamayim. (5) What does YHWH, the God of Israel, the King of Glory do? The Great and Fearful God, mighty in strength, covers His face. (6) In Araboth (highest heaven) are 660,000 times ten-thousand angels of glory standing over against the Throne of Glory and the divisions of flaming fire. And the King of Glory covers His face; for else the Araboth (highest heaven) of Raqia (heaven) would be torn apart from its center because of the majesty, splendor, beauty, radiance, loveliness, brilliancy, brightness and Excellency of the appearance of (the Holy One,) blessed be He. (7) There are innumerable ministering angels carrying out his will, many kings and princes in the Araboth (highest heaven) of His delight. They are angels who are revered among the rulers in heaven, distinguished, adorned with song and they bring love to the minds of those who are frightened by the splendor of Shekina, and their eyes are dazzled by the shining beauty of their King, their faces grow black and their strength fails. (8) There are rivers of joy, streams of gladness, rivers of happiness, streams of victory, rivers of life, streams of friendship and they flow over and go out from in front of the

Throne of Glory and grow large and wend their way through the gates on the paths to Araboth (highest heaven) of Raqia (heaven) at the voice of shouting and music of the CHAYYOTH, at the voice of the rejoicing of the cymbals of his OPHANNIM and at the melody of the cymbals of His Cherubim. And they grow great and go out with noise and with the sound of the hymn: "HOLY, HOLY, HOLY, IS THE LORD OF HOST; THE WHOLE EARTH IS FULL OF HIS GLORY!"

CHAPTER 22 -C

Rabbi Ishmael said: Metatron, the Prince of the Presence said to me: (1) What is the distance between one bridge and another? Tens of thousands of parasangs. They rise up tens of thousands of parasangs , and the go down tens of thousands of parasangs. (2) The distance between the rivers of dread and the rivers of fear is 22 times ten-thousand parasangs; between the rivers of hail and the rivers of darkness 36 times ten-thousand paragangs; between the chambers of lightnings and the clouds of compassion 42 times ten-thousand parasangs; between the clouds of compassion and the Merkaba (chariot) 84 times ten-thousand parasangs; between the Merkaba (chariot) and the Cherubim 148 times ten-thousand parasangs; between the Cherubim and the Ophannim 24 times ten-thousand parasangs; between the chambers of chambers and the Holy Chayoth 40,000 times ten-thousand parasangs; between one wing (of the Chayoth) and another 12 times ten-thousand parasangs; and the breadth of each one wing is of that same measure; and the distance between the Holy Chayoth and the Throne of Glory is 30,000 times ten-thousand parasangs. (3) And from the foot of the Throne to the seat there are 40,000 times ten-thousand parasangs. And the name of Him that sits on it: let the name be sanctified! (4) And the arches of the Bow are set above the Araboth (highest heaven), and they are 1000 thousands and 10,000 times ten thousands of parasangs high. Their measure is after the measure of the 'Irin and Qaddishin (the Watchers and the Holy Ones). As it is written, *(Gen. 9:13),* "My bow I have set in the cloud." It is not written here "I will set" but "I have set," that is to say; I have already set it in the clouds that surround the Throne of Glory. As His clouds pass by, the angels of hail turn into burning coal. (5) And a voice of fire goes down from the Holy Chayoth. And because of the breath of that voice they *run (Ezek. 1:14)* to another place, fearing that it could command them to go; and they return for fear that it may injure them from the other side. Therefore "they run and return." (6) And these arches of the Bow are more beautiful and radiant than the radiance of the sun during the summer solstice. And they are brighter (whiter) than a flaming fire and they are large and beautiful. (7) Above the arches of the Bow are the wheels of the Ophannim. Their height is 1000 thousand and 10,000 times 10,000 units of measure after the measure of the Seraphim and the Troops (Gedudim).

The Irin *and* Qaddishin *are the highest ranked of all the angels. They constitute the supreme council of heaven. These angels are the twin sentinels. The Irin decrees while the Qaddishin sentences every case in the court of heaven. In Daniel 4:14 we find references. "By decree of the sentinels is this decided, by order of the holy ones, this sentence, that all who live may know that the most High rules over the kingdom of men: he can give it to whom he will, or set over it the lowliest of men. For the words rendered "of the holy god," we read in Chaldee, the language in which Daniel was composed, the words* elain cadisin, *which mean "holy gods," not "holy God."(*St. Jerome, *Commentary on Daniel.)*

CHAPTER 23
The winds are blowing under the wings of the Cherubim

Rabbi Ishmael said: Metatron, the Angel, the Prince of the Presence, said to me: (1) There are numerous winds blowing under the wings of the Cherubim. There blows "the Brooding Wind," for it is written *(Gen. 1: 2):* "and the wind of God was brooding upon the face of the waters." (2) There blows "the Strong Wind," as it is said *(Ex.14: 21):* "and the Lord caused the sea to go back by a strong east wind all that night." (3) There blows "the East Wind" for it is written *(Ex. 10: 13):* "the east wind brought the locusts." (4) There blows "the Wind of Quails for it is written *(Num. 9: 31):* "And there went forth a wind from the Lord and brought quails." (5) There blows "the Wind of Jealousy" for it is written (Num. 5:14): "And the wind of jealousy came upon him." (6) There blows the "Wind of Earthquake" and it is written *(I Kings. 19: 11):* "and after that the wind of the earthquake; but the Lord was not in the earthquake." (7) There blows the "Wind of YHWH" for it is written *(Ex. 37: 1):* "and he carried me out by the wind of YHWH and set me down." (8) There blows the "Evil Wind" for it is written *(I Sam. 14: 23):* "and the evil wind departed from him." (9) There blows the "Wind of Wisdom" and the "Wind of Understanding" and the "Wind of Knowledge" and the "Wind of the Fear of YHWH" for it is written *(Is. 11: 2):* "And the wind of YHWH shall rest upon him; the wind of wisdom and understanding, the wind of counsel and might, the wind of knowledge and the fear of YHWH." (10) There blows the "Wind of Rain," for it is written *(Prov. 25: 23)* "the north wind brings forth rain." (11) There blows the "Wind of Lightning," for it is written (Jer. 10: 13): "he makes lightning for the rain and brings forth the wind out of his storehouses." (12) There blows the "Wind, Which Breaks the Rocks," for it is written *(1 Kings 19: 11):* "the Lord passed by and a great and strong wind (rent the mountains and break in pieces the rocks before the Lord.) (13) There blows the Wind of Assuagement of the Sea," for it is written *(Gen. 7:1):* "and God made a wind to pass over the earth, and the waters assuaged." (14) There blows the "Wind of Wrath," for it is written *(Job1: 19):* 'and behold there came a great wind from the wilderness and smote the four corners of the house and it fell." (15) There blows the "Wind of Storms," for it is written *(Ps. 148: 8):* "Winds of the storm, fulfilling his word." (16) And Satan is standing among these winds, for "the winds of the storm" is nothing else but "Satan" and all these winds do not blow but under the wings of Cherubim, for it is written *(Ps. 18.11):* "and he rode upon a cherub and flew, yes, and he flew with speed upon wings of the wind." (17) And where do all these winds go? The Scripture teaches us, that they go out from under the wings of the Cherubim and descend on the globe of the sun, for it is written *(Eccl. 1:6):* "The wind goes toward the south and turns around to the north; it turns around over and over in its course and the wind returns again to its route." And from the orb of the sun they return and go down on to the rivers and the seas, then up on the mountains and up on the hills, for it is written *(Amos 4:12-13):* "For lo, he that forms the mountains and creates the wind." (18) And from the mountains and the hills they return and go down again to the seas and the rivers; and from the seas and the rivers they return and go up to the cities and provinces: and from the cities and provinces they return and go down into the Garden, and from the Garden they return and descend to Eden, for it is written *(Gen. 3:8)* "walking in the Garden in the wind (cool) of day." In the middle of the Garden they come together and blow from one side to the other. In the Garden they are perfumed with spices from the Garden in its most remote parts, until the winds again separate from each other. Filled with the odor of the pure spices, the winds bring the aroma from the most remote parts of Eden. They carry the spices of the Garden to the righteous and godly who in time to come will inherit the Garden of Eden and the Tree of life, for it is written *(Songs of Solomon 4:16):* "Awake, O north wind; and come you south; blow upon my garden and eat his precious fruits."

The same word used for "wind" is also used for "spirit." It is interesting to read the same verses using the word "spirit." It should also be noted that when certain attributes are associated with "wind," such as the wind of jealousy, it could be seen to be an agent of God, such as an angel or demon.

CHAPTER 24
The different chariots of the Holy One, blessed be He

Rabbi Ishmael said: Metatron, the Angel, the Prince of the Presence, the glory of all heaven, said to me: (1) The Holy One blessed be He, has innumerable chariots. He has the "Chariots of the Cherubim," for it is written *(Ps. 18:11, 2 Sam 22: 11):* " And he rode upon a cherub and did fly." (2) He has the "Chariots of Wind," for it is written: "and he flew swiftly upon the wings of the wind." (3) He has the "Chariots of the Swift Cloud," for it is written *(Is.19:1):* "Behold, the Lord rides upon a swift cloud:. (4) He has "Chariots of Clouds," for it is written *(Ex. 19:9):* "Lo, I come unto you in a cloud." (5) He has the "Chariots of the Altar," for it is written, " I saw the Lord standing upon the Altar." (6) He has the "Chariots of Ribbotaim," for it is written *(Ps. 68:18):* "The chariots of God are Ribbotaim; thousands of angels."

Ribbotaim appear to be used as the chariot and are a type of Cherub.

(7) He has the "Chariots of the Tent," for it is written *(Deut. 31:15):* "And the Lord appeared in the Tent in a pillar of cloud." (8) He has the "Chariots of the Tabernacle," for it is written *(Lev. 1:1):* "And the Lord spoke unto him out of the tabernacle." (9) He has the "Chariots of the Mercy-Seat," for it is written *(Num. 7:89):* "then he heard the Voice speaking unto him from upon the mercy-seat." (10) He has the "Chariots of Sapphire," for it is written *(Ex. 24:10):* "and there was under his feet a paved street of sapphires." (11) He has the "Chariots of Eagles," for it is written *(Ex. 19:4):* "I bare you on eagles' wings." It is not Eagles that are not meant here but "they that fly as swiftly as the eagles." (12) He has the "Chariots of a Shout," for it is written: "God is gone up with a shout." (13) He has the "Chariots of Araboth (highest heaven)," for it is written *(Ps 68 :5):* " Praise Him that rides upon the Araboth (highest heaven)." (14) He has the "Chariots of Thick Clouds," for it is written *(Ps. 106:3):* "who makes the thick clouds His chariot." (15) He has the "Chariots of the Chayoth," for it is written *(Ezek. 1:14):* "and the Chayoth ran and returned." They run by permission and return by permission, for Shekina is above their heads. (16) He has the "Chariots of Wheels (Galgallim)," for it is written *(Ezek. 10: 2):* "And he said: Go in between the whirling wheels." (17) He has the "Chariots of a Swift Cherub," for it is written, "riding on a swift cherub." And at the time when He rides on a swift cherub, as he sets one of His feet upon his back, and before he sets the other foot upon his back, he looks through eighteen thousand worlds at one glace. And he perceives and understands and sees into them all and knows what is in all of them, and then he sets down the other foot upon the cherub, for it is written *(Ezek. 48:35):* " Round about eighteen thousand." How do we know that He looks through every one of them every day? It is written (Ps. 14: 2): "He looked down from heaven upon the children of men to see if there were any that understand, that seek after God." (18) He has the "Chariots of the Ophannim," for it is written *(Ezek. 10:12):* "and the Ophannim were full of eyes round about." (19) He has the "Chariots of His Holy Throne," for it is written *(Ps. 67:8):* "God sits upon his holy throne" (20) He has the "Chariots of the Throne of Yah (Jah)," for it is written *(Ex. 17:16):* "Because a hand is lifted up upon the Throne of Jah (Yah)." (21) He has the "Chariots of the Throne of Judgment," for it is written *(Is. 5: 16):* "but the Lord of hosts shall be exalted in judgment." (22) He has the "Chariots of the Throne of Glory," for it is written *(Jer. 17:12):* "The Throne

of Glory, set on high from the beginning, is the place of our sanctuary." (23) He has the "Chariots of the High and exalted Throne," for it is written *(Is. 6: 1):* "I saw the Lord sitting upon the high and exalted throne."

CHAPTER 25
Ophphanniel, the Prince of the Ophannim and a description of the Ophannim

Rabbi Ishmael said: Metatron, the Angel, the Prince of the Presence, said to me: (1) Above these there is one great prince, highly honored, fit to rule, fearful, ancient and powerful. OPHAPHANNIEL YHWH is his name. (2) He has sixteen faces, four faces on each side, also 100 wings on each side. And he has 8466 eyes, corresponding to the days of the year and sixteen on each side. (Other sources have it as: corresponding to the hours in a year.)

The number of 8,466 is difficult to understand in a 365 day year. The lunar year was calculated to be 352.5 days at the time of the writing of 3 Enoch. But 8466 is the number of hours in a lunar year. This makes sense and makes the alternate rendering the correct one. However, other places in the texts may refer to the number 8766, which is exact number of hours is a solar year of 365.25 days.

(3) And in those two eyes of his face, in each one of them lightning is flashing, and from each one of them burning staves are burning; and no creature is able to look at them: for anyone who looks at them is burned up instantly. (4) His height is the distance of 2500 years' journey. No eye can see and no mouth can tell of the mighty power of his strength except the King of kings, the Holy One, blessed be He. He alone can tell.

The number 2,500 yields the number 7, as the digits are added together. This pattern will occur again is these types of measurements. It is a way Jewish mystics reenforce the perfection of the template of heaven.

(5) Why is he called OPHPHANNIEL? Because he rules over the Ophannim and the Ophannim are given over to his authority. He stands every day and attends to them and makes them beautiful. And he raises them up and determines their activity. He polishes the place where they stand and makes their dwelling place bright. He even makes the corners of their crowns and their seats spotless. And he waits upon them early and late, by day and by night, in order to increase their beauty and make their dignity grow. He keeps them diligent in the praise of their Creator. (6) And all the Ophannim are full of eyes, and they are full of brightness; seventy-two sapphires are fastened to their garments on their right side and seventy-two sapphire are fastened to their garments on their left side.

Note the number 72 again, representing the nations of the world.

(7) And four carbuncle stones are fastened to the crown of every single one, the splendor of which shines out in the four directions of Araboth (the highest heaven) even as the splendor of the orb of the sun shines out in all the directions of the universe. And why is it called Carbuncle (Bare'qet)? Because its splendor is like the appearance of a lightning (Baraq). And tents of splendor, tents of brilliance, tents of brightness as of sapphire and carbuncle enclose them because of the shining appearance of their eyes.

Carbuncle is an archaic name given to red garnet. The word occurs in four places in most English translations of the Bible. Each use originates from the Greek term Anthrax – meaning coal, in reference to the color of burning coal. A carbuncle is usually taken to mean a gem, particularly a deep-red garnet, which has no facet and is convex. In the same place in the masoretic text is the Hebrew word "nofech (no'-fekh)." In Exdodus 28:17 and again in Exodus 39:10 the carbuncle is used as the third stone in the breastplate of the Hoshen. Ezekiel 28:13 refers to the carbuncle's presence in the Garden of Eden.

CHAPTER 26
The Prince of the Seraphim. Description of the Seraphim

Rabbi Ishmael said: Metatron, the Angel, the Prince of the Presence, said to me: (1) Over them there is one prince, who is wonderful, noble, of great honor, powerful and terrible, a chief leader and a fast scribe. He is glorified, honored and loved. (2) He is completely filled with splendor, and full of praise. He shines and he is totally full of the brightness of light and beauty. He is full of goodness and greatness. (3) His face is identical to that of angels, but his body is like an eagle's body. (4) His is magnificent like lightning, his appearance like burning staves. His beauty like sparks. His honor burns bright like glowing coal. His majesty like chashmals, His radiance like the light of the planet Venus. His image is like the Sun. His height is as high as the seven heavens. The light from his eyebrows is seven times as bright.

Chasmal *is the fiery substance, which makes up the pillars on which the world rests. It is a mysterious substance or entity illuminating the heart of Ekekiel's chariot vision. Midrash Konen designated* chashmal *another class of angelic being.*

(5) The sapphire on his head is as large as the entire universe and as splendid as the great heavens in radiance. (6) His body is full of eyes like the stars of the sky, innumerable and cannot be known. Every eye is like the planet Venus. But there are some of them like the Moon and some of them like the Sun. From His ankles to his knees they are like stars twinkling (of lightning). From his knees to his thighs is like the planet Venus, across his

thighs like the moon, from his thighs to his neck is like the sun. From his neck to his head is like the Eternal Light. (7) The crown on his head is like the splendor of the Throne of Glory. The size of the crown is the distance of 502 years' journey. There is no kind of splendor, no kind of brilliance, no kind of radiance, no kind of light in the universe that is not affixed to the crown.

As in the prior chapter, the number seven is the result of the addition of the digits in the measurement, which in this case is 502.

(8) The name of that prince is SERAPHIEL YHWH. And the crown on his head, its name is "the Prince of Peace." And why is he called by the name of SERAPHIEL YHWH? Because he is assigned to rule over the Seraphim. And the flaming Seraphim are under his authority. And he presides over them by day and night and teaches them to sing, praise, and proclaim the beauty, power and majesty of their King. They proclaim the beauty of their King through all types of Praise and Sanctification. (Kedushah - Sacred Salutation of Holy, Holy, Holy). (9) How many Seraphim are there? Four, equating to the four winds of the world. And how many wings have each one of them? Six, relating to the six days of Creation. And how many faces do they have? Each one of them have four faces. (10) The height measurement of the Seraphim is the height of the seven heavens. The size of each wing is like the span of all Raqia (heaven). The size of each face is like the face of the East. (11) And each one of them gives out light, adding to the splendor of the Throne of Glory, so that not even the Holy Chayoth, the honored Ophannim, nor the majestic Cherubim are able to look on it. Anyone who gazes at it would be blinded because of its great splendor. (12) Why are they called Seraphim? Because they burn (saraph) the writing tables of Satan: Every day Satan sits together with SAMMAEL, the Prince of Rome, and with DUBBIEL, the Prince of Persia, and they write down the sins of Israel on their writing tables, which they hand over to the Seraphim, so that the Seraphim can present them to the Holy One, blessed be He, so that He should eliminate (destroy) Israel from the world. But the Seraphim know the secrets of the Holy One, blessed be He. They know that He does not want the people Israel to perish. What do the Seraphim do about this? Every day they receive the tablets from the hand of Satan and they burn them in the burning fire, which is near the high and exalted Throne. They do this in order that the tablet should not come before the Holy One, blessed be He, when he is sitting upon the Throne of Judgment, judging the entire world in truth.

Satan and Sammael are not allowed to approach the throne of God, but their accusations are taken by a Seraph, who destroys the tablet with the accusations against Israel and burns it. The tablet is not given to God, who would have to judge Israel, since the Seraph knows God does not wish to judge or punish Israel. Dubbiel is the guardian angel of Persia and one of the special accusers of Israel. Dubbiel is an angel who was ranked among angels who were said to act as guardians over the 70 nations. Dubbiel was counted as the protector of Persia and as such defended its interests against its enemy Israel, a role that naturally put him at odds with the Chosen People and their special patron, St. Michael the Archangel. Sammael is an angel whose name has been interpreted as meaning "angel" or "god" (el) *of "poison"* (sam). *He is the guardian angel of Rome, another enemy of Israel. He is considered in legend a member of the heavenly host who fell. He is equated with Satan and the chief of the evil spirits. He is the angel of death. In this capacity he is a fallen angel but remains the Lord's servant, or at least under His control. As a good angel, Sammael resided in the seventh heaven, although he is declared to be the chief angel of the fifth heaven.*

Seraphim are among the highest and most splendid of the nine accepted angelic orders as developed by the sixth-century theologian Dionysius. They are the closest in all of heaven to the throne of God. They are said to glow as if they are on fire so brightly they no mortal can endure the sight.

CHAPTER 27
RADWERIEL, the keeper of the Book of Records

Rabbi Ishmael said: Metatron, the Angel of YHWH, the Prince of the Presence, said to me: (1) Above the Seraphim there is one prince, exalted above all princes. He is more wonderful than all the servants. His name is RADWERIEL YHWH who is assigned to rule over the treasuries of the books.

Radweriel *is appointed over the treasury of book of records or remembrances. (See Mal.3:16). He is an angelic scribe, fluent in reading and writing. He reads the records in the* Beth Din, *(house/court) of justice. This is another name for the Sanhedrin.*

(2) He couriers the Case of Writings, which has the Books of Records in it, and he brings it to the Holy One, blessed be He. And he breaks the seals of the case, opens it, and takes out the books and delivers them before the Holy One, blessed be He. And the Holy One, blessed be He, receives them out of his hand and gives them to the Scribes to see so they may read them in the Great Beth (house) Din in the height of Araboth (highest heaven) of Raqia (heaven), before the household of heaven. (3) And why is he called RADWERIEL? Because from every word going out of his mouth an angel is created. He stands in the service of the company of the ministering angels and sings a song before the Holy One, blessed be He, as the time draws near for the recitation of the Thrice Holy One.

CHAPTER 28

The 'Irin and Qaddishin (Watchers and Holy Ones)

Rabbi Ishmael said: Metatron, the Angel, the Prince of the Presence, said to me: (1) Above all these there are four great princes. Their names are Irin and Qaddishin. They are highly honored, revered, loved, wonderfully glorious, and greater than any of the heavenly children. There is none like them among all the princes of heaven (sky). There are none equal to them among any Servants. Each one is equal to all the rest of the heavenly servants put together. (2) And their dwelling is near the Throne of Glory and their standing place near the Holy One, blessed be He. The brightness of their dwelling is a reflection from the brightness from the Throne of Glory. Their face is magnificent and is a reflection of the magnificence of Shekina. (3) They are elevated by the glory of the Divince Majesty (Gebura) and praised by (through) the praise of Shekina. (4) And not only that, but the Holy One, blessed be He, does nothing in his world without first consulting them. Only after He consults them does He perform it. As it is written *(Dan. 4: 17):* "The sentence is by the decree of the Irin and the demand by the word of the Qaddishin." (5) The Irin are two (twins) and the Qaddishin are two (twins). In what fashions standing before the Holy One, blessed be He? We should understood, that one Ir is standing on one side and the other 'Ir on the other side. Also, one Qaddish is standing on one side and the other on the other side. (6) And they exalt the humble forever, and they humble and bring to the ground those that are proud. They exalt to the heights those that are humble. (7) And every day, as the Holy One, blessed be He, is sitting upon the Throne of Judgment and judges the entire world, and the Books of the Living and the Books of the Dead are opened in front of Him all the children of heaven are standing before Him in fear and dread. They are in awe and they shake. When the Holy One, blessed be He, is sitting on the Throne of Judgment to execute His judgment , His garment is white as snow, the hair on his head is like pure wool and the His entire cloak is shining with light. He is covered with righteousness all over, like He is wearing a coat of mail. (8) And those Irin and Qaddishin (Watchers and Holy Ones) are standing before Him like court officers before the judge. And constantly they begin and argue a case and close the case that comes before the Holy One, blessed be He, in judgment, according for it is written *(Dan. 4. 17):* "The sentence is by the decree of the 'Irin and the demand by the word of Qaddishin."

This section explains the function of the Irin and Qaddishin. They are two pairs of angels forming the apex of angelic power. They are the holy counselors and they have authority over all things terrestrial. They are judge and executioner. Another tradition has the Irin and Qaddishin as two classes of angels but many in number. Yet, they seem to come in sets of two each, like twins. Again, this may represent the balance of mercy and justice always sought in heaven.

(9) Some of them argue the case and others pass the sentence in the Great Beth Din (Great House of the Sanhedrin) in Araboth (the highest heaven). Some of them make requests in the presence of the Divine Majesty and some close the cases before the Most High. Others finish by going down and confirming the judgment and executing the sentences on earth below. According for it is written *(Dan. 4. 13, 14):* "Behold an Ir and a Qaddish came down from heaven and cried aloud and said , "Chop down the tree, and cut off his branches, shake off his leaves, and scatter his fruit: let the beasts escape from under it, and the fowls from his branches." (10) Why are they called Irin and Qaddishin (Watchers and Holy Ones)? Because they sanctify the body and the spirit with beatings with fire on the third day of the judgment, for it is written (Hos. 6: 2): "After two days will he revive us: on the third he will raise us up, and we shall live before him."

Irin and Qaddishin or ministering spirits receive men from the Angel of Death. They judge him with angels arguing for him. This takes two days. On the third day they pass judgment. The sentence is based on the man's character and how closely he followed the Torah. They beat them accordingly.

CHAPTER 29
Description of a class of angels

Rabbi Ishmael said: Metatron, the Angel, the Prince of the Presence, said to me: (1) Each one of the Angels has seventy names corresponding to the seventy languages (nations) of the world. And all of them are based upon the name of the Holy One, blessed be He. And every several name is written with a flaming pen of iron on the Fearful Crown (Kether Nora), which is on the head of the high and exalted King.

Metatron was said to have names based upon the names of God. Fearful Crown refers to the crown of a sitting king, thus God.

(2) And each one of them projects sparks and lightning. Each one of them is covered with horns of splendor all over. Lights shine from each of them, and each one is surrounded by tents of brilliance so that not even the Seraphim and the Chayoth who are greater than all the children of heaven are able to look at them.

CHAPTER 30
The 72 princes of kingdoms and the Prince of the World are at the Great Sanhedrin.

Rabbi Ishmael said: Metatron, the Angel, the Prince of the Presence, said to me: (1) Whenever the Great Beth Din (House of the Sanhedrin) is seated in the Araboth (highest heaven) of Raqia (heaven) there no one speaks. No mouth opens for anyone in the world except those great princes who are called YHWH by the name of the Holy One, blessed be He. (2) How many are those Princes are there? Seventy-two princes of the kingdoms of the world besides the Prince of the World who pleads in favor of the world before the Holy One, blessed be He. Every day at the appointed hour the book with the records of all the deeds of the world is opened. For it is written *(Dan. 7:10):* " The judgment was set and the books were opened."

The highest classes of angels are marked with the Tetragrammaton. Each nation has its own angel appointed to guard and plea for its cause. What is odd about this is the equal and universal appeal to justice. There is no difference in how the court is conducted between Gentile or Jew. In this scenario, Metatron is the Prince of the world.

CHAPTER 31
The attributes of Justice, Mercy and Truth

Rabbi Ishmael said: Metatron, the Angel, the Prince of the Presence, said to me: (1) At the time when the Holy One, blessed be He, is sitting on the Throne of Judgment, Justice is standing on His right and Mercy on His left and Truth in front of His face, (2) then man (Some sources say "wicked man" but this is to be read as mankind) enters before Him for judgment, then , a staff comes out from the splendor of Mercy towards him and it stands in front of the man. Then man falls upon his face, and all the angels of destruction are fearful and they shake before him. For it is written *(Is. 16:5):* "And with mercy shall the throne be established, and he shall sit upon it in truth."

The fundamental balance of justice and mercy is only possible through truth, including the truth of what the real intent of the person being judged was. This is only possible with God. The angels of destruction are there to execute man but Mercy stops them and makes the angels fear. The wording of the verse makes this point unclear.

CHAPTER 32
The execution of judgment on the wicked
God's sword

Rabbi Ishmael said: Metatron, the Angel, the Prince of the Presence, said to me: (1) When the Holy One, blessed be He, opens the Book, half of it is fire and half of it is flames. Then the angels of destruction go out from Him continually to execute the judgment on the wicked by His sword, which is drawn from its sheath and it shines like magnificent lightning and pervades the world from one end to the other. For it is written *(Is. 66:16):* "For by fire will the Lord plead by His sword with all flesh." (2) And all those who come into the world fear and shake before Him, when they behold His sharpened sword like lightning from one end of the world to the other, and sparks and flashes of the size of the stars of Raqia (heaven) going out from it; according for it is written *(Deut. 32: 41):* If I whet the lightning of my sword."

CHAPTER 33
The Angels of Mercy, of Peace, and of Destruction are by the Throne of Judgment.

Rabbi Ishmael said: Metatron, the Angel, the Prince of the Presence, said to me: (1) At the time that the Holy One, blessed be He, is sitting on the Throne of Judgment, then the angels of Mercy are standing on His right, the angels of Peace are standing on His left and the angels of Destruction are standing in front of Him. (2) And there is one scribe standing beneath Him, and another scribe standing above Him. (3) And the glorious Seraphim surround the Throne on all four of its sides with walls of lightning. And the Ophannim surround them with burning staves all around the Throne of Glory. And clouds of fire and clouds of flames surround them to the right and to the left. The Holy Chayoth carry the Throne of Glory from below. Each one uses only three fingers. The length of each fingers is 800,000 and 700 times one hundred, and 66,000 parasangs. (4) And underneath the feet of the Chayoth there are seven rivers of fire running and flowing. And the distance across of each river is 365 thousand parasangs and its depth is 248 thousand times ten-thousand parasangs. Its length cannot be known and is immeasurable. (5) And each river turns round in a bow in the four directions of Araboth (the highest heaven) of Raqia (heaven), and from there it falls down to Maon and is stopped, and from Maon (some sources have "Velum") to Zebul, from Zegul to Shechaqim, from Shechaqim to Raqia (heaven) to Shamayim and from Shamayim it fows on the heads of the wicked who are in Gehenna, for it is written *(Jer. 23:19):* "Behold a whirlwind of the Lord, even His fury, is gone, yes, a whirling tempest; it shall burst upon the head of the wicked."

Maon *or* Velum *is the name of the first heaven. The river flows down from heaven and all of its levels, to* Gehenna, *which is the burning hell. Speculation on the meaning of the numbers contained in this chapter are random. In general, 3 is the number of spiritual completeness, and 8 is the number of judgment. The number of man and his shortcomings is 6. The number 7 represents spiritual perfection. 5 represents grace and spirit.*

CHAPTER 34
The different concentric circles around the Chayoth consist of fire, water, hailstones.

Rabbi Ishmael said: Metatron; the Angel, the Prince of the Presence, said to me: (1) The hoofs of the Chayoth are surrounded by seven clouds of burning coals. The clouds of burning coals are surrounded on the outside by seven walls of flames. The seven walls of flames are surrounded on the outside by seven walls of hailstones (stones of El-gabish, *Ezek.13: 11, 13, 28: 22)*. The hailstones are surrounded on the outside by boulders (stones) of hail. The boulders (stones) of hail are surrounded on the outside by stones of "the wings of the tempest." The stones of "the of the winged tempest" are surrounded by the outside by flames of fire. The chambers of the whirlwind are surrounded on the outside by the fire and water. (2) Around the fire and the water are those who sing the "Holy." Around about those who sing the "Holy" are those who sing the "Blessed." Around about those who sing the "Blessed" are the bright clouds. The bright clouds are surrounded on the outside by coals of burning juniper wood. There are thousands of camps of fire and ten thousand hosts of flames. And between every camp and every host there is a cloud, so that they may not be burned by the fire.

The stones of hail are made of the two opposite substances of fire and ice. This, like the reference to fire and water, represent a balance of forces which, if applied within the spiritual realm, brings blessings.

CHAPTER 35
The camps of angels in Araboth (the highest heaven) of Raqia (heaven); Angels performing the Kedushah (Sacred salutation of Holy, Holy, Holy)

Rabbi Ishmael said: Metatron, the Angel, the Prince of the Presence, said to me: (1) 506 (other sources have 496) thousand times ten-thousand camps has the Holy One, blessed be He, in the height of Araboth (the highest heaven) of Raqia (heaven). And each camp is composed of 496 thousand angels.

The Gematria *for 506 is "kingdom" and for 496 it is "kingdoms."*

(2) And every single angel is as tall as the width of the great sea; and the appearance of their face is like the appearance of lightning. Their eyes are like lamps of fire, and their arms and their feet were the color of polished brass and when they spoke words their voice roared and sounded like the voice of a multitude of them. (3) They all stand before the Throne of Glory in four rows. And the princes of the army are standing at the beginning of each row. (4) Some of them sing the "Holy" and others sing the "Blessed." Some run as messengers while others stand in attendance. For it is written *(Dan. 7: 10)*: "Thousands of thousands ministered unto Him, and ten thousand times ten thousand stood before Him. The judgment was set and the books were opened."

The singing or chanting of "Holy, Holy, Holy" is returned by the phrase, "Blessed be Thou and blessed is the name of the Lord forever and ever."

(5) When the time nears and the hour comes to say the "Holy," first a whirlwind from before the Holy One, blessed be He, goes out and bursts on the camp of Shekina and there arises a great noise and confusion among them. For it is written *(Jer. 30: 23):* "Behold, the whirlwind of the Lord goes forth with fury, a continuing commotion." (6) At that moment thousands of thousands of them are changed into sparks, thousands of thousands of them ignite into burning staves, thousands of thousands flashes, thousands of thousands burst into flames, thousands of thousands change into males, thousands of thousands change into females, thousands of thousands burst into winds, thousands of thousands burst into burning fires, thousands of thousands burst into flames, thousands of thousands turn into sparks, thousands of thousands turn into chashmals of light; until they take upon themselves the yoke of the kingdom of heaven, the high and lifted up, of the Creator of them all with fear, dread, awe, and trembling, with commotion, anguish, terror and trepidation. Then they are changed again into their former shape to have the fear of their King before them always, as they have set their hearts on saying the Song continually, for it is written *(Is. 6:3):* "And one cried unto another and said Holy, Holy, Holy."

The phrase, "…thousands of thousands change into males, thousands of thousands change into females …" is suspect and may have been added later. The idea of taking onto oneself the yoke of heaven may refers to the fact that the angels are reciting the "Holy" and "Blessed" discourse, which means they understand and acknowledge the ways of heaven and the place and power of God. Judgment comes accordingly.

CHAPTER 36
The angels bathe in the river of fire before they recite the song

Rabbi Ishmael said: Metatron, the Angel, the Prince of Presence, said to me: (1) At the time when the ministering angels desire to sing (the) Song, (then) Nehar di-Nur (the stream of fire) rises with many "thousand thousands and ten-thousand ten-thousands" (of angels) of power and strength of fire (the intensity of the radiant fire of the angels flows) and it runs and passes under the Throne of Glory, between the camps of the ministering angels and the troops of Araboth (highest heaven). (2) And all the ministering angels first go down into Nehar di-Nur (stream of fire), and they dip themselves in the fire and dip their tongue and their mouth seven times; *(2Kings 5:14*) and after that they go up and put on the garment of Machaqe Samal and cover themselves with cloaks of chashmal (the zenith of heaven) and stand in four rows over near the side of the Throne of Glory, in all the heavens.

No meaning for the term Machaqe Samal *could be found.*

CHAPTER 37
The Four Camps of Shekina and Their Surroundings

Rabbi Ishmael said: Metatron, the Angel, the Prince of the Presence, said to me: (1) In the seven halls four chariots of Shekina are standing. Before each one stands the four camps of Shekina. Between (or behind) each camp a river of fire is continually flowing. (2) Between (or behind) each river there are bright clouds surrounding them, and between (or behind) each cloud there are pillars of brimstone erected. Between one pillar and another there stands flaming wheels, which surround them. And between one wheel and another there are flames of fire all around. Between the flames there are storehouses of lightning. Behind the storehouses of lightning there are the wings of the Wind of the Storm. Behind the wings of the Wind of the Storm are the chambers of the tempest. Behind the chambers of the tempest there are winds, voices, thunder, and sparks emitting from sparks and earthquakes within earthquakes.

The original intent of the verse may have been to draw a picture of the rivers running in concentric circles through the heavens and beside the river, in rows are clouds, lightning, and wind.

CHAPTER 38
The fear in heavens at the sound of the "Holy" is appeased by the Prince of the World

Rabbi Ishmael said: Metatron, the Angel, the Prince of the Presence, said to me: (1) At the time, when the ministering angels sing (the Thrice) Holy, then all the pillars of the heavens and their sockets shake, and the gates of the Halls of Araboth (the highest heaven) of Raqia (heaven) are shaken and the foundations of Shechaqim and the universe are moved, and the orders (secrets) of Maon and the chambers of Makon quiver, and all the orders of Raqia (heaven) and the constellations and the planets are distressed. The orbs of the sun and the moon rush away and run out of their pattens and run 12,000 parasangs and the wish to throw themselves down from heaven, (2) because of the roaring voice (sound) of their song, and the noise of their praise and the sparks and lightning that proceed from their faces. For it is written *(Ps. 77: 18)*: "The voice of your thunder was in the heaven (the lightning illuminated the world, the earth trembled and shook)." (3) Until the Prince of the World calls them, saying; Be quiet in your place! Do not fear because of the ministering angels who sing the Song before the Holy One, blessed be He." As it is written *(Job. 38: 7)*: "When the morning stars sang together and all the children of heaven shouted for joy."

As the appointed times approached to sing the Holy, Holy, Holy, all of heaven became anxious. Metatron quieted them and gave them focus.

CHAPTER 39

The explicit names fly from the Throne.

Rabbi Ishmael said: Metatron, the Angel, the Prince of the Presence, said to me: (1) When the ministering angels sing the "Holy" then all the explicit names that are engraved with a flaming iron pen on the Throne of Glory go flying off like eagles, each with sixteen wings. And they surround and hover around the Holy One, blessed be He, on all four sides of the place of His Shekina. (2) And the angels of the host, and the flaming Servants, the mighty Ophannim, the Cherubim of the Shekina, the Holy Chayoth, the Seraphim, the Er'ellim, the Taphsarim, the troops of burning fire, the armies of fire, the flaming hosts, and the holy princes, adorned with crowns, clothed in kingly majesty, wrapped in glory, tied with high honor, fall on their faces three times, saying: "Blessed be the name of His glorious kingdom forever and ever."

Taphsarim *are the troupes of flames.* Er'el, *more commonly referred to in the plural as the* Erelim, *are a rank of angels in Jewish Kabbala (Cabbalah) and mythology. The name is seen to mean "the valiant/courageous." They are generally seen as the third highest rank of divine beings/angels below God. The description in the verse seems to say that letters fly off of the Torah like eagles when it is burned.*

CHAPTER 40

The ministering angels rewarded and punished

Rabbi Ishmael said: Metatron, the Angel, the Prince of the Presence, said to me: (1) When the ministering angels say "Holy" before the Holy One, blessed be He, in the proper way, then the servants of His Throne, the attendants of His Glory, go out with much happiness from under the Throne of Glory. (2) And each one carries in their hands thousands and ten thousand times ten thousand crowns of stars, similar in appearance to the planet Venus, and put them on the ministering angels and the great prince who sing the "Holy." They place three crowns on each one of them: one crown because they say "Holy," and another crown, because they say "Holy, Holy," and a third crown because they say "Holy, Holy, Holy, is the Lord of Hosts." (3) But in the moment that they do not sing the "Holy" in the right order, a consuming fire flashes out from the little finger of the Holy One, blessed be He, and descends into the middle of their ranks, which is divided into 496 thousand parts corresponding to the four camps of the ministering angels, and the fire burns up in a single moment those who did not say the "Holy" correctly. For it is written *(Ps. 92:3):* "A fire goes before him and burns up his adversaries round about." (4) After that the Holy One, blessed be He, opens His mouth and speaks one word and creates other new ones like them to replace them. And each one stands before His Throne of Glory, signing the "Holy," as it written *(Lam. 12:23)*: "They are new every morning; great is your faithfulness."

Here we see the full extent of the phrase, "taking on the yoke of heaven." One is rewarded for proper worship and ceremony or annihilated if God disapproves. The text indicates that all of the angels in the offending group are destroyed. Angels are created, nullifying the six days of the creation of everything.

CHAPTER 41
Letters engraved on the Throne of Glory created everything

Rabbi Ishmael said: Metatron, the Angel, the Prince of the Presence, said to me: (1) Come and see the letters by which the heaven and earth were created. These are the letters by which were created the mountains and hills. These are the letters by which were created the seas and rivers, these are the letters by which were created the trees and herbs, these are the letters by which were created the planets and the constellations, these are the letters by which were created the globe of the earth and the orb of the moon and the orb of the sun, as well as Orion, the Pleiades and all the different luminaries of Raqia (heaven) were created. (2) These are the letters by which were created the Throne of Glory and the Wheels of the Merkaba (chariot) , the letters by which were created the necessities of the worlds, (3) the letters by which were created wisdom, understanding, knowledge, prudence, meekness and righteousness by which the entire world is sustained. (4) And I walked by his side and he took me by his hand and raised me up on his wings and showed me those letters, all of them, that are engraved with a flaming iron pen on the Throne of Glory. Sparks go out from them and cover all the chambers of Araboth (the highest heaven).

Jewish tradition has it that God and angels spoke Hebrew, and thus all things came into existence when God spoke them into existence in Hebrew. It is a very short leap of logic to assume the written word would have the same power and effect. This means within the various combinations of the 22 Hebrew letters all things were created and are sustained.

CHAPTER 42
Opposites Kept in Balance by Several Divine Names

Rabbi Ishmael said: Metatron, the Angel, the Prince of the Presence, said to me: (1) Come and I will show you, where the waters are suspended in the highest place, where fire is burning in the midst of hail, where lightning flashes forth from out of the middle of snowy mountains, where thunder is roaring in the heights of the skies, where a flame is burning in the burning fire, and where voices make themselves heard within (in spite of) thunder and earthquake.

The balance indicated herein reminds one of a Zen koan – "See the sun in the midst of the rain. Scoop clear water from the heart of the fire." This chapter reveals a fundamental truth. All things are created in heaven by His word, sustained by His word, and reflected in the lower world where we live only after being created in heaven.

(2) Then I went to his side and he took me by his hand and lifted me up on his wings and showed me all those things. I saw the waters suspended on high in Araboth (the highest heaven) of Raqia (heaven) by the power of the name YAH EHYE ASHER EHYE (Jah, I am that I am), and their fruits (rain) was falling down from heaven and watering the face of the world, for it is written *(Ps. 104:13):* "(He waters the mountains from his chambers:) the earth is satisfied with the fruit of your work." (3) And I saw fire and snow and hail that were mingled together within each other and yet were undamaged. This was accomplished by the power of the name ESH OKELA (consuming fire). For it is written *(Deut. 55: 24):* "For the Lord, your God, is a consuming fire." (4) And I saw lightning flashing out of mountains of snow and yet the lightning was not extinguished, by the power of the name YA SUR OLAMIM (Jah, the everlasting rock). For it is written (Is. 26: 4): "For Jah, YHWH is the everlasting rock." (5) And I saw thunder and heard voices that were roaring within flames of fire and they were not silenced. This is accomplished by the power of the name EL-SHADDAI RABBA (the Great God Almighty) for it is written *(Gen. 17:1):* "I am God Almighty." (6) And I saw a flame glowing in the middle of burning fire, and yet it was not devoured. This was done by the power of the name YA.D. AL KES YAH (the hand upon the Throne of the Lord.) For it is written *(Ex. 17: 16):* " And he said: for the hand is upon the Throne of the Lord." (7) And I looked and saw rivers of fire within of rivers of water and they were not extinguished. All of this was done by the power of the name OSE SHAlOM (Maker of Peace) for it is written *(Job 25: 2):* "He makes peace in high places." For he makes peace between fire and water, and between hail and fire, and between the wind and cloud, and between earthquakes and sparks.

CHAPTER 43
The Abode of the Unborn Spirits and of the Spirits of the Righteous Dead

Rabbi Ishmael said: Metatron said to me: (1) Come and I will show you where the spirits of the righteous are that have been created and those that have returned, and the spirits of the righteous that have not yet been created (born). (2) And he lifted me up to his side, took me by his hand and sat me near the Throne of Glory by the place of the Shekina; and he revealed the

Throne of glory to me, and he showed me the spirits that have been created and had returned as well as those who were flying above the Thorne of Glory in front of the Holy One, blessed be He. (3) After that I went to interpret the following verse of Scripture and I found what is written *(Isa. 57: 16)*: "for the spirit clothed itself before me.") It refers to the spirits that have been created in the chamber of creation of the righteous and that have returned before the Holy One, blessed be He; (and the (His) words.) "The souls I have made" refers to the spirits of the righteous that have not yet been created in the chamber (GUPH).

Within the entire book of 3 Enoch, this chapter could be the most important to all "children of the book:" Jews, Christians, and Moslems. The story of creation has God creating everything in six days. Everything must also include all of the souls that are ever to be born. These souls are housed in a chamber near the throne of God, called the Guph (Guf). This chapter tells us the souls of the righteous are housed.

The righteous souls are housed in the Guph, waiting to be clothed in flesh for their incarnation. But if the righteous souls are here, where are the unrighteous souls kept? If there were another place where the unrighteous souls are kept the distinction would indicate predestination. If the character of the soul is already determined and they are stored accordingly then how is the determination made? Are we created as righteous and unrighteous beings? Does God simply look ahead and see us as we are to be?

As the next two chapters unfold, we see hints that the Guph may not be the place where all of the souls are housed but possibly it is where the souls of the righteous are conducted to be clothed in flesh and dispatched to earth through birth. The wicked soul finds his home in Sheol. If this were true it would still indicate predestination or foreknowledge are at work.

Mystical writings, such as the Zohar, describe God as a burning flame from where sparks fly outward. These sparks are the souls of the Jewish people. When these sparks return to the primal flame, time will come to an end. Another tradition states that when the Guph is emptied time will end. Souls leaving the Guph are born and return to God after death.

CHAPTER 44

Metatron shows Rabbi Ishmael the abode of the wicked and the intermediate in Sheol

Rabbi Ishmael said: Metatron, the Angel, the Prince of the Presence, said to me: (1) Come and I will show you the spirits of the wicked and the spirits of those in between (intermediate) where they are standing, and the spirits of those in between (intermediate), where they go down, and the spirits of the wicked, where they go down.

The text tells us there are three classes of souls: the righteous, the intermediate, and the unrighteous. The obvious questions are, where were the souls of the "intermediates" kept and from where were they dispatched? Are these the souls of the "lukewarm?"

(2) And he said to me: The spirits of the wicked go down to Sheol by the hands of two angels of destruction: ZAAPHIEL and SIMKIEL. (3) SIMKIEL is assigned to rule over the intermediate to support them and purify them because of the great mercy of the Prince of the Place (The Divine Majesty). ZAAPHIEL is assigned to rule over the spirits of the wicked in order to cast them down from the presence of the Holy One, blessed be He, and from the magnificence of the Shekina, and he casts them into Sheol, to punish them in the fire of Gehenna with rods of burning coal. (4) And I went by his side, and he took me by his hand and pointed them all out to me. (5) And I saw the faces of children of men and the way they looked. Their bodies were like eagles. And not only that but the color of the complexion of the intermediate was like pale grey because of their deeds. They were stained until they become cleansed from their iniquity in the fire.

It is interesting to note this indirect reference to Purgatory in a Jewish book written between the second and fifth centuries A.D.

(6) And the color of the wicked was like the bottom of a pot (burned black) because of the wickedness of their deeds. (7) And I saw the spirits of the Patriarchs Abraham, Isaac, and Jacob and the rest of the righteous, whom they have brought up out of their graves and who have ascended to Heaven. And they were praying before the Holy One, blessed be He, saying in their prayer: "Lord of the Universe! How long will you sit upon your Throne like a mourner in the days of his mourning with your right hand behind you and not deliver your children and reveal your Kingdom in the world? And how long will you have no pity upon your children who are made slaves among the nations of the world? Your right hand is behind you. Why do you not stretch out the heavens and the earth and the heavens of the highest heavens? When will you have compassion?"

The right hand is the symbol of power and authority. To have the right hand behind your back means you are not using the power or authority available to you.

(8) Then the Holy One, blessed be He, answered every one of them, saying: "Since these wicked commit sins on and on, and transgress with sins again

and again against Me, how could I deliver my great Right Hand when it would mean their downfall would be caused by their own hands.

The reason God does not bring judgment upon the world is because many Jews were among the unrepentant sinners. He wishes to await their return to him before judging them. This is the ultimate mercy.

(9) In that moment Metatron called me and spoke to me: "My servant! Take the books, and read their evil deeds!" Then I took the books and read their deeds and there were 36 transgressions to be found written down regarding each wicked one and besides that they have transgressed all the letters in Torah, for it is written *(Dan. 55: 11)*: "Yea, all Israel have transgressed your Law." It is not written, "for they have transgressed from Aleph to Taw (A to Z) 36 (40) statutes have they transgressed for each letter?"

Some sources have "40 statues." Forty is the number of severe trials and testing. The implication of the verse is that the souls have broken 40 major laws and many minor ones.

(10) Then Abraham, Isaac and Jacob wept. Then the Holy One, blessed be He said to them: "Abraham, my beloved, Isaac, my Elect one, Jacob, my firstborn, how can I deliver them from among the nations of the world at this time?" And immediately MIKAEL (Michael), the Prince of Israel, cried and wept with a loud voice and said *(Ps. 10:1)*: "Why stand you afar off, O Lord?"

CHAPTER 45
Past and future events recorded on the curtain of the Throne

Rabbi Ishmael said: Metatron said to me: (1) Come, and I will show you the Curtain of The Divine Majesty which is spread before the Holy One, blessed be He. On it are written all the generations of the world and all their deeds (actions/doings), both what they have done and what they will do until the end of all generations. (2) And I came, and he showed it to me pointing it out with his fingers like a father who teaches his children the letters of Torah. And I saw each generation and within the generations I saw the rulers, the leaders, the shepherds, the oppressors (despots), the keepers, the punisher, the counselors, the teachers, the supporters, the bosses, the presidents of academies, the magistrates, the princes, the advisors, the noblemen, and the warriors, the elders, and the guides of each generation.

In the ancient world, these represent all major groups that have influence over the lives of people.

(3) And I saw Adam, his generation, their deeds (actions/doings) and their thoughts, Noah and his generation, their deeds and their thoughts, and the generation of the flood, their deeds and their thoughts, Shem and his generation, their deeds and their thoughts, Nimrod and the generation of the confusion of tongues, and his generation, their deeds and their thoughts, Abraham and his generation, their deeds and their thoughts, Isaac and his generation, their deeds and their thoughts, Ishmael and his generation, their deeds and their thoughts, Jacob and his generation, their deeds and their thoughts, Joseph and his generation , their deeds and their thoughts, the tribes and their generation, their deeds and their thoughts, Amram and his generation, their deeds and their thoughts, Moses and his generation, their deeds and their thoughts, (4) Aaron and Mirjam their accomplishments and actions, the princes and the elders, their works and deeds, Joshua and his generation, their works and deeds, the judges and their generation, their works and deeds, Eli and his generation, their works and deeds, Phinehas, their works and deeds, Elkanah and his generation, their accomplishments and actions, Samuel and his generation, their works and deeds, the kings of Judah with their generations, their works and their doing, the kings of Israel and their generation, their accomplishments and actions, the princes of Israel, their accomplishments and actions; the princes of the nations of the world, their accomplishments and actions, the heads of the councils of Israel, their accomplishments and actions; the heads of the councils in the nations of the world, their generations, their accomplishments and actions; the rulers of Israel and their generation, their accomplishments and actions; the noblemen of Israel and their generation, their works and their deeds; the noblemen of the nations of the world and their generations, their accomplishments and actions; the men of reputation in Israel, their generation, their accomplishments and actions; the judges of Israel, their generation, their accomplishments and actions; the judges of the nations of the world and their generation, their accomplishments and actions; the teachers of children in Israel, their generations, their accomplishments and actions: the teachers of children in the nations of the world, their generation, their accomplishments and actions; the interpreters) of Israel, their generation, their accomplishments and actions; the interpreters of the nations of the world, their generation, their accomplishments and actions; (5) and all the fights and wars that the nations of the world worked against the people of Israel in the time of their kingdom. And I saw Messiah, the son of Joseph, and his generation and their accomplishments and actions that they will do against the nations of the world. And I saw Messiah, the son of David, and his generation, and all the fights and wars, and their accomplishments and actions that they will do with Israel both for good and evil. And I saw all the fights and wars that Gog and Magog will fight with Israel in the days of Messiah, and all that the Holy One, blessed be He, will do with them in the time to come.

This is the first mention of two Messiahs. However, the dual functions of the Messiah can be seen as the impetus to this idea. The Messiah is seen as a peacemaker and teacher, who brings mercy. The Messiah is also seen as a warrior, destroyer, and bringer of justice. One comes in peace and the other is determined to do war to avenge God and Israel. It appears the Messiah, son of David, is truculent compared to the son of Joseph, who will be killed for his attempt to make peace. Christians believe the same Messiah will perform both functions because he came as peacemaker and teacher but will return from heaven as the warrior of God. The text here indicates there will be two separate Messiahs.

(6) And all the rest of all the leaders of the generations and all the works of the generations both in Israel and in the nations of the world, both what is done and what will be done hereafter to all generations until the end of time all were written on the Curtain of The Divine Majesty. And I saw all these things with my eyes; and after I had seen it, I opened my mouth in praise of The Divine Majesty saying, *(Eccl. 8:4, 5):* "For the King's word has power and who may say unto Him, What do you do? Whoever keeps the commandments shall know no evil thing." And I said *(Ps. 104:24):* "O Lord how manifold (multi-colored/multifaceted) are your works!"

Rabbi Ishmael was shown all of the deeds and works of mankind for all generations. This implies predestination or foreknowledge. The reader must decide for himself or herself.

CHAPTER 46
The place of the stars shown to Rabbi Ishmael

Rabbi Ishmael said: Metatron said to me: (1) Come and I will show you the distance between the stars that are standing in the Raqia (heaven), for they stand there night after night in fear of the Almighty and The Divine Majesty. I will show you where they go and where they stand. (2) I walked by his side, and he took me by his hand and pointed out all of them to me with his finger. And they were standing on sparks of flames around the Merkaba (chariot) of the Almighty, The Divine Majesty. What did Metatron do? At that moment he clapped his hands and chased them off from their place. Then they flew off on flaming wings, rose and fled from the four sides of the Throne of Merkaba (chariot), and as they flew he told me the names of ever-single one. As it is written, *(Ps. 137:4)* "He tells the number of the stars; he gives them all their names," teaching, that the Holy One, blessed be He, has given a name to each one of them. (3) And by the authority of RAHATIEL they enter in a numbered order to Raqia (heaven) ha-shamayim (the second of the seven heavens) to serve the world. And they go out in numbered order to praise the Holy One, blessed be He, with songs and hymns, for it is written *(Ps. 19: 1):* "The heavens declare the glory of God." (4) But in the age to come the Holy One, blessed be He, will create them anew. For it is written *(Lam. 52: 23):* "They are new every morning." And they open their mouth and sing a song. Which is the song that they sing? *(Ps. 8:3):* "When I consider your heavens."

Rahatiel is the angelic ruler of the stars and constellations. The Ophannim is the class of angels that move the celestial sphere. Stars were considered by many cultures to be spiritual entities, or angels. This was a Babylonian concept that was absorbed. It is in this light that the stars would sing. They leave the second heaven and proceed through the heavens to the seventh heaven where they end their journey at the throne.

CHAPTER 47
Metatron shows Rabbi Ishmael the spirits of punished angels

Rabbi Ishmael said: Metatron said to me: (1) Come and I will show you the souls of the angels and the spirits of the servants that served, whose bodies have been burned up in the fire of The Divine Majesty of the Almighty, that projects from his little finger. And they have been made into burning and glowing coals in the midst of the river of fire (Nehar di-Nur). But their spirits and their souls are standing behind the Shekina. (2) Whenever the angel servants sing a song at a wrong time or they sing what was not appointed to be sung they are burned and consumed by the fire of their Creator and by a flame from their Maker from the rooms of the whirlwind. The fire blows on them and drives them into the river of fire (Nehar di-Nur). There they become mountains of burning coal. But their spirit and their soul return to their Creator, and all are standing behind their Master. (3) And I went by his side and he took me by his hand, and he showed me all the souls of the angels and the spirits of the attending servants who were standing behind the Shekina and were standing on the wings of a whirlwind with walls of fire all around them. (4) At that moment Metatron opened the gates of the walls within which they were standing behind the Shekina for me to see. And I raised my eyes and I saw them. I saw what of every one of the angels looked like and I saw their wings were like birds made out of flames. And it looked as if they were fashioned from burning fire. In that moment I opened my mouth in praise of The Divine Majesty and said *(Ps. 92: 5):* "How great are your works, O Lord."

The river of fire or Nehar di-Nur *is presented here as a place of resurrection of the angels since their bodies were burnt but the spirit continues and ends up again with God. However, this idea is contradicted in most Jewish mystic writings. It is possible the text here is somehow corrupted or missunderstood.*

CHAPTER 48A
Rabbi Ishmael sees the Right Hand of the Most High

Rabbi Ishmael said: Metatron said to me: (1) come, and I will show you the Right Hand of The Divine Majesty, which He keeps behind Him because of the destruction of the Holy Temple; from which all kinds of splendor and light shine forth and by which the 955 heavens were created; and whom not even the Seraphim and the Ophannim are permitted to experience until the day that salvation shall arrive.

God became inactive because of the destruction of the temple between March and September of 70 A.D. and onward. Why God would choose the sacking of his temple to mark his quiescence might be understood by looking at the reason given for the destruction. If the Jewish people believed themselves to be the only chosen people of God then God must be their protector. To have a heathen army come in and defeat them so soundly, looting and destroying the temple of the God that was supposed to protect them, brought into question their position in the divine scheme. Since the fault could not be with God, it must have been with his people. The Jewish nation must have failed God by falling away from Him or sinning badly enough to cause God to turn them over to their enemy. Since this would be a great and grievous sin, God has chosen not to become active, since that would mean having to judge His apostate people. He awaits his people to return to Him in a righteous state.

(2) and I went by his side and he took me by his hand and showed me the Right Hand of The Divine Majesty, with all types of praises, joyous singing. No mouth can articulate its worth, and no eye can look at it because of its greatness, and dignity and its majesty, and splendid beauty. (3) Not only that, but all the souls of the righteous who are counted worthy to see the joy of Jerusalem are standing by it, praising and praying before it three times every day, saying (Is. 51: 9): "Awake, awake, put on strength, O arm of the Lord" according for it is written *(Is. 63: 12):* "He caused his glorious arm to go at the right hand of Moses." (4) In that moment the Right Hand of The Divine Majesty was weeping. And there flew out from its five fingers, five rivers of tears and fell they flowed down into the great sea and it shook the entire world. For it is written *(Is. 24: 19,20):* "The earth is utterly broken, the earth is totally dissolved, the earth is moved greatly, the earth shall stagger like a drunken man and shall be moved back and froth like a hut, five times corresponding to the fingers of His Great Right Hand. " (5) But when the Holy One, blessed be He, saw that there is not a righteous man in that generation, and no pious man on the entire earth, and no men doing justice, and that there is no one like Moses, and no intercessor like Samuel who could pray before The Divine Majesty for the salvation and deliverance of His Kingdom, His great Right Hand was revealed in the entire world that that He put it out from Himself again to work great salvation by it for Israel,

(6) then the Holy One, blessed be He, will remember His own justice, favor, mercy and grace, and He will deliver His great Arm by himself, and His righteousness will support Him. For it is written *(Is. 59: 16):* "And he saw, that there was no man" that is like Moses who prayed countless times for Israel in the desert and averted the Divine decrees from them – "and he wondered why there was no intercessor" – like Samuel who entreated the Holy One, blessed be He, and called unto Him and He answered him and fulfilled his desire, even if it did not fit into the Divine plan. For it is written *(I Sam. 12: 17):* "Is it not wheat-harvest today? I will call unto the Lord." (7) And not only that, but He joined fellowship with Moses in every place, for it is written *(Ps. 99: 6):* "Moses and Aaron among His priest." And again it is written, *(Jer. 15: 1):* "Though Moses and Samuel stood before Me" *(Is. 63: 5):* "Mine own arm brought salvation unto Me." (8) The Holy One, blessed be He said at that time, "How long do I have to wait for the children of men to obtain salvation according to their righteousness for My power and authority? For My own sake and for the sake of My worthiness and righteousness will I deliver My power and authority and by it I will redeem my children from among the nations of the world. For it is written *(Is. 48: 11):* "For My own sake will I do it. For how should My name be profaned."

At this point, God has waited as long as he wished for Israel to come back to Him in righteousness by their own power. He has decided to take them back from the heathen nations.

(9) In that moment the Holy One, blessed be He, will reveal His Great Power and Authority (Arm) and show it to the nations of the world. Its length is the length of the entire world and its width is the width of the world. And its splendor looks like the splendor of the sunshine in its power in the summer solstice. (10) Then Israel will be saved from among the nations of the world. And Messiah will appear unto them and He will bring them up to Jerusalem with great joy. And not only that but they will eat and drink for they will glorify the Kingdom of Messiah, of the house of David, in the four corners of the world.

This is the time, not for the Messiah of the house of Joseph, but for the Messiah of the house of David. This is the time of war and leadership of the nation in a physical sense.

And the nations of the world will not prevail against them, for it is written *(Is. 52: 10):* "The Lord has made bare His holy arm in the eyes of all the nations; and all the ends of the earth shall see the salvation of our God." And again *(Deut. 32: 12):* "The Lord alone did lead him, and there was no strange god with him." *(Zech. 14: 9):* "And the Lord shall be king over all the earth."

"Heaven" is the number 955 using Gematria. The meaning seems to be that of all heavens and all worlds.

CHAPTER 48B

The Divine names that go forth from the Throne of Glory and pass through the heavens and back again to the Throne

Many of the names are not decipherable. Attempting to place the letters into any kind of Latinized form or alphabet made the meanings even more obscure. For this reason, the names that could be interpreted with any certainty were listed. Those that yielded only meaningless letters were marked with only a dash.

These are the seventy-two names written on the heart of the Holy One, Blessed be He: Righteousness, - , Righteous (one) -, Lord of Host, God Almighty, God, YHWH - - - Living (one) - Riding upon the Araboth (highest heaven), - Life Giver - King of Kings, Holy One - - Holy, Holy, Holy, - - - Blessed be the Name of His glorious kingdom forever and ever, - - Complete, King of the Universe, - - The beginning of Wisdom for the children of men, - -. Blessed be He who gives strength to the weary and increases strength to them that have no might, *(Is. 40:29)* that go forth adorned with many flaming crowns with many flames, with innumerable crowns of chashmal (celestial substance), with many, many crowns of lightning from before the Throne of Glory. And with them there are hundreds of hundreds of powerful angels who escort them like a king with trembling and dread, with amazement and shivering, with honor and majesty and fear, terror, greatness and dignity, and with glory and power, with wisdom and knowledge and with a pillar of fire and flame and lightning—and their light is as lightning flashesof light—and with the likeness of the chashmal (the substance of heaven). (2) And they give glory to them and they answer and cry before them, " Holy, Holy, Holy." And they lead them in a single line through every heaven as powerful and honorable princes. And when they bring them all back to the place of the Throne of Glory, then all the Chayoth by the Merkaba (chariot) open their mouth in praise of His glorious name, saying: "Blessed be the name of His glorious kingdom forever and ever."

CHAPTER 48C

An Enoch-Metatron piece

(1)"I seized him, and I took him and I appointed him"—that is Enoch, the son of Jared, whose name is Metatron (2) and I took him from among the children of men (5) and made him a Throne over near and beside My Throne. What is the size of that Throne? Seventy-thousand parasangs all of fire. (9) I committed to him 70 angels symbolizing the nations of the world and I gave into his authority all the household above and below. (7) And I imparted to him Wisdom and Intelligence more than all the angels. And I called his name "the LESSER YAH," whose name is by Gematria 71.

To refresh memory, Gematria was the ancient art of numerology. Each letter is given a number, usually determined by where it occurs in the alphabet. Numbers go from one to nine, then from 10 to 90, and, if there were enough letters, from100 to 900. However, there are only 22 letters. Numbers are then summed. When the numbers are added they total seventy-one.

And I arranged all the works of creation for him. And I made him more powerful than all the ministering angels. (3) He gave Metatron—that is Enoch, the son of Jared— the authority over all the storehouses and treasuries, and appointed him over all the stores (reserves) in every heaven. And I assigned the keys of each store into him. (4) I made him the prince over all the princes and a minister of the Throne of Glory and the Halls of Araboth (the highest heaven). I appointed him over the Holy Chayoth for him to open their doors of the Throne of Glory to me, to exalt and arrange it, and I gave to him wreathe crowns to place upon their heads. I sent him to the majestic Ophannim, to crown them with strength and glory. I sent him to the honored Cherubim, to clothe them in majesty covered with radiant sparks, to make them to shine with splendor and bright light over the flaming Seraphim, to cover them with highness. I sent him to the Chashmallim of light, to make them radiant with light and to prepare the seat for me every morning as I sit upon the Throne of Glory. I have given him the secrets above and below, which are the heavenly secrets and earthly secrets so that he can praise and magnify my glory in the height of my power). (5) I made him higher than all. The height of his stature stood out in the midst of all who are of high of stature. I made seventy thousand parasangs. I made his Throne great by the majesty of my Throne. And I increased its glory by the honor of My glory. (6) I transformed his flesh into torches of fire, and all the bones of his body into burning coals; and I made his eyes look like lightning, and the light of his eyebrows as a light that will never be quenched. I made his face as bright as the splendor of the sun, and his eyes like the splendor of the Throne of Glory.

The description of Metatron is that of an angel and specifically a Seraphim, who is a fiery creature. A wreathe means victory.

(7) I made his clothing honor and majesty, beauty and highness. I covered him with a cloak and a crown of a size of 500 by 500 parasangs and this was his diadem. And I put My honor, My majesty and the splendor of My glory that is on My Throne of Glory upon him. I called him the "LESSER YHWH," the Prince of the Presence, the Knower of Secrets:. I revealed every secret to him as a father and as a friend, and all mysteries I spoke to him in truth. (8) I

set up his throne at the door of My hall that he may sit and judge the heavenly household on high. And I made every prince subject to him, so that they will receive his authority and perform his will. (9) I took Seventy names from my names and called him by them to enhance his glory. I placed Seventy princes into his hand so that he can command them to do my laws and obey my words in every language. And the proud will be brought to the ground by his word, and by the speech of his mouth he will exalt the humble to high places. He is to strike kings by his speech, to turn kings away from their own plans, and he is to set up the rulers over their dominion for it is written *(Dan. 51: 21):* "and he changes the times and the seasons, "and to give wisdom unto all the wise of the world and understanding and knowledge to all who understand *(Dan. 51: 21):* "and knowledge to them that know understanding." He is to reveal to them the secrets of my words and to teach them the command of my judgment in righteousness.

God is the God of the universe. He is the God of all. His names are infinite. Names reveal power, authority, personality traits, and character. Metatron is given authority over the nations. There are 70 nations and Metatron has 70 names.

(10) It is written *(Is. 55: 11):* "so shall My word be that goes forth out of my mouth; it shall not return unto me void but shall accomplish that which I please." I shall accomplish that which is not written here, but " he shall accomplish. Every word and every speech that goes out from the Holy One, blessed be He, Metatron stands and carries out. And he establishes the orders of the Holy One, blessed be He. (11) "And he shall make to prosper that which I sent." I will make to prosper what is not written here but he shall make to prosper teaching, that whatever decree proceeds from the Holy One, blessed be He, concerning a man, as soon as he makes repentance, they do not execute it upon him but they execute it upon another wicked man, for it is written *(Prov. 9:8):* "The righteous is delivered out of trouble, and the wicked comes in his place."

If a man repents and is no longer wicked, the angels inflicts his punishment on a person who is still wicked and has not repented.

(12) And not only that but Metatron sits three hours every day in the high heavens, and he gathers all the souls of those dead who died in their mothers womb, and the nursing baby who died on their mother's breast, and of the scholars who died over the five books of the Law. And he brings them under the Throne of Glory and places them in companies, divisions and classes round the Presence, and there he teaches them the Law, and the books of Wisdom, and Haggada and Tradition and completes their education for them. It is written *(Is. 28: 9)* "Whom will he teach knowledge?

And whom will he make to understand tradition? Them that are weaned from the milk and draw from the breast."

Ancient Jews viewed learning as one way to approach God. To study the Torah is almost as good as worship and prayer. Unborn, sucklings, and those who die while studying the Torah are guiltless.

CHAPTER 48D
The names of Metatron.

The names fall into three major categories: those which are built upon the name El, *those that are based on the name* Metatron, *and those based on the name* Yah. *The reader will notice the letters EL, ON, and YAH or YA in the names. Although the text states there are 70 names, there are in fact 105 names listed. The Latinized version of the 1928 work is referenced in this list however the parsing and pronunciations are unique to this work in order to accent the holy names found within most of the 105 names..*

(1)Seventy names has Metatron which the Holy One, blessed be He, took from His own name and put upon him. And these they are: 1 Yeho-EL Yah, 2 Yeho-EL, 3 Yofi-EL and 4 Yophphi-EL, and 5 Hafifi-EL and 6 Margezi-EL, 7 Gippyu-EL, 8 Pahazi-EL, 9 Hahah, 10 Pepri-EL, 11 Tatri-EL, 12 Tabki-EL, 13 Haw, 14 YHWH, 15 Dah 16, WHYH, 17 Hebed, 18 DiburiEL, 19 Hafhapi-EL, 20 Spi-EL, 21 Paspasi-EL, 22 Senetron, 23 Metatron, 24 Sogdin, 25 HadriGon, 26 Asum, 27 Sakhpam, 28 Sakhtam, 29 Mig-on, 30 Mitt-on, 31 Mot-tron, 32 Rosfim, 33 Khinoth, 34 KhataTiah, 35 Degaz-Yah, 36 Pisf-YaH, 37 Habiskin-Yah, 38 Mixar, 39 Barad, 40 Mikirk, 41 Mispird, 42 Khishig, 43 Khishib, 44 Minret, 45 Bisyrym, 46 Mitmon, 47 Titmon 48 Piskhon, 49 SafsafYah, 50 Zirkhi, 51 ZirkhYah 52 'B', 53 Be-Yah, 54 HiBhbe-Yah, 55 Pelet, 56 Pit-Yah, 57 Rabrab-YaH, 58 Khas, 59 Khas-Yah, 60 Tafaf-Yah, 61 Tamtam-Yah, 62 Sehas-Yah, 63 Hirhur-Yah, 64 Halhal-Yah, 65 BazrId-Yah, 66 Satsatk-Yah, 67 Sasd-Yah, 68 Razraz-Yah, 69 BaZzraz-Yah, 70 Harim-Yah, 71 Sibh-Yah, 72 Sibibkh-Yah, 73 Simkam, 74 Yah-Se-Yah, 75 Sibib-Yah, 76 Sabkasbe-Yah, 77 khelil-khil-Yah, 78 Kih, 79 HHYH, 80 WH, 81 WHYH, (letters in the holy YHWH) 82 Zakik-Yah, 83 Turtis-Yah, 84 Sur-Yah, 85 Zeh, 86 Penir-Yah, 87 ZihZih, 88 Galraza-Yah, 89 Mamlik-Yah, 90 Hitt-Yah, 91 Hemekh, 92 Kham-Yah, 93 Mekaper-Yah, 94 Perish-Yah, 95 Sefam, 96 Gibir, 97 Gibor-Yah, 98 Gor, 99 Gor-Yah, 100 Ziw, 101 Hokbar, the 102 LESSER YHWH, after the name of his Master, *(Ex. 23: 21)* "for My name is in him,"103 Rabibi-EL, 104 TUMIEL, 105 Segansakkiel, the Prince of Wisdom.

(2) And why is he called by the name Sagnesakiel? Because all the storehouses of wisdom are committed in to his hand. (3) And all of them were opened to Moses on Sinai, so that he learned them during the 40 days, while he remained. He learned the Torah in the seventy ways it applies to

the seventy nations, and the Prophets and the seventy application of the seventy tongues, the writings in the seventy variations of the seventy tongues, the Halakas (Jewish law and ritual) in the seventy applications of the seventy nations, the Traditions in the seventy aspects of the seventy nations, the Haggadas (Passover Seder) in the seventy aspects of the seventy tongues and the Toseftas (Secondary compilation of Jewish oral laws) in the seventy aspects of the seventy tongues. (4) But as soon as the 40 days were completed, he forgot all of them in one moment. Then the Holy One, blessed be He, called Yephiphyah, the Prince of the Law, and (through him) they were given to Moses as a gift, for it is written *(Deut. 10:4)*: "and the Lord gave them to me." And after that it remained with him. And how do we know that it remained in his memory? Because it is written ***(Mal. 4:5-6):*** "Remember the Law of Moses my servant which I commanded unto him in Horeb for all Israel, even my statues and judgments." 'The Law of Moses': that is the Torah, the Prophets and the Writings, 'statues': that is the Halakas and Traditions, 'judgments'; that is the Haggadas and the Toseftas. And all of them were given to Moses on high on Sinai. (5) These seventy names are a reflection of the Explicit names and given to the name of Metatron: seventy Names of His by which the ministering angels call the King of the kings of kings, blessed be He, in the high heavens, and twenty-two letters (of the Hebrew alphabet) that are on the ring placed on his finger with which are sealed the destinies of the high, powerful and great princes of kingdoms and with which are sealed along with the future of the Angel of Death, and the destinies of every nation and tongue. (6) Metatron, the Angel, the Prince of the Presence said; the Angel who is the Prince of the Wisdom and the Angel who the Prince of the Understanding, and the Angel who the Prince of the Kings, and the Angel who the Prince of the Rulers, and the angel who is the Prince of the Glory, and the angel who is the Prince of the high ones and of the princes, all of which are the exalted, greatly honored ones in heaven and on earth: (7) "YHWH, the God of Israel, is my witness that I revealed this secret to Moses and when I did all the host all the high heavens were enraged against me. (8) They asked me, saying, "Why do you reveal this secret to a son of man, born of woman, who is tainted and unclean, a man of the putrefying drop? You gave him the secret by which heaven and earth, sea and land, mountains and hills, rivers and springs, Gehenna of fire and hail, the Garden of Eden and the Tree of Life were all created and by which Adam and Eve, and the cattle, and the wild beasts, the birds of the air, and the fish of the sea, and Behemoth and Leviathan, and the crawling things, the snakes, the dragons of the sea, and the creeping things of the deserts; and Torah and Wisdom and Knowledge and Thought and the imparted knowledge and the Gnosis of things above and of heaven and the fear of heaven were all created. Why did you reveal this to flesh and blood? I answered them: Because the Holy One, blessed be He, has given me authority. And furthermore, I have obtained permission from the high and exalted throne, from which all the Explicit names go forth with lightning and fire and flaming chashmallim.

Verse 7 makes a statement that when the complete gnosis or revealed knowledge was given to Moses (through Metatron) all the heavenly host was enraged at the act. This Knowledge was not even available to all the host of heaven but was given to a human. Verse 8 asks the question in a direct and insulting way. To slightly paraphrase, it asked, "Why did You give the secrets of creation to this human who was conceived by a woman, through the transfer of semen, which spoils and putrefies and then gives birth, when blood from birth and menses is considered unclean, as is the woman herself for a time after a ritual cleansing. In light of this, all the heavenly hosts consider humans to be inferior, unclean, animals. Still, God chose to transmit to Moses the secret gnosis of creation.

Behemoth is the primal unconquerable monster of the land. Leviathan is the primal monster of the waters of the sea. Ziz is their counterpart in the sky. There is a legend that the Leviathan and the Behemoth shall hold a battle at the end of the world. The two will finally kill each other, and the surviving men will feast on their meat. Behemoth also appears in the 1 Enoch, giving a description of this monster's origins there mentioned as being male, as opposed to the female Leviathan. See Job, chapter 40 for further information.

(9) But they (the hosts) were not appeased or satisfied, until the Holy One, blessed be He, scorned them and drove them away from Him with contempt and said to them: "I delight in him, and have set my love on him, and have entrusted to him and given unto Metatron, my Servant, and I have given to him alone, for he is Unique among all the children of heaven. (10) And Metatron brought them out from his house and storehouses and gave these secrets to Moses, and Moses gave them to Joshua, and Joshua gave them to the elders, and the elders to gave them the prophets and the men of the Great Synagogue, and the men of the Great Synagogue gave them to Ezra and Ezra the Scribe gave them to Hillel the elder, and Hillel the elder gave them to Rabbi Abbahu and Rabbi Abbahu to Rabbi Zera, and Rabbi Zera to the men of faith, and the men of faith gave them to give warning and to heal by them all disease that ravaged the world, for it is written *(Ex. 15: 26)*: "If you will diligently hearken to the voice of the Lord, your God, and will do that which is right in His eyes, and will give ear to His commandments, and keep all his statues, I will put none of the disease upon you, which I have put on the Egyptians, for I am the Lord that heals you."

(Ended and finished. Praise be unto the Creator of the World.)

Hillel was said to be one of the greatest and wisest rabbis.

A Narrative of Fallen Angels, the Watchers, and the Nephilim

Composed From Various Sacred Texts.

The Alpha

The origins of evil are planted deeply within each of us. Evil is innocent as a child and monstrously vicious. It feeds upon the same flesh and breathes the same air as saint and martyr. Free will and personal choice direct our steps to heaven or hell and mark us as good or evil. Whether we are angel, watcher, nephilim, or man, evil is a choice many give themselves over to, fully and completely.

What is evil? Could it be as simple as pernicious selfishness? Could it be the drive for immediate gratification without regard for others? Man's life is limited; 100 years or less. But, the souls of angel and watcher are eternal. Consider how much evil can be wrought through the millennia of immediate gratification on an eternal scale.

It continues to be pride that keeps us from seeing the truth of our own nature. Pride itself blinds us to our own pride. Pride, arrogance, and selfishness are the seeds and flowers arising from the same root of evil. Evil is the manifestation of the same, all too common, human condition; a condition afflicting angels and watchers alike.

"The fear of the Lord is to hate evil: pride, and arrogance, and the evil way, and the froward mouth, do I hate." Proverbs 8:13

The root and cause of all evil arise from a self-centered viewpoint that takes no one else into consideration. It is the drive to control, dominate, and consume. The condition comes from tunnel vision so narrow as to include only the person and his desires. This calls into question the nature of evil.

Does evil have a reasoned intent to hurt, kill, and destroy or is there an egomaniacal innocence to evil? Could it be that complete evil is actually a blind selfishness? Does evil not arise from a refusal to consider the life, position, or feelings of others? Evil thoughts, actions, and feelings are based on fulfilling one's own desires at the expense or destruction of all others. Feelings and welfare of others do not come into play, nor do they cross the mind of an evil being. The nature of evil is a twisted, childish, innocence; a self-centered and myopic view.

How strange and paradoxical; how appropriate Satan should take what was so much a part of his own nature and assist man in finding it so abundantly in himself.

As it is written of Satan in the Book of Isaiah:

"How art thou fallen from heaven, O Lucifer, son of the morning! How art thou cut down to the ground, which didst weaken the nations! For thou hast said in thine heart, I will ascend into heaven, I will exalt my throne above the stars of God: I will sit also upon the mount of the congregation, in the sides of the north: I will ascend above the heights of the clouds; I will be like the most High." *(Isaiah 14:12-14)*

As it is written in the records of man, in the most ancient books of Enoch, Jasher, and Jubilees:

Look the children of men have become evil because the building of a city and a tower in the land of Shinar was for an evil purpose. They built the city and the tower, saying, "Go to, let us rise up thereby into heaven." And whilst they were building against the Lord God of heaven, they imagined in their hearts to war against him and to ascend into heaven.

And all these people and all the families divided themselves in three parts; the first said, "We will ascend into heaven and fight against him;" the second said, "We will ascend to heaven and place our own gods there and serve them;" and the third part said, "We will ascend to heaven and strike him with bows and spears." God knew all their works and all their evil thoughts, and he saw the city and the tower which they were building.

Ancient texts reveal the history of evil

Yet this is only the beginning of the story. Hidden within the most ancient texts are the footprints of evil's origins. Spread through these books are threads of truth left here and there in racial memories and oral histories dating back to the first recollections of man. In this primal state, evil was born and the story was recorded.

By contrasting and comparing ancient texts containing the creation of angels, demons, and man, a full and panoramic history of evil is produced. In this history the startling revelation of the descent of man and angels, and the evolution of evil on earth is clearly revealed.

The books selected for this purpose are First and Second Adam and Eve, Jasher, Jubilees, First and Second Enoch, the War Scrolls, The Book of Giants, the Bible, and other ancient texts. Each of these ancient texts carries within it a piece of the story. By weaving the stories together, the origins of evil are brought into focus.

Holy Scriptures and Jewish oral traditions are inserted

Related scriptures are interwoven to add detail to the history of evil. In these cases scriptures may be inserted non-chronologically. However, these are digressions used to emphasize certain points within the ancient texts.

Certain familiar Jewish oral traditions and myths were inserted at the appropriate places in the timeline. Since myths are given less weight of authenticity, the passages are included in italics to distinguish them from the more accepted texts. The Fragment of the Book of Giants is also italicized and noted due to the unique and fragmented information.

Although there were fragments from over 600 separate scrolls found in the caves of Quman, only a few fragments were used in tracing the history of evil. The War Scroll is one such scroll.

The Dead Sea Scrolls and the War Scroll

The Dead Sea Scrolls comprise documents, including texts from the Hebrew Bible, discovered between 1947 and 1956 in 11 caves in and around the Wadi Qumran on the northwest shore of the Dead Sea. They are Biblical and religious documents of great historical value dating from before A.D. 100.

In 1955, the War Scroll was found in Cave 1 at Qumran. Other fragments were found in Cave 4. The 19 columns of the scroll were badly mutilated. After great pains, the fragments were deciphered and published by the Hebrew University in Jerusalem

The War Scroll is thought to have been written sometime after the mid-first century B.C.E to the beginning of the 1st Century CE. The author of the manuscript made use of the Book of Daniel. The War Scroll contains rules for the military, religious preparations, and how the fighting was to be conducted.

In the War Scroll we see the sons of light, who are the remnants of the Jewish faithful, exiled into the wilderness by an ever-darkening world. Out of the wilderness of Jerusalem they return to fight against the sons of darkness, the children of Belial, in the last days. This fits in very well with our accepted prophecies in the book of Revelation.

No story is complete without a resolution to the problem. Essene literature sees the conclusion in the person of the "teacher of righteousness." This figure was the Messiah who would come to teach and guide them into the new kingdom. This figure is fulfilled in the person of Jesus as he establishes his eternal kingdom at his second coming. Thus, the story of evil and man's conquest over Satan or Mastema ends when he is overcome and destroyed by the teacher of righteousness, Jesus, the Messiah. The story presented here is an abbreviated one drawn from the New Testament books of Matthew, Mark, Luke, John, Acts, and Revelation.

From the beginning of man's oral history, through our present age, and ending with prophecies some say will occur in this generation, the story of evil is told. Its origins and its abolition are laid out before us in the words of historians, priests, and prophets, to be read as a warning of our own susceptibility to enemies unseen.

The listing and description of all sources used in the telling of our story can be found at the end of our tale. Some sources are but fragments and when placed within the story, their missing pieces may add a disjointed or staccato-like rendering to the story. In those places a note is placed and the patience of the reader is requested. When condensing thousands of lines of unaltered texts into a compact storyline some leeway will hopefully be given.

Preface

What you are about to read is not in any Bible. It is a story drawn from the pages of some of the oldest writings on earth. The stories told in these ancient pages were both historical and prophetic. All of them spoke of the same occurrences, those of the birth, history, and destruction of evil.

From the books of First and Second Adam and Eve, Jasher, Jubilees, First and Second Enoch, the War Scrolls, The Book of Giants, the Bible, and other ancient texts, each narrator tells a version of the same events, rich in detail. By combining all the narratives and removing repetitive events we come to a place of awe, where the specific aspects before us are amazing and finely painted.

The majority of the narrative sources are mixed. In these sections the reader is informed of the multiple sources. The reader is never told what line, word, or phrase came from any particular book. The story is written, as any story should be, without pause. Only the myth of Lilith and a fragment of the Book of Giants is set apart by being printed in italicized font. This was done to distinguish Lilith, a traditional oral myth of the Middle Ages from those books honored in the halls of much greater antiquity. The Book of Giants is italicized and labeled to alert the readers to the fragmented information and thus some disjointed sentences.

The history of evil begs the deepest and most profound questions. Was evil created, or discovered within us as a consequence of free will? Did God, who created everything, create evil? Did He who is omniscient realize what would happen when He gave all sentient beings the ability to choose? How did it begin, and where will it end? Let us read what the prophets say.

The Fallen Angels, The Watchers, and The Origins of Evil

In the beginning, God created the heavens and the earth, and the earth was formless, vacant, and chaotic. Darkness was everywhere and no light was seen except God, Himself. God formed the earth, divided the lands and waters, and set the clouds, sky, and earth in place. He made the sun and moon and all the planets and set their courses, dividing day from night. All heavenly bodies were assigned their times and paths and none varied from God's word.

God created all things living, and then he created man. He created a man and a woman and gave them dominion over all things. God named the man Adam, and the woman He named Lilith. Both were formed from the dust of the earth and in both God breathed the breath of life. They became human souls and God endowed them with the power of speech.

Created at the same time, in the same way, there was no master, no leader, and only bickering between them. Lilith said, "I will not be below you, in life or during sex. I want the superior position." But Adam would not relent and insisted God had created him to be the head of the family and in the affairs of earth. Lilith was enraged and would not submit.

Then God communed with Adam in the cool of the evening and as he entered into His presence, Adam appealed to God. As God fellowshipped with them, they reasoned together, Adam, Lilith, and the living God. But Lilith would not listen to God or Adam. Seeing that with two people of equal authority there could be no solution, Lilith became frustrated, angry, and intractable. Finally, enraged and defiant, she pronounced the holy and ineffable name of God. Corrupting the power of the name, she flew into the air, changing form, and disappeared, soaring out of sight.

Adam stood alone, confused, praying. "Lord of the universe," he said, "The woman you gave me has run away." At once, three holy angels were dispatched to bring her back to Adam. The angels overtook Lilith as she passed over the sea, in the area where Moses would later pass through. The angels ordered Lilith to come with them in the name and by the authority of the most high God, but she refused. As her rebellion increased, she changed, becoming more and more ugly and demonic.

God spoke into Lilith's heart, saying, "You have chosen this evil path, and so shall you become evil. You are cursed from now until the end of days." Lilith spoke to the angels and said, "I have become this, created to cause sickness, to kill children, which I will never have, and to torment men." With these words, she completed her demonic transformation. Her form was that of a succubus.

Confined to the night, she was destined to roam the earth, seeking newborn babes, stealing their lives, and strangling them in their sleep. She torments men even now, causing lust and evil dreams. Her rebellious and evil spirit forever traps her. Bound in the darkness of her own heart, Lilith became the mistress and lover to legions of demons. And Adam's countenance fell and he mourned for he had loved Lilith, and he was again alone and lonely.

God said, "It is not good for man to be alone." And the Lord God caused a deep sleep to fall on him, and he slept, and He took from Adam a rib from among his ribs for the woman, and this rib was the origin of the woman. And He built up the flesh in its place, and created the woman. He awakened Adam out of his sleep. On awakening Adam rose on the sixth day, and God brought her to Adam, and he knew her, and said to her, "This is now bone of my bones and flesh of my flesh; she shall be called woman for she was taken from man, and she shall be called my wife; because she was taken from her husband."

Her name will be Eve, for she will be the mother of all. Therefore shall man and wife become one. Because of this a man shall leave his father and his mother, and cling to his wife, and they shall be one flesh.

In the first week of creation Adam was created, and from his rib, his wife was formed.

(Here begins The Gnostic Gospels)

And the whole kingdom of the first (head) archon (power) quaked, and the foundations of the abyss shook. And the underside of waters, which are above material world, were illuminated by the appearance of his image which had been revealed. When all the authorities and the head archon looked, they saw the whole region of the underside (of the waters) that was illuminated. And through the light they saw the form of the image (reflected) in the water.

And he (Yaldaboth) said to the authorities of him, "Come, let us make a man using the image of God as a template to our likeness, that his image may become a light for us." And they created by the means of their various powers matching the features which were given to them. And each authority supplied a feature in the form of the image which Yaldaboth had seen in its natural form. He created a being according to the likeness of the first, perfect Man. And they said, "Let us call him Adam (man), that his name may be a power of light for us."

(Here begins the Apocryphon of John) -

And the powers began to create.

The first one, Goodness, created a bone essence; and the second, Foreknowledge, created a sinew essence; the third, Divinity, created a flesh essence; and the fourth, the Lordship, created a marrow essence; the fifth, Kingdom created a blood essence; the sixth, Envy, created a skin essence; the seventh, Understanding, created a hair essence. And the multitude of the angels were with him and they received from the powers the seven elements of the natural (form) so they could create the proportions of the limbs and the proportion of the buttocks and correct functioning of each of the parts together.

The first one began to create the head. Eteraphaope-Abron created his head; Meniggesstroeth created the brain; Asterechme created the right eye; Thaspomocha, the left eye; Yeronumos, the right ear; Bissoum, the left ear; Akioreim, the nose; Banen-Ephroum, the lips; Amen, the teeth; Ibikan, the molars; Basiliademe, the tonsils; Achcha, the uvula; Adaban, the neck; Chaaman, the vertebrae; Dearcho, the throat; Tebar, the right shoulder; the left shoulder; Mniarcon, the right elbow; the left elbow; Abitrion, the right underarm; Evanthen, the left underarm; Krys, the right hand; Beluai, the left hand; Treneu, the fingers of the right hand; Balbel, the fingers of the left hand; Kriman, the nails of the hands; Astrops, the right breast; Barroph, the left breast; Baoum, the right shoulder joint; Ararim, the left shoulder joint; Areche, the belly; Phthave, the navel; Senaphim, the abdomen; Arachethopi, the right ribs; Zabedo, the left ribs; Barias, the right hip; Phnouth the left hip; Abenlenarchei, the marrow; Chnoumeninorin, the bones; Gesole, the stomach; Agromauna, the heart; Bano, the lungs; Sostrapal, the liver; Anesimalar, the spleen; Thopithro, the intestines; Biblo, the kidneys; Roeror, the sinews; Taphreo, the spine of the body; Ipouspoboba, the veins; Bineborin, the arteries; Atoimenpsephei, theirs are the breaths which are in all the limbs; Entholleia, all the flesh; Bedouk, the right buttock; Arabeei, the penis; Eilo, the testicles; Sorma, the genitals; Gorma-Kaiochlabar, the right thigh; Nebrith, the left thigh; Pserem, the kidneys of the right leg; Asaklas, the left kidney; Ormaoth, the right leg; Emenun, the left leg; Knyx, the right shin-bone; Tupelon, the left shin-bone; Achiel, the right knee; Phnene, the left knee; Phiouthrom, the right foot; Boabel, its toes; Trachoun, the left foot; Phikna, its toes; Miamai, the nails of the feet; Labernioum.

And those who were appointed over all of these are: Zathoth, Armas, Kalila, Jabel, (Sabaoth, Cain, Abel). And those who are particularly active in the limbs are the head Diolimodraza, the neck Yammeax, the right shoulder Yakouib, the left shoulder Verton, the right hand Oudidi, the left one Arbao, the fingers of the right hand Lampno, the fingers of the left hand Leekaphar, the right breast Barbar, the left breast Imae, the chest Pisandriaptes, the right shoulder joint Koade, the left shoulder joint Odeor, the right ribs Asphixix, the left ribs Synogchouta, the belly Arouph, the womb Sabalo, the right thigh Charcharb, the left thigh Chthaon, all the genitals Bathinoth, the right leg Choux, the left leg Charcha, the right shin-bone Aroer, the left shin-bone Toechtha, the right knee Aol, the left knee Charaner, the right foot Bastan, its toes Archentechtha, the left foot Marephnounth, its toes Abrana.

(Note: Could this be those constructing human DNA or a the blueprint to the human form? Were we created as an experiment of another race?)

Seven have power over all of these: Michael, Ouriel, Asmenedas, Saphasatoel, Aarmouriam, Richram, Amiorps. And the ones who are in charge of the senses are Archendekta; and he who is in charge of the receptions is Deitharbathas; and he who is in charge over the imagination is Oummaa; and he who is over creativity Aachiaram, and he who is over the whole impulse Riaramnacho.

The origin of the demons that are in the entire body is known to be these four: heat, cold, wetness, and dryness. And the mother of all of them is the material creation. And he who rules over the heat is Phloxopha; and he who rules over the cold is Oroorrothos; and he who rules over what is dry is Erimacho; and he who rules over the wetness is Athuro. And the mother of all of these is Onorthochrasaei, who stands in with them without limits, and she covorts with all of them. She is truly material and they are sustained by her.

The four ruling demons are: Ephememphi, who is attached to pleasure,

Yoko, who is attached to desire, Nenentophni, who is attached to grief,

Blaomen, who is attached to fear, and the mother of them all is Aesthesis-Ouch-Epi-Ptoe. And from the four demons passions was created. And grief spawned envy, jealousy, distress, trouble, pain, callousness, anxiety, mourning, and more. Pleasure spawned wickedness, vanity, pride, and similar things. Desire spawned anger, wrath, and bitterness, and driving passion, the inability to be satisfied, and similar things. Fear spawned dread, subservience, agony, and shame. These are both good and evil, but the understanding of their nature is attributed to Anaro, who is over the material soul. It belongs with the seven senses, which are controlled by Ouch-Epi-Ptoe.

This is the number of the angels: together they are 365. They all worked on it from limb to limb, until the physical (material) body was completed by them.

In the second week God showed her to him. For this reason the commandment was given to keep in the times of their defilement (from birth). A male should be purified in seven days and for a female twice seven days. After Adam had completed forty days in the land where he had been created, the angels brought him into the garden of Eden to till and keep it, but his wife the angels brought in on the eightieth day, and after this she entered into the garden of Eden.

And God spoke to Adam and Eve and said, "Be fruitful, multiply, and replenish the earth."

In these days there was a great war in heaven. Lucifer, who is known as the son of the morning, amassed one third of the angels of heaven and fought for supremacy. In righteous anger, God arose and spoke to Lucifer, "Hell from beneath is moved for thee to meet thee at thy coming; it stirreth up the dead for thee, even all the chief ones of the earth; it hath raised up from their thrones all the kings of the nations.

"All shall speak and say unto thee, Art thou also become weak as we? Art thou become like unto us? Thy pomp is brought you down to the grave, and the noise of thy viols. The worm is spread under thee, and the worms cover thee. How art thou fallen from heaven, O Lucifer, son of the morning! How art thou cut down to the ground, you who didst weaken the nations! For thou hast said in thine heart, I will ascend into heaven, I will exalt my throne above the stars of God: I will sit also upon the mount of the congregation, in the sides of the north.

"I will ascend above the heights of the clouds; I will be like the most High. Yet thou shalt be brought down to hell, to the sides of the pit."

But Lucifer did not heed the words of God, and the war in heaven began.

Michael and his host fought against Lucifer and his army and Michael prevailed. And Lucifer, whose name became Satan, the devil, and Mastema, was thrown down to the earth in defeat and dishonor. And Jesus, who is the word of God and with him from the beginning, watched as Lucifer was defeated in heaven and cast down. And he said unto them, "I beheld Satan as lightning fall from heaven." Thus, the war in heaven would be waged on earth for the prize of the souls of man.

Then Satan entered into the serpent, for the serpent was willing. And he waited until the time of deceit was at hand.

After the completion of exactly seven years there, and in the second month, on the seventeenth day of the month, the serpent, which God had created with them in the earth, came to Eve to incite them to go contrary to the command of God which he had given them. The serpent approached the woman, and the serpent said to the woman, "Has God commanded you saying, you shall not eat of every tree of the garden?"

She said to it, "God said to us, 'Of all the fruit of the trees of the garden, eat; but of the fruit of the tree which is in the middle of the garden,' God said to us, 'You shall not eat of it, neither shall you touch it, or you shall die.'"

The serpent said to the woman, "You shall not surely die. God knows if you were to eat the fruit of the tree your eyes would be opened and you would become as a god." And the woman saw the tree that it was beautiful and pleasant to the eye, and that its fruit was good for food. And the serpent enticed and persuaded the woman to eat from the tree of knowledge, and the woman listened to the voice of the serpent, and she went contrary to the word of God, and took from the tree of the knowledge of good and evil. And she took of it and ate. And she took from it and gave also to her husband and he ate. For, the serpent said, "You will not surely die. God knows that on the day you shall eat of it, your eyes will be opened, and you will be as gods, and you will know good and evil."

And Adam and his wife went contrary to the command of God which he commanded them, and God knew it, and his anger was set ablaze against them and he cursed them.

And the Lord God drove them that day from the Garden of Eden, to till the ground from which they were taken, and they went and lived at the east of the garden of Eden.

First, Eve covered her shame with fig leaves and then she gave the fruit to Adam and he ate, and his eyes were opened, and he saw that he was naked.

He took fig leaves and sewed them together, and made an apron for himself, and covered his shame.

God cursed the serpent, and was very angry at it forever. And He was very angry with the woman, because she listened to the voice of the serpent, and ate; and He said to her, "I will vastly multiply your sorrow and your pains, in sorrow you will bring forth children, and your master shall be your husband, and he will rule over you."

To Adam also he said, "Because you have listened to the voice of your wife, and have eaten of the tree of which I commanded you not to eat, cursed be the ground for your sake, thorns and thistles shall it produce for you, and you will eat your bread in the sweat of your face, until you return to the earth from where you were taken; for earth you are, and to earth will you return."

And God made for them coats of skin, and clothed them, and sent them out from the Garden of Eden.

(Here begins the Books of Adam and Eve)

God said to Adam, "I have ordained days and years on this earth, and you and your descendants shall live and walk in them until the days and years are fulfilled. Then I shall send the Word that created you and against which you have transgressed the Word that made you come out of the garden and that raised you when you were fallen. Yes, this is the Word that will again save you when the five and a half days are fulfilled."

But when Adam heard these words from God, and of the great five and a half days he did not understand the meaning of them. For Adam was thinking there would be only five and a half days for him until the end of the world. And Adam cried and prayed to God to explain it to him. Then God in his mercy for Adam who was made after His own image and likeness explained to him that these were 5,000 and 500 years and how (the) One would then come and save him and his descendants. But before that, God had made this covenant with our father, Adam, in the same terms before he came out of the garden, when he was by the tree where Eve took of the fruit and gave it to him to eat. Because, when our father, Adam, came out of the garden he passed by that tree and saw how God had changed the appearance of it into another form and how it had shriveled.

And as Adam went to it he feared, trembled, and fell down. But God in His mercy lifted him up and then made this covenant with him. Also, when Adam was by the gate of the garden he saw the cherub with a sword of flashing fire in his hand, and the cherub grew angry and frowned at him. Both Adam and Eve became afraid of the cherub and thought he meant to put them to death. So they fell on their faces, trembling with fear. But he had pity on them and showed them mercy. And turning from them, he went up to heaven and prayed to the Lord, and said; "Lord, You sent me to watch at the gate of the garden, with a sword of fire. But when Your servants, Adam and Eve, saw me, they fell on their faces, and were as dead. O my Lord, what shall we do to Your servants?"

Then God had pity on them, and showed them mercy, and sent His Angel to keep the garden. And the Word of the Lord came to Adam and Eve, and raised them up. And the Lord said to Adam, "I told you that at the end of the five and a half days I will send my Word and save you. Therefore, strengthen your heart and stay in the Cave of Treasures, of which I have spoken to you before." And when Adam heard this Word from God he was comforted with that which God had told him. For He had told him how He would save him.

But God had said to him, of your own free will have you transgressed through your desire for divinity, greatness, and an exalted state, such as I have; therefore I deprived you of the bright nature which you had then, and I made you come out of the garden to this land, rough and full of trouble. If only you had not transgressed My commandment and had kept My law, and had not eaten of the fruit of the tree which I told you not to come near! And there were fruit trees in the garden better than that one.

But the wicked Satan did not keep his faith and had no good intent towards Me, and although I had created him he considered Me to be useless, and he sought the Godhead for himself. For this I hurled him down from heaven so that he could not remain in his first estate. It was he who made the tree appear pleasant to your eyes until you ate of it by believing his words. Thus have you transgressed My commandment, and therefore I have brought on you all these sorrows. For I am God the Creator, who, when I created My creatures, did not intend to destroy them. But after they had greatly roused My anger I punished them with grievous plagues until they repent. But, if on the contrary they still continue hardened in their transgression they shall be under a curse forever." But Adam and Even continued to seek God and Pray with fervent hearts.

Satan, the hater of all that is good, saw how they continued in prayer, and how God communed with them, and comforted them, and how He had accepted their offering. Then Satan made a phantasm. He began by transforming his hosts. In his hands was a shining, glimmering fire, and they were in a huge light. Then, he placed his throne near the mouth of the cave, because he could not enter it due to their prayers. And he shown light into the cave until the cave glistened over Adam and Eve while his hosts began to sing praises. Satan did this so that when Adam saw the light he would think to himself that it was a heavenly light and that Satan's hosts were angels and that God had sent them to watch at the cave, and give him light in the darkness.

Satan planned that when Adam came out of the cave and saw them and Adam and Eve bowed to Satan, then he would overcome Adam and humble him before God a second time. When, therefore, Adam and Eve saw the light, thinking it was real, they strengthened their hearts. Then, as they were trembling, Adam said to Eve: "Look at that great light, and at those many songs of praise, and at that host standing outside who won't come into our cave. Why don't they tell us what they want or where they are from or what the meaning of this light is or what those praises are or why they have been sent to this place, and why they won't come in? If they were from God, they would come into the cave with us and would tell us why they were sent."

Then Adam stood up and prayed to God with a burning heart and said: "O Lord, is there in the world another god besides You who created angels and filled them with light, and sent them to keep us, who would come with them? But, look, we see these hosts that stand at the mouth of the cave. They are in a great light and they sing loud praises. If they are of some other god(s) than You, tell me, and if they are sent by you, inform me of the reason for which You have sent them." No sooner had Adam said this, than an angel from God appeared to him in the cave, who said to him, "O Adam, fear not. This is Satan and his hosts. He wishes to deceive you as he deceived you at first. For the first time, he was hidden in the serpent, but this time he is come to you in the likeness of an angel of light in order that, when you worshipped him, he might enslave you in the very presence of God."

Then the angel went from Adam and seized Satan at the opening of the cave, and stripped him of the false image (lie/pretense) he had assumed and brought him in his own hideous form to Adam and Eve who were afraid of him when they saw him.

But Satan, the hater of all that is good, thought to himself: "God has promised salvation to Adam by covenant, and promised that He would deliver him from all the hardships that have befallen him, but God has not promised me by covenant, and will not deliver me out of my hardships. He has promised Adam that He should make him and his descendants live in the kingdom that I once lived in. I will kill Adam. The earth shall be rid of him. The earth shall be left to me alone. When he is dead he will not have any descendants left to inherit the kingdom and it will remain my own realm. God will then be wanting me, and He will restore it to me and my hosts." And so Satan never stopped seeking to destroy Adam and Eve.

After this Satan, the hater of all that is good, took the form of an angel, and two others with him. So, they looked like the three angels who had brought to Adam gold, incense, and myrrh. They came to Adam and Eve while they were under the tree, and greeted Adam and Eve with friendly words that were full of deceit. But when Adam and Eve saw their friendly countenance and heard their sweet speech, Adam rose, welcomed them, and brought them to Eve and they remained all together. Adam's heart was happy all the while because he thought that they were the same angels, who had brought him gold, incense, and myrrh. This was because when they came to Adam the first time peace and joy came over him from them because they brought him good gifts.

So Adam thought that they had come a second time to give him other gifts to make him rejoice. He did not know it was Satan, therefore he received them with joy and associated with them. Then Satan, the tallest of them, said, "Rejoice, Adam, and be glad. Look, God has sent us to you to tell you something." And Adam said, "What is it?" Then Satan said, "It is a simple thing, but it is the Word of God. Will you accept it from us and do it? If you will not accept it, we will return to God and tell Him that you would not receive His Word." And Satan continued, saying to Adam, "Don't be afraid and don't shake. Don't you know us?" But Adam said, "I do not know you." Then Satan said to him, "I am the angel that brought you gold and took it to the cave. This other angel is the one that brought you incense. And that third angel is the one who brought you myrrh when you were on top of the mountain. It was he who carried you to the cave. It was our other fellow angels who lifted you to the cave. God has not sent them with us this time because He said to us, 'You will be enough.'"

So when Adam heard these words he believed them, and said to the angels, "Speak the Word of God, and I will receive it." And Satan said to him, "Swear and promise me that you will receive it." Then Adam said, "I do not know how to swear and promise." And Satan said to him, "Hold out your hand and put it inside my hand."

Then Adam held out his hand, and put it into Satan's hand. Satan said to him, "Now say this; As God who raised the stars in heaven, and established the dry ground on the waters, and has created me out of the four elements, and out of the dust of the earth, and is logical and true does speak, I will not break my promise, nor abandon my word." And Adam swore.

Then Satan said to him, "Look, some time has passed since you came out of the garden, and you do not know wickedness or evil. But now God says to you, to take Eve who came out of your side, and marry her so that she will bear you children to comfort you and to drive from you trouble and sorrow. This thing is not difficult and there is nothing morally wrong in it for you. But when Adam heard these words from Satan, he sorrowed much, because of his oath and his promise. And he said, "Shall I commit adultery with my flesh and my bones, and shall I sin against myself, so that God will destroy me blot me out from the face of the earth?

But from that day Adam struggled in his mind about marrying Eve, because he was afraid that if he did it, God would be angry with him. Then Adam and Eve went to the river of water, and sat on the bank, as people do when they enjoy themselves. But Satan was jealous of them and planned to destroy them.

Therefore Satan worked this apparition before Adam and Eve, because he sought to kill him, and to make him disappear from off the face of the earth. Meanwhile the fire of immorality came over Adam and he thought of committing transgression. But he restrained himself, fearing that if he followed the advice of Satan, God would put him to death. Then Adam and Eve got up and prayed to God, while Satan and his hosts went down into the river in front of Adam and Eve so they would see them going back to their own world.

Then Adam and Eve went back to the Cave of Treasures, as they usually did around evening time. And they both got up and prayed to God that night. Adam remained standing in prayer but did not know how to pray because of the thoughts in his heart about marrying Eve. And he continued this way until morning. When light came up, Adam said to Eve, "Get up, let us go below the mountain where they brought us gold and let us ask the Lord concerning this matter." Then Eve said, "What is that matter, Adam?" And he answered her, "That I may request the Lord to inform me about marrying you because I will not do it without His permission or else He will kill you and me. For those devils have set my heart on fire with thoughts of what they showed us in their sinful visions. Then Eve said to Adam, "Why do we need to go to the foot of the mountain? Let us rather stand up and pray in our cave to God to let us know whether this advice is good or not."

Then Adam rose up in prayer and said, "O God, you know that we transgressed against you, and from the moment we sinned we were stripped of our bright nature, and our body became brutish, requiring food and drink, and with animal desires. Command us, O God, not to give way to them without Your permission, for fear that You will turn us into nothing. If you do not give us permission we will be overcome and follow that advice of Satan, and You will again kill us. If not, then take our souls from us and let us be rid of this animal lust. And if You give us no order about this thing then separate Eve from me and me from her, and place us each far away from the other.

Then, O God, if You separate us from each other the devils will deceive us with their apparitions that resemble us, and destroy our hearts, and defile our thoughts towards each other. If our heart is not toward each other it will be toward them, through their appearance when the devils come to us in our likeness." Here Adam ended his prayer.

Then God considered the words of Adam that they were true, and that he could not wait long for His order, respecting the counsel of Satan. And God approved Adam in what he had thought concerning this, and in the prayer he had offered in His presence; and the Word of God came to Adam.

After that, God sent His angel who had brought gold, and the angel who had brought incense, and the angel who had brought myrrh to Adam, that they should inform him respecting his marriage to Eve. Then those angels said to Adam, "Take the gold and give it to Eve as a wedding gift, and promise to marry her; then give her some incense and myrrh as a present; and be you both will be one flesh." Adam obeyed the angels, and took the gold and put it into Eve's bosom in her garment; and promised to marry her with his hand. Then the angels commanded Adam and Eve to get up and pray forty days and forty nights; when that was done, then Adam was to have sexual intercourse with his wife; for then this would be an act pure and undefiled; so that he would have children who would multiply, and replenish the face of the earth. And God spoke to Adam and Eve and said, "Be fruitful, multiply, and replenish the earth."

(Here begins the Book of Jubilees)

Adam knew his wife Eve and she bore two sons and three daughters. In the third week in the second jubilee she gave birth to Cain, and in the fourth jubilee she gave birth to Abel, and in the fifth jubilee she gave birth to her daughter Awan.

In the first year of the third jubilee, Cain talked with Abel his brother. It was at the expiration of a few years, that they had brought a first-fruit offering to the Lord, and Cain brought from the fruit of the ground, and Abel brought from the firstlings of his flock from the fat thereof, and God turned and inclined to Abel and his offering, and a fire came down from the Lord from heaven and consumed it. And to Cain and his offering the Lord did not turn, and he did not incline to it, for he had brought from the inferior fruit of the ground before the Lord, and Cain was jealous against his brother Abel on account of this, and he sought an opportunity to kill him.

And in some time after, Cain and Abel his brother, went one day into the field to do their work; and they were both in the field, Cain farming and plowing his ground, and Abel feeding his flock; and the flock passed through that part which Cain had plowed in the ground, and it sorely grieved Cain on this account. And Cain approached his brother Abel in anger, and he said to him, "What gives you the right to come and live here and bring your flock to feed in my land?" And Abel answered his brother Cain and said to him, "What gives you the right to eat the flesh of my flock and clothe yourself with their wool? Take off the wool of my sheep with which you have clothed yourself, and pay me for their resources you have used and flesh which you have eaten, and when you shall have done this, I will then go from your land as you have said."

And Cain said to his brother Abel, "Certainly if I kill you this day, who will require your blood from me?" And Abel answered Cain, saying, "Certainly God who has made us in the earth, he will avenge my cause, and he will require my blood from you should you kill me, for the Lord is the judge and arbiter, and it is he who will repay man according to his evil, and the wicked man according to the wickedness that he may do upon earth. And now, if you should kill me here, certainly God knows your secret views, and will judge you for the evil which you declared to do to me this day."

And when Cain heard the words which Abel his brother had spoken, the anger of Cain was set ablaze against his brother Abel for declaring this thing. And Cain hurried and rose up, and took the iron part of his plowing instrument, with which he suddenly struck his brother and he killed him, and Cain spilled the blood of his brother Abel upon the earth, and the blood of Abel streamed upon the earth before the flock. And after this Cain repented of having slain his brother, and he was sadly grieved, and he wept over him and it troubled him exceedingly. And Cain rose up and dug a hole in the field, wherein he put his brother's body, and he turned the dust over it.

And the Lord said unto Cain, "Where is Abel thy brother?" And he said, "I know not: Am I my brother's keeper?" And he said, "What hast thou done? The voice of thy brother's blood crieth unto me from the ground. And now art thou cursed from the earth, which hath opened her mouth to receive thy brother's blood from thy hand; When thou tillest the ground, it shall not henceforth yield unto thee her strength; a fugitive and a vagabond shalt thou be in the earth."

"For you have slain your brother and have lied before me, and imagined in your heart that I saw you not, nor knew all your actions. But you did this thing and did kill your brother for naught, for he spoke rightly to you, and now therefore, cursed be you from the ground which opened its mouth to receive your brother's blood from your hand, and wherein you did bury him."

"And it shall be when you shall till it, it shall no more give you its strength as in the beginning, for thorns and thistles shall the ground produce, and you shall be moving and wandering in the earth until the day of your death." So, the Lord blamed Cain, because he had killed Abel, and He made him a fugitive on the earth because of the blood of his brother, and He cursed him on the earth.

Because of this it is written on the heavenly tablets, "Cursed is he who kills his neighbor treacherously, and let all who have seen and heard say, 'So be it', and the man who has seen and not reported it, let him be accursed as the one committing it." For this reason the angels announce when they come before the Lord our God all the sin that is committed in heaven and on earth, and in light and in darkness, and everywhere.

It was in this day that God prepared a place for the dead of man, for until now no one had died that was a living soul. And Enoch would later prophesy about this place. And Enoch, when he was taken up to God saw there was a place and in it four hollow places, deep and wide and very smooth. How smooth are the hollow places and looked deep and dark. And he asked the angel regarding these places.

Then Raphael, one of the holy angels, answered and said, "These hollow places have been created for this very purpose, that the spirits of the souls of the dead should be gathered here, that all the souls of the children of men should be brought together here. And these places have been made to receive them until the day of their judgment and until the period appointed, until the great judgment comes on them."

Enoch saw the spirit of a dead man, and his voice went out to heaven and made petitions. Raphael the angel said to him, "This spirit petitions heaven." Enoch said, "Whose voice goes up and petitions heaven?"

Raphael said, "This is the spirit which went out from Abel, whom his brother Cain slew, and he makes his suit against him until his offspring is destroyed from the face of the earth, and his offspring are annihilated from among the children of men."

And Adam and his wife mourned for Abel four weeks of years, and in the fourth year of the fifth week they became joyful, and Adam knew his wife again, and she gave birth to a son, and he called his name Seth, for he said "God has raised up a second offspring to us on the earth instead of Abel; for Cain killed him."

In the sixth week he begat his daughter Azura. And Cain took Awan his sister to be his wife and she gave birth to Enoch at the close of the fourth jubilee. In the first year of the first week of the fifth jubilee, houses were built on the earth, and Cain built a city, and called its name after the name of his son Enoch.

Adam knew Eve his wife and she gave birth to a total of nine sons. In the fifth week of the fifth jubilee Seth took Azura his sister to be his wife, and in the fourth year of the sixth week she gave birth to Enos.

He began to call on the name of the Lord on the earth. In the seventh jubilee in the third week Enos took Noam his sister to be his wife, and she gave birth to a son in the third year of the fifth week, and he called his name Kenan.

At the close of the eighth jubilee Kenan took Mualeleth his sister to be his wife, and she gave birth to a son in the ninth jubilee, in the first week in the third year of this week, and he called his name Mahalalel.

In the second week of the tenth jubilee Mahalalel took to him to wife Dinah, the daughter of Barakiel the daughter of his father's brother, and she gave birth to a son in the third week in the sixth year. And he called his name Jared, for in his days the angels of the Lord descended on the earth, those who are named the Watchers, that they should instruct the children of men, and that they should do judgment and uprightness on the earth.

And it came to pass when the children of men had multiplied that in those days were born to them beautiful and fair daughters. And when men began to multiply on the face of the earth, and daughters were born unto them, the sons of God saw the daughters of men that they were fair; and they took them wives of all which they chose. And the Lord said, "My spirit shall not always strive with man, for that he also is flesh yet his days shall be an hundred and twenty years."

(Here begins the Book of 1 Enoch)

And the angels, the sons of heaven, saw and lusted after them, and said to one another, "Come, let us choose us wives from among the children of men and have children with them." And Semjaza, who was their leader, said to them, "I fear you will not agree to do this deed and I alone shall have to pay the penalty of this great sin." And they all answered him and said, "Let us all swear an oath, and all bind ourselves by mutual curses so we will not abandon this plan but to do this thing."

Then they all swore together and bound themselves by mutual curses. And they were in all two hundred who descended in the days of Jared on the summit of Mount Hermon, and they called it Mount Hermon, because they had sworn and bound themselves by mutual curses on the act.

I will therefore put you in remembrance, though ye once knew this, how that the Lord, having saved the people out of the land of Egypt, afterward destroyed them that believed not. And the angels who kept not their first estate, but left their own habitation, he hath reserved in everlasting chains under darkness unto the judgment of the great day. And these are the names of their leaders: Samlazaz, their leader, Araklba, Rameel, Kokablel, Tamlel, Ramlel, Danel, Ezeqeel, Baraqijal, *(Author's note: Samlazaz could be another spelling of Semjaza, and possibly be the same entity.)*, Asael, Amaros, Batarel, Ananel, Zaqiel, Samsapeel, Satarel, Turel, Jomjael, Sariel. These are their chiefs of tens.

And all of them together went and took wives for themselves, each choosing one for himself, and they began to go in to them and to defile themselves with sex with them.

There were giants in the earth in those days; and also after that, when the sons of God came in unto the daughters of men, and they gave birth to children to them, the same became mighty men which were of old, men of renown (of legend).

(Here begins the fragments of the Book of the Giants)

And they knew the secrets of the angels and sin was great in the earth and there were the Watchers and they killed man and took to themselves the daughters of men they begat] giants. The angels exploit (consumed) the fruits (fruitfulness) of the earth (consumed all the foods of the earth,) and everything that the earth produced even the great fish. And they ate everything from the seas to the sky with all that grew even the fruit of the earth and all kinds of grain and all the trees and their fruits. They consumed beasts and reptiles and all creeping things of the earth and they observed all uncleanness.

And they preformed every harsh deed and blasphemous utterance and sexual deeds on male and female, and among humans and on animals.

Note: The 200 angels chose animals on which to perform unnatural acts on men, women, and animals.

Two hundred donkeys, two hundred asses, two hundred rams of the flock, two hundred goats, two hundred beasts of the field from every animal, from every bird for sexual acts regardless of species. The outcome of the demonic corruption was violence, perversion, and a brood of monstrous beings.

They defiled [themselves]; they begot giants and monsters. They begot, and, behold, all the earth was corrupted with its blood and by the hand of the angels. And there was sin and death committed by the offspring of the angels, which are giants. And the giants began to devour the animals, which did not suffice for them and they were seeking to devour many humans. So sacrifices of animals were offered, and when an animal was offered, the monsters attacked it.

Monsters defiled all flesh. There were offspring of the monsters and they would arise, lacking in true knowledge and because of them the earth grew more corrupt.

Note: The giants begin to be troubled by a series of dreams and visions. Mahway, the titan son of the angel Barakel, reports the first of these dreams to his fellow giants. He sees a tablet being immersed in water. When it emerges, all but three names have been washed away. The dream evidently symbolizes the destruction of all but Noah and his sons by the Flood.

And one of the giants dreamed a dream… In the dream they drenched the tablet in the water and the waters went up over the tablet and they lifted out the tablet from the water of [. . .] The giant goes to the others and they discuss the dream.

And he said this vision is for cursing and sorrow. I am the one who confessed the whole group of the castaways. (In this dream I saw that) I shall go to the spirits of the slain complaining about their killers and crying out. (Now I know that) we shall die together and be made an end of. In the vision and also I entered into the gathering of the giants, Ohya said to Mahway without trembling. Who showed you all this vision, [my] brother? Barakel, my father, was with me. Before Mahway had finished telling what [he had seen Ohya said] to him, Now I have heard wonders! As if a barren woman gives birth.

[The sons of Shemihaza were Ohya and Hahya.] [There] upon Ohya said to Hahya we are destined to be [destroyed] from upon the earth and then [. . .] they wept before [the giants . . .]

Thereupon Ohya [said] to Hahya we do not have enough strength. Then he answered, It is not for us, but for Azaiel, for he did [. . .lead us to create the children of] angels who are the giants, and they would not let all their loved ones] be neglected [. . . we have] not been cast down; you have strength [. . .]

And he answered, I am a giant, and by the mighty strength of my arm and my own great strength [I can defeat] anyone mortal, and I have made war against them; but I am not [strong enough for our heavenly opponent or to be] able to stand against them, for my opponents [. . .] reside in Heaven, and they dwell in the holy places. And not [on the earth and they] are stronger than I. [. . .] The time of the wild beast has come, and the wild man calls me. Then Ohya said to him, I have been forced to have a dream and the sleep of my eyes vanished in order to let me see a vision. Now I know that on Gilgamesh [our futures rest.]

Note: The first speaker may be Gilgamesh. He has realized the futility of warring against the forces of heaven.

[I had a dream about a tree and three of its roots. [While] I was [watching,] there came and they moved the tree but left its roots in the ground. They planted the tree in this garden, but left the root, all of them.

Note: Ohya's dream vision is of a tree that is uprooted except for three of its roots; the vision's primary meaning is the same as that of the first dream.

[This dream concerns the death of our souls [Gilgamesh] and all his comrades, and Ohya told them what Gilgamesh said to him. And it was said [by Gilgamesh] "concerning [the meaning of the dream that it was about] the leader [of the watcher named Azael.] He has cursed the authorities and rulers" and the giants were glad at his words. Then he turned and left.

Note: Ohya tries to avoid the implications of the visions. Above he stated that it referred only to the demon Azazel; here he suggests that the destruction is for the earthly rulers alone.

And the sleep of their eye fled from them, and they arose and came and told their dreams, and said in the assembly of their peers, the monsters, "In my dream I was watching this very night [and there was a garden, and in it were] gardeners and they were watering [. . . two hundred trees and] large shoots came out of their root [

. . .] all the water, and a fire burned all [the garden . . .] They found the giants to tell them [the dream . . .]

Note: More dreams afflict the giants. The details of this vision are obscure, but it does not bode well for the giants. The dreamers speak first to the monsters, then to the giants. Two of them have had visions or dreams.

Note: Someone suggests that Enoch should be found to interpret the vision.

[Go to Enoch], the noted scribe, and he will interpret for us the dream. Thereupon his fellow Ohya declared and said to the giants, I too had a dream this night, O giants, and, behold, the Ruler of Heaven came down to earth [and destroyed all of us] and such is the end of the dream. [Thereupon] all the giants [and monsters] grew afraid and called Mahway. He came to them and the giants pleaded with him and sent him to Enoch [the noted scribe]. They said to him, Go [. . .] to you that [. . .] you have heard his voice. And he said to him, He will [. . . and] interpret the dreams [. . .] [and he will tell you] how long the giants have to live. [. . .]

Note: After a journey through time and space, Mahway comes to Enoch and makes his request.

So [he soared up in the air] like strong winds, and flew with his hands (flapping) like eagles . . . he left behind] the inhabited world and passed over Desolation, the great desert [and he found Enoch] and Enoch saw him and hailed him, and Mahway said to him [and he yelled] here and there a second time to Mahway [and Mahway said] . . . The giants await your words, and all the monsters of the earth. Regarding the dreams and visions, we would know from you their meaning. [In one of the visions] two hundred trees that from heaven [came down. . .]

Three of its roots [were cut away] [while] I was [watching,] there came [angels] and they moved the roots into this garden, all of them, and not [the tree.]

Note: Enoch sends back a tablet with its grim message of judgment, but with hope for repentance.

The scribe [Enoch wrote] a copy of the second tablet that he sent [. . .] in the very handwriting of Enoch the noted scribe [. . .] In the name of God the great and holy one, to Shemihaza and all [his companions . . .] let it be known to you that not [one of you will be left] and the things you have done, and that your wives, they and their sons and the wives of [their sons,] by your licentiousness on the earth, and there has been upon you [. . .a curse and the land is crying out] and complaining about you and the deeds of your children [. . .] and the harm that you have done to it. [. . .] And the earth will not cease until Raphael arrives. Behold, destruction [is coming, in the form a great flood, and it will destroy all living things] and whatever is in the deserts and the seas. And the meaning of the matter [is that judgement is] upon you for evil. But now, loosen the bonds binding you to evil . [repent] and pray.

(Here begins excerpts from the Book of Jasher and the Book of Jubilees)

And God saw that the wickedness of man was great in the earth, and that every imagination of the thoughts of his heart was only evil continually. And it repented the Lord that he had made man on the earth, and it grieved him at his heart.

And the angels began to teach the men of earth charms and spells, and the cutting of roots, and made them acquainted with plants.

And the women became pregnant, and they gave birth to large giants, whose height was three thousand cubits (ells). The giants consumed all the work and toil of men. And when men could no longer sustain them, the giants turned against them and devoured mankind.

And they began to sin against birds, and beasts, and reptiles, and fish, and to devour one another's flesh, and drank the blood. Then the earth laid accusation against the lawless ones.

And Azazel taught men to make swords, and knives, and shields, and breastplates, and taught them about metals of the earth and the art of working them, and bracelets, and ornaments, and the use of antimony, and the beautifying of the eyelids, and all kinds of precious stones, and all coloring and dyes. And there was great impiety, they turned away from God, and committed fornication, and they were led astray, and became corrupt in all their ways.

Semjaza taught the casting of spells, and root-cuttings, Armaros taught counter-spells (release from spells), Baraqijal taught astrology, Kokabel taught the constellations (portents), Ezeqeel the knowledge of the clouds, Araqiel the signs of the earth, Shamsiel the signs of the sun, and Sariel the course of the moon. And as men perished, they cried, and their cry went up to heaven.

And then Michael, Uriel, Raphael, and Gabriel looked down from heaven and saw much blood being shed on the earth, and all lawlessness being done on the earth. And they said to each other: "Let the cries from the destruction of Earth ascend up to the gates of heaven." And now to you, the holy ones of heaven, the souls of men make their petition, saying, "Bring our cause before the Most High."

And they said to the Lord of the ages, "Lord of lords, God of gods, King of kings, and God of the ages, the throne of your glory endures through all the generations of the ages, and your name holy and glorious and blessed to all the ages! Which in his times he shall show, who is the blessed and only Potentate, the King of kings, and Lord of lords; Who only hath immortality, dwelling in the light which no man can approach unto;

whom no man hath seen, nor can see: to whom be honor and power everlasting. Amen.

You have made all things, and you have power over all things: and all things are revealed and open in your sight, and you see all things, and nothing can hide itself from you.

Look at what Azazel has done, who hath taught all unrighteousness on earth and revealed the eternal secrets which were made and kept in heaven, which men were striving to learn: And Semjaza, who taught spells, to whom you gave authority to rule over his associates."

And it was in the hundred and thirtieth year of the life of Adam upon the earth, that he again knew Eve his wife, and she conceived and gave birth to a son and he looked like Adam, and she called his name Seth, saying, "Because God has appointed me another offspring in the place of Abel, for Cain has slain him."

And Seth lived one hundred and five years, and he begat a son; and Seth called the name of his son Enosh, saying, "Because in that time the sons of men began to reproduce, and to afflict their souls and hearts by disobeying and rebelling against God."

And it was in the days of Enosh that the sons of men continued to rebel and go contrary, against God, to increase the anger of the Lord against the sons of men.

And the sons of men went and they served other gods, and they forgot the Lord who had created them in the earth: and in those days the sons of men made images of brass and iron, wood and stone, and they bowed down and served them.

And every man made his god and they bowed down to them, and the sons of men turned away from the Lord all the days of Enosh and his children; and the anger of the Lord was set ablaze on account of their works and abominations which they did in the earth.

And the Lord caused the waters of the river Gihon to overwhelm them, and he destroyed and consumed them, and he destroyed the third part of the earth. Notwithstanding this, the sons of men did not turn from their evil ways, and their hands were yet extended to do evil in the sight of the Lord.

And in those days there was neither sowing nor reaping in the earth; and there was no food for the sons of men and the famine was very great in those days.

And the offspring which they sowed in those days in the ground became thorns, thistles and briers; for from the days of Adam was this declaration concerning the earth, of the curse of God, which he cursed the earth, on account of the sin which Adam sinned before the Lord.

And it was when men continued to rebel and go contrary, against God, and to corrupt their ways, that the earth also became corrupt.

And Enosh lived ninety years and he begat Cainan;

And Cainan grew up and he was forty years old, and he became wise and had knowledge and skill in all wisdom, and he reigned over all the sons of men, and he led the sons of men to wisdom and knowledge; for Cainan was a very wise man and had understanding in all wisdom, and with his wisdom he ruled over spirits and demons;

And Cainan knew by his wisdom that God would destroy the sons of men for having sinned upon earth, and that the Lord would in the latter days bring upon them the waters of the flood. And in those days Cainan wrote upon tablets of stone what was to take place in the time to come, and he put them in his treasures. And Cainan reigned over the whole earth, and he turned some of the sons of men to the service of God.

And Lamech, the son of Methusael, became related to Cainan by marriage, and he took his two daughters for his wives, and Adah conceived and gave birth to a son to Lamech, and she called his name Jabal. And she again conceived and gave birth to a son, and called his name Jubal; and Zillah, her sister, was barren in those days and had no offspring. For in those days the sons of men began to trespass against God, and to transgress the commandments, which he had commanded to Adam, to be fruitful and multiply in the earth.

And some of the sons of men caused their wives to drink a potion that would render them barren, in order that they might retain their figures and therefore their beautiful appearance might not fade. And when the sons of men caused some of their wives to drink, Zillah drank with them.

And the child-bearing women appeared abominable in the sight of their husbands as widows, whilst their husbands lived, for to the barren ones only they were attached. And in the end of days and years, when Zillah became old, the Lord opened her womb. And she conceived and had a son and she called his name Tubal Cain, saying, "After I had withered away have I obtained him from the Almighty God." And she conceived again and gave birth to a daughter, and she called her name Naamah, for she said, "After I had withered away have I obtained pleasure and delight."

And Lamech was old and advanced in years, and his eyes were dim that he could not see, and Tubal Cain, his son, was leading him into the field and Tubal Cain his son was with him, and whilst they were walking in the field, Cain the son of Adam advanced towards them; for Lamech was very old and could not see much, and Tubal Cain his son was very young.

And Tubal Cain told his father to draw his bow, and with the arrows he smote Cain, who was yet far off, and he slew him, for he appeared to them to be an animal. And the arrows entered Cain's body although he was distant from them, and he fell to the ground and died. And the Lord requited Cain's evil according to his wickedness, which he had done to his brother Abel, according to the word of the Lord which he had spoken.

And it came to pass when Cain had died, that Lamech and Tubal went to see the animal which they had slain, and they saw, and behold Cain their grandfather was fallen dead upon the earth. And Lamech was very much grieved at having done this, and in clapping his hands together he struck his son and caused his death. And the wives of Lamech heard what Lamech had done, and they sought to kill him. And the wives of Lamech hated him from that day, because he slew Cain and Tubal Cain, and the wives of Lamech separated from him, and would not hearken to him in those days.

And Lamech came to his wives, and he pressed them to listen to him about this matter. And he said to his wives Adah and Zillah, "Hear my voice O wives of Lamech, attend to my words, for now you have imagined and said that I slew a man with my wounds, and a child with my stripes for their having done no violence, but surely know that I am old and grey-headed, and that my eyes are heavy through age, and I did this thing unknowingly."

And the wives of Lamech listened to him in this matter, and they returned to him with the advice of their father Adam, but they bore no children to him from that time, knowing that God's anger was increasing in those days against the sons of men, to destroy them with the waters of the flood for their evil doings. And Mahlallel the son of Cainan lived sixty-five years and he begat Jared; and Jared lived sixty-two years and he begat Enoch.

In the eleventh jubilee Jared took to himself a wife, and her name was Baraka, the daughter of Rasujal, a daughter of his father's brother, in the fourth week of this jubilee, and she gave birth to a son in the fifth week, in the fourth year of the jubilee, and he called his name Enoch.

He was the first among men that are born on earth who learned writing and knowledge and wisdom and who wrote down the signs of heaven according to the order of their months in a book, that men might know the seasons of the years according to the order of their separate months.

He was the first to write a testimony and he testified to the sons of men among the generations of the earth, and recounted the weeks of the jubilees, and made known to them the days of the years, and set in order the months and recounted the Sabbaths of the years as we made them known to him.

And Enoch was a righteous man who walked with God. And Enoch did not die but God took him up into heaven.

And Enoch lived sixty and five years, and begat Methuselah: And Enoch walked with God after he begat Methuselah three hundred years, and begat sons and daughters: And all the days of Enoch were three hundred sixty and five years: And Enoch walked with God: and he was not; for God took him. And Methuselah lived an hundred eighty and seven years, and begat Lamech. And Methuselah lived after he begat Lamech seven hundred eighty and two years, and begat sons and daughters: And all the days of Methuselah were nine hundred sixty and nine years: and he died. And Lamech lived an hundred eighty and two years, and begat a son:

And he called his name Noah, saying, This same shall comfort us concerning our work and toil of our hands, because of the ground which the LORD hath cursed.

Then, the angels prayed to God saying, "You know all things before they come to pass, and you see these things and you have permitted them, and say nothing to us about these things. What are we to do with them about these things?"

At this time, Noah was five hundred years old, and Noah begat Shem, Ham, and Japheth.

Then said the Most High, the Great and Holy One, "Go to the son of Lamech, Uriel. Say to him: Go to Noah and tell him in my name hide yourself and reveal to him the end that is approaching; that the whole earth will be destroyed, and a flood is about to come on the whole earth, and will destroy everything on it."

"For yet seven days, and I will cause it to rain upon the earth forty days and forty nights; and every living substance that I have made will I destroy from off the face of the earth. And now instruct him as to what he must do to escape that his offspring may be preserved for all the generations of the world."

And God said unto Noah, "The end of all flesh is come before me; for the earth is filled with violence through them. And, behold, I will destroy them with the earth. Make thee an ark of gopher wood; rooms shalt thou make in the ark, and shalt pitch it within and without with pitch."

And again the Lord said to Raphael, "Bind Azazel hand and foot, and cast him into the darkness and split open the desert, which is in Dudael, and cast him in. And fill the hole by covering him rough and jagged rocks, and cover him with darkness, and let him live there forever, and cover his face that he may not see the light."

"And on the day of the great judgment he shall be hurled into the fire. And heal the earth which the angels have ruined, and proclaim the healing of the earth, for I will restore the earth and heal the plague, that not all of the children of men may perish through all the secret things that the Watchers have disclosed and have taught their sons."

"For I reckon that the sufferings of this present time are not worthy to be compared with the glory which shall be revealed in us. For the earnest expectation of the creature waiteth for the manifestation of the sons of God. For the creature was made subject to vanity, not willingly, but by reason of him who hath subjected the same in hope; because the creature itself also shall be delivered from the bondage of corruption into the glorious liberty of the children of God."

The whole earth has been corrupted through the works that were taught by Azazel: to him ascribe ALL SIN. And all the sons of men departed from the ways of the Lord in those days as they multiplied upon the face of the earth with sons and daughters, and they taught one another their evil practices and they continued sinning against the Lord. And every man made unto himself a god, and they robbed and plundered every man his neighbor as well as his relative, and they corrupted the earth, and the earth was filled with violence.

And their judges and rulers went to the daughters of men and took their wives by force from their husbands according to their choice.

And the sons of men in those days took from the cattle of the earth, the beasts of the field and the fowls of the air, and taught the mixture of animals of one species with the other, in order therewith to provoke the Lord; and God saw the whole earth and it was corrupt, for all flesh had corrupted its ways upon earth, all men and all animals.

To Gabriel said the Lord, "Proceed against the bastards and the reprobates, and against the children of fornication and destroy the children of fornication and the children of the Watchers. Cause them to go against one another that they may destroy each other in battle: Shorten their days."

And the Lord said, "I will destroy man whom I have created from the face of the earth; both man, and beast, and the creeping thing, and the fowls of the air; for it repenteth me that I have made them."

And the Lord said to Michael, "Go, bind Semjaza and his team who have associated with women and have defiled themselves in all their uncleanness. When their sons have slain one another, and they have seen the destruction of their beloved ones, bind them fast for seventy generations under the hills of the earth, until the day of the consummation of their judgment and until the eternal judgment is accomplished."

(Note: Noah was 500 years old. 70 generations of 500 years=35,000 years.)

"In those days they shall be led off to the abyss of fire and to the torment and the prison in which they shall be confined forever. Then Semjaza shall be burnt up with the condemned and they will be destroyed, having been bound together with them to the end of all generations. Destroy all the spirits of lust and the children of the Watchers, because they have wronged mankind."

For God spared not the angels that sinned, but cast them down to hell, and delivered them into chains of darkness, to be reserved unto judgment. And After judgment these fallen ones, these Grigori, shall mourn and lament for all eternity and weep forever without ceasing.

"Destroy all wrong from the face of the earth and let every evil work come to an end and let (the earth be planted with righteousness) the plant of righteousness and truth appear (Messiah); and it shall prove a blessing, the works of righteousness and truth shall be planted in truth and joy forevermore."

And the Lord said, "I will destroy man whom I have created from the face of the earth; both man, and beast, and the creeping thing, and the fowls of the air; for it repenteth me that I have made them. And then shall all the righteous survive, and shall live until they beget thousands of children, and all the days of their youth and their old age shall they complete in peace. While the earth remaineth, seedtime and harvest, and cold and heat, and summer and winter, and day and night shall not cease."

And God blessed Noah and his sons, and said unto them, "Be fruitful, and multiply, and replenish the earth. And then shall the whole earth be tilled in righteousness. And all desirable trees shall be planted on it, and they shall plant vines on it. And the vine which they plant shall yield fruit in abundance, and as for all the seed which is sown, each measurement (of it) shall bear a thousand, and each measurement of olives shall yield ten presses of oil. You shall cleanse the earth from all oppression, and from all unrighteousness, and from all sin, and from all godlessness, and all the uncleanness that is brought on the earth you shall destroy from off the earth."

Because of these three things came the flood on the earth, namely, the fornication that the Watchers committed against the law of their ordinances when they went whoring after the daughters of men, and took themselves wives of all they chose, and they made the beginning of uncleanness. And they begat sons, the Nephilim, and they were all dissimilar, and they devoured one another, and the Giants killed the Naphil, and the Naphil killed the Eljo, and the Eljo killed mankind, and one man killed one another.

Every one committed himself to crime and injustice and to shed much blood, and the earth was filled with sin. After this they sinned against the beasts and birds, and all that moved and walked on the earth, and much blood was shed on the earth, and men continually desired only what was useless and evil.

And the Lord destroyed everything from the face of the earth. Because of the wickedness of their deeds, and because of the blood they had shed over all the earth, He destroyed everything.

And against the angels whom He had sent on the earth, He had boiling anger, and He gave commandment to root them out of all their dominion, and He commanded us to bind them in the depths of the earth, and look, they are bound in the middle of the earth, and are kept separate. And against their sons went out a command from His mouth that they should be killed with the sword, and be left under heaven.

He sent His sword into their presence that each should kill his neighbor, and they began to kill each other until they all fell by the sword and were destroyed from the earth. And their fathers were witnesses of their destruction, and after this they were bound in the depths of the earth forever, until the day of the great condemnation, when judgment is executed on all those who have corrupted their ways and their works before the Lord.

He destroyed all wherever they were, and there was not one left of them whom He judged according to all their wickedness. Through His work He made a new and righteous nature, so that they should not sin in their whole nature forever, but should be all righteous each in his own way always.

The judgment of all is ordained and written on the heavenly tablets in righteousness, even the judgment of all who depart from the path that is ordained for them to walk; and if they do not walk it, judgment is written down for every creature and for every kind. There is nothing in heaven or on earth, or in light or in darkness, or in the abode of the dead or in the depth, or in the place of darkness that is not judged. All their judgments are ordained and written and engraved.

He will judge all, the great according to his greatness, and the small according to his smallness, and each according to his way. He is not one who will regard the position of any person, nor is He one who will receive gifts, if He says that He will execute judgment on each. If one gave everything that is on the earth, He will not regard the gifts or the person of any, nor accept anything at his hands, for He is a righteous judge. Of the children of Israel it has been written and ordained, if they turn to him in righteousness He will forgive all their transgressions and pardon all their sins. It is written and ordained that He will show mercy to all who turn from all their guilt once each year.

And as for all those who corrupted their ways and their thoughts before the flood, no person was acceptable to God except Noah. His sons were saved in deference to him, and these God kept from the waters of the flood on his account; for Noah's heart was righteous in all his ways. He upheld the laws and did as God commanded him and he had not departed from anything that was ordained for him.

The Lord said that he would destroy everything on the earth, both men and cattle, and beasts, and birds of the air, and that which moves on the earth. And He commanded Noah to make an ark, so that he might save himself from the waters of the flood. And Noah made the ark in all respects as He commanded him, in the twenty-seventh jubilee of years, in the fifth week in the fifth year on the new moon of the first month. He entered in the sixth year of it, in the second month, on the new moon of the second month, until the sixteenth; and he entered, and all that we brought to him, into the ark, and the Lord closed it from the outside on the seventeenth evening.

And the Lord opened seven floodgates of heaven, and He opened the mouths of the fountains of the great deep, seven mouths in number. And the floodgates began to pour down water from the heaven forty days and forty closets. And the fountains of the deep also sent up waters, until the whole world was full of water.

The waters increased on the earth, by fifteen cubits (a cubit is about 18 inches) the waters rose above all the high mountains. And the ark was lifted up from the earth. And it moved on the face of the waters.

And the water covered the face of the earth five months, which is one hundred and fifty days. And all flesh was destroyed, but the spirits of the evil ones were not destroyed. Having sought out the flesh of animals in which to live after their bodies were killed, the spirits of the giants and the children of the Watchers escaped and waited.

And the ark went and rested on the top of Lubar, one of the mountains of Ararat. On the new moon in the fourth month the fountains of the great deep were closed and the floodgates of heaven were restrained; and on the new moon of the seventh month all the mouths of the bottomless gulfs of the earth were opened, and the water began to flow down into the deep below. On the new moon of the tenth month the tops of the mountains were seen, and on the new moon of the first month the earth became visible. The waters disappeared from the earth in the fifth week in the seventh year of it, and on the seventeenth day in the second month the earth was dry.

On the twenty-seventh of it he opened the ark, and sent out beasts, and cattle, and birds, and every moving thing. And the spirits of the evil ones began to inhabit animals and men once again.

And it would come to pass in the future that there would arise war at Gezer with the Philistines; at which time Sibbechai the Hushathite would kill Sippai, who was of the children of the giant, and they were subdued. And there would be war again with the Philistines; and Elhanan the son of Jair would slay Lahmi the brother of Goliath the Gittite, whose spear staff was like a weaver's beam. And yet again there was war at Gath, where there was a man of great stature, whose fingers and toes were four and twenty, six on each hand, and six on each foot and he also was the son of the giant. These would be born unto the giant in Gath, being descended from the Watchers; and they would fall by the hand of David, and by the hand of his servants. Thus the evil of the Watchers would continue to plague the children of God.

On the new moon of the third month Noah went out of the ark, and built an altar on that mountain. And he made atonement for the earth, and took a kid and made atonement by its blood for all the guilt of the earth; for every thing that had been on it had been destroyed, except those that were in the ark with Noah.

He placed the fat of it on the altar, and he took an ox, and a goat, and a sheep and kids, and salt, and a turtle-dove, and the young of a dove, and placed a burnt sacrifice on the altar, and poured on it an offering mingled with oil, and sprinkled wine and frankincense over everything, and caused a good and pleasing odor to arise, acceptable before the Lord.

And the Lord smelled the good and pleasing odor, and He made a covenant with Noah that there should not be any more floods to destroy the earth; that all the days of the earth seed-time and harvest should never cease; cold and heat, and summer and winter, and day and night should not change their order, nor cease forever.

"Increase and multiply on the earth, and become many, and be a blessing on it. I will inspire the fear of you and the dread of you in everything that is on earth and in the sea." And the earth was cleaned of the sins of the flesh, but spirits of the evil Watchers and their accursed offspring cannot die.

In the twenty-ninth jubilee, in the beginning of first week, Arpachshad took to himself a wife and her name was Rasu'eja, the daughter of Susan, the daughter of Elam, and she gave birth to a son in the third year in this week, and he called his name Kainam. The son grew, and his father taught him writing, and he went to seek for himself a place where he might seize a city for himself. He found writing which former generations had carved on a rock, and he read what was on it, and he transcribed it and sinned because of it, for it contained the teaching of the Watchers, which they had used to observe the omens of the sun and moon and stars in all the signs of heaven.

He wrote it down and said nothing of it, for he was afraid to speak to Noah about it or he would be angry with him because of it. In the third week of this jubilee the unclean demons began to lead astray the children of the sons of Noah, and to make them sin and to destroy them. The sons of Noah came to Noah their father, and they told him about the demons that were leading astray and blinding and slaying his sons' sons.

(Here begins the Book of 1 Enoch.)

And Noah said, "I see the demons have begun their seductions against you and against your children and now I fear on your behalf, that after my death you will shed the blood of men on the earth, and that you, too, will be destroyed from the face of the earth.

"For whoever sheds man's blood, and who ever eats the blood of any flesh, shall all be destroyed from the earth."

And he prayed before the Lord his God, and said, "God of the spirits of all flesh, who have shown mercy to me and have spared me and my sons from the waters of the flood, and have not caused me to die as You did the sons of perdition; For your grace has been great toward me, and great has been your mercy to my soul."

"Let your grace be lifted up on my sons, and do not let the wicked spirits rule over them or they will destroy them from the earth. But bless me and my sons, so that we may increase and multiply and replenish the earth. You know how your Watchers, the fathers of these spirits, acted in my day, and as for these spirits which are living, imprison them and hold them fast in the place of condemnation, and let them not bring destruction on the sons of your servant, my God; for these are like cancer and are created in order to destroy.

Let them not rule over the spirits of the living; for You alone can exercise dominion over them. And let them not have power over the sons of the righteous from now and forever." And the Lord our God commanded the angels to bind all of them.

And the Watchers came to Enoch, whom God had taken up into heaven, and begged him to intercede before God on their behalf.

Then God answered and said, "No request that the Watchers, or their children make of you shall be granted them on their behalf; for they hope to live an eternal life, and that each one of them will live five hundred years."

And God answered and said to Enoch, "Do not be afraid, Enoch, you righteous man and scribe of righteousness. Approach and hear my voice. Go and say to the Watchers of heaven, for whom you have come to intercede: You should intercede for men, and not men for you. Why and for what cause have you left the high, holy, and eternal heaven, and had sex with women, and defiled yourselves with the daughters of men and taken to yourselves wives, and done like the children of earth, and begotten giants (as your) sons? Though you were holy, spiritual, living the eternal life, you have defiled yourselves with the blood of women, and have begotten children with the blood of flesh, and, as the children of men, you have lusted after flesh and blood like those who die and are killed.

This is why I have given men wives that they might impregnate them, and have children by them, that deeds might continue on the earth. But you were formerly spiritual, living the eternal life, and immortal for all generations of the world. Therefore I have not appointed wives for you. You are spiritual beings of heaven, and in heaven was your dwelling place. Only after death will man know what you have known.

"For the children of this world marry, and are given in marriage: But they which shall be accounted worthy to obtain that world, and the resurrection from the dead, neither marry, nor are given in marriage, neither can they die any more. For they are equal unto the angels, and are the children of God, being the children of the resurrection."

And now, the giants, who are produced from the spirits and flesh, shall be called evil spirits on the earth, and shall live on the earth. Evil spirits have come out from their bodies because they are born from men and from the holy Watchers, their beginning is of primal origin, and they shall be called spirits of the evil ones. As for the spirits of heaven, in heaven shall be their dwelling, but as for the spirits of the earth which were born on the earth, on the earth shall be their dwelling.

And the spirits of the giants afflict, oppress, destroy, attack, war, destroy, and cause trouble on the earth. Their spirits take no food, but do not hunger or thirst. They cause offences but are not seen. And these spirits shall rise up against the children of men and against the women, because they have proceeded from them in the days of the slaughter and destruction.

And at the death of the giants, spirits will go out and shall destroy without incurring judgment. Coming from their bodies, their flesh shall be destroy until the day of the consummation, the great judgment in which the age shall be consummated, over the Watchers and the godless, and shall be wholly consummated.

These evil spirits shall torment men without restraint, inhabiting animals and possessing men until the days of the Messiah come.

And now as to the Watchers who have sent you to intercede for them, who had been in heaven before, (Say to them), "You were in heaven, but all the mysteries of heaven had not been revealed to you, and you knew worthless ones, and these in the hardness of your hearts you have made known to the women, and through these mysteries women and men work much evil on earth."

Say to them therefore, "You have no peace." The chief of the spirits, Mastema (Satan), came and said, "Lord, Creator, let some of them remain before me, and let them listen to my voice, and do all that I shall say to them; for if some of them are not left to me, I shall not be able to execute the power of my will on the sons of men, for these are for corruption and leading astray before my judgment, for great is the wickedness of the sons of men."

He said, "Let one-tenth of them remain before him, and let nine-tenths of them descend into the place of condemnation."

Then God commanded one of the angels to teach Noah all their medicines, for He knew that the Watchers would not walk in uprightness, nor strive in righteousness.

The angels did according to all His words. Then they bound all the malignant evil ones in the place of condemnation and a tenth part of them we left that they might be subject in the presence of Satan on the earth. The angels explained to Noah all the medicines of their diseases, together with their seductions, how he might heal them with herbs of the earth. Noah wrote down all things in a book as they instructed him concerning every kind of medicine. Thus the evil spirits were precluded from hurting the sons of Noah.

But, the sons of Noah began to war with each other, to take captives and kill each other, and to shed the blood of men on the earth, and to eat blood, and to build strong cities, and walls, and towers, and individuals began to exalt themselves above the nation, and to establish kingdoms, and to go to war, people against people, and nation against nation, and city against city, and all began to do evil, and to acquire arms, and to teach their sons war, and they began to capture cities, and to sell male and female slaves.

(Here begin excerpts from the Book of Jubilees and the Book of Jasher.)

In the three and thirtieth jubilee, in the first year in the second week, Peleg took to himself a wife, whose name was Lomna the daughter of Sina'ar, and she gave birth to a son for him in the fourth year of this week, and he called his name Reu, for he said, "Look, the children of men have become evil because they conceived building, a city, and a tower in the land of Shinar for an evil purpose." For they departed from the land of Ararat eastward to Shinar, for in his days they built the city and the tower, saying, "Let us build this now so that we may rise into heaven."

And in these days King Nimrod reigned securely, and all the earth was under his control, and all the earth was of one tongue and words of union.

And all the princes of Nimrod and his great men took counsel together; Phut, Mitzraim, Cush and Canaan with their families, and they said to each other, "Come let us build ourselves a city and in it a strong tower, and its top reaching heaven, and we will make ourselves famed, so that we may reign upon the whole world, in order that the evil of our enemies may cease from us, that we may reign mightily over them, and that we may not become scattered over the earth on account of their wars."

And they all went before the king, and they told the king these words, and the king agreed with them in this affair, and he did so.

And all the families assembled consisting of about six hundred thousand men, and they went to seek an extensive piece of ground to build the city and the tower, and they sought in the whole earth and they found none like one valley at the east of the land of Shinar, about two days' walk, and they journeyed there and they lived there. And they began to make bricks and burn fires to build the city and the tower that they had imagined to complete. And the building of the tower was to them a transgression and a sin, and they began to build it, and whilst they were building against the Lord God of heaven, they imagined in their hearts to war against him and to ascend into heaven.

They began to build, and in the fourth week they made brick with fire, and the bricks served them for stone, and the clay with which they cemented them together was asphalt which comes out of the sea, and out of the fountains of water in the land of Shinar. They built it, forty-three years were they building it. Its breadth was 203 bricks, and the height of a brick was the third of one; its height amounted to 5433 cubits and 2 palms, and the extent of one wall was 13 times 600 feet and of the other thirty times 600 feet.

And all these people and all the families divided themselves in three parts. The first said, "We will ascend into heaven and fight against him;" the second said, "We will ascend to heaven and place our own gods there and serve them;" and the third part said, "We will ascend to heaven and strike him with bows and spears;" and God knew all their works and all their evil thoughts, and he saw the city and the tower which they were building.

And when they were building they built themselves a great city and a very high and strong tower; and on account of its height the mortar and bricks did not reach the builders in their ascent to it, until those who went up had completed a full year, and after that, they reached to the builders and gave them the mortar and the bricks; thus was it done daily. And behold these ascended and others descended the whole day; and if a brick should fall from their hands and get broken, they would all weep over it, and if a man fell and died, none of them would look at him.

And the Lord knew their thoughts, and it came to pass when they were building they cast the arrows toward the heavens, and all the arrows fell upon them filled with blood, and when they saw them they said to each other, "Certainly we have slain all those that are in heaven." For this was from the Lord in order to cause them to err, and in order to destroy them from off the face of the earth.

And they built the tower and the city, and they did this thing daily until many days and years were elapsed.

And the Lord our God said to the angels, "Look, they are one people, and they begin to do this, and now nothing will be withheld from them. Let us go down and confound their language, that they may not understand one another's speech, and they may be dispersed into cities and nations, and they will not be in agreement together with one purpose until the Day of Judgment."

And God said to the seventy angels who stood foremost before him, to those who were near to him, saying, "Come let us descend and confuse their tongues, that one man shall not understand the language of his neighbor." And they did so.

And from that day following, they forgot each man his neighbor's tongue, and they could not understand to speak in one tongue, and when the builder took from the hands of his neighbor lime or stone which he did not order, the builder would cast it away and throw it upon his neighbor, that he would die. And they did so many days, and they killed many of them in this manner.

And the Lord struck the three divisions that were there, and he punished them according to their works and designs. Those who said, "We will ascend to heaven and serve our gods," became like apes and elephants; and those who said, "We will strike the heaven with arrows," the Lord killed them, one man through the hand of his neighbor; and the third division of those who said, "We will ascend to heaven and fight against him," the Lord scattered them throughout the earth.

And those who were left amongst them, when they knew and understood the evil which was coming upon them, they turned away from the building, and they also became scattered upon the face of the whole earth. And they ceased building the city and the tower; therefore he called that place Babel, for there the Lord confounded the language of the whole earth; behold it was at the east of the land of Shinar.

And the Lord descended, and the angels descended with him to see the city and the tower that the children of men had built. He confounded their language, and they no longer understood one another's speech, and they then ceased to build the city and the tower. For this reason the whole land of Shinar is called Babel, because the Lord confounded all the language of the children of men there, and from that place they were dispersed into their cities, each according to his language and his nation.

Then, the Lord sent a mighty wind against the tower and it fell to the earth, and behold it was between Asshur and Babylon in the land of Shinar, and they called its name "Overthrow." And as to the tower which the sons of men built, the earth opened its mouth and swallowed up one third part thereof, and a fire also descended from heaven and burned another third, and the other third is left to this day, and it is of that part which was aloft, and its circumference is three days' walk. And many of the sons of men died in that tower, a people without number.

In the fourth week in the first year in the beginning of it in the four and thirtieth jubilee, were they dispersed from the land of Shinar. Ham and his sons went into the land that he was to occupy, which he acquired as his portion in the land of the south. Ur, the son of Kesed, built the city of Ara of the Chaldees, and called its name after his own name and the name of his father.

And they made themselves molten images, and they worshipped the idols and the molten image they had made for themselves, and they began to make graven images and unclean and shadowy presence, and malevolent and malicious spirits assisted and seduced them into committing transgression and uncleanness.

Prince Mastema exerted himself to do all this, and he sent out other spirits, which were put under his control, to do all manner of wrong and sin, and all manner of transgression, to corrupt and destroy, and to shed blood on the earth.

For this reason he called the name of Seroh, Serug, for every one turned to do all manner of sin and transgression.

He grew up, and dwelt in Ur of the Chaldees, near to the father of his wife's mother, and he worshipped idols, and he took to himself a wife in the thirty-sixth jubilee, in the fifth week, in the first year of it, and her name was Melka, the daughter of Kaber, the daughter of his father's brother.

She gave birth to Nahor, in the first year of this week, and he grew and dwelt in Ur of the Chaldees, and his father taught him the sciences of the Chaldees to divine and conjure, according to the signs of heaven. In the thirty-seventh jubilee in the sixth week, in the first year of it, he took to himself a wife, and her name was 'Ijaska, the daughter of Nestag of the Chaldees. And she gave birth to Terah in the seventh year of this week.

Prince Mastema sent ravens and birds to devour the seed that was sown in the land, in order to destroy the land, and rob the children of men of their labors. Before they could plow in the seed, the ravens picked it from the surface of the ground. This is why he called his name Terah because the ravens and the birds reduced them to destitution and devoured their seed.

The years began to be barren because of the birds, and they devoured all the fruit from the trees, it was only with great effort that they could harvest a little fruit from the earth in their days.

In the seventh year of this week she gave birth to a son, and called his name Abram, by the name of the father of his mother, for he had died before his daughter had conceived a son. And the child began to understand the errors of the earth that all went astray after graven images and after uncleanness. His father taught him writing, and he was two weeks of years old when he separated himself from his father, that he might not worship idols with him. He began to pray to the Creator of all things that He might spare him from the errors of the children of men, and that his portion should not fall into error after uncleanness and vileness.

The time came for the sowing of seed in the land, and they all went out together to protect their seed against the ravens, and Abram, a lad of fourteen, went out with those that went. A cloud of ravens came to devour the seed and Abram ran to meet them before they settled on the ground, and cried to them before they settled on the ground to devour the seed, and said, "Descend not, return to the place from where you came," and they began to turn back. And he caused the clouds of ravens to turn back that day seventy times, and of all the ravens throughout all the land where Abram was there settled not so much as one.

All who were with him throughout all the land saw him cry out, and all the ravens turn back, and his name became great in all the land of the Chaldees. There came to him this year all those that wished to sow, and he went with them until the time of sowing ceased, and they sowed their land, and that year they brought enough grain home to eat and they were satisfied.

In the first year of the fifth week Abram taught those who made implements for oxen, the artificers in wood, and they made a vessel above the ground, facing the frame of the plow, in order to put the seed in it, and the seed fell down from it on the share of the plow, and was hidden in the earth, and they no longer feared the ravens. After this manner they made vessels above the ground on all the frames of the plows, and they sowed and tilled all the land, according as Abram commanded them, and they no longer feared the birds.

In the sixth week, in the seventh year of it, Abram said to Terah his father, "Father!" And Terah said, "Look, here am I, my son." He said to his father, "What help and profit have we from those idols which you worship, and in the presence of which you bow yourself? There is no spirit in them.

They are dumb forms, and they mislead the heart. Do not worship them, Worship the God of heaven, who causes the rain and the dew to fall on the earth and does everything on the earth, and has created everything by His word, and all life is from His presence.

Why do you worship things that have no spirit in them? For they are the work of men's hands, and you bear them on your shoulders, and you have no help from them, but they are a great cause of shame to those who make them, and they mislead the heart of those who worship them. Do not worship them."

His father replied, "I also know it, my son, but what shall I do with a people who have made me serve them? If I tell them the truth, they will kill me, because their soul clings to them so they worship them and honor them. Keep silent, my son, or they will kill you." And these words he spoke to his two brothers, and they were angry with him and he kept silent.

In the fortieth jubilee, in the second week, in the seventh year of it, Abram took to himself a wife, and her name was Sarai, the daughter of his father, and she became his wife. Haran, his brother, took to himself a wife in the third year of the third week, and she gave birth to a son in the seventh year of this week, and he called his name Lot. Nahor, his brother, took to himself a wife. In the sixtieth year of the life of Abram, that is, in the fourth week, in the fourth year of it, Abram arose in the night and burned the house of the idols, and he burned all that was in the house and no man knew it.

And they arose and sought to save their gods from the fire. Haran hasted to save them, but the fire flamed over him, and he was burnt in the fire, and he died in Ur of the Chaldees before Terah his father, and they buried him in Ur of the Chaldees. Terah went out from Ur of the Chaldees, he and his sons, to go into the land of Lebanon and into the land of Canaan, and he dwelt in the land of Haran, and Abram dwelt with Terah his father in Haran two weeks of years.

In the sixth week, in the fifth year of it, Abram sat up all night on the new moon of the seventh month to observe the stars from the evening to the morning, in order to see what would be the character of the year with regard to the rains, and he was alone as he sat and observed. And a word came into his heart and he said, "All the signs of the stars, and the signs of the moon and of the sun are all in the hand of the Lord. Why do I search them out? If He desires, He causes it to rain, morning and evening, and if He desires, He withholds it, and all things are in his hand." He prayed in the night and said, "My God, God Most High, You alone are my God, and You and your dominion have I chosen.

And You have created all things, and all things that are the work of Your hands. Deliver me from the hands of evil spirits who have dominion over the thoughts of men's hearts, and let them not lead me astray from You, my God.

And establish me and my offspring forever so that we do not go astray from now and forever." He said, "Shall I return to Ur of the Chaldees who are trying to find me? Should I return to them? Am I to remain here in this place? The right path is before You. Make it prosper in the hands of your servant that he may fulfill it and that I may not walk in the deceitfulness of my heart, O my God." He stopped speaking and stopped praying.

Then the word of the Lord was sent to him through an angel, saying, "Get out of your country, and from your kindred and from the house of your father and go to a land which I will show you, and I shall make you a great and numerous nation. And I will bless you and I will make your name great, and you will be blessed in the earth, and in You shall all families of the earth be blessed, and I will bless them that bless you, and curse them that curse you. I will be a God to you and your son, and to your son's son, and to all your offspring, fear not, from now on and to all generations of the earth I am your God."

The Lord God said to the angel, "Open his mouth and his ears, that he may hear and speak with his mouth, with the language which has been revealed." For it had ceased from the mouths of all the children of men from the day of the overthrow of Babel. And the angel opened his mouth, and his ears and his lips, and the angel began to speak with him in Hebrew in the tongue of the creation. He took the books of his fathers, and these were written in Hebrew, and he transcribed them, and he began from then on to study them, and the angel made known to him that which he could not understand, and he studied them during the six rainy months.

In the seventh year of the sixth week he spoke to his father and informed him that he would leave Haran to go into the land of Canaan to see it and return to him. Terah his father said to him, "Go in peace. May the eternal God make your path straight. And the Lord be with you, and protect you from all evil, and grant to you grace, mercy, and favor before those who see you, and may none of the children of men have power over you to harm you. Go in peace. If you see a land pleasant to your eyes to dwell in, then arise and take me with you and take Lot with you, the son of Haran your brother as your own son, the Lord be with you. Nahor your brother leave with me until you return in peace, and we go with you all together."

And Peleg the son of Eber died in those days, in the forty-eighth year of the life of Abram son of Terah, and all the days of Peleg were two hundred and thirty-nine years.

Abram journeyed from Haran, and he took Sarai, his wife, and Lot, his brother Haran's son and they went to the land of Canaan, and he came into Asshur, and proceeded to Shechem, and dwelt near a tall oak. He saw the land was very pleasant from the border of Hamath to the tall oak. The Lord said to him, "To you and to your offspring I will give this land." He built an altar there, and he offered on it a burnt sacrifice to the Lord, who had appeared to him.

He left from that place and went to the mountain Bethel on the west and Ai on the east, and pitched his tent there. He saw the land was very wide and good, and everything grew on it, vines, and figs, and pomegranates, oaks, and ilexes, and turpentine and oil trees, and cedars and cypresses, and date trees, and all trees of the field, and there was water on the mountains. And he blessed the Lord who had led him out of Ur of the Chaldees, and had brought him to this land.

And God established the covenant of circumcision with Abraham and said, "Every one that is born, the flesh of whose foreskin is not circumcised on the eighth day, does not belong to the children of the covenant which the Lord made with Abraham, but instead they belong to the children of destruction. Nor is there any other sign on him that he is the Lord's, but he is destined to be destroyed and killed from the earth, and to be rooted out of the earth, for he has broken the covenant of the Lord our God. All the angels of the presence (of the Lord) and all the angels of sanctification have been created already circumcised from the day of their creation, and before the angels of the presence (of the Lord) and the angels of sanctification He has sanctified Israel, that they should be with Him and with His holy angels.

Command the children of Israel and let them observe the sign of this covenant for their generations as an eternal law, and they will not be rooted out of the land. For the command is ordained for a covenant, that they should observe it forever among all the children of Israel. For Ishmael and his sons and his brothers, and Esau, the Lord did not cause them to come to Him, and he did not choose them. Although they are the children of Abraham, He knew them, but He chose Israel to be His people.

He sanctified them, and gathered them from among all the children of men; for there are many nations and many peoples, and all are His, and over all nations He has placed spirits in authority to lead them astray from Him. But over Israel He did not appoint any angel or spirit, for He alone is their ruler, and He will preserve them and require them at the hand of His angels and His spirits, and at the hand of all His powers in order that He may preserve them and bless them, that they may be His and He may be theirs from now on forever.

I announce to you that the children of Israel will not keep true to this law, and they will not circumcise their sons according to all this law; for in the flesh of their circumcision they will omit this circumcision of their sons, and all of the sons of Beliar will leave their sons uncircumcised as they were born.

There will be great wrath from the Lord against the children of Israel because they have forsaken His covenant and turned aside from His word, and provoked (God) and blasphemed, because they do not observe the ordinance of this law; for they have treated their genitalia like the Gentiles, so that they may be removed and rooted out of the land. And there will no more be pardon or forgiveness to them for all the sin of this eternal error."

(Here begin excerpts from the Holy Bible)

Then, in the days of King Saul, the spirits of the evil ones, the sons of the Watchers inhabited the people and animals of the land of Amalek. And God sent the prophet Samuel to speak to the king. Samuel said unto Saul, "The Lord sent me to anoint thee to be king over his people, over Israel; now therefore hearken thou unto the voice of the words of the Lord."

Thus saith the Lord of hosts, "I remember that which Amalek did to Israel, how he laid wait for him in the way, when he came up from Egypt. Now go and smite Amalek, and utterly destroy all that they have, and spare them not; but slay both man and woman, infant and suckling, ox and sheep, camel and ass." And Saul gathered the people together, and numbered them in Telaim, two hundred thousand footmen, and ten thousand men of Judah.

And Saul came to a city of Amalek, and laid wait in the valley. And Saul said unto the Kenites, "Go, depart, get you down from among the Amalekites, lest I destroy you with them, for ye shewed kindness to all the children of Israel, when they came up out of Egypt." So the Kenites departed from among the Amalekites. And Saul smote the Amalekites from Havilah until thou comest to Shur, that is over against Egypt. And he took Agag the king of the Amalekites alive, and utterly destroyed all the people with the edge of the sword.

But Saul and the people spared Agag, and the best of the sheep, and of the oxen, and of the fatlings, and the lambs, and all that was good, and would not utterly destroy them, but every thing that was vile and refuse, that they destroyed utterly.

Then came the word of the Lord unto Samuel, saying, "It repenteth me that I have set up Saul to be king, for he is turned back from following me, and hath not performed my commandments." And it grieved Samuel; and he cried unto the Lord all night. And when Samuel rose early to meet Saul in the morning, and it was told Samuel, "Saul came to Carmel, and, behold, he set him up a place, and is gone about, and passed on, and gone down to Gilgal."

And Samuel came to Saul and Saul said unto him, "Blessed be thou of the Lord, I have performed the commandment of the Lord." And Samuel said, "What meaneth then this bleating of the sheep in mine ears, and the lowing of the oxen which I hear?"

And Saul said, "They have brought them from the Amalekites, for the people spared the best of the sheep and of the oxen, to sacrifice unto the Lord thy God; and the rest we have utterly destroyed." Then Samuel said unto Saul, "Stay, and I will tell thee what the Lord hath said to me this night." And Saul said unto him, "Say on." And Samuel said, "When thou wast little in thine own sight, wast thou not made the head of the tribes of Israel, and the Lord anointed thee king over Israel?"

"And the Lord sent thee on a journey, and said, 'Go and utterly destroy the sinners the Amalekites, and fight against them until they be consumed.' Wherefore then didst thou not obey the voice of the Lord, but didst fly upon the spoil, and didst evil in the sight of the Lord?"

And Saul said unto Samuel, "Yea, I have obeyed the voice of the Lord, and have gone the way which the Lord sent me, and have brought Agag the king of Amalek, and have utterly destroyed the Amalekites. But the people took of the spoil, sheep and oxen, the chief of the things which should have been utterly destroyed, to sacrifice unto the Lord thy God in Gilgal."

And Samuel said, "Hath the Lord as great delight in burnt offerings and sacrifices, as in obeying the voice of the Lord? Behold, to obey is better than sacrifice, and to hearken than the fat of rams. For rebellion is as the sin of witchcraft, and stubbornness is as iniquity and idolatry. Because thou hast rejected the word of the Lord, he hath also rejected thee from being king."

And Saul said unto Samuel, "I have sinned for I have transgressed the commandment of the Lord, and thy words because I feared the people, and obeyed their voice." And Saul spared the animals and the some of the people of the land and brought the evil spirits into the land of the Israelites to dwell and spread there. And evil was let loose to plague and possess the souls of man until the day when Messiah came.

And it came to pass in those days that Jesus came from Nazareth of Galilee, and was baptized by John in Jordan. And straightway coming up out of the water, he saw the heavens opened, and the Spirit like a dove descending upon him. And there came a voice from heaven, saying, "Thou art my beloved Son, in whom I am well pleased." And immediately the spirit driveth him into the wilderness.

Then was Jesus led up of the Spirit into the wilderness to be tempted of the devil. And when he had fasted forty days and forty nights, he was afterward hungered. And when the tempter came to him, he said, "If thou be the Son of God, command that these stones be made bread." But he answered and said, "It is written, 'Man shall not live by bread alone, but by every word that proceedeth out of the mouth of God.'"

Then the devil taketh him up into the holy city, and setteth him on a pinnacle of the temple, and saith unto him, "If thou be the Son of God, cast thyself down; for it is written, 'He shall give his angels charge concerning thee and in their hands they shall bear thee up, lest at any time thou dash thy foot against a stone.'"

Jesus said unto him, "It is written again, 'Thou shalt not tempt the Lord thy God.'"

Again, the devil taketh him up into an exceeding high mountain, and sheweth him all the kingdoms of the world, and the glory of them, and saith unto him, "All these things will I give thee, if thou wilt fall down and worship me."

Then saith Jesus unto him, "Get thee hence, Satan, for it is written, 'Thou shalt worship the Lord thy God, and him only shalt thou serve.'"

Then the devil leaveth him, and, behold, angels came and ministered unto him. For it is written, "Submit yourselves to God. Resist the devil, and he will flee from you."

And Jesus could not be tempted by anything of this world for it is written in the Gospel of Thomas, "Become passers by." And again in the Gospel of Thomas is it written, "If you have found the world, you have found a corpse."

Now when Jesus had heard that John was cast into prison, he departed into Galilee. Leaving Nazareth, he came and dwelt in Capernaum, which is upon the sea coast, in the borders of Zabulon and Nephthalim; that it might be fulfilled which was spoken by Esaias the prophet, saying, "The land of Zabulon, and the land of Nephthalim, by the way of the sea, beyond Jordan, Galilee of the Gentiles, the people which sat in darkness saw great light; and to them which sat in the region and shadow of death light is sprung up."

And his fame went throughout all Syria and they brought unto him all sick people that were taken with diverse diseases and torments, and those who were possessed with devils, and those who were lunatic, and those that had the palsy; and he healed them. And there followed him great multitudes of people from Galilee, and from Decapolis, and from Jerusalem, and from Judea, and from beyond Jordan.

And Jesus came over unto the other side of the sea, into the country of the Gadarenes. And when he was come out of the ship, there were two possessed with devils, coming out of the tombs, exceeding fierce, so that no man might pass by that way. And, behold, they cried out, saying, "What have we to do with thee, Jesus, thou Son of God? Art thou come hither to torment us before the time?"

And one of the men came of the tombs with an unclean spirit, who had his dwelling among the tombs; and no man could bind him, no, not with chains; because he had been often bound with fetters and chains, and the chains had been plucked asunder by him, and the fetters broken in pieces, neither could any man tame him. And always, night and day, he was in the mountains, and in the tombs, crying and cutting himself with stones.

But when he saw Jesus afar off, he ran and worshipped him, crying with a loud voice, and said, "What have I to do with thee, Jesus, thou Son of the most high God?"

"I adjure thee by God, that thou torment me not." For he said unto him, "Come out of the man, thou unclean spirit." And he asked him, "What is thy name?" And he answered, saying, "My name is Legion for we are many." And he besought him much that he would not send them away out of the country.

Now there was there nigh unto the mountains a great herd of swine feeding. And all the devils besought him, saying, "Send us into the swine, that we may enter into them."

And forthwith Jesus gave them leave. And the unclean spirits went out, and entered into the swine and the herd ran violently down a steep place into the sea, (they were about two thousand;) and were choked in the sea. And they that fed the swine fled, and told it in the city, and in the country. And they went out to see what it was that was done. And they came to Jesus, and saw him that was possessed with the devil, and had the legion, sitting, and clothed, and in his right mind: and they were afraid.

They that saw it told them how it befell to him that was possessed with the devil and also concerning the swine. And they began to pray him to depart out of their coasts.

And when he was come into the ship, he that had been possessed with the devil prayed him that he might be with him. Howbeit Jesus suffered him not, but saith unto him, "Go home to thy friends, and tell them how great things the Lord hath done for thee, and hath had compassion on thee."

And he departed, and began to publish in Decapolis how great things Jesus had done for him and all men did marvel. And when Jesus was passed over again by ship unto the other side, much people gathered unto him and he was nigh unto the sea. And, behold, there cometh one of the rulers of the synagogue, Jairus by name; and when he saw him, he fell at his feet, And besought him greatly, saying, "My little daughter lieth at the point of death I pray thee, come and lay thy hands on her, that she may be healed and she shall live."

And Jesus went with him; and much people followed him, and thronged him.

And there was a certain woman, which had an issue of blood twelve years, and had suffered many things of many physicians, and had spent all that she had, and was nothing bettered, but rather grew worse. When she had heard of Jesus, she came in the press behind, and touched his garment. For she said, "If I may touch but his clothes, I shall be whole."

But the Pharisees stopped him because it was not legal to heal anyone on the Sabbath. But Jesus said to them, "Ought not this woman, being a daughter of Abraham, whom Satan hath bound, lo, these eighteen years, be loosed from this bond on the Sabbath day?" And straightway the fountain of her blood was dried up; and she felt in her body that she was healed of that plague. And Jesus, immediately knowing in himself that virtue had gone out of him, turned him about in the press, and said, "Who touched my clothes?"

And his disciples said unto him, "Thou seest the multitude thronging thee, and sayest thou, 'Who touched me?'" And he looked round about to see her that had done this thing. But the woman fearing and trembling, knowing what was done in her, came and fell down before him, and told him all the truth. And he said unto her, "Daughter, thy faith hath made thee whole; go in peace, and be whole of thy plague."

While he yet spake, there came from the ruler of the synagogue's house certain which said, "Thy daughter is dead, why troublest thou the Master any further?" As soon as Jesus heard the word that was spoken, he saith unto the ruler of the synagogue, "Be not afraid, only believe."

And having chosen twelve disciples, Jesus taught them and empowered them.

And as he sat upon the Mount of Olives, the disciples came unto him privately, saying, "Tell us, when shall these things be? And what shall be the sign of thy coming, and of the end of the world?"

And Jesus answered and said unto them, "Take heed that no man deceive you. For many shall come in my name, saying, 'I am Christ;' and shall deceive many. And ye shall hear of wars and rumors of wars, see that ye be not troubled for all these things must come to pass, but the end is not yet.

For nation shall rise against nation and kingdom against kingdom; and there shall be famines, and pestilences, and earthquakes, in diverse places. All these are the beginning of sorrows.

Then shall they deliver you up to be afflicted, and shall kill you and you shall be hated of all nations for my name's sake. And then shall many be offended, and shall betray one another, and shall hate one another.

And many false prophets shall rise, and shall deceive many. And because iniquity shall abound, the love of many shall wax cold. But he that shall endure unto the end, the same shall be saved.

And this gospel of the kingdom shall be preached in all the world for a witness unto all nations; and then shall the end come.

When you therefore shall see the abomination of desolation, spoken of by Daniel the prophet, stand in the holy place, whoso readeth, let him understand. Then let them which be in Judea flee into the mountains. Let him which is on the housetop not come down to take any thing out of his house. Neither let him which is in the field return back to take his clothes.

And woe unto them that are with child, and to them that give suck in those days! But pray ye that your flight be not in the winter, neither on the Sabbath day. For then shall be great tribulation, such as was not since the beginning of the world to this time, no, nor ever shall be.

And except those days should be shortened, there should no flesh be saved but for the elect's sake those days shall be shortened. Then if any man shall say unto you, 'Lo, here is Christ, or there;' believe it not. For there shall arise false Christs and false prophets, and shall shew great signs and wonders; insomuch that, if it were possible, they shall deceive the very elect.

Behold, I have told you before. Wherefore if they shall say unto you, 'Behold, he is in the desert;' go not forth. 'Behold, he is in the secret chambers;' believe it not. For as the lightning cometh out of the east, and shineth even unto the west; so shall also the coming of the Son of Man be. For wheresoever the carcass is, there will the eagles be gathered together."

Immediately after the tribulation of those days shall the sun be darkened, and the moon shall not give her light, and the stars shall fall from heaven, and the powers of the heavens shall be shaken. And then shall appear the sign of the Son of Man in heaven and then shall all the tribes of the earth mourn, and they shall see the Son of Man coming in the clouds of heaven with power and great glory.

And he shall send his angels with a great sound of a trumpet, and they shall gather together his elect from the four winds, from one end of heaven to the other. And while he had called unto him his twelve disciples, he gave them power against unclean spirits, to cast them out, and to heal all manner of sickness and all manner of disease.

Now the names of the twelve Apostles are these: the first, Simon who is called Peter; Andrew his brother; James the son of Zebedee; and John his brother; Philip; Bartholomew; Thomas; Matthew the publican; James the son of Alphaeus; Lebbaeus, whose surname was Thaddaeus; Simon the Canaanite, and Judas Iscariot, who also betrayed him.

These twelve Jesus sent forth, and commanded them, saying, "Go not into the way of the Gentiles, and into any city of the Samaritans enter ye not. But go rather to the lost sheep of the house of Israel. And as ye go, preach, saying, 'The kingdom of heaven is at hand.' Heal the sick, cleanse the lepers, raise the dead, cast out devils; freely ye have received, freely give."

But the heart of Judas was greedy, for he was the treasurer and kept the money bag. And Judas wished to have Jesus establish his kingdom so that he could control the money for the nation. So he conceived a plan that would force Jesus to act or die.

Now the feast of unleavened bread drew nigh, which is called the Passover. And the chief priests and scribes sought how they might kill Jesus; for they feared the people.

Then entered Satan into Judas surnamed Iscariot, being of the number of the twelve. And he went his way, and communed with the chief priests and captains, how he might betray Jesus unto them. And they were glad, and covenanted to give him money.

And Judas said unto them, "What will ye give me, and I will deliver him unto you?" And they covenanted with him for thirty pieces of silver. And he promised, and sought opportunity to betray him unto them in the absence of the multitude.

Then came the day of unleavened bread, when the Passover must be killed. And from that time Judas sought opportunity to betray him. Now, on the first day of the feast of unleavened bread the disciples came to Jesus, saying unto him, "Where wilt thou that we prepare for thee to eat the Passover?"

And he said, "Go into the city to such a man, and say unto him, 'the Master saith, my time is at hand, I will keep the Passover at thy house with my disciples.'" And the disciples did as Jesus had appointed them; and they made ready the Passover.

Now when the even was come, he sat down with the twelve. And as they did eat, he said, "Verily I say unto you, that one of you shall betray me. The Son of Man goeth as it is written of him but woe unto that man by whom the Son of Man is betrayed! It had been good for that man if he had not been born."

And they were exceeding sorrowful, and began every one of them to say unto him, "Lord, is it I?" Jesus answered, "He it is, to whom I shall give a sop, when I have dipped it." And when he had dipped the sop, he gave it to Judas Iscariot, the son of Simon.

And after the sop Satan entered into him. Then said Jesus unto him, "That thou doest, do quickly."

Now no man at the table knew for what intent he spake this unto him. For some of them thought, because Judas had the bag, that Jesus had said unto him, "Buy those things that we have need of against the feast;" or, that he should give something to the poor.

Judas then having received the sop went immediately out and it was night.

(The Gospel of Judas, once deemed an apostate book by the bishops of Rome, states that Jesus asked Judas to betray him so that the mission of both men might be fulfilled. This view has gained further examination of late as the "forbidden books" are drawing attention again.)

Therefore, when he was gone out, Jesus said, "Now is the Son of Man glorified, and God is glorified in him. If God be glorified in him, God shall also glorify him in himself, and shall straightway glorify him.

"Little children, yet a little while I am with you. Ye shall seek me and as I said unto the Jews, 'Whither I go, ye cannot come;' so now I say to you.

"A new commandment I give unto you. That ye love one another as I have loved you. By this shall all men know that ye are my disciples, if ye have love one to another."

Simon Peter said unto him, "Lord, whither goest thou?" Jesus answered him, "Whither I go, thou canst not follow me now; but thou shalt follow me afterwards."

When Jesus had spoken these words, he went forth with his disciples over the brook Cedron where there was a garden, into which he entered, and his disciples.

And Judas also, who betrayed him, knew the place, for Jesus ofttimes resorted thither with his disciples. Judas then, having received a band of men and officers from the chief priests and Pharisees, cometh thither with lanterns and torches and weapons.

Jesus therefore, knowing all things that should come upon him, went forth, and said unto them, "Whom seek ye?" They answered him, "Jesus of

Nazareth." Jesus saith unto them, "I am he."

And Judas also, which betrayed him, stood with them. As soon then as he had said unto them, I am he, they went backward, and fell to the ground. Then asked he them again, "Whom seek ye?" And they said, "Jesus of Nazareth." Jesus answered, "I have told you that I am he; if therefore ye seek me, let these go their way that the saying might be fulfilled, of which he spake. Of them which thou gavest me have I lost none."

When the morning was come, all the chief priests and elders of the people took counsel against Jesus to put him to death. And when they had bound him, they led him away, and delivered him to Pontius Pilate the governor.

Then Judas, who had betrayed him, when he saw that he was condemned, repented himself, and brought again the thirty pieces of silver to the chief priests and elders, saying, "I have sinned in that I have betrayed the innocent blood." And they said, "What is that to us? See thou to that."

And he cast down the pieces of silver in the temple, and departed, and went and hanged himself.

(Again, the Gospel of Judas presents the notion that Jesus had told Judas before his betrayal that Judas would be a man most reviled and hated, but he had been chosen by God for what could be considered a selfless act.)

And the chief priests took the silver pieces, and said, "It is not lawful for to put them into the treasury, because it is the price of blood." And they took counsel, and bought it with them to the potter's field. Wherefore that field was called the field of blood unto this day. Then was fulfilled that which was spoken by Jeremy the prophet, saying, "And they took the thirty pieces of silver, the price of him that was valued, whom they of the children of Israel did value; and gave them for the potter's field, as the Lord appointed me."

Then they took Jesus and beat him and laid a crown of thorns on his head and spit on him. And they crucified him, and parted his garments, casting lots that it might be fulfilled which was spoken by the prophet, "They parted my garments among them, and upon my vesture did they cast lots."

And set up over his head this accusation written, THIS IS JESUS THE KING OF THE JEWS. Then were there two thieves crucified with him, one on the right hand, and another on the left. And they that passed by reviled him, wagging their heads saying, "If thou be the Son of God, come down from the cross."

Likewise also the chief priests mocked him, with the scribes and elders, and said, "He saved others; himself he cannot save. If he be the King of Israel, let him now come down from the cross, and we will believe him."

"He trusted in God; let him deliver him now, if he will have him: for he said, 'I am the Son of God.'"

Now from the sixth hour there was darkness over all the land unto the ninth hour. And about the ninth hour Jesus cried with a loud voice, saying, "Eli, Eli, lama sabachthani?" That is to say, "My God, my God, why hast thou forsaken me?"

Some of them that stood there, when they heard that, said, "This man calleth for Elias." And straightway one of them ran, and took a sponge, and filled it with vinegar, and put it on a reed, and gave him to drink.

The rest said, "Let be, let us see whether Elias will come to save him." Jesus, when he had cried again with a loud voice, yielded up the ghost.

And, behold, the veil of the temple was rent in twain from the top to the bottom; and the earth did quake, and the rocks rent; and the graves were opened; and many bodies of the saints which slept arose.

Now when the centurion, and they that were with him, watching Jesus, saw the earthquake, and those things that were done, they feared greatly, saying, "Truly this was the Son of God."

The first day of the week cometh Mary Magdalene early, when it was yet dark, unto the sepulcher, and seeth the stone was taken away from the sepulcher. Then she runneth, and cometh to Simon Peter, and to the other disciple, whom Jesus loved, and saith unto them, "They have taken away the Lord out of the sepulcher, and we know not where they have laid him."

And returned from the sepulcher, and told all these things unto the eleven, and to all the rest. It was Mary Magdalene and Joanna, and Mary the mother of James, and other women that were with them, which told these things unto the Apostles. And their words seemed to them as idle tales, and they believed them not.

Peter therefore went forth, and that other disciple, and came to the sepulcher. So they ran both together and the other disciple did outrun Peter, and came first to the sepulcher.

And he stooping down, and looking in, saw the linen clothes lying; yet went he not in. Then cometh Simon Peter following him, and went into the sepulcher, and seeth the linen clothes lie, and the napkin, that was about his head, not lying with the linen clothes, but wrapped together in a place by itself.

Then went in also that other disciple, which came first to the sepulcher, and he saw, and believed. For as yet they knew not the scripture, that he must rise again from the dead. Then the disciples went away again unto their own home.

But Mary stood without at the sepulcher weeping and as she wept, she stooped down, and looked into the sepulcher, and seeth two angels in white sitting, the one at the head, and the other at the feet, where the body of Jesus had lain. And they say unto her, "Woman, why weepest thou?" She saith unto them, "Because they have taken away my Lord, and I know not where they have laid him." And when she had thus said, she turned herself back, and saw Jesus standing, and knew not that it was Jesus.

Jesus saith unto her, "Woman, why weepest thou? "Whom seekest thou?" She, supposing him to be the gardener, saith unto him, "Sir, if thou have borne him hence, tell me where thou hast laid him, and I will take him away."

Jesus saith unto her, "Mary." She turned herself, and saith unto him, "Rabboni," which is to say, Master. Jesus saith unto her, "Touch me not for I am not yet ascended to my Father but go to my brethren, and say unto them, 'I ascend unto my Father, and your Father and to my God, and your God.'"

Mary Magdalene came and told the disciples that she had seen the Lord, and that he had spoken these things unto her.

And, behold, Peter and another of them went that same day to a village called Emmaus, which was from Jerusalem about threescore furlongs. And they talked together of all these things which had happened. And it came to pass, that while they communed together and reasoned, Jesus himself drew near, and went with them. But their eyes were holden that they should not know him.

And he said unto them, "What manner of communications are these that ye have one to another, as ye walk, and are sad? And the one of them, whose name was Cleopas, answering said unto him, Art thou only a stranger in Jerusalem, and hast not known the things which are come to pass there in these days?

And he said unto them, "What things?" And they said unto him, "Concerning Jesus of Nazareth, which was a prophet mighty in deed and word before God and all the people. And how the chief priests and our rulers delivered him to be condemned to death, and have crucified him.

But we trusted that it had been he which should have redeemed Israel and beside all this, today is the third day since these things were done. Yea, and certain women also of our company made us astonished, which were early at the sepulcher. And when they found not his body, they came, saying, that they had also seen a vision of angels, which said that he was alive.

And certain of them which were with us went to the sepulcher, and found it even so as the women had said but him they saw not."

Then he said unto them, "O fools, and slow of heart to believe all that the prophets have spoken. Ought not Christ to have suffered these things, and to enter into his glory?"

And beginning at Moses and all the prophets, he expounded unto them in all the scriptures the things concerning himself. And they drew nigh unto the village, whither they went and he made as though he would have gone further. But they constrained him, saying, "Abide with us for it is toward evening, and the day is far spent." And he went in to tarry with them.

And it came to pass, as he sat at meat with them, he took bread, and blessed it, and break, and gave to them. Then the same day at evening, being the first day of the week, when the doors were shut where the disciples were assembled for fear of the Jews, came Jesus and stood in the midst, and saith unto them, "Peace be unto you."

And when he had so said, he shewed unto them his hands and his side. Then were the disciples glad, when they saw the Lord. And he said unto them, "Thus it is written, and thus it behooved Christ to suffer, and to rise from the dead the third day. And that repentance and remission of sins should be preached in his name among all nations, beginning at Jerusalem. And ye are witnesses of these things."

"And, behold, I send the promise of my Father upon you; but tarry ye in the city of Jerusalem, until ye be imbued with power from on high."

Then said Jesus to them again, "Peace be unto you; as my Father hath sent me, even so send I you." And when he had said this, he breathed on them, and saith unto them, "Receive ye the Holy Ghost." And their eyes were opened, and they knew him.

And he led them out as far as to Bethany, and he lifted up his hands, and blessed them. And it came to pass, while he blessed them, he was parted from them, and carried up into heaven.

Jesus Christ is the faithful witness, and the first begotten of the dead, and the prince of the kings of the earth. Unto him that loved us, and washed us from our sins in his own blood, And hath made us kings and priests unto God and his Father; to him be glory and dominion forever and ever.

Behold, he cometh with clouds; and every eye shall see him, and they also which pierced him and all kindreds of the earth shall wail because of him.

"I am the Alpha and the Omega, the beginning and the ending," saith the Lord, "Which is and which was and which is to come; the Almighty. I am he that liveth and was dead; and, behold, I am alive forevermore, and have the keys of hell and of death."

And an angel came down from heaven, having the key of the bottomless pit and a great chain in his hand. And he laid hold on the dragon, that old serpent, which is the Devil, and Satan, and bound him a thousand years, And cast him into the bottomless pit, and shut him up, and set a seal upon him, that he should deceive the nations no more, till the thousand years should be fulfilled: and after that he must be loosed a little season.

And I saw thrones and they sat upon them, and judgment was given unto them. And I saw the souls of them that were beheaded for the witness of Jesus, and for the word of God, and which had not worshipped the beast, neither his image, neither had received his mark upon their foreheads, or in their hands; and they lived and reigned with Christ a thousand years. But the rest of the dead lived not again until the thousand years were finished.

This is the first resurrection.

Blessed and holy is he that hath part in the first resurrection, on such the second death hath no power, but they shall be priests of God and of Christ, and shall reign with him a thousand years.

And when the thousand years are expired, Satan shall be loosed out of his prison, and shall go out to deceive the nations which are in the four quarters of the earth, Gog, and Magog, to gather them together to battle, the number of whom is as the sand of the sea.

And they went up on the breadth of the earth, and compassed the camp of the saints about, and the beloved city. And those faithful to the Lord God were resolved to meet the force of darkness in battle. And their priests said to them, "Strengthen yourselves and do not fear them. Their craving for your death is formlessness and empty and their staff is as though it were not. Israel is all that is and shall be. It is in the eternal times to be. Today is God's appointed time to subdue and to abase the prince of wickedness. And God shall send eternal help to all of His redeemed by the might of an angel. He made the dominion of Michael magnificent in eternal light and has enlightened the covenant of Israel with happiness. Peace and blessing are in store for those who follow God.

We shall exalt Him among all the gods and the dominion of Michael and the rule of Israel will be exalted among all flesh. And righteousness shall be happy on high and all the sons of His truth shall rejoice in eternal knowledge. And you who are sons of His covenant, strengthen yourselves in the crucible of God until He waves His hand and fills His crucibles, His mysteries will be revealed to you according to your place and time.

You are the God of our covenant and we are your people, an eternal people, and you placed us in the source of light to see for your truth. And from the days of old you appointed a prince of light as our helper and all the spirits of truth are in his rule. It was you who (destined) made Belial for the pit, for he is an angel of enmity.

In darkness is his dominion. It is his way to make wicked and to make men guilty. And all the spirits of his kingdom are angels of violence. They walk in places of darkness and together their desire is for it. But we are the appointed of your truth. We shall rejoice in the hand of your might and we shall be glad in your salvation and we shall celebrate your help in our times of need. We desire your peace.

Who is like you in power, O God of Israel? Yet the poor you protect with your mighty hand. And which angel or prince is like the help of your might? For of old you appointed for yourself a day of battle to help with truth and to destroy guilt, to abase darkness, and to give might and light to your people. The sons of darkness are destined to an eternal place of annihilation. And happiness shall be the appointment of the sons of light."

Then their words were heard in the ears of God. And I looked, and behold a white cloud, and upon the cloud one sat like unto the Son of Man, having on his head a golden crown, and in his hand a sharp sickle. And another angel came out of the temple, crying with a loud voice to him that sat on the cloud, "Thrust in thy sickle, and reap for the time is come for thee to reap, for the harvest of the earth is ripe."

And he that sat on the cloud thrust in his sickle on the earth; and the earth was reaped. And another angel came out of the temple which is in heaven, he also having a sharp sickle. And another angel came out from the altar, which had power over fire and cried with a loud cry to him that had the sharp sickle, saying, "Thrust in thy sharp sickle, and gather the clusters of the vine of the earth; for her grapes are fully ripe."

And the angel thrust in his sickle into the earth, and gathered the vine of the earth, and cast it into the great winepress of the wrath of God. And the winepress was trodden without the city, and blood came out of the winepress, even unto the horse bridles, by the space of a thousand and six hundred furlongs.

And the devil that deceived them was cast into the lake of fire and brimstone, where the beast and the false prophet are, and shall be tormented day and night forever and ever.

And I saw a great white throne, and him that sat on it, from whose face the earth and the heaven fled away; and there was found no place for them. And I saw the dead, small and great, stand before God; and the books were opened and another book was opened, which is the Book of Life, and the dead were judged out of those things which were written in the books, according to their works.

And the sea gave up the dead who were in it; and death and hell delivered up the dead who were in them: and they were judged every man according to their works.

And death and hell were cast into the lake of fire. This is the second death. And whosoever was not found written in the Book of Life was cast into the lake of fire.

And I saw a new heaven and a new earth; for the first heaven and the first earth were passed away. And there was no more sea. I saw the holy city, new Jerusalem, coming down from God out of heaven, prepared as a bride adorned for her husband. And I heard a great voice out of heaven saying, "Behold, the tabernacle of God is with men, and he will dwell with them, and they shall be his people, and God himself shall be with them, and be their God."

And God shall wipe away all tears from their eyes; and there shall be no more death, neither sorrow, nor crying, neither shall there be any more pain, for the former things are passed away.

And he that sat upon the throne said, "Behold, I make all things new." And he said unto me, "Write, for these words are true and faithful."

He said unto me, "It is done. I am the Alpha and the Omega, the beginning and the end. I will give unto him that is athirst of the fountain of the water of life freely."

"He that overcometh shall inherit all things and I will be his God, and he shall be my son."

The Omega

Evil walked the earth when angels fell. Evil stalks us now in disembodied spirits; immortal wraiths once clothed in flesh when angels and women bred; spirits released from their fleshly prisons when their bodies were destroyed for drinking the blood of men.

Evil also lives inside of the common man; set free when pride kills reason and eats integrity whole.

There is evil that entraps us and evil that tugs from within. But neither have control until we choose to relent. Evil is a choice of action, of thoughts entertained too long, of arrogance pushing aside the last vestiges of compassion. When angels or men think of themselves first, this is evil being born afresh. When outcome is not considered, empathy abandoned, or compassion dismissed, evil has come of age.

.

About the Ancient Texts

The Dead Sea Scrolls found in the caves of Qumran are of great interest in the task of clarifying the history and doctrine in existence between biblical times and the fixing of canon. The scrolls were penned in the second century B.C. and were in use at least until the destruction of the second temple in 70 A.D. Similar scrolls to those found in the 11 caves of Qumran were also found at the Masada stronghold which fell to the Romans in 73 A.D.

Fragments of every book of the Old Testament except Esther were found in the caves of Qumran, as were many other ancient books. Some of these books are considered to have been of equal importance and influence to the people of Qumran and to the writers and scholars of the time. Writers of the New Testament were among those studying the scrolls found in Qumran. Knowing this, one might ask which of the dozens of non-canonical books most influenced the writers of the New Testament.

It is possible to ascertain the existence of certain influences within the Bible context by using the Bible itself. The Bible can direct us to other works in three ways. The work can be mentioned by name, as is the Book of Jasher. The work can be quoted within the Bible text, as is the case with the Book of Enoch. The existence of the work can be alluded to, as is the case of the missing letter from the apostle Paul to the Corinthians.

In the case of those books named in the Bible, one can compile a list. The list is lengthier than one might suspect. Most of these works have not been found. Some have been unearthed but their authenticity is questioned. Others have been recovered and the link between scripture and scroll is generally accepted. Let us now take a look at the texts used to trace the history of evil.

All texts used or referenced in this book may be purchased from Fifth Estate Publishers. http://www.fifthestatepub.com

The First Book of Adam and Eve: The Conflict With Satan

The First Book of Adam and Eve is an apocryphal story, written in a midrash style, detailing the life of Adam and Eve from the time God planted the Garden of Eden to the time that Cain killed his brother, Abel.

The story is an embellishment of the Genesis story up to the point of the cursing of Cain for the murder of Abel.

Of the numerous apocryphal works that were written regarding Adam and Eve this text seems to have most influenced early theologians. This is evident in the widespread popularity of the book from the third to the 13th century. Even though the book was widely read in the Middle Ages, and considered to shine light on what actually took place in the time of creation, today it is considered fiction and thus relegated to a collection of texts called the *Pseudepigrapha*, or "false writings."

The text shows some cobbling together of various works, combined into a single storyline. Although the foundation of the text can be traced to combined oral traditions thousands of years old, the primary story was likely created around 200 to 300 years before Christ. Additions and details were added over many years, leading to this version being penned around the thirdcentury A.D.

The text presented here is an embellishment of the Jewish storyline from Genesis that is "Christianized" by additions of allusions and references to the New Testament. Quite often the details of the story are made to foreshadow the birth, death, and resurrection of Jesus. The result is the text before you.

The central part of the text focuses on the conflict between Good and Evil in the form of Satan's endeavor to destroy God's creations, Adam and Eve. The story begs the eternal question:How does one know whether God or Satan guides the opportunity, situation, or person confronting us? The fight between good and evil, as well as the question of who is influencing our surroundings, are eternal, and the story attempts to answer in metaphor.

The creation story and the tale of Adam and Eve pervaded the thoughts of writers throughout the ancient world. Evidence is seen in the large number of versions that exist in various languages and cultures. Indeed, it is due to the amazing popularity of the text that it has survived in six languages: Greek, Latin, Armenian, Georgian, and Slavonic, as well as a fragment in Coptic. The stories may also be traced through the writings of Greeks, Syrians, Egyptians, Abyssinians, Hebrews, and other ancient peoples.

Most scholars agree that the text was written originally in Greek and that all of the six versions show evidence of Greek linguistic roots. Those

Greek manuscripts we posses seem to be no more accurate to the original than any of the other translations, having been so many generations removed from the source document.

The foundation of our modern English translation began with the work of, Vicar of Broadwindsor, Dr. S. C. Malan, who worked from the Ethiopic edition edited by, Professor at the University of Munich. Dr. Trumpp, who had the advantage of having an older version at his disposal.

From an ancient oral tradition, to a third century codex, through the hands of Dr. E. Trumpp and Dr. S. C. Malan, to our modern English version, the First Book of Adam and Eve has survived, just as mankind has survived the struggles written of in the book itself.

The Malan translation of the text was penned in a rather stilted and formal style of English resembling that of the King James Bible. The Malan translation was then taken and re-written with word choices and sentence structure altered to make it more palatable and understandable to the modern reader, while keeping the poetic flow of the text.

The Second Book of Adam and Eve

The Second Book of Adam and Eve expands on the time from Cain's act of murder to the time Enoch was taken by God. It is, above all, a continuation of the story of The First Book of Adam and Eve.

Like the first book, this book is also part of the "Pseudepigrapha," which is a collection of historical biblical works that are considered to be fiction. Although considered to be *Pseudepigrapha,* it carries significance in that it provides insight into what was considered acceptable religious writing and ideas of the time.

This book is a composite of oral versions of an account handed down by word of mouth, from generation to generation until an unknown author pieced the stories together into a written form.

This particular version is the work of unknown Egyptians. The lack of historical allusion makes it difficult to date the writing. Using other *Pseudepigrapha* works as a reference only slightly narrows the probable dates to a range of a few hundred years. Parts of the text were probably included in an oral tradition, 200 to 300 years before the birth of Christ. Certainly, book two was written after book one.

Sections of the text are found in the Jewish Talmud, and the Islamic Koran. Although some think this shows how the books of Adam and Eve played a vital role in ancient literature, it could just as well expose the fact that the authors of the Adam and Eve stories borrowed heavily from accepted holy books.

The Egyptian author wrote in Arabic, but later translations were found written in Ethiopic. The present English translation was completed in the late 1800's by Dr. S. C. Malan and Dr. E. Trumpp. They translated the text into King James English from both the Arabic version and the Ethiopic version, which was then published in The Forgotten Books of Eden in 1927 by The World Publishing Company. The version presented here takes the 1927 version, written in King James style English, and renders it into wording more familiar to the modern reader. Tangled sentence structure and archaic words were replaced with a more clear, crisp, 21st century English.

The Book of Jasher

Jasher is not the author's name. Rather, it carries the meaning of something straight, true, or upright. The meaning could be the upright book or the faithful record, or it could refer to the character and reliability of the person(s) making the record.

The Bible references The Book of Jasher as a source of information and history in at least two places.

In the Book of Joshua is the account of an event that staggers the mind.

"And the sun stood still, and the moon stayed, until the people had avenged themselves upon their enemies. Is not this written in the book of Jasher? So the sun stood still in the midst of heaven, and hasted not to go down about a whole day." *(Joshua 10:13)*

One translation of a parallel chapter in the Book of Jasher states as follows:

"And when they were smiting, the day was declining toward evening, and Joshua said in the sight of all the people, Sun, stand thou still upon Gibeon, and thou moon in the valley of Ajalon, until the nation shall have revenged itself upon its enemies. And the Lord hearkened to the voice of Joshua, and the sun stood still in the midst of the heavens, and it stood still six and thirty moments, and the moon also stood still and hastened not to go down a whole day." *(Jasher 88:63-64)*

Another Biblical reference to Jasher shows David teaching archery to his army:

"Also he bade them teach the children of Judah the use of the bow; behold, it is written in the book of Jasher." *(2 Samuel 1:18)*

The Jews of the first century A.D. held the Book of Jasher as a reliable historical document, although not "inspired." When Titus destroyed Jerusalem in A.D. 70, one of his officers discovered a hidden library complete with a scholar hiding there. The officer had mercy on the man and took him and the books to his residence at Seville, Spain, (which was at that time the capital of the Roman province Hispalensis). The manuscript was later donated to the Jewish college at Cordova, Spain; and after printing was invented, the Jewish scholars had the book printed in Hebrew in Venice in 1625.

Confusion arose when another book of the same title was translated and released. This book, known now as Pseudo-Jasher, was discovered to be a hoax. Scholars turned against that book but continued to confuse it with the older document of the same name.

One of the printed manuscripts of Jasher from Spain was acquired by a British citizen named Samuel. Samuel set about to translate the book into English. When the British scholars heard of this, they made no distinction between the two books of Jasher and Pseudo-Jasher and the climate for publication turned stormy. Samuel sold his translation to Mordecai M.

Noah, a New York publisher, who published it in 1840 as the first English translation. The copyright was later obtained by J. H. Parry and Company of Salt Lake City, Utah in 1887. It is a modern rendition of this version presented here.

The book seems to contain authentic Hebrew traditions and phraseology. Jasher, being a record, was added to and updated by each Hebrew historian as the book was handed down.

The Book of Jasher we possess today was likely composed by an author compiling many old Jewish traditions (called Midrash) dating back to around the time of Christ. This included the source from the rescue of 70 A.D. Scholars agree that the Book of Jasher was likely last updated in Spain about the 12th century A.D. It is difficult to know if Jasher is quoting Midrash literature, or if Midrash literature was quoting the real Book of Jasher, which was also quoted in the Old Testament.

"Midrash" refers to writings containing extra-legal material of anecdotal or allegorical nature, designed either to clarify historical material, or to teach a moral point.

The names of the countries in which the sons of Noah are reported to have settled can definitely be dated to the 11th century in Spain. This does not make it conclusive that the entire work must have been authored at that time. As books are copied, scribes can take it upon themselves to place the current names in the text.

Although Jasher was not considered inspired, it was considered to be a historical record reliable enough to be quoted by prophets and kings.

There are differences in authority and weight given to various types of records. Civil and historical records may serve the same historical purpose or record, but texts thought to be inspired have both historical and spiritual function.

When Ptolemy, king of Egypt, requested the Jewish holy books, the Israelites felt they could not give the Gentiles their sacred texts, so they sent him the Book of Jasher. He cherished it but later found it had a lesser status than the scriptures. Angry about the hoax, he confronted the Jews. Now with their heads at risk, they agreed to translate their Old Testament into Greek, which became known as the Septuagint.

The Books of Enoch

Of all books used in the preceding narrative, the books of Enoch, especially 1 Enoch, was used to draw out the greatest amount of information. Here, I will spare the reader from redundant information. Please refer to the introductions of 1 Enoch, 2 Enoch, and 3 Enoch for more information regarding each of the books.

The Book of Jubilees

The Book of Jubilees, also known as The Little Genesis and The Apocalypse of Moses, opens with an extraordinary claim of authorship. It is attributed to the very hand of Moses; penned while he was on Mount Sinai, as an angel of God dictated to him regarding those events that transpired from the beginning of the world. The story is written from the viewpoint of the angel.

The angelic monolog takes place after the exodus of the children of Israel out of Egypt. The setting is atop Mount Sinai, where Moses was summoned by God. The text then unfolds as the angel reveals heaven's viewpoint of history. We are led through the creation of man, Adam's fall from grace, the union of fallen angels and earthly women, the birth of demonic offspring, the cleansing of the earth by flood, and the astonishing claim that man's very nature was somehow changed, bringing about a man with less sinful qualities than his antediluvian counterpart.

The story goes on to fill in many details in Israel's history, ending at the point in time when the narrative itself takes place, after the exodus.

Scholars believe Jubilees was composed in the second century B.C. The Hebrew fragments found at Qumran are part of a Jewish library that contained other supporting literature such as 1 Enoch and others.

An analysis of the chronological development in the shapes of letters in the manuscripts confirms that Jubilees is pre-Christian in date and seems to have been penned between 100 and 200 B.C. The book of Jubilees is also cited in the Qumran Damascus Document in pre-Christian texts.

The author was a Pharisee (a doctor of the law), or someone very familiar with scripture and religious law. Since the scrolls were found in what is assumed to be an Essene library, and were dated to the time the Essene community was active, the author was probably a member of that particular religious group. Jubilees represents a hyper-legalistic and midrashic tendency, which was part of the Essene culture at the time.

Jubilees represents a midrash on Genesis 1:1 through Exodus 12 depicting the episodes from creation with the observance of the Sabbath by the angels and men; to Israel's escape from Egyptian bondage.

Although originally written in Hebrew, the Hebrew texts were completely lost until the find at Qumran. Fragments of Jubilees were discovered among the Dead Sea Scrolls. At least fourtee14 copies of the Book of Jubilees have been identified from caves 1, 2, 3 and 11 at Qumran. This makes it clear that the Book of Jubilees was a popular and probably authoritative text for the community whose library was concealed in the caves. These fragments are actually generations closer to the original copies than most books in our accepted Bible. Unfortunately, the fragments found at Qumran were only pieces of the texts and offered the briefest of glimpses of the entire book. The only complete versions of the Book of Jubilees are in Ethiopic, which in turn were translations of a Greek version.

Four Ethiopian manuscripts of Jubilees were found to be hundreds of years old. Of these, the fifteenth and sixteenth century texts are the truest and least corrupted when compared to the fragments found at Qumran. There are also citations of Jubilees in Syriac literature that may reflect a lost translation from Hebrew. Pieces of Latin translations have also been found.

Other fragments of a Greek version are quoted or referenced by Justin Martyr, Origen, Diodorus of Antioch, Isidore of Alexandria, Isidore of Seville, Eutychius, Patriarch of Alexandria, John of Malala, and Syncellus. This amount of varied information and translations is enough to allow us to reconstruct the original to a great degree. The internal evidence of Jubilees shows very little tampering by Christians during its subsequent translations, allowing a clear view of certain Jewish beliefs propagated at the time of its origin. By removing certain variances, we can isolate Christian alterations and mistakes in translations with a reasonable degree of confidence. Due to the poor condition of the fragments of Qumran, we may never be able to confirm certain key phrases in Hebrew. Thus, as with many texts, including the Bible, in the end we must trust in the accuracy of the ancient translators.

It should be noted that the books of Jubilees, Enoch, and Jasher present stories of "The Watchers," a group of angels sent to earth to record and teach, but who fell by their own lust and pride into a demonic state. Both Enoch and Jubilees refer to a solar-based calendar. This may show a conflict or transition at the time of their penning since Judaism now uses a lunar-based calendar.

Laws, rites, and functions are observed and noted in Jubilees. Circumcision is emphasized in both humans and angels. Angelic observance of Sabbath laws as well as parts of Jewish religious laws are said to have been observed in heaven before they were revealed to Moses.

To the Qumran community, complete obedience to the Laws of Moses entailed observing a series of holy days and festivals at a particular time according to a specific calendar. The calendar described in Jubilees is one of 364 days, divided into four seasons of three months each with 13 weeks to a season. Each month had 30 days with one day added at certain times for each of the four seasons. With 52 weeks in a year, the festival and holy days recur at the same point each year. This calendar became a hallmark of an orthodox Qumran community.

The adherence to a specific calendar is one of many ways the Book of Jubilees shows the devotion to religious law. The law had been placed at the pinnacle of importance in the lives of the community at Qumran. All aspects of life were driven by a seemingly obsessive compliance to every jot and tittle of the law. The Book Of Jubilees confirms what can only be inferred from the books of Ezra, Nehemiah, and Zechariah, that the law and those who carried it out were supreme.

As the law took hold, by its nature, it crystallized the society. Free expression died, smothered under a mantle of hyper-orthodoxy. Since free thought invited accusations of violations of the law or claims of heresy, prudence, a closed mind, and a silent voice prevailed. Free thought was limited to religious or apocryphal writings, which upheld the orthodox positions of the day. The silent period between Malachi and Mark may be a reflection of this stasis. Jubilees, Enoch, and other apocryphal books found in the Qumran caves are a triumph over the unimaginative mindset brought on by making religious law supreme and human expression contrary to the law and punishable by death. It may be an odd manifestation that such a burst of creativity was fueled by the very search for order that suppressed free thought in the first place.

The Book of Jubilees seems to be an attempt to answer and explain all questions left unanswered in the Book of Genesis as well as to bolster the position of the religious law. It attempts to trace the source of religious laws back to an ancient beginning thereby adding weight and sanction.

In the Book of Jubilees, we discover the origin of the wife of Cain. There is information offered about angels and the beginnings of the human race, how demons came into existence, and the place of Satan in the plans of God. Information is offered in an attempt to make perfect sense of the vagaries left in Genesis. For the defense of order and law and to maintain religious law as the center point of Jewish life, Jubilees was written as an answer to both pagan Greeks and liberal Jews. From the divine placement of law and order to its explanation of times and events, Jubilees is a panorama of legalism.

The name "Jubilees" comes from the division of time into eras known as Jubilees. One Jubilee occurs after the equivalent of 49 years, or seven Sabbaths of weeks of years have passed. It is the numerical perfection of seven sevens. In a balance and symmetry of years, the Jubilee occurs after seven cycles of seven or 49 years have been completed. Thus, the fiftieth year is a Jubilee year. Time is told by referencing the number of Jubilees that have transpired from the time the festival was first kept. For example, Israel entered Canaan at the close of the fiftieth jubilee, which is about 2450 B.C.

The obsession with time, dates, and the strict observance of festivals are all evidence of legalism taken to the highest level.

Based on the approximate time of writing, Jubilees was created in the time of the Maccabees, in the high priesthood of Hyrcanus. In this period of time the appearance of the Messiah and the rise of the Messianic kingdom were viewed as imminent. Followers were preparing themselves for the arrival of the Messiah and the establishment of His eternal kingdom.

Judaism was in contact with the Greek culture at the time. The Greeks were known to be philosophers and were developing processes of critical thinking. One objective of Jubilees was to defend Judaism against the attacks of the Hellenists and to prove that the law was logical, consistent, and valid. Attacks against paganism and non-believers are embedded in the text along with defense of the law and its consistency through proclamations of the law being observed by the angels in heaven from the beginning of creation.

Moral lessons are taught by use of the juxtaposition of the "satans" and their attempts to test and lead mankind into sin against the warning and advice of scriptural wisdom from Moses and his angels.

Mastema is mentioned only in The Book of Jubilees and in the Fragments of a Zadokite Work. Mastema is Satan. The name Mastema is derived from the Hebrew, "Mastim," meaning "adversary." The word occurs as singular and plural. The word is equivalent to satan (adversary or accuser). This is similar to the chief Satan and his class of "satans" in 1 Enoch 40,7.

Mastema is subservient to God. His task is to tempt men to sin and if they do, he accuses them in the presence of the Throne of God. He and his minions lead men into sin but do not cause the sin. Once men have chosen to sin, they lead them from sin to destruction. Since man is given free will, sin is a choice, with Mastema simply encouraging and facilitating the decision. The choice, we can assume, is our own and the destruction that follows is "self-destruction."

Beliar is also mentioned. Beliar is the Greek name for Belial/Beliaal. The name in its Hebrew equivalent means "without value." This was a demon known by the Jews as the chief of all the devils. Belial is the leader of the Sons of Darkness. Belial and Mastema are mentioned in a Zadokite fragment saying that at the time of the Antichrist, Belial shall be let loose against Israel; as God spoke through Isaiah the prophet. Belial is sometimes presented as an agent of God's punishment although he is considered a "satan."

It is important to mention that Judaism had no doctrine of original sin. The fall of Adam and Eve may have removed man from the perfect environment and the curses that followed may have shortened his lifespan, but propagation of sin through the bloodline was not considered. Sin seemed to affect only man and the animals he was given dominion over. Yet man continued to sin, and to increase in his capacity and modes of sin. The explanation offered for man's inability to resist is the existence of fallen angels; spiritual, superhuman creatures whose task it was to teach us but who now tempted and misled men. In the end, the world declines and crumbles under the evil influence of the fallen angels turned demons called, "The Watchers."

With the establishment of the covenant between Abraham and God, we are told that God had appointed spirits to "mislead" all the nations but would not assign a spirit to lead or mislead the children of Isaac as God himself would be leading them.

The angels converse in Hebrew as it is the heavenly tongue. The law is written by God using this alphabet thus the law is also holy. All men spoke Hebrew until the time of Babel when the Hebrew language was lost. However, when Abraham dedicated himself to God, his ears were opened and his tongue was sanctified and Hebrew was again spoken and understood.

Finally, the entire text is based on the numbers of 49 and 50. Forty-nine represents the pinnacle of perfection, being made up of seven times seven. The number 50, which is the number of the Jubilee, is the number of grace. In the year of Jubilee slaves were to be set free, debts were forgiven, and grace filled the land and people.

Drawing from the theology and myths at the time, the Book of Jubilees expands and embellishes on the creation story, the fall of Adam and Eve, and the fall of the angels. The expanded detail written into the text may have been one reason it was eventually rejected. However, the effects of the book can still be seen throughout the Judeo-Christian beliefs of today. The theology espoused in Jubilees can be seen in the angelology and demonology taught in the Christian churches of today and widely held by many Jews.

In an attempt to answer questions left unaddressed in Genesis the writer confronts the origin and identification of Cain's wife. According to the Book Of Jubilees, Cain married his sister, as did all of the sons of Adam and Eve, except Abel, who was murdered. This seemed offensive to some, since it flies in the face of the very law it was written to defend. Yet this seemed to the writer to be the lesser of evils, given the problematic questions. Inbreeding was dismissed with the observation that the law was not fully given and understood then. The effects of the act were moot due to the purity of the newly created race.

The seeming discrepancy between the divine command of Adam's death decree and the timing of his death is addressed. Seeing that Adam continued to live even after he ate the fruit, which was supposed to bring on his death, the writer set about to clarify God's actions. The problem is explained away in a single sentence. Since a day in heaven is as a thousand years on earth and Adam died having lived less than a thousand years this meant he died in the same heavenly day. Dying within the same day of the crime was acceptable.

In an astonishing parallel to 1 Enoch, written at about the same time as Jubilees, the Watchers, or sons of God mentioned in Genesis 6, fell from grace when they descended to earth and had sex with the daughters of men.

In 1 Enoch, the angels descended for the purpose of seducing the women of earth.

However, in The Book of Jubilees, the angels were sent to teach men, but after living on earth for a while, they were tempted by their own lust and fell from heaven. The offspring of this unholy union were bloodthirsty and cannibalistic giants.

The Book of Jubilees indicates that each of the offspring was somehow different. Because of this, they are divided into categories of the Nephilim (or Naphidim, depending on the transliteration), the Giants, and the Eljo. The Nephil are mentioned however this word is the singular of Nephilim. Therefore, we have these classifications or species living on the earth: Angels, also referred to as Watchers; Nephilim; Eljo; Giants; and Human.

The Nephilim seem to be a being that contains an evil spirit much like their fathers. The giants, although coming from the same union of angel and woman, were carnal creatures. We have little information about the Eljo except they lived to kill men. They could be the "men of renown" mentioned in the Bible. These may have been the beings that brought about the myths of the violent and angry creatures such as the Cyclops or gods of war.

As sin spread throughout the world and the minds of men were turned toward evil, God saw no alternative but to cleanse the earth with a flood and establish a "new nature" in man that does not have to sin. It is this new nature that the Messiah will meet in mankind when He comes. As far as this author is aware, the re-creation of man's nature is mentioned in no other book. This idea of human nature being altered as it existed before the flood is found nowhere else but in Jubilees.

The angelic narrator tells us there were times in Israel's history when no evil existed and all men lived in accord. We are also told when and where the satans were allowed to attack and confound Israel. In this narrative, God uses his satans to harden the hearts of the Egyptians so they pursued Israel and were destroyed.

"The Apocalypse of Moses" also denotes the same work. This title seems to have been used for only a short period of time. It refers to the revelation given to Moses as the recipient of all the knowledge disclosed in the book. The term "Apocalypse" means to make known or to reveal. Another title of Jubilees is "Little Genesis." This refers to the lesser, non-canon status of the book. With the exception of minor differences picked up through translation and copying, the three titles represent the same text.

The War Scroll

In 1955, the War Scroll was found in Cave 1 at Qumran. Other fragments were found in Cave 4. The 19 columns of the scroll were badly mutilated. After great pains, the fragments were deciphered and published by the Hebrew University in Jerusalem

The War Scroll is thought to have been written sometime after the mid-first century B.C.E to the beginning of the 1st Century CE. The author of the manuscript made use of the Book of Daniel. The War Scroll contains rules for the military, religious preparations, and how the fighting was to be conducted.

In the War Scroll we see the sons of light, who are the remnants of the Jewish faithful, exiled into the wilderness by an ever-darkening world. Out of the wilderness of Jerusalem they return to fight against the sons of darkness, the children of Belial, in the last days. This fits in very well with our accepted prophecies in the book of Revelation.

The Book of Genesis

Genesis is the first book of the Old Testament in both the Jewish and Christian Bibles. Genesis means the act or process of producing, thus the text is named for the creation story.

The first 11 chapters are adapted from Mesopotamian and Canaanite traditions regarding the creation of earth. Other story lines were added to account for the existence of man by incorporating stories about Adam and Eve. The story of the flood is brought into Genesis, although it is difficult to know exactly which region the story was taken from as practically every culture has such a story. It is generally assumed the Deluge story was acquired from the same culture the creation story element was taken.

Although traditionally The Book of Genesis is attributed to Moses, most modern scholars agree that the book is a composite of at least three different literary strands: J (10th century B.C.), E (ninth century), and P (fifth century). Oddly, one of the contributors seems to have a "feminine" voice and could have been penned, or at least influenced by a woman.

At the time of the "J" document, a despot ruled over the Jews around 560 B.C. The writer of "J" may have written the book to document the people's oral history. Fearing their own destructions, he thus give them hope and ensured there would be a record of their connection to their God.

Since three stories were being interwoven, the writer of Genesis took the J,P, and E stories and combined them, removing parts that were contrary to the religious beliefs of the day. One set of writings used the Canaanite term, "Elohim," as the name of the creator God. A second used the more ancient Judean word transliterated from Hebrew and rendered "Jehovah" in English, to describe its God.

By removing inconsistencies and repetitions a smooth storyline emerged. The story coming from the Canaanite culture contained polytheistic beliefs. Traces of the two different gods and their differing personalities, as well as the Canaanite belief in polytheism may remain, but since the Jews had come to embrace monotheism at that time, the writer attempted to remove traces of such variances.

For a more complete picture it is always best to keep all stories and books in context. The complete translations of the non-biblical books used in this work can be obtained in *The Lost Books of the Bible: The Great Rejected Texts* by Joseph Lumpkin, published by Fifth Estate.

The Lost Books of the Bible: The Great Rejected Texts

Eighteen of the most sought after books available, which shed light on the evolution of our faith, our theology, and our church. Translations and commentary by the author of the best selling book, *The Lost Book of Enoch*, Joseph B. Lumpkin.

Section One: Lost Scriptures of the Old Testament- First Book of Adam and Eve, Second Book of Adam and Eve, First Book of Enoch, Second Book of Enoch (Secrets of Enoch), Jubilees, Jasher, The Story of Ahikar

Section Two: Apocalyptic Writings and the End of Days-Apocalypse of Abraham, Apocalypse of Thomas 4 Ezra, 2 Baruch, War Scroll (Sons of Dark vs. Sons of Light)

Section Three: Lost Scriptures of the New Testament-Gospel of Philip, Gospel of Mary Magdalene, Apocryphon of John, Gospel of Thomas, Gospel of Judas, Acts Chapter 29

The books of **Apocryphon of John, Gospel of Thomas, and Gospel of Judas** are Gnostic Gospels. The Gospel of Thomas and the Gospel of Judas may be purchased separately from Fifth Estate Publishers. All books quoted in these work may be purchased via the Fifth Estate web site at:

Fifthestatepub.com

or

Apocryphalbooks.org

Names and Station of Angels

The following list is of traditional angel names gathered from different religions, mythologies and lore. These angels are those considered to be good and not fallen angels or demons.

Abasdarhon - angel of the fifth hour of the night.
Abraxos - ancient name attributed to an angel.
Adnachiel - angel who rules November.
Adonael - an archangel.
Adonai - one of seven angels of the presence, or elohim; creator.
Aeshma - Persian archangel.
Af - angel of light.
Agla - angel who saved Lot and his family.
Akriel - angel who aids those with infertility.
Amitiel - angel of truth.
Amriel - angel of the month of May.
Anael - angel influencing love, passion and sexuality.
Anapiel - angel whose name means "branch of God."
Anahel - angel who rules the third heaven.
Anpiel - angel who protects birds.
Ansiel - name of an angel known as "the constrainer."
Arael - variation of Uriel; prince over the people.
Araqiel - angel with dominion over the earth.
Araton - one of seven ruling angels over the provinces of heaven.
Ariel - "lion of God;" angel of protection.
Armisael - angel of the womb.
Asariel - "whom God has bound;" rules the moon.
Asroilu - guardian angel of the seventh heaven.
Astanphaeus - one of the seven angels of the presence; third gate guardian.
Asteraoth - name of an angel who thwarts power.
Atrugiel - great prince of the seventh heaven.
Ayil - angel of the zodiac sign Sagittarius.
Azbogah - name of the high ranking angel of judgment.
Azrael - archangel of death.
Azriel - name for the angel of destruction.
Balthioul - angel with the power to thwart distress.
Baradiel - angel of hail.
Barakiel - angel of lightning.
Barrattiel - angel of support.
Barbiel - angel of October.
Bariel - ruling angel of the 11th hour of the day.
Barman - angel of intelligence.

Barquiel - ruling angel of the seventh hour of the day.
Baruchiel - angel with power over strife.
Bath Kol - female angel of divine prophecy.
Bazazath - archangel of the second heaven.
Bethor - one of seven ruling angels of the province of heaven.
Briathos - name of an angel who thwarts demons.
Cahethal - seraphim angel over agriculture.
Camael - angel name that means "he who sees God;" chief angel of powers.
Cassiel - angel of Saturn.
Cerviel - angel ruler of the principalities.
Chamuel - archangel whose name means "he who seeks God."
Chayyliel - angel whose name means "army;" a powerful angel.
Cochabiel - angel prince who stands before God.
Dabriel - angel of the first heaven who rules over Monday.
Dagiel - angel who has dominion over fish.
Dalquiel - angel prince of the third heaven.
Damabiath - angel of naval construction.
Dardariel - ruling angel of the 11th hour.
Diniel - angel who protects infants.
Domiel - angel who guards the sixth hall of the seventh heaven.
Dubbiel - guardian angel of Persia; name means "bear-God."
Duma - angel prince of dreams.
Dumah - angel of silence.
Eae - angel who thwarts demons.
Eiael - angel with dominion over the occult sciences.
Elyon - ministering angel who brought the plague of hail upon Egypt.
Emmanuel - angel whose name means "God with us."
Erathaol - one of seven great archon angels.
Eremiel - great angel who presides over the Abyss and Hades.
Gabriel - archangel whose name means "man or hero of God."
Gadriel - angel who rules the fifth heaven.
Galgaliel - prince angel of the sun, like Raphael.
Galizur - great angel who rules the second heaven.
Gamaliel - angel who takes the elect unto heaven.
Gazardiel - angel who supervises the east.
Geburatiel - angel prince who guards the seventh heaven.
Guriel - angel of the zodiac sign of Leo.
Gzrel - angel who revokes any evil decree against another in heaven.
Hadraniel - angel standing at the second gate in heaven; "majesty of God."Hadriel - guardian angel of the gates of the east wind.
Hagith - one of the seven ruling angels of the provinces of heaven.
Halaliel - archangel known as "the lord of karma."
Hamaliel - angel who rules the order of virtues.
Hamon - a great, honored, beautiful prince angel in heaven.

Haniel - an archangel who guards the tree of life.
Harahel - angel who oversees libraries.
Hasdiel - angel of benevolance.
Hasmal - fire speaking angel of the throne of God.
Hayliel - angel prince in the seventh heaven.
Haziel - angel whose name means "vision of God."
Heman - angel leader of the heavenly choir, whose name means "trust."
Hermesiel - angel who leads one of the heavenly choirs.
Hofniel - ruling angel of the bene elohim; name means "fighter of God."
Iaoel - an angel of the lord; angel of visions.
Iaoth - archangel who has power to thwart demons.
Leo - an angel who thwarts demons
Iofiel - archangel whose name means "beauty of God."
Israfil - Islamic angel whose name means "the burning one."
Jael - cherub who guards the ark of the covenant.
Jahoel - one of the angels of the presence and chief of the seraphim.
Jaoel - guardian angel who lives in the seventh heaven.
Jeduthun – angel, name means "master of howling" or chanting to God.
Jefischa - ruling angel of the fourth hour of the night.
Jehudiel - archangel who rules the movements of the heavenly spheres.
Jeremiel - archangel whose name means "mercy of God."
Kabshiel - angel of grace and favor.
Kafziel - archangel who rules the planet Saturn.
Kakabel - angel who rules over stars and constellations.
Kalaziel - angel who has the power to thwart demons of disease.
Karael - angel who has the power to thwart demons.
Kemuel - archon angel and chief of the seraphim.
Kerubiel - prince angel of the Cherubim.
Kokabiel - prince angel of the stars.
Kutiel - angel of water and the use of diving rods.
Labbiel - angel whose name was changed to Raphael.
Lahabiel - angel who protects against evil spirits.
Lamechial - angel who thwarts deception.
Lassuarium - angel who rules the tenth hour of the night.
Laylah - angel who oversees and protects childbirth.
Machidiel - angel governing the zodiac sign of Aries, the month of March
Marmaroth - angel who has power to thwart fate.
Mendrion - angel who rules the seventh hour of the night.
Metatron - one of the greatest archangels, second only to God.
Michael - great archangel whose name means "who is as God."
Mihr - angel of divine mercy; angel that governs September.
Miniel - angel invoked to induce love.
Mitatron - an angel of the third heaven.
Morael - angel of awe that rules the months of August-September.

Moroni - brought messages to Joseph Smith, founder of Mormonism.
Muriel - angel who rules the dominions and the month of June.
Naaririel - great prince angel of the seventh heaven.
Nahaliel - angel who governs running streams; "valley of God."
Nanael - angel who governs the sciences, and philosophy.
Narcariel - angel that rules the eighth hour of the night.
Nasargiel - good angel with a lion head that rules hell.
Nathanael - angel ruling over hidden things, fire and vengeance.
Naya'il - angel of testing.
Nelchael - angel of the schemhamphorae.
Nuriel - angel of spellbinding power and of hail storms.
Och - one ruling angel of the provinces of heaven.
Omael - angel of chemistry and species perpetuation.
Onoel - name of an archon angel...
Ophaniel - prince angel over the ophanim.
Ophiel - one ruling angel of the provinces of heaven and Mercury.
Oriel - ruling angel of the tenth hour of the day.
Orifiel - archangel over thrones, and the second hour of the day.
Orphamiel - angel known as the "great finger of the Father."
Osmadiel - ruling angel of the eighth hour of the day.
Ouriel - archangel who commands demons.
Pamyel - ruling angel of the ninth hour of night.
Pathiel - angel whose name means "opener of God."
Peliel - angel who rules the virtues.
Peniel - angel who rules Friday and resides in the third heaven.
Pesagniyah - angel who ushers prayers of grief to heaven.
Phaleg - one of the seven ruling angels of the provinces of heaven.
Phanuel - archangel who is an interpreter of revelations.
Phounebiel - disease thwarting angel.
Phul one of the seven ruling angels of the provinces of heaven.
Pravuil - an archangel who keeps all the records of heaven.
Pronoia - an archon angel who helped make mankind.
Purah - angel of forgetfulness.
Puriel - angel whose name means "the fire of God;" angel of punishment.
Qaspiel - angel who rules the moon.
Quabriel - ruling angel of the ninth hour of the day.
Rachiel - ophanim angel who rules Venus and governs sexuality.
Rachmiel - angel of mercy whose name also means the same.
Radueriel - angel who can create other angels and oversees archives.
Raguel - angel who watches over the behavior of angels; "friend of God."
Rahab - angel of death, destruction, but also the sea.
Rahatiel - angel prince of the constellations; name means "to run."
Rahmiel - angel of mercy and love.
Ramiel - angel who oversees visions and souls during the day ofjudgment.

Raphael - great archangel whose name means "the shining one who heals."
Rathanael - angel of the third heaven and thwarter of demons.
Raziel - angel chief over the thrones, guarding the secrets of the universe.
Remiel - angel who leads souls to judgment; name means "mercy of God."
Rikbiel - angel who oversees the divine chariot; chief of wheels.
Rizoel - angel with power to thwart demons.
Rogziel - angel of punishment whose name means "the wrath of God."
Ruman - angel who takes account of evil men's deeds while in hell.
Sabaoth - archon angel of the presence.
Sabathiel - angel or intelligence who communicates divine light.
Sablo - angel of graciousness and protection.
Sabrael - archangel who guards the first heaven.
Sabrathan - ruling angel of the first hour of the night.
Sachiel - ruling angel of Jupiter whose name means "covering of God."
Sagnessagiel - angel who guards the fourth hall of the seventh heaven.
Sahaqiel - angel prince of the fourth heaven.
Salathiel - rescuing angel of Adam and Eve.
Samkiel - angel of destruction and purifier of souls from sheol.
Samuel - Ruling angel of the first hour of the day.
Sandalphon - giant angel whose name means "co-brother" (of Metratron).
Saniel - ruling angel of the sixth hour of the day.
Sarakiel - angel who rules the ministering angels.
Sarandiel - ruling angel of the 12th hour of the night.
Satqiel - angel prince of the fifth heaven.
Seraphiel - chief angel of the seraphim angels.
Shamsiel - angel whose name means "light of day."
Shepherd - angel of repentance.
Shoftiel - angel whose name means "the judge of God."
Sidqiel - angel prince of the ophanim; ruler of Venus.
Sidriel - angel prince of the first heaven.
Simiel - archangel.
Sizouze - angel of prayer.
Sophia - angel whose name means "wisdom."
Soqedhozi - angel who weighs the merits of of men before God.
Sorath - angel who is the spirit of the sun.
Sorush - angel who punishes souls on judgment day.
Soterasiel - angel whose name means "who stirs up the fire of God."
Sraosha - angel who sets the world in motion.
Suriel - angel of healing whose name means "God's command."
Tagas - governing angel of singing angels.
Tartys - ruling angel of the second hour of the night.
Tatrasiel - great angelic prince.
Temeluch - angel caretaker who protects newborn babies and children.
Temperance - angel of the elixir of life.

Theliel - angel prince of love.
Tubiel - angel of summer.
Tzadkiel - angel of justice and guardian of the gates of the east wind.
Ubaviel - angel of the zodiac sign of Capricorn.
Umabel - angel of physics and astronomy.
Uriel - great archangel whose name means "God is my light."
Usiel - an angel who stands before the throne of God.
Uzziel - Cherubim angel whose name means "strength of God."
Varhmiel - ruling angel of the fourth hour of the day.
Vequaniel - ruling angel of the third hour of the day.
Verchiel - ruling angel of the month of July and of the zodiac sign Leo.
Vretiel - swift in wisdom archangel responsible for recording God's deeds.
Xathanael - the sixth angel created by God.
Yabbashael - an angel of the earth whose name means "the mainland."
Yefefiah - archangel who is the prince of the Torah.
Yehudiah - benevolant angel of death.
Yerachmiel - an archangel who rules earth.
Yeshamiel - angel who rules the zodiac sign of Libra.
Yofiel - angel prince of the Torah commanding 53 legions of angels.
Zaapiel - angel punisher of wicked souls.
Zaazenach - ruling angel of the sixth hour of the night.
Zabkiel - angel who rules over the thrones.
Zachariel - angel governor of Jupiter.
Zachriel - angel who governs memories.
Zadkeil - archangel who rules heaven and stands in the presence of God.
Zagzagel - angel prince of the Torah and of wisdom.
Zakzakiel - angel of the seventh heaven who records good deeds.
Zaphiel - angel ruler of the Cherubim.
Zaphkiel - archangel whose name means "knowledge of God."
Zarall - cherub angel who guards the ark of the covenant.
Zazriel - angel whose name means "strength of God."
Zehanpuryu - high ranking angel whose name means "one who sets free."
Zerachiel - angel of the month of July and the sun.
Zophiel - angel whose name means "God's spy."
Zuriel - ruler of the principalities whose name means "my rock is God."

Evil Angels, Fallen Angels, or Demons:

AGLÆCA: An Old English dictionary defines áglaeca as follows: "wretch, miscreant, monster, demon, fierce enemy, fierce combatant, miserable being." In the Anglo-Saxon epic Beowulf, Grendel, Grendel's mother and Beowulf are all three referred to by this name for each is a "fierce combatant." Variant spelling of Anglo-Saxon unisex Aglæca, meaning both "demon, monster, fiend," and "hero, warrior."

NUKPANA: Native American Hopi unisex name meaning "evil."

ABADDON : Greek name derived from Hebrew abaddown, meaning "destruction, ruination." In the New Testament bible, this is the name of the place of destruction. And it is a name given to the angel of the bottomless pit, the Destroyer Apollyon. An Anglicized form of Greek Abaddon, meaning "destruction, ruination." In the New Testament bible, this is the name of the place of destruction. And it is a name given to the angel of the bottomless pit, the Destroyer Apollyon.

ADDANC: In Welsh legend, this is the name of a lake monster that King Arthur (or Percival) killed. It is variously described as a demon, a dwarf, beaver, or crocodile. It was said to prey upon anyone foolish enough to swim in its lake.

AHRIMAN: Middle Persian form of Old Persian Angra Mainyu, meaning "devil; evil spirit." In mythology, this is the name of the god of darkness, death and destruction, and the number one enemy of Ahura Mazda.

ALIAH: Variant of Hebrew Alvah (having the letters transposed), meaning "evil, iniquity." In the bible, this is the name of a duke of Edom.

ALVA: Variant spelling of Hebrew Alvah, meaning "evil, iniquity." Compare with feminine forms of Alva.

ALVAH: Hebrew name meaning "evil, iniquity." In the bible, this is the name of a duke of Edom. Also spelled Aliah.

ANGRA MAINYU: Old Persian myth name of the source of all evil, the twin brother and main enemy of Ahura Mazda, meaning "evil spirit; devil."

APEP: Egyptian name, possibly connected to the root pp, meaning "to slither." In mythology, Apep is the personification of evil, seen as a giant snake, serpent or dragon. Known as the Serpent of the Nile or Evil Lizard, he was an enemy of the sun god.

AZA'ZEL: Hebrew word meaning "entire removal" and "scapegoat." In the bible, this word is found in the law of the day of atonement (Leviticus 16:8, 10, 26). It refers to a goat used for sacrifice for the sins of the people. In modern times, Azazel was interpreted as a Satanic, goat-like demon. The name has even been used for the "Angel of Death."

AZAZEL: Anglicized form of Hebrew Aza'zel, meaning "entire removal" and "scapegoat." In the bible, this word is found in the law of the day of atonement (Leviticus 16:8, 10, 26). It refers to a goat used for sacrifice for the sins of the people. In modern times, Azazel was interpreted as a Satanic, goat-like demon. The name has even been used for the "Angel of Death."

CERBERUS: Latin form of Greek Kerberos, meaning "demon of the pit." In mythology, this is the name of the three-headed dog that guards the entrance to Hades.

□ERNOBOG: Czech form of Russian Chernobog, meaning "black god." In Slavic mythology, this is the name of a god of evil and darkness, the counterpart of Belobog ("white god").

CHERNOBOG: Russian form of Slavic Crnobog, composed of the elements cherno "black" and bog "god," hence "black god." In Slavic mythology, this is the name of a god of evil and darkness, the counterpart of Belobog ("white god").
CRNOBOG: Variant form of Russian Czernobog, meaning "black god." In mythology, this is the name of a god of evil and darkness, the counterpart of Belobog ("white god").
CZERNOBOG: Russian form of Slavic Zherneboh, meaning "black god."
DEMOGORGON: Greek myth name of a god of the underworld, thought to be a name for Satan, possibly composed of the Greek elements daimon "demon, devil" and gorgos "grim," hence "grim demon."
DEMON: Ancient Greek name derived from the word demos, meaning "the people."
DEVIL: English form of Greek Diabolos, meaning "accuser, slanderer." In the bible, this is a title for Satan, the prince of demons and author of evil, who estranges men from God and entices them to sin. Figuratively, the devil is a man who, by opposing the cause of God, may be said to act the part of the devil or to side with him.
DIABOLOS: Greek name meaning "accuser, slanderer." In the bible, this is a title for Satan, the prince of demons and author of evil, who estranges men from God and entices them to sin. Figuratively, the devil is a man who, by opposing the cause of God, may be said to act the part of the devil or to side with him.
DRACUL: Romanian name meaning "devil" or "dragon."
KARAWAN: An expression used to avert the evil eye, transferred to forename use.
KERBEROS: Greek name meaning "demon of the pit." In mythology, this is the name of the three-headed dog that guards the entrance to Hades.
MATCHITEHEW: Native American Algonquin name meaning "he has an evil heart."
MUKESH: Hindi myth name of a demon in the form of a boar who was killed by Shiva, meaning "ruler of Muka."
NAZAR: Turkish name derived from the word nazar, the name of an amulet known as the "evil eye stone" used to ward off evil. Compare with another form of Nazar.
RAVANA: Hindi name meaning "person with ten necks." In Hindu mythology, this is the name of a demon king of Ceylon who kidnapped Rama's wife, Sita.
SAMA'EL: Variant spelling of Hebrew Samael, the name of an Angel of Death, meaning "whom God makes" and "venom of God."
SAMAEL: In Jewish mythology, this is the name of an archangel, a fallen angel, the Angel of Death or Poison, the accuser, seducer, and destroyer famously known as The Grim Reaper. He is said to be both good and evil, having been one of the heavenly host. He rules over seven habitations called

Sheba Ha-yechaloth, infernal realms of the Earth. The Talmud states: "the evil Spirit, Satan, and Sama'el the Angel of Death, are the same"; and Samael is also therein equated with the biblical serpent who tempted Eve in the Garden of Eden. He is called the Prince of Darkness and chief of the Dragons of Evil and is held responsible for the scorching wind of the desert called the simoom. It is probably the Hebrew form of Syrian Shemal ("left"), but composed of 'el "god" and suwm "to create" or "to place, to set," hence "whom God makes." It is also sometimes rendered "venom of God." Also spelled Samil and Sammael.
SAMIL: Variant form of Hebrew Samael, the name of an Angel of Death, meaning "whom God makes" and "venom of God."
SAMMAEL: Variant spelling of Hebrew Samael, the name of an Angel of Death, meaning "whom God makes" and "venom of God."
SATAN: Greek form of Hebrew satan, meaning "adversary." In the bible, this is the name of the inveterate enemy of God. In the New Testament, Hebrew satan is translated once into Greek Diabolos, and once using the word epiboulos, meaning "plotter." This is also the Late Latin and Old English form of Hebrew satan.
SATANAS: Greek name of Aramaic origin, corresponding to Greek Satan, from Hebrew satan, meaning "adversary." In the bible, this is the name of the inveterate enemy of God.
SET: Another form of Egyptian Sutekh, possibly meaning "one who dazzles." In mythology, this is the name of an ancient evil god of Chaos, storms, and the desert, who slew Osiris.
SETH: Greek form of Egyptian Set, possibly meaning "one who dazzles." In mythology, this is the name of an ancient evil god of Chaos, storms, and the desert, who slew Osiris. Compare with other forms of Seth.
SETHOS: Greek form of Egyptian Sutekh, possibly meaning "one who dazzles." In mythology, this is the name of an ancient evil god of Chaos, storms, and the desert, who slew Osiris.
SHEMAL: Syrian name meaning "left." In mythology, this is the name of the Lord of the genii and demons.
SUTEKH: Egyptian name, possibly meaning "one who dazzles." In mythology, this is the name of an ancient evil god of Chaos, storms, and the desert, who slew Osiris.
TEIVEL: Yiddish name meaning "devil."
TJERNOBOG: Danish form of Slavic Crnobog, meaning "black god." In Slavic mythology, this is the name of a god of evil and darkness, the counterpart of Belobog ("white god").
TŠERNOBOG: Finnish form of Slavic Crnobog, meaning "black god." In Slavic mythology, this is the name of a god of evil and darkness, the counterpart of Belobog ("white god").
VRITRA: Hindi myth name of a dragon or serpent, the personification of drought and enemy of Indra, meaning "the enveloper."

ZERNEBOG: Variant form of Russian Czernobog, meaning "black god."
ZHERNEBOH: Slavic name meaning "black god."
ZLOGONJE: Slavic name meaning "expels evil."

Female Demons:
HECATE: Latin form of Greek Hekate, meaning "worker from far off." In mythology, this is the name of a goddess of witchcraft, demons, graves, and the underworld.
HEKATE : Variant spelling of Greek Hekabe, meaning "worker from far off." In mythology, this is the name of a goddess of witchcraft, demons, graves, and the underworld.
IEZABEL : Greek form of Hebrew Iyzebel ("Ba'al exalts," "unchaste," or "without cohabitation"), but meaning "chaste, intact." In the bible, this is the name of the evil wife of King Ahab. She was eaten by dogs as prophesied by Elijah.
IYZEBEL: Hebrew name meaning "Ba'al exalts," "unchaste," or "without cohabitation." In the bible, this is the name of the evil wife of King Ahab. She was eaten by dogs as prophesied by Elijah.
JEZEBEL: Anglicized form of Hebrew Iyzebel ("Ba'al exalts," "unchaste," or "without cohabitation") and Greek Iezabel ("chaste, intact"). In the bible, this is the name of the evil wife of King Ahab. She was eaten by dogs as prophesied by Elijah.
LAMIA: Greek myth name of an evil spirit who abducts and devours children, meaning "large shark." The name means "vampire" in Latin and "fiend" in Arabic.
LILIT: Variant spelling of Hebrew Lilith, meaning "of the night."
LILITH: Hebrew form of Sumerian Lilitu, meaning "of the night." In mythology, this is the name of a Mesopotamian storm demon associated with the wind and thought to bear disease and death. In ancient Semitic folklore, it is the name of a night demon. The oldest story considers Lilith to be Adam's first wife. In the bible, this is simply a word for a "screech owl."
LILITU: Sumerian name meaning "of the night."
PANDORA: Greek name composed of the elements pan "all" and doron "gift," hence "all-gift." In mythology, this is the name of the first mortal woman whose curiosity unleashed evil into the world.
USHA: Female Hindi myth name of a demon princess, daughter of heaven, and sister of night, meaning "dawn."

About the Author

Joseph Lumpkin has a Doctor of Ministry degree from Battlefield Baptist Institute. He has written for various newspapers and has authored over 20 books including commentary and reflections on the books of Jubilees, Jasher, 1, 2, and 3 Enoch, as well as an *Encyclopedia of Rejected Scripture*, which contains over 40 ancient texts. Joseph apprears regularly on L.A. Talk Radio with "Max and Friends" hosted by Max Tucci, as well as "Rain Making Time" with host Kim Greenhouse. He is the CEO of Fifth Estate Publishing. http://www.fifthestatepub.com

Look for other books by Joseph Lumpkin, including:

Banned From The Bible: Books Banned, Rejected, And Forbidden

ISBN-10: 193358047X

The Lost Books of the Bible: The Great Rejected Texts

ISBN-10: 1933580666

The Gospel of Thomas: A Contemporary Translation

ISBN: 0976823349

Dark Night of the Soul - A Journey to the Heart of God

ISBN: 0974633631

The Book of Jubilees; The Little Genesis, The Apocalypse of Moses

ISBN: 1933580097

A complete catalog can be seen at fifthestatepub.com or apocryphalbooks.org

Printed in Great Britain
by Amazon